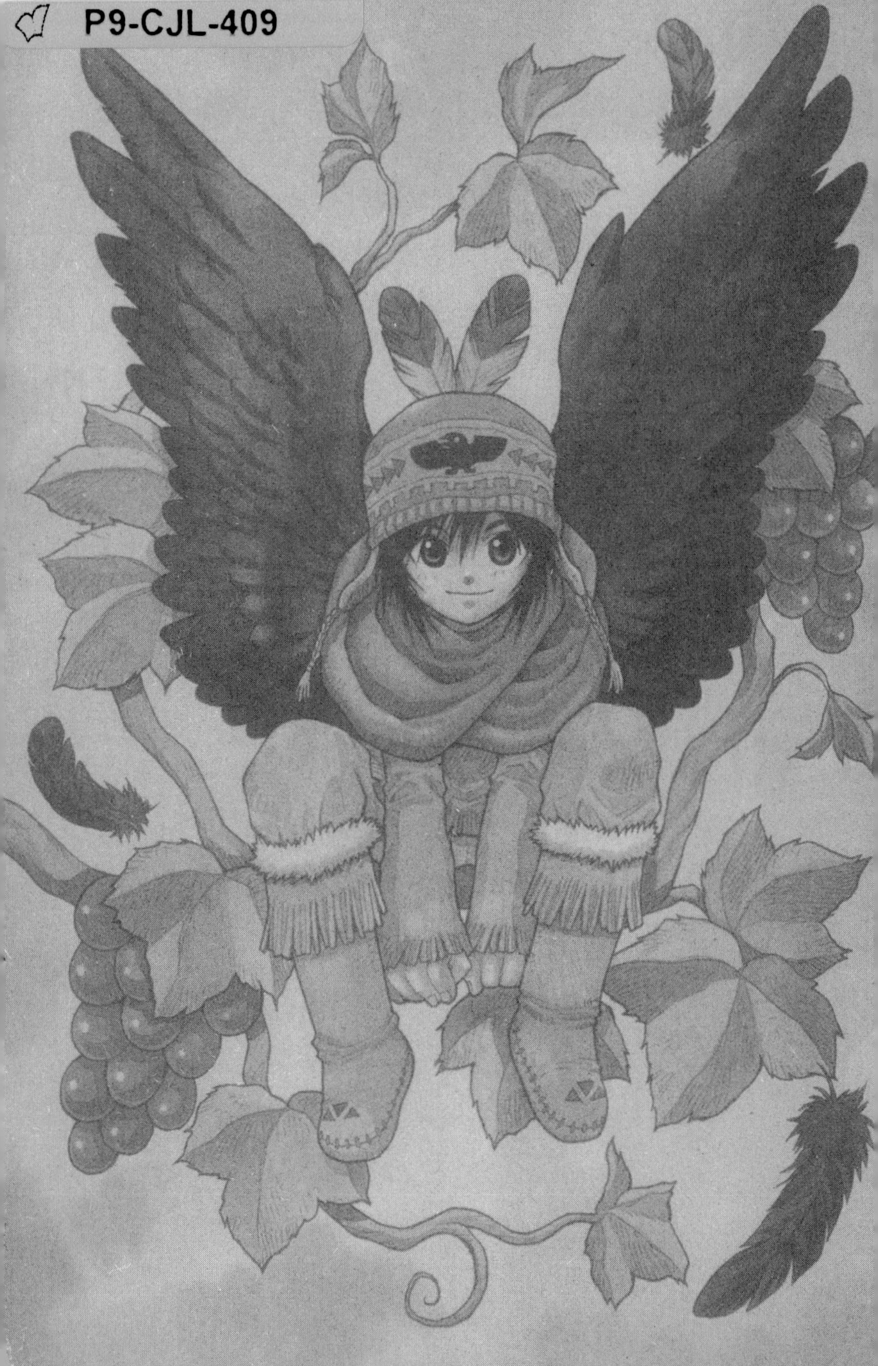

+ANIMA Volume 6
Created by Natsumi Mukai

Translation - Alethea & Athena Nibley
English Adaptation - Karen S. Ahlstrom
Copy Editor - Sarah Mercurio
Retouch and Lettering - Star Print Brokers
Production Artist - Vicente Rivera, Jr.
Graphic Designer - James Lee

Editor - Troy Lewter
Digital Imaging Manager - Chris Buford
Pre-Production Supervisor - Erika Terriquez
Production Manager - Elisabeth Brizzi
Managing Editor - Vy Nguyen
Creative Director - Anne Marie Horne
Editor-in-Chief - Rob Tokar
Publisher - Mike Kiley
President and C.O.O. - John Parker
C.E.O. and Chief Creative Officer - Stuart Levy

A  **TOKYOPOP** Manga

TOKYOPOP and are trademarks or registered trademarks of TOKYOPOP Inc.

TOKYOPOP Inc.
5900 Wilshire Blvd. Suite 2000
Los Angeles, CA 90036

E-mail: info@TOKYOPOP.com
Come visit us online at www.TOKYOPOP.com

ISBN: 978-1-59816-352-0

First TOKYOPOP printing: December 2007
10 9 8 7 6 5 4 3 2 1
Printed in the USA

Volume 6
by Natsumi Mukai

HAMBURG // LONDON // LOS ANGELES // TOKYO

+ A N I M A

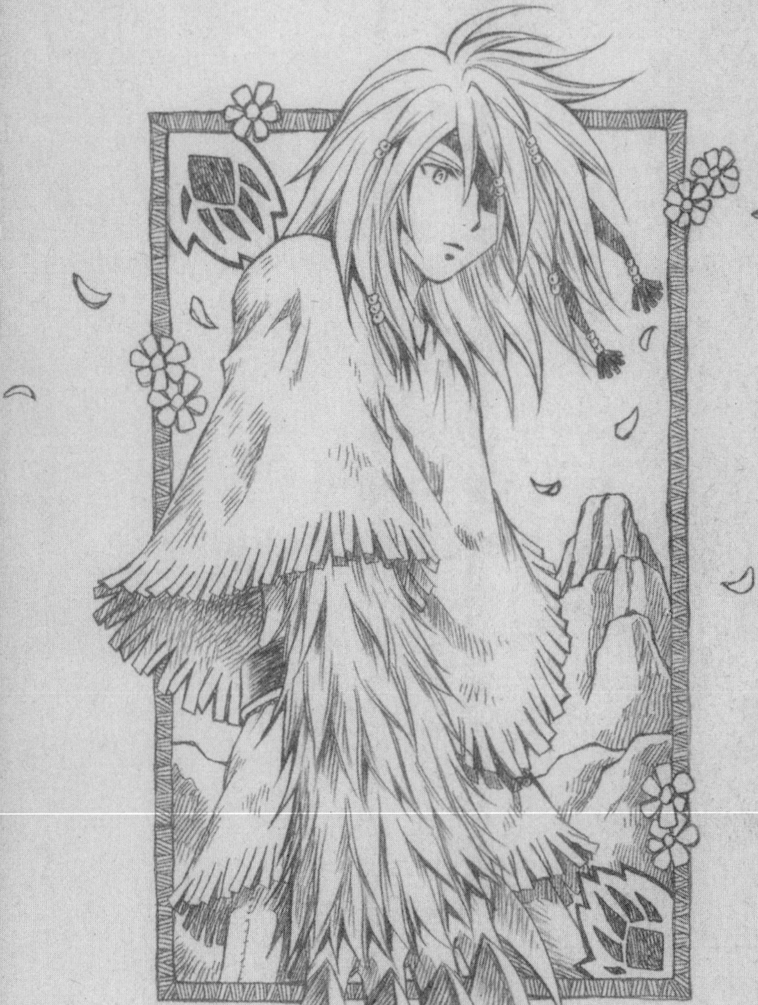

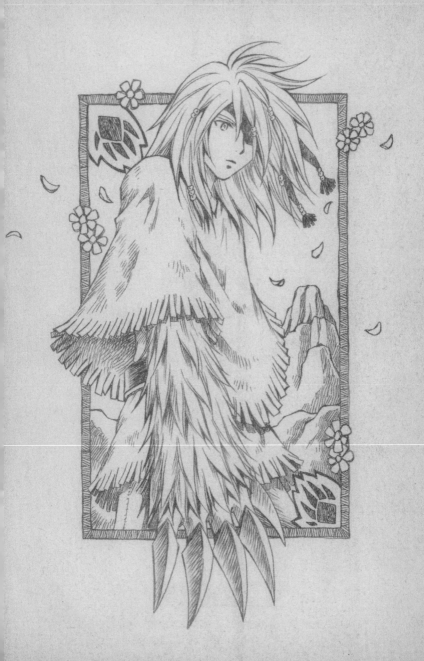

+ANIMA

プラスアニマ

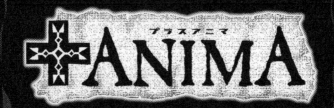

迎夏生

NATSUMI MUKAI

STORY & CHARACTERS

The +Anima are beings who possess animal-like powers.

Cooro, a crow +Anima, meets Husky, a fish +Anima, at the circus. The two of them travel together and are soon joined by new companions: Senri, a bear +Anima, and Nana, a bat +Anima. And so, the four children's adventures begin...

Cooro and company meet a girl named Marca who is traveling alone in search of +Anima. Not knowing what her intentions are, the four keep their powers secret.

A... MERMAID...?

ハスキー[Husky]

Fish +Anima. He can swim freely through water like a merman. He's a little stubborn--and he hates girls.

クーロ[Cooro]

Crow +Anima. When he spreads his pitch-black wings, he can fly freely in the sky. He's also a bit of a glutton!

LIKE ME... SEE?

ナナ[Nana]

Bat +Anima. She can fly and emit an ultrasonic screech. A fashion-conscious girl, she is scared of forests at night.

センリ[Senri]

Bear +Anima. His arms bear sharp claws, not to mention he has amazing strength. He doesn't talk very much.

While searching the town for +Anima, Marca gets herself mixed up in some trouble. Cooro feels like she's somehow familiar, so he spreads his black wings and helps her out. Now that she knows Cooro's a +Anima, Marca decides to follow him for a while. While in the forest searching for food, Cooro and Senri discover an apple orchard. Cooro, overjoyed, starts eating apples...but when the owner named Emma surprises him, he falls from a tree and hurts his head. Emma tends to his wound and the four decide to help harvest the apples to repay her. Emma is very kind to Cooro, which leads him to happily state, "Being here is like a dream." But Nana and Husky feel uncomfortable and leave the house with Senri early one morning. When Cooro catches up to them, he decides to continue his travels with the others, and bids farewell to Emma. As he leaves, Emma is reminded of her son, who left home a year ago, never to return.

マルカ[Marca]

They next travel to Sandra, the largest city in western Astaria.
Senri helps a girl with a teddy bear run away from her pursuers, but it turns out that she is the daughter of the Giesrieg family that governs Sandra. She's also the fiancée of Arthur, an officer in the Astarian military.

The four then make their way to a port town on the southern coast. Husky spots a man named Kevin drowning in the ocean, and rescues him. Thinking he was rescued by a mermaid princess, Kevin decides he's in love with the mermaid. Husky tries to avoid Kevin so he won't realize that Husky is the "mermaid princess," but Kevin continues going out into the ocean to see the mermaid. But when his boat sinks, Husky rescues him again and finally sets the record straight.

Igneous and his troops have come to Moss Mountain to make a treaty with the Kim-un-kur. Astaria's leaders want the Kim-un-kur to assist them in opposing the warmongering Sailand. Due to past ill feelings, the Kim-un-kur will not talk with Igneous, so he conscripts Senri, a Kim-un-kur, to be his emissary. Cooro and the others are forced to travel with the Astarian military for their talks. However, along the way, there is a change in Senri...

イグナス[Igneous]

CONTENTS

Chapter 27:
That Which Sleeps

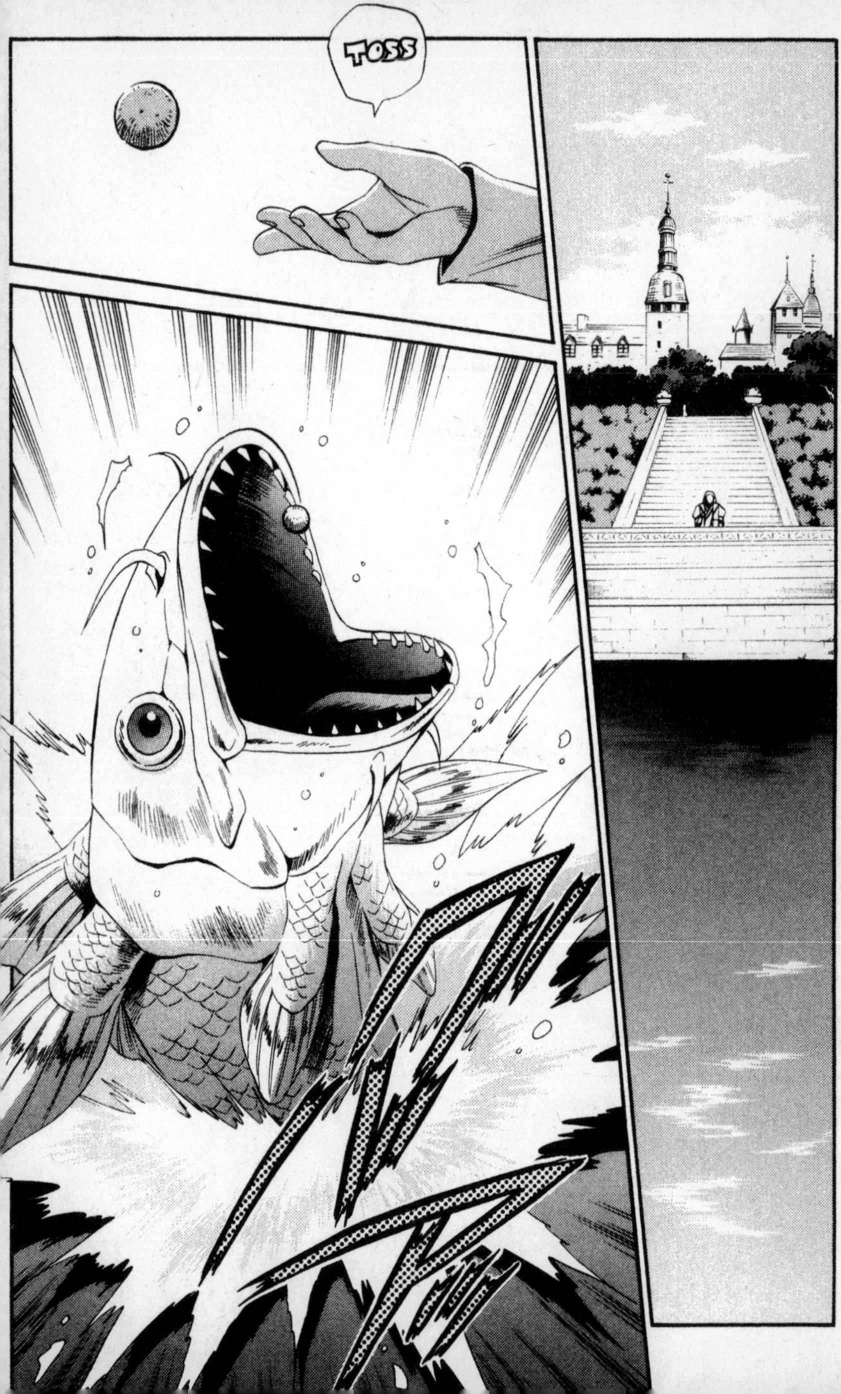
TOSS

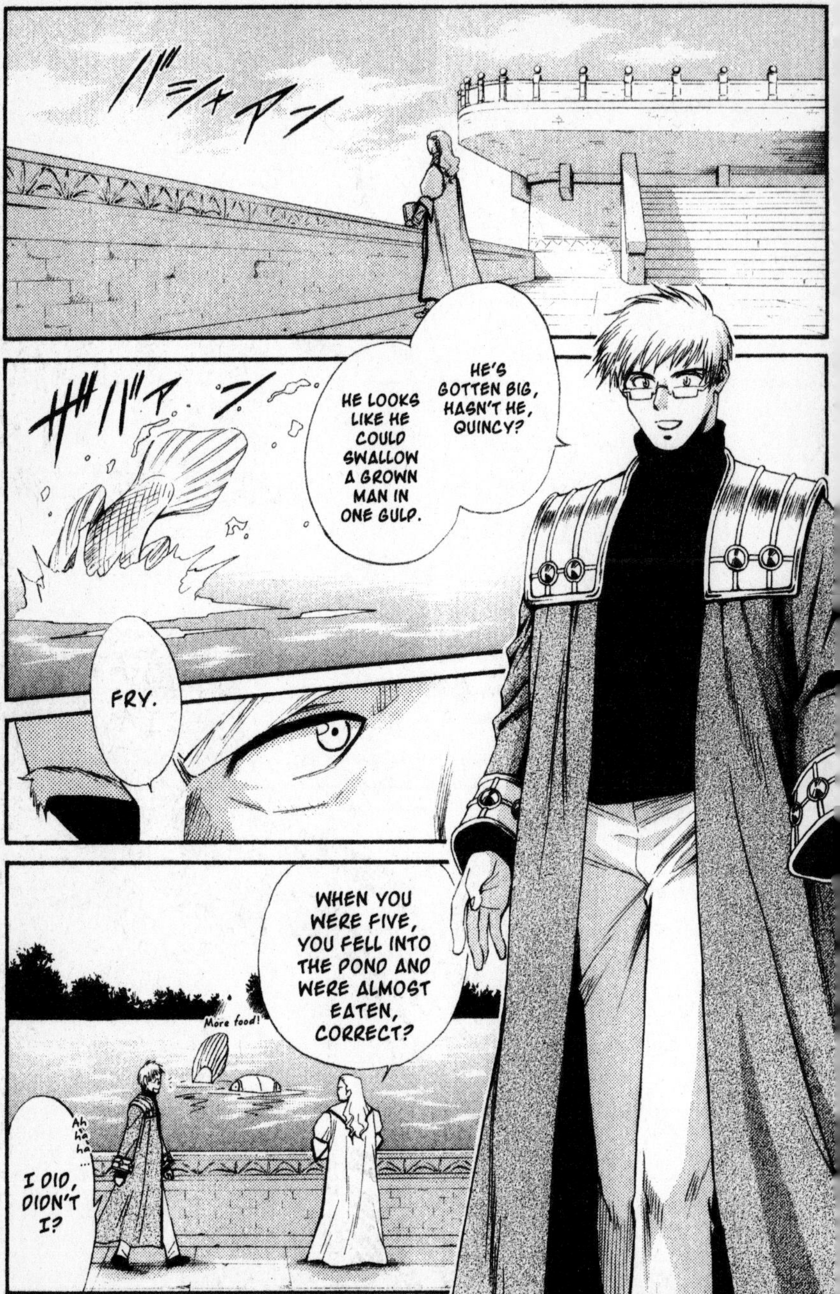
バシャアン
ザバァン
HE'S GOTTEN BIG, HASN'T HE, QUINCY?
HE LOOKS LIKE HE COULD SWALLOW A GROWN MAN IN ONE GULP.
FRY.
WHEN YOU WERE FIVE, YOU FELL INTO THE POND AND WERE ALMOST EATEN, CORRECT?
More food!
Ah ha ha...
I DID, DIDN'T I?

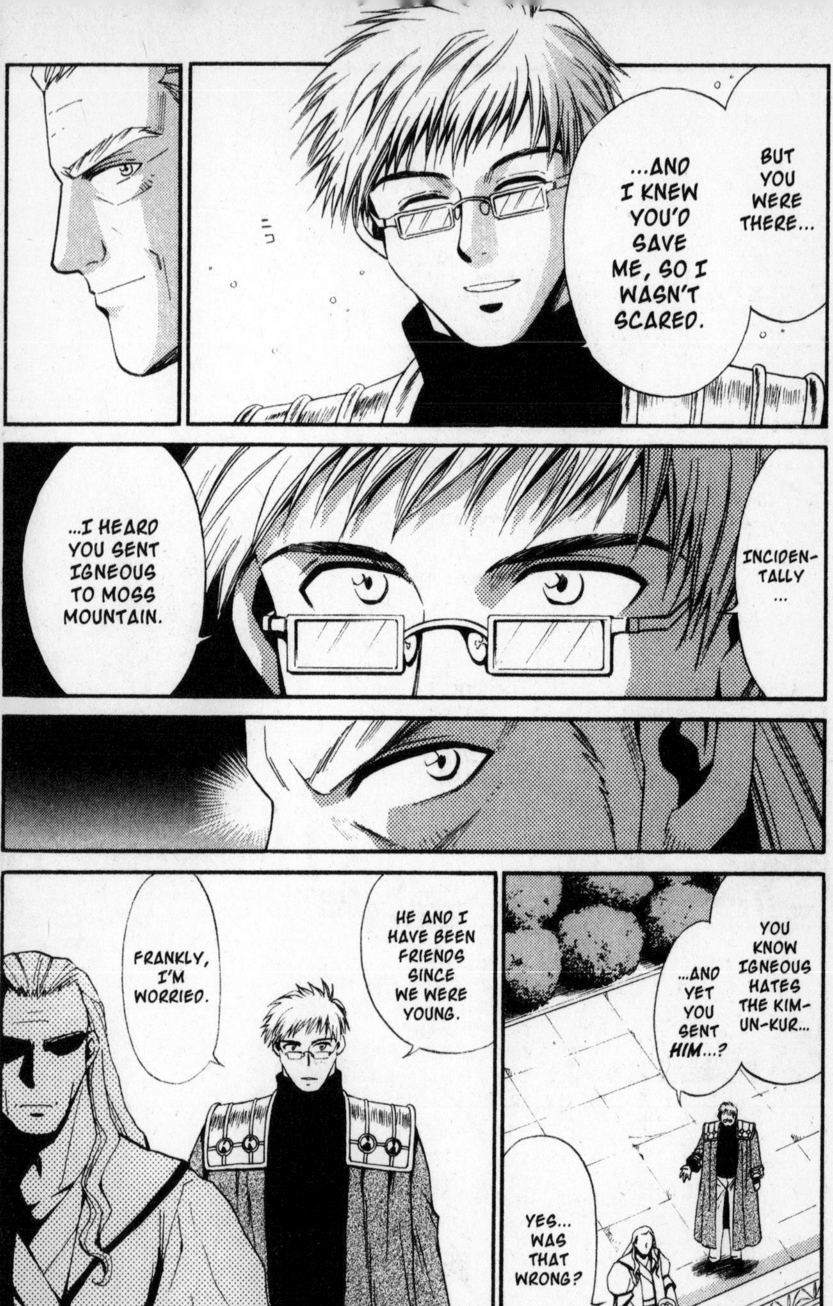
BUT YOU WERE THERE...
...AND I KNEW YOU'D SAVE ME, SO I WASN'T SCARED.
INCIDEN-TALLY ...
...I HEARD YOU SENT IGNEOUS TO MOSS MOUNTAIN.
YOU KNOW IGNEOUS HATES THE KIM-UN-KUR...
...AND YET YOU SENT *HIM*...?
YES... WAS THAT WRONG?
HE AND I HAVE BEEN FRIENDS SINCE WE WERE YOUNG.
FRANKLY, I'M WORRIED.

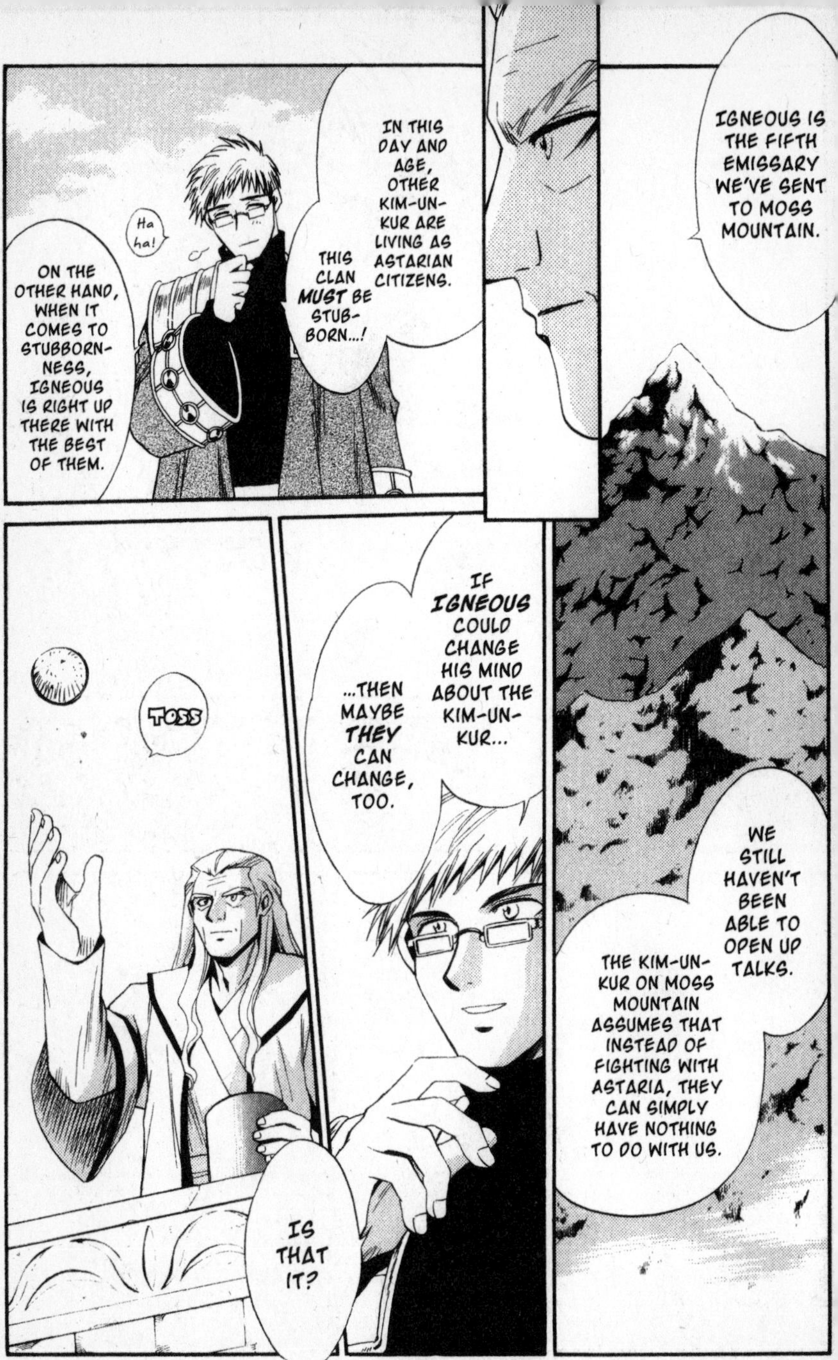
IGNEOUS IS THE FIFTH EMISSARY WE'VE SENT TO MOSS MOUNTAIN.
WE STILL HAVEN'T BEEN ABLE TO OPEN UP TALKS.
THE KIM-UN-KUR ON MOSS MOUNTAIN ASSUMES THAT INSTEAD OF FIGHTING WITH ASTARIA, THEY CAN SIMPLY HAVE NOTHING TO DO WITH US.
IN THIS DAY AND AGE, OTHER KIM-UN-KUR ARE LIVING AS ASTARIAN CITIZENS.
THIS CLAN MUST BE STUB-BORN...!
Ha ha!
ON THE OTHER HAND, WHEN IT COMES TO STUBBORN-NESS, IGNEOUS IS RIGHT UP THERE WITH THE BEST OF THEM.
IF IGNEOUS COULD CHANGE HIS MIND ABOUT THE KIM-UN-KUR...
...THEN MAYBE THEY CAN CHANGE, TOO.
TOSS
IS THAT IT?

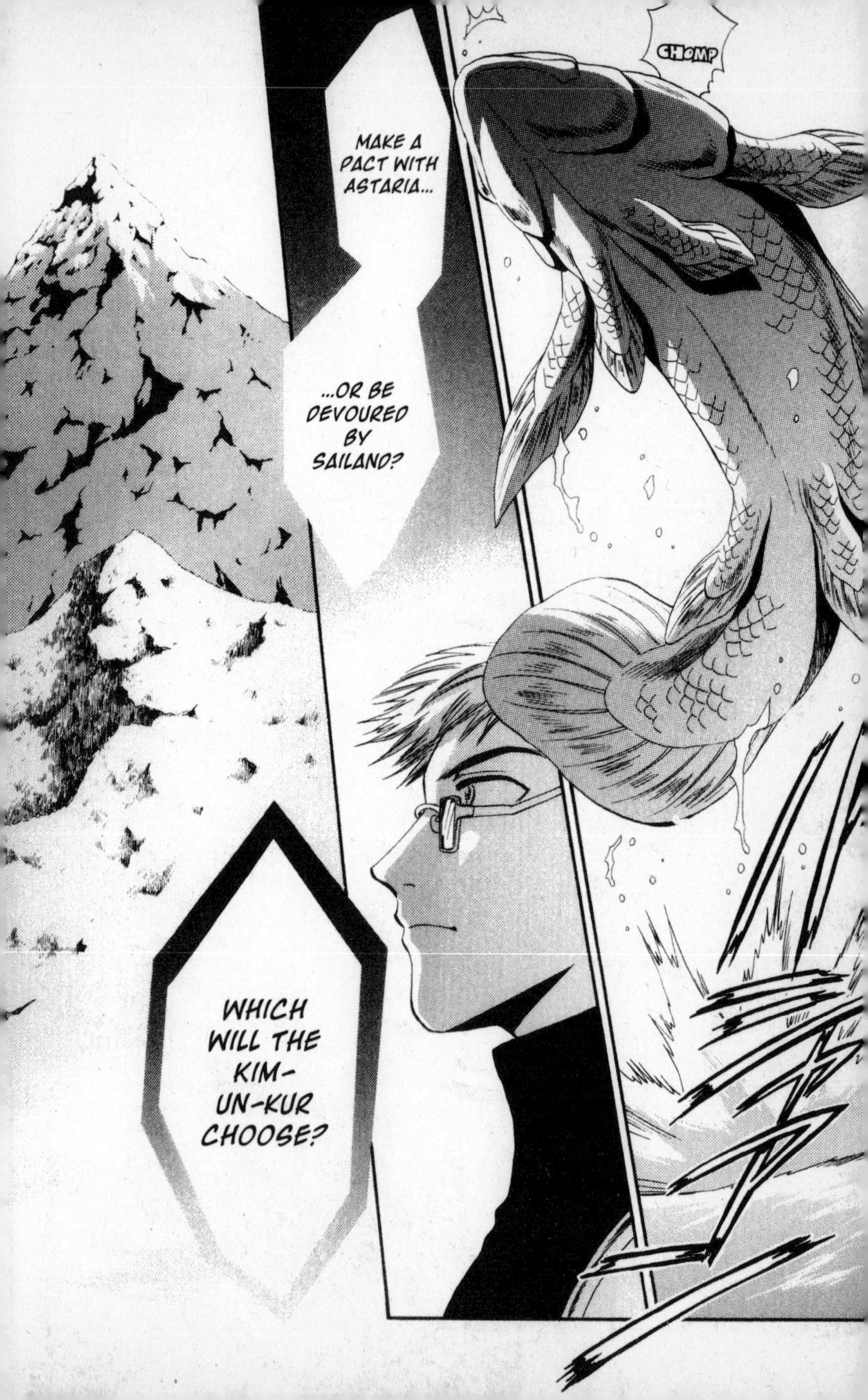
CHOMP
MAKE A PACT WITH ASTARIA...
...OR BE DEVOURED BY SAILANO?
WHICH WILL THE KIM-UN-KUR CHOOSE?

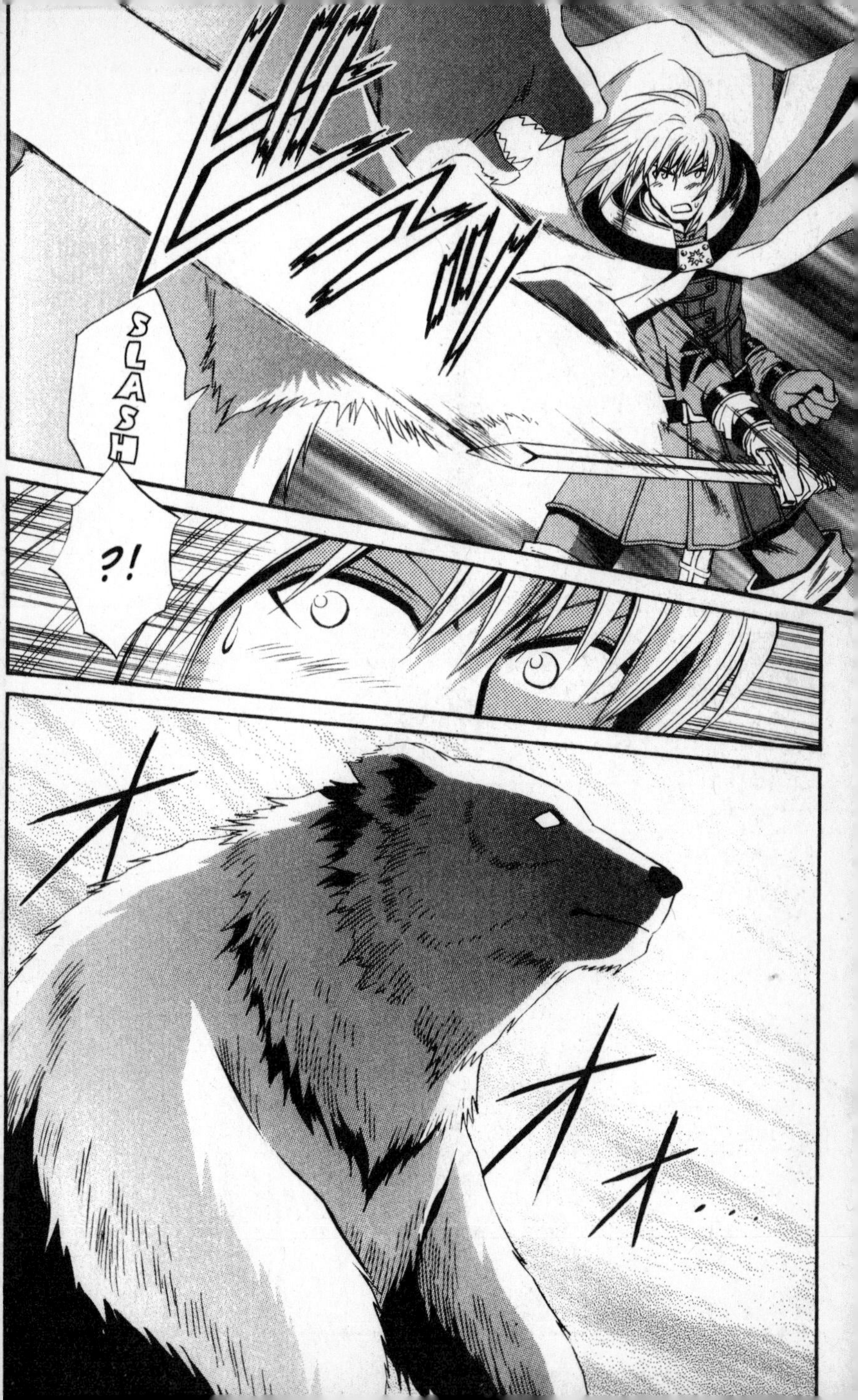
SLASH
?!
オオオ…

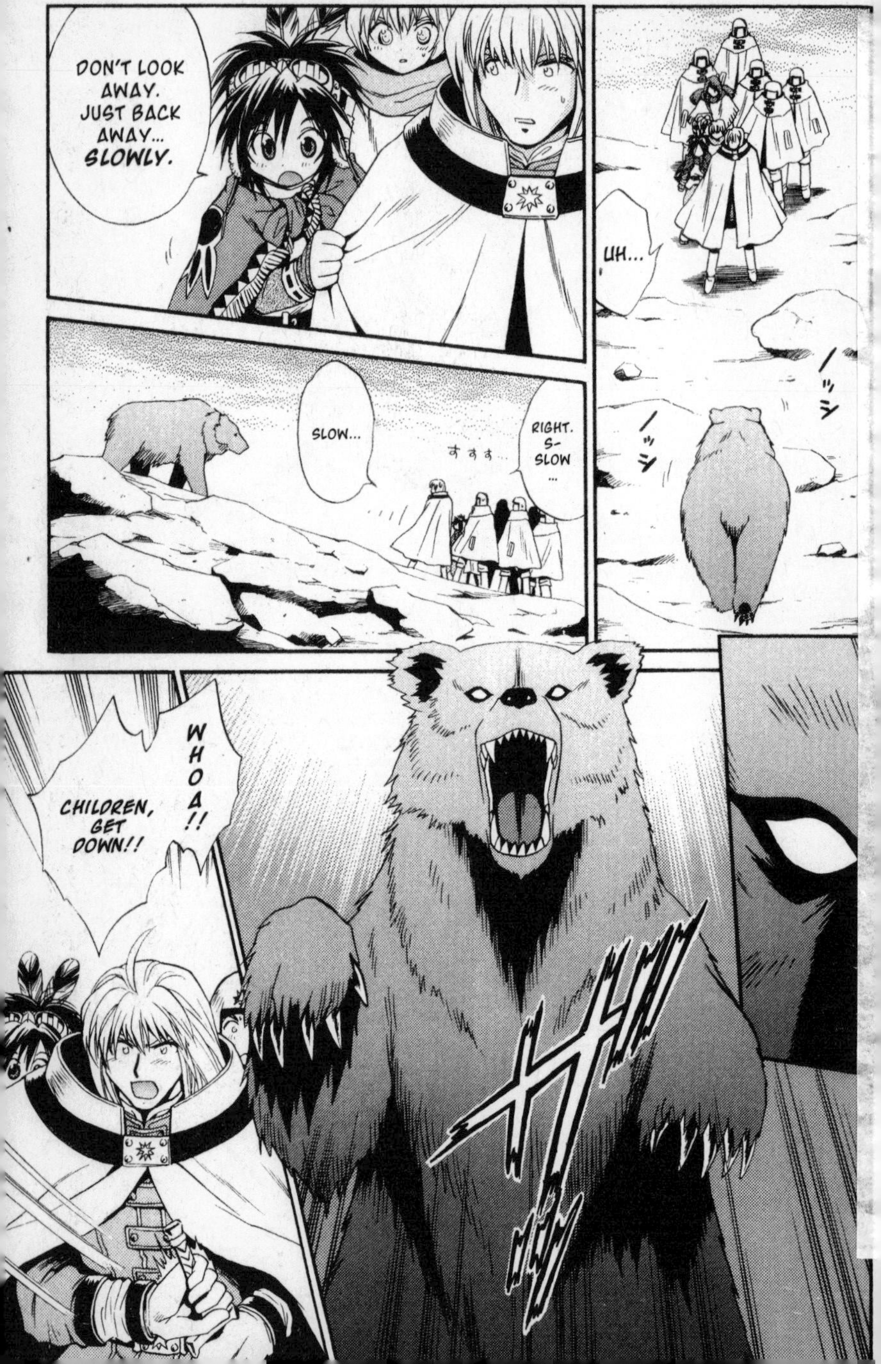
UH...
ノッシ
ノッシ
DON'T LOOK AWAY. JUST BACK AWAY... SLOWLY.
RIGHT. S-SLOW...
すすす...
SLOW...
WHOA!!
CHILDREN, GET DOWN!!

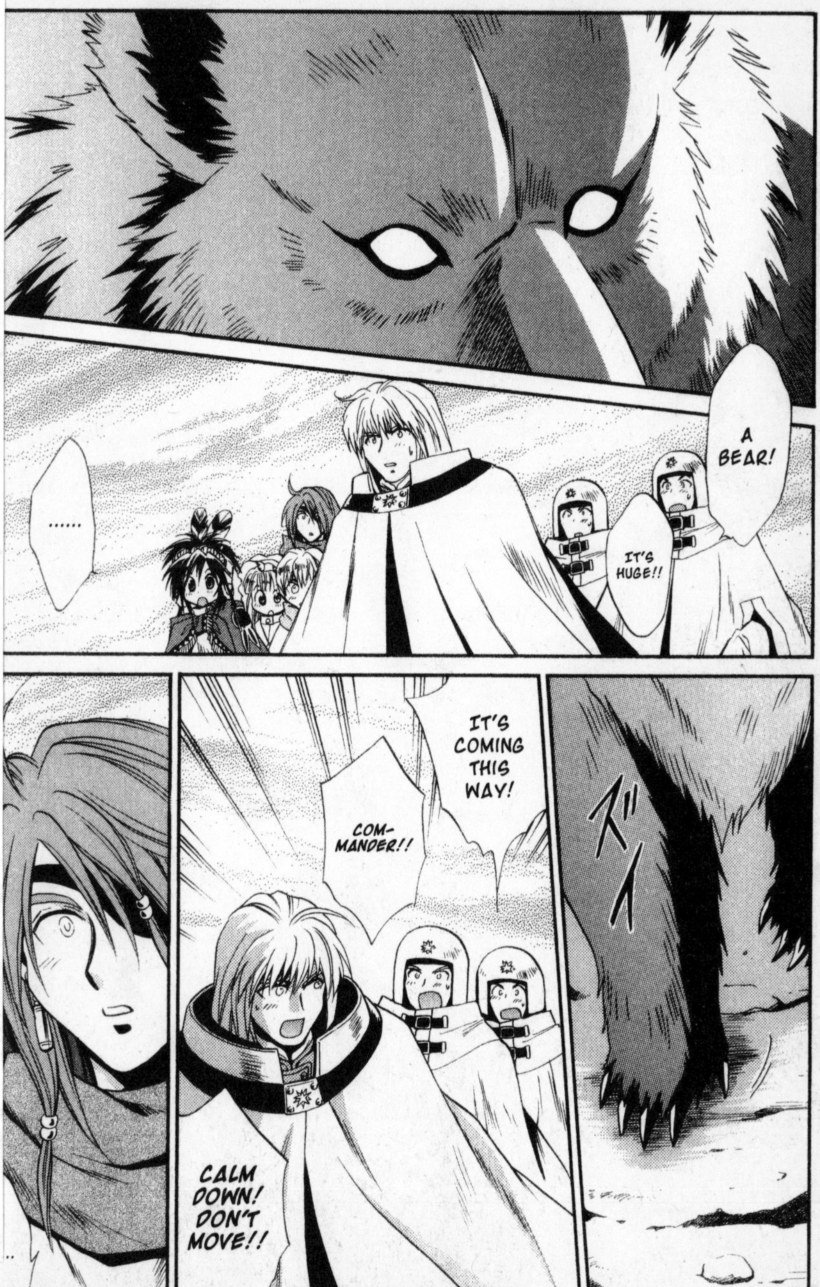
A BEAR!
IT'S HUGE!!
......
ズイ
IT'S COMING THIS WAY!
COM-MANDER!!
CALM DOWN! DON'T MOVE!!

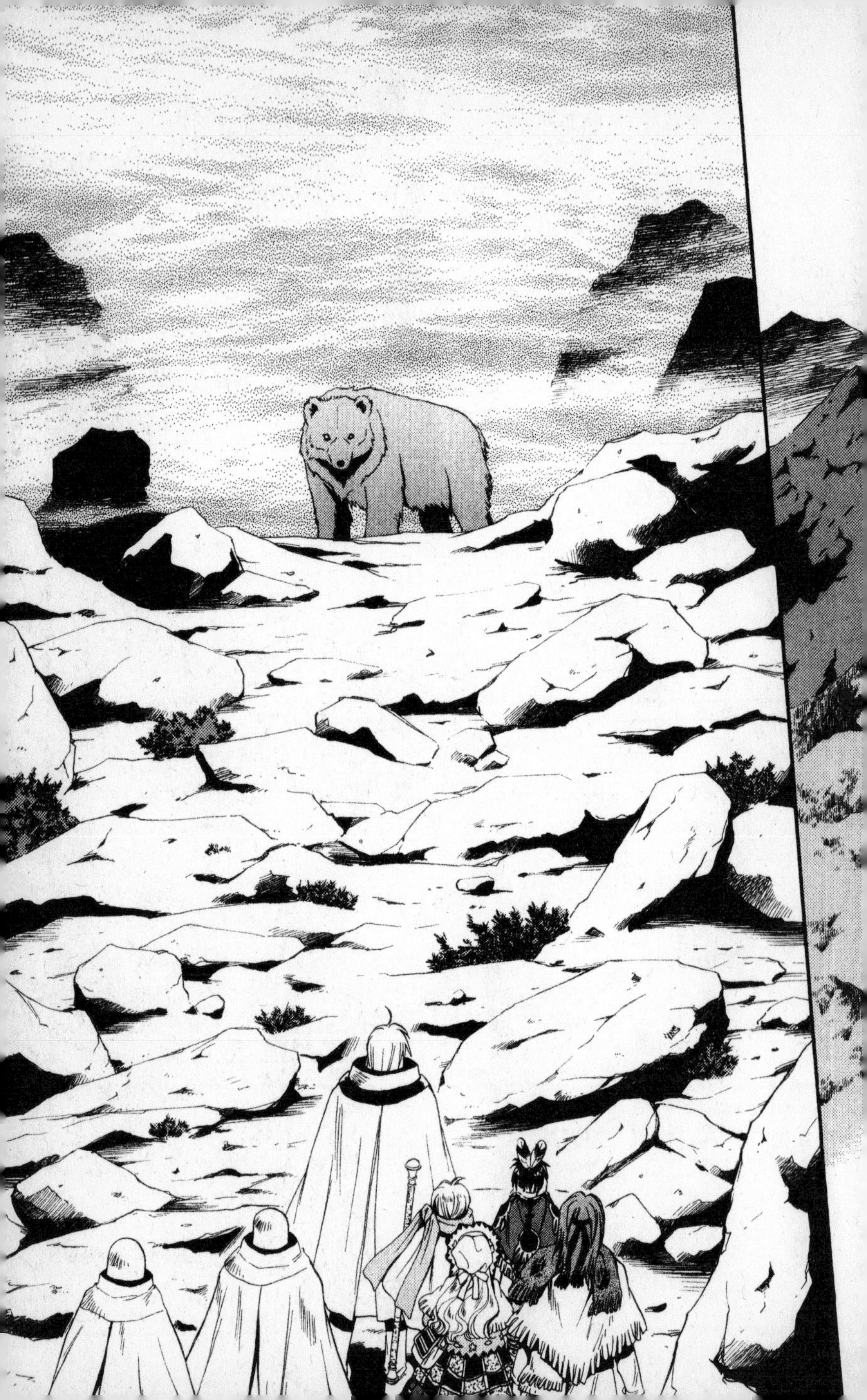

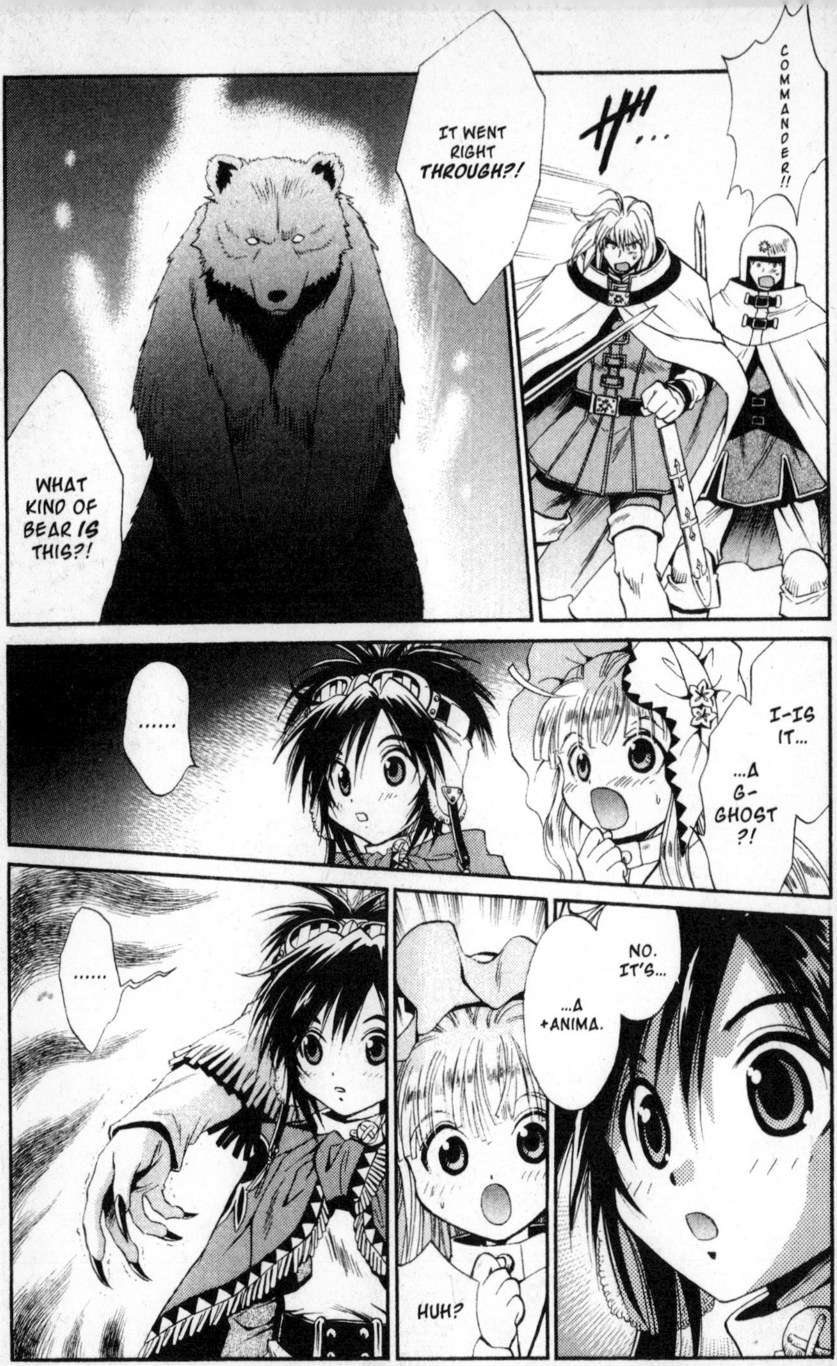
COMMANDER!!
IT WENT RIGHT THROUGH?!
WHAT KIND OF BEAR IS THIS?!
I-IS IT...
...A G-GHOST?!
......
NO. IT'S...
...A +ANIMA.
HUH?
......

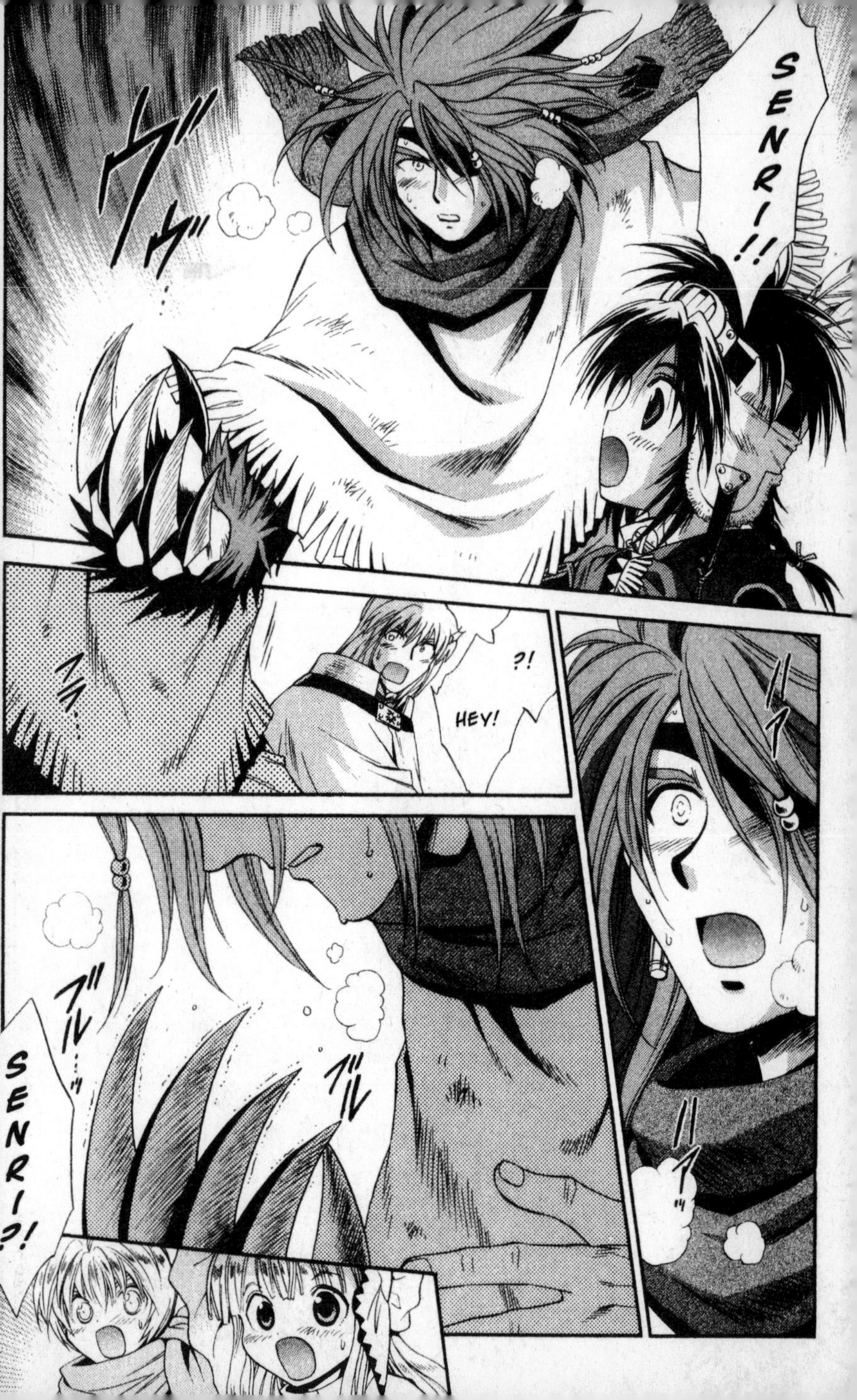
SENRI!!
?!
HEY!
SENRI?!

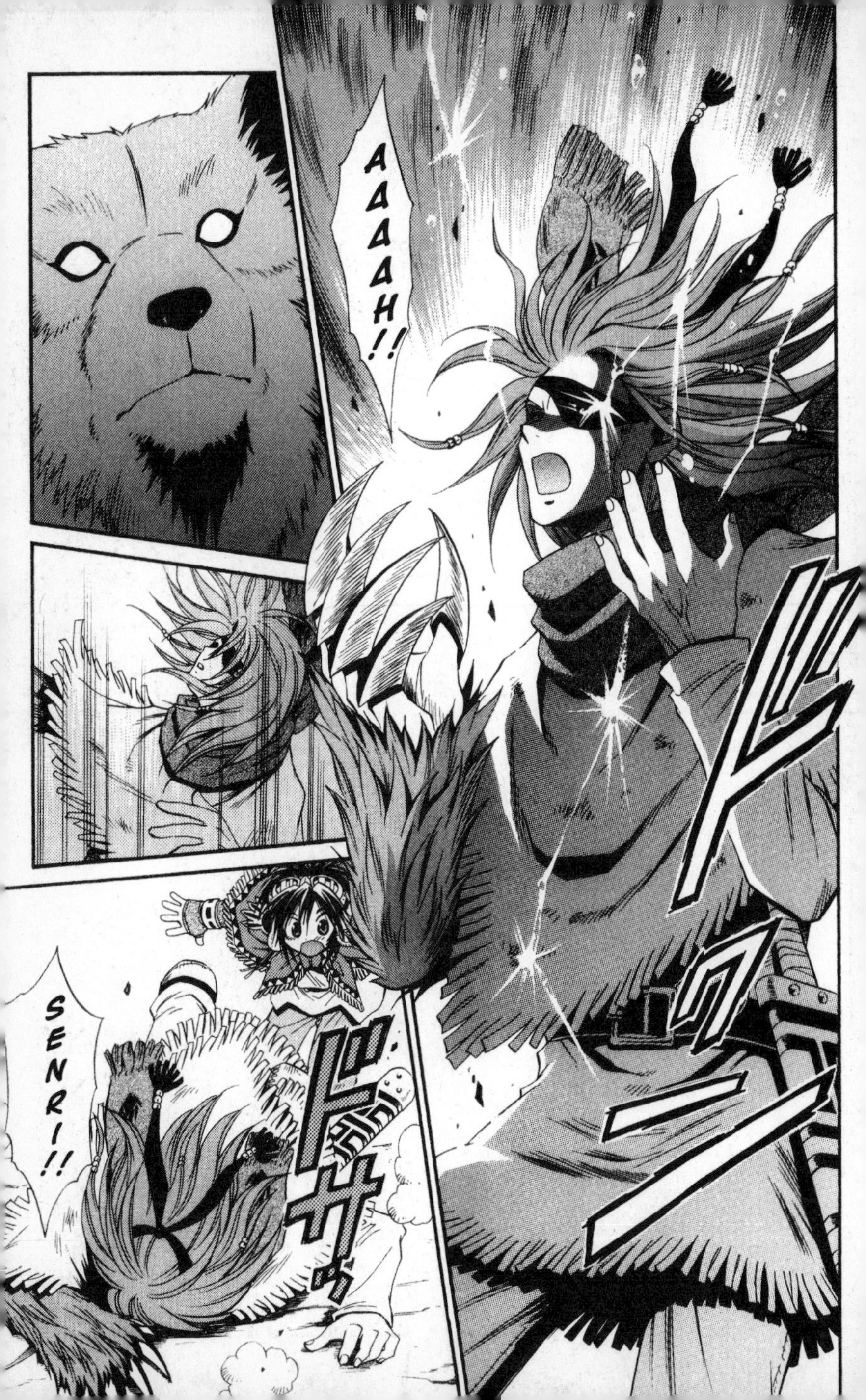
AAAAAH!!
SENRI!!

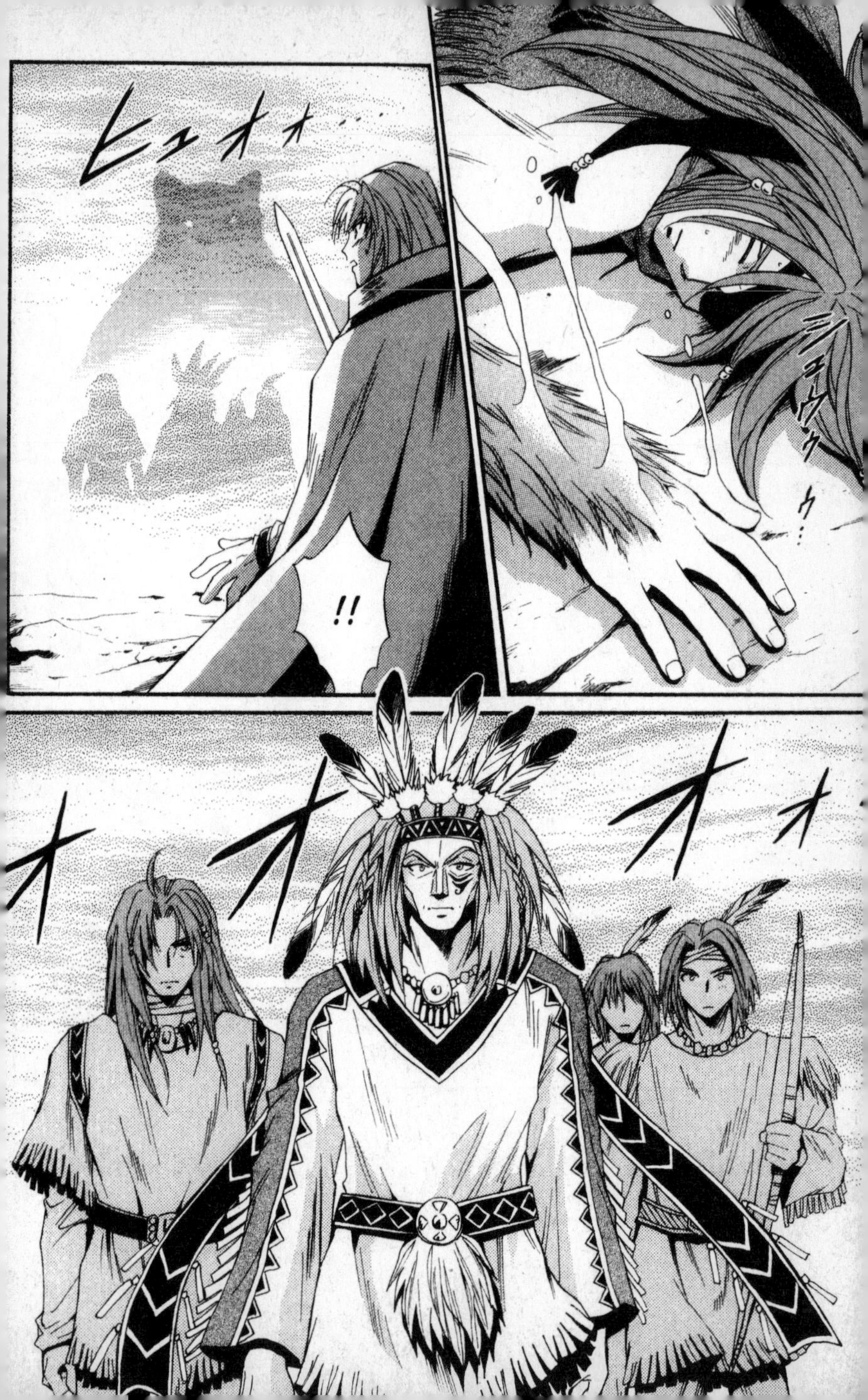
ヒュオオ……
!!
オオオオ

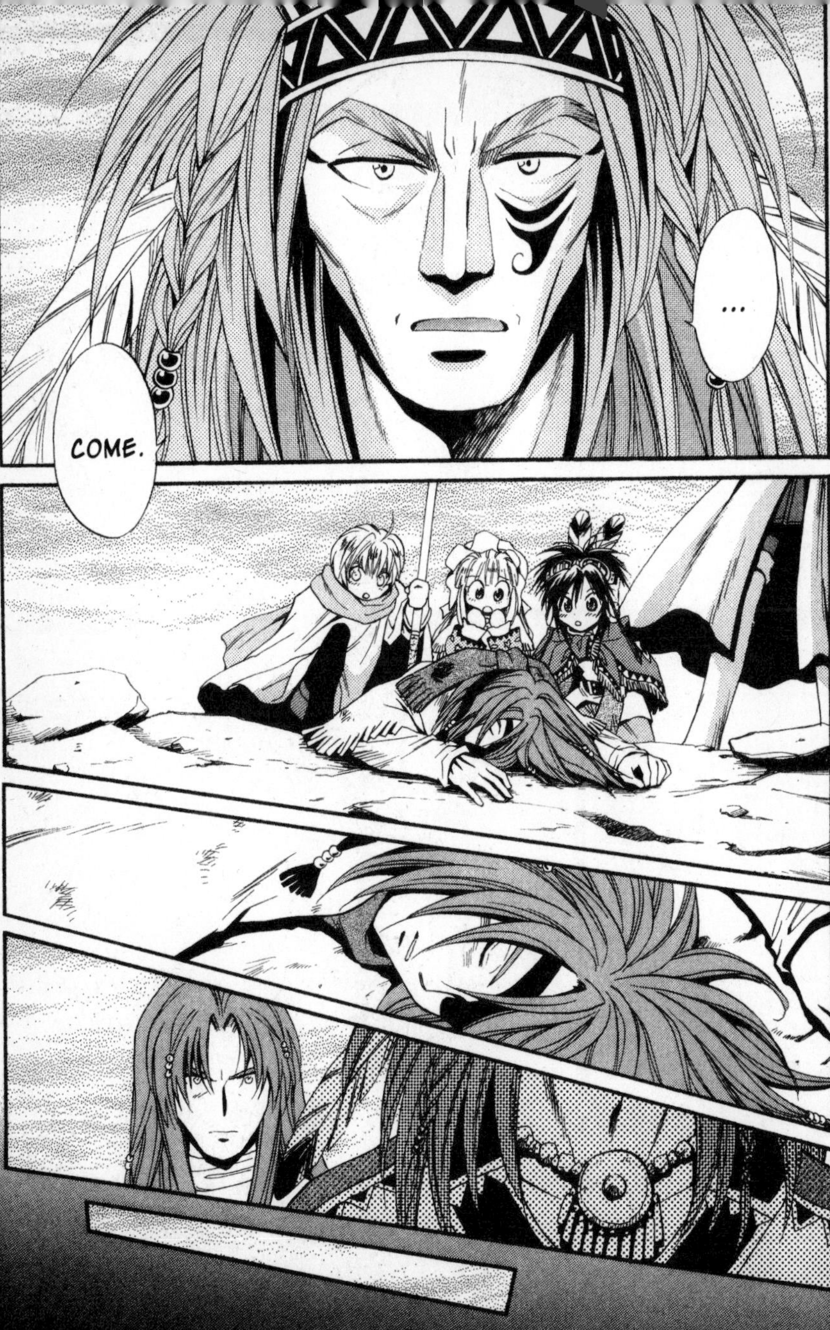
...
COME.

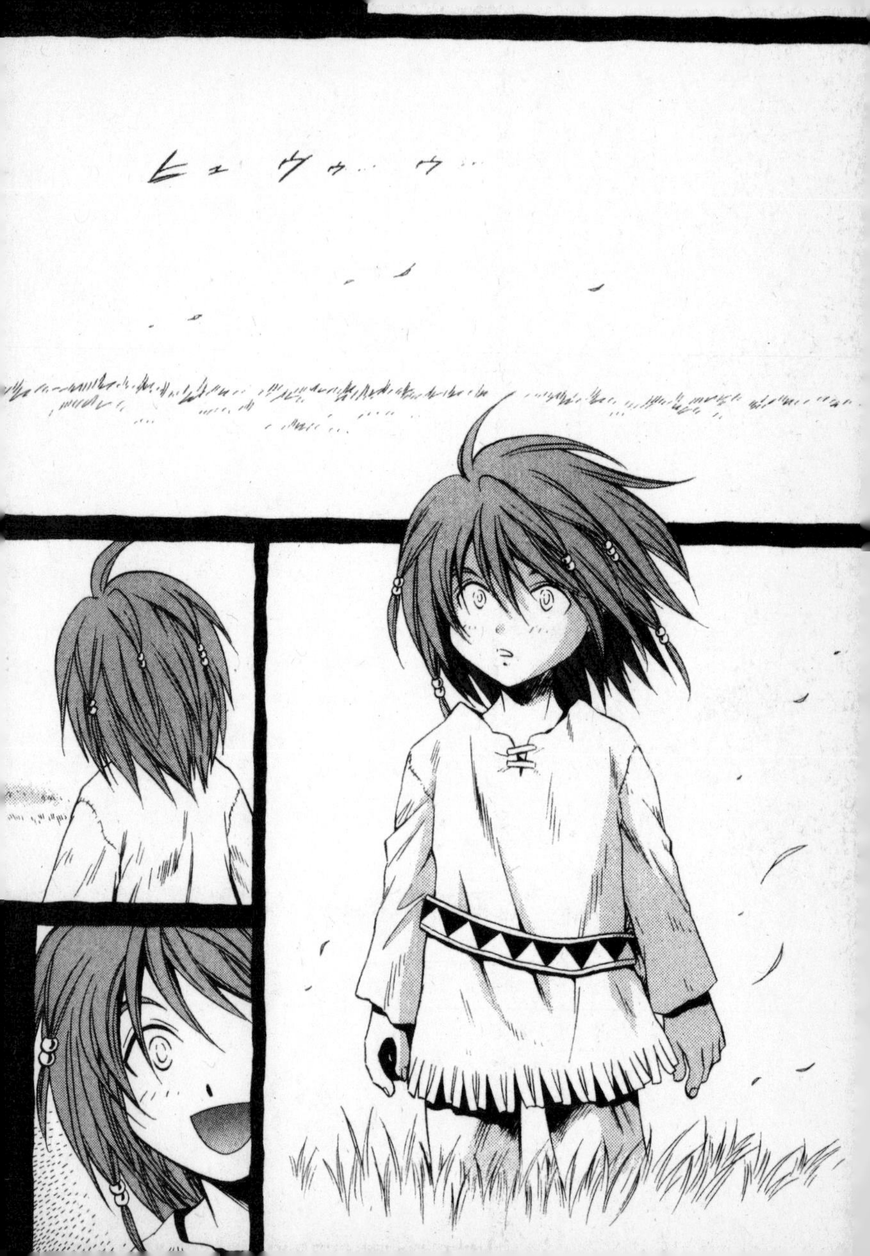
ヒュヴゥ‥ウ‥

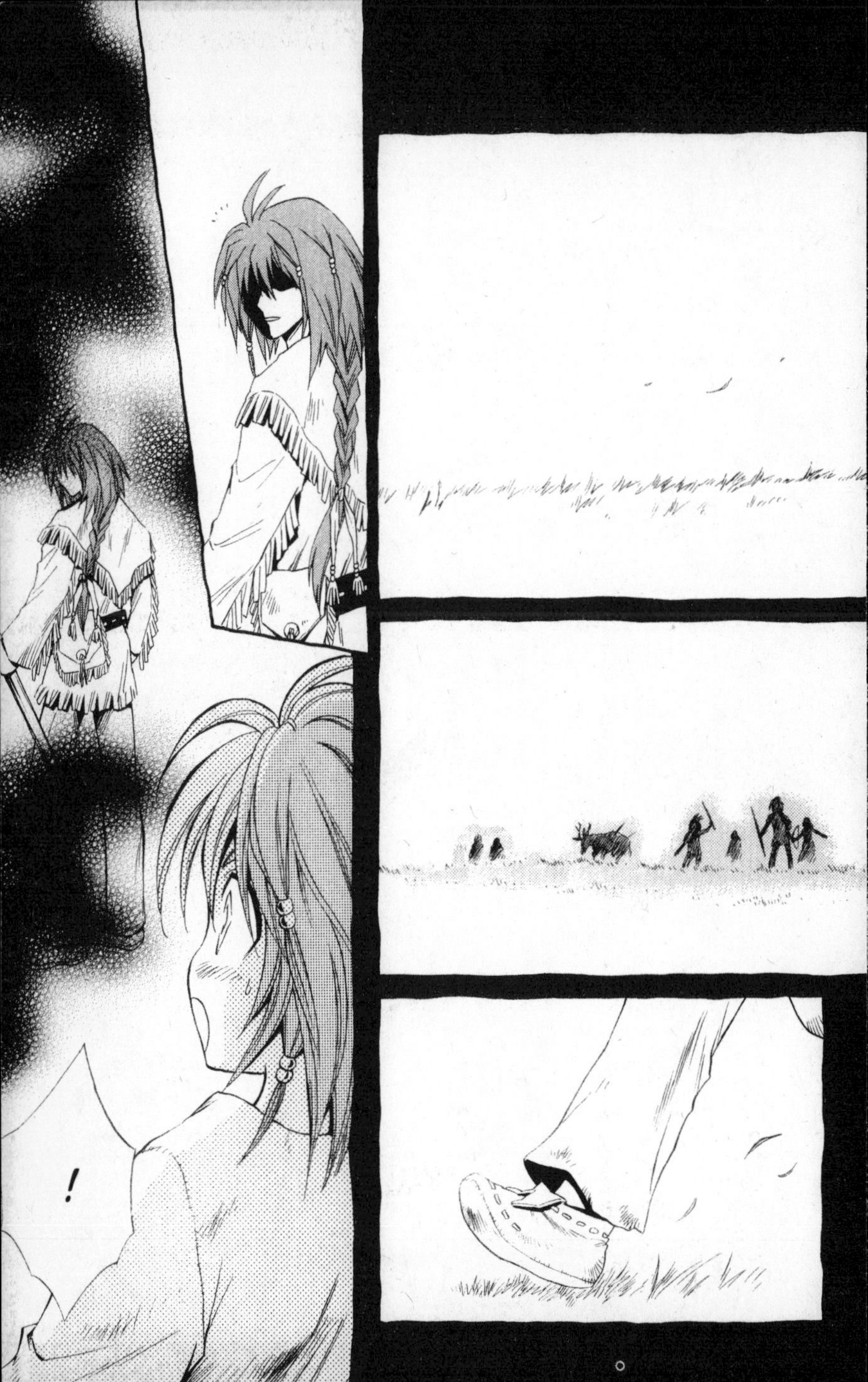
!

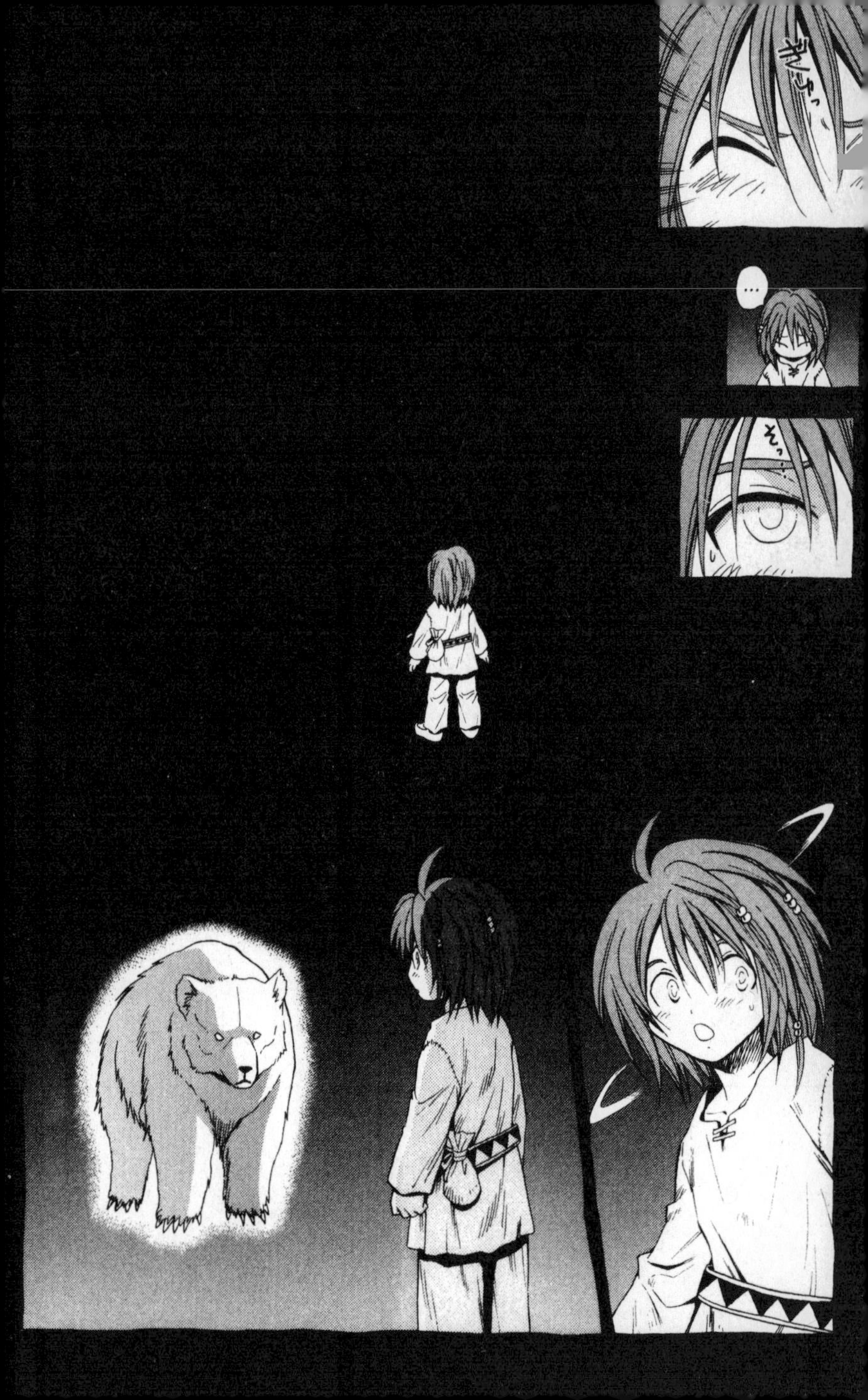
ぎゅっ
…
ぞっ

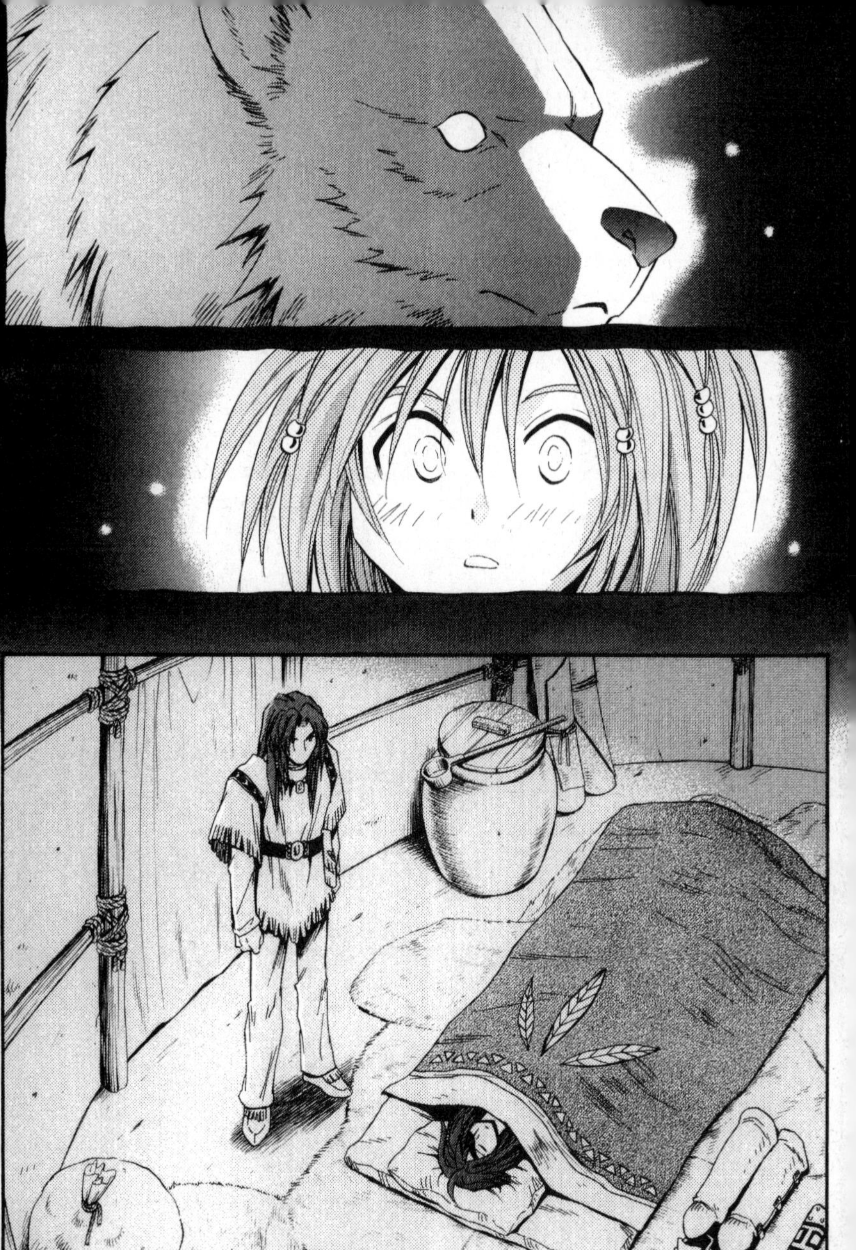

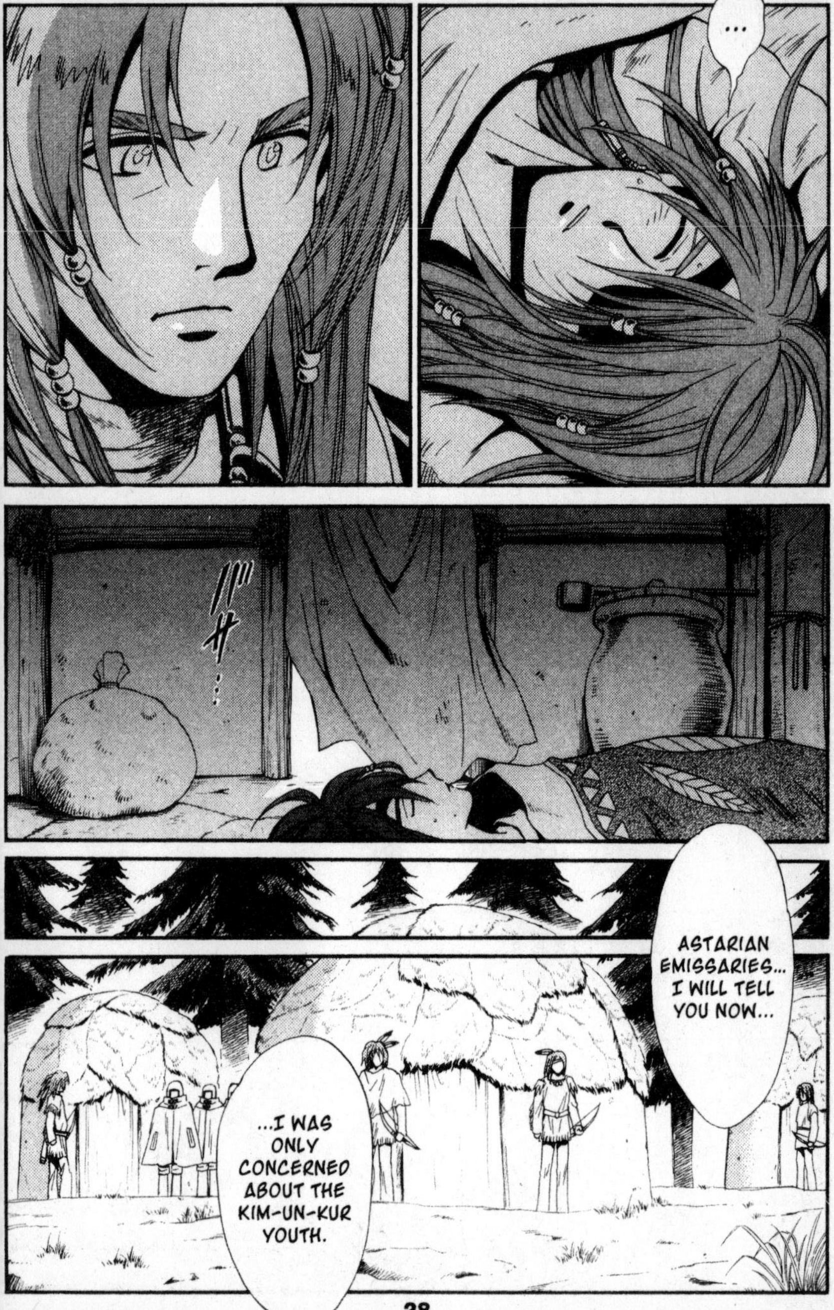
...
ASTARIAN EMISSARIES... I WILL TELL YOU NOW...
...I WAS ONLY CONCERNED ABOUT THE KIM-UN-KUR YOUTH.

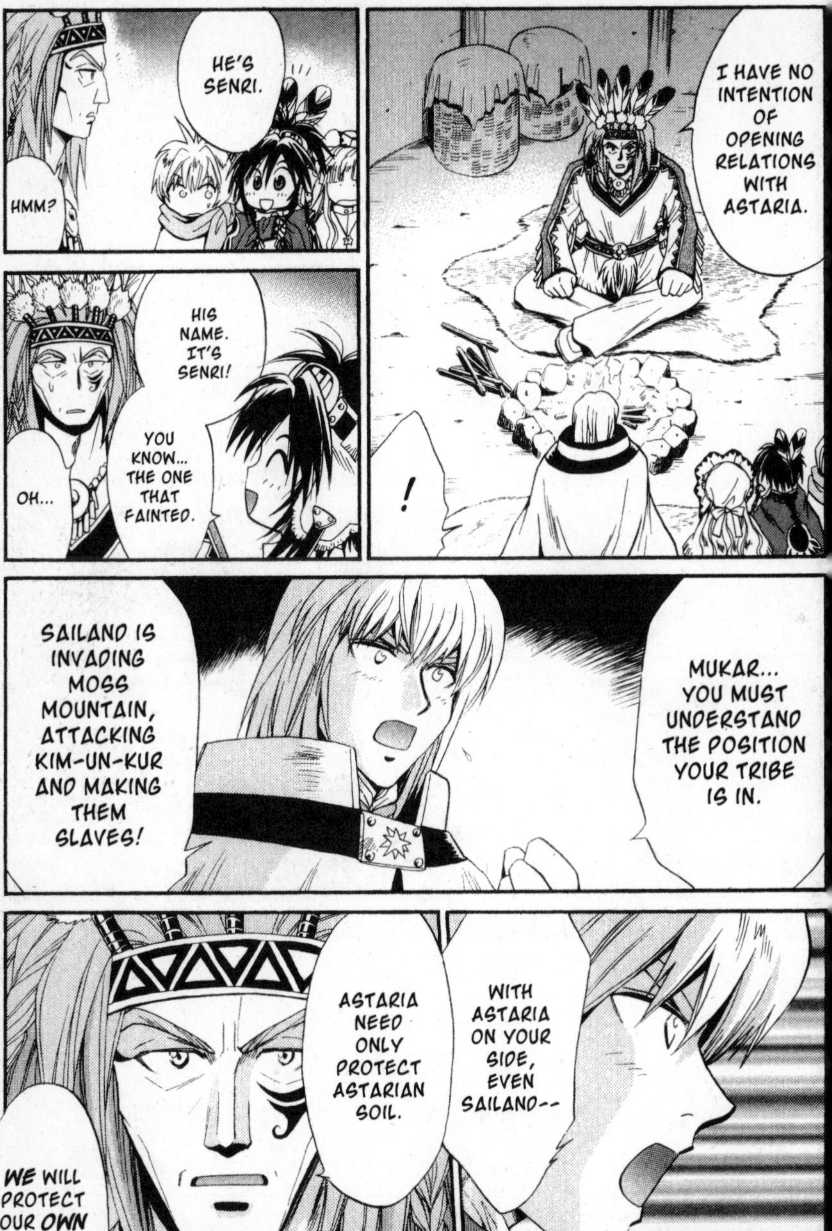
I HAVE NO INTENTION OF OPENING RELATIONS WITH ASTARIA.
!
HE'S SENRI.
HMM?
HIS NAME. IT'S SENRI!
YOU KNOW... THE ONE THAT FAINTED.
OH...
MUKAR... YOU MUST UNDERSTAND THE POSITION YOUR TRIBE IS IN.
SAILAND IS INVADING MOSS MOUNTAIN, ATTACKING KIM-UN-KUR AND MAKING THEM SLAVES!
WITH ASTARIA ON YOUR SIDE, EVEN SAILAND--
ASTARIA NEED ONLY PROTECT ASTARIAN SOIL.
WE WILL PROTECT OUR OWN LAND.

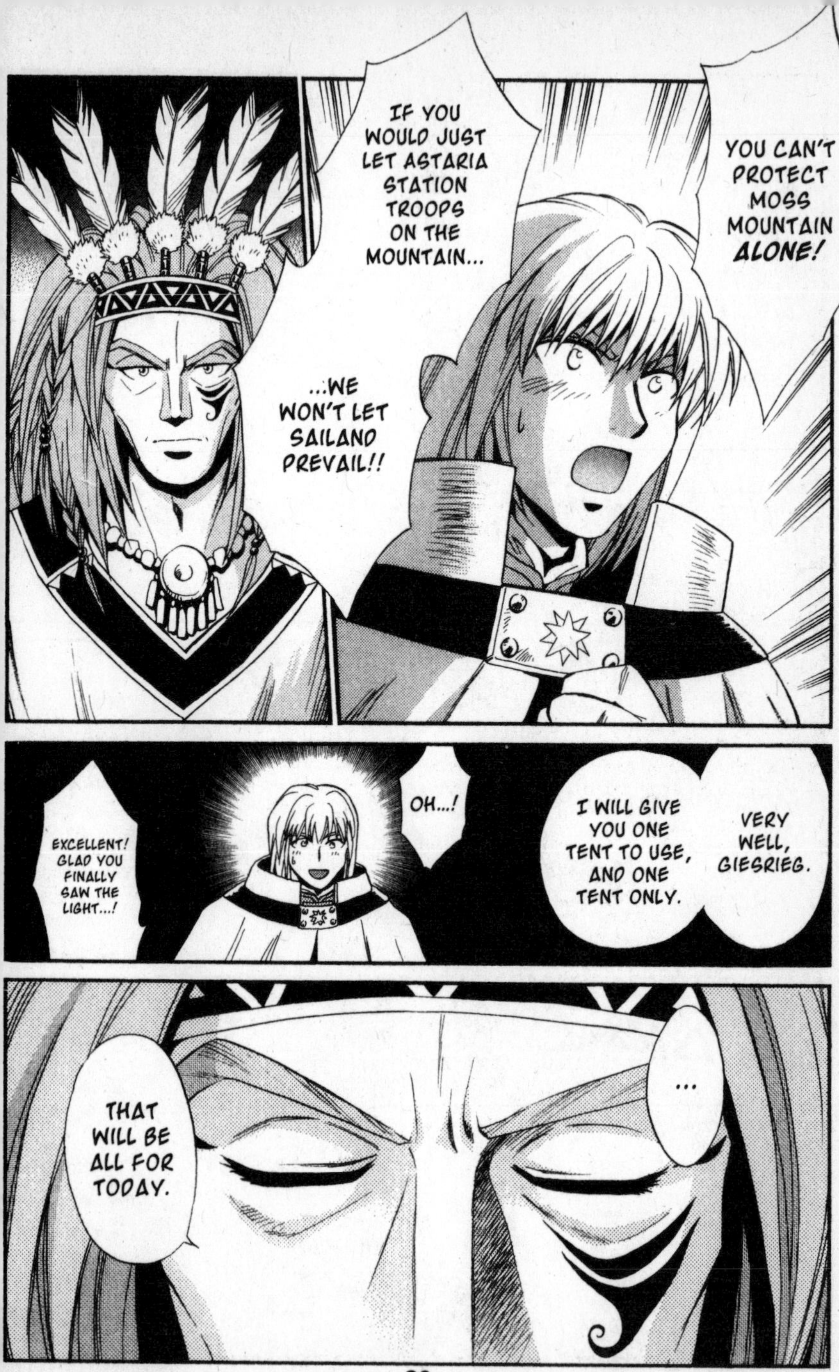
YOU CAN'T PROTECT MOSS MOUNTAIN ALONE!
IF YOU WOULD JUST LET ASTARIA STATION TROOPS ON THE MOUNTAIN...
...WE WON'T LET SAILAND PREVAIL!!
VERY WELL, GIESRIEG.
I WILL GIVE YOU ONE TENT TO USE, AND ONE TENT ONLY.
OH...!
EXCELLENT! GLAD YOU FINALLY SAW THE LIGHT...!
...
THAT WILL BE ALL FOR TODAY.

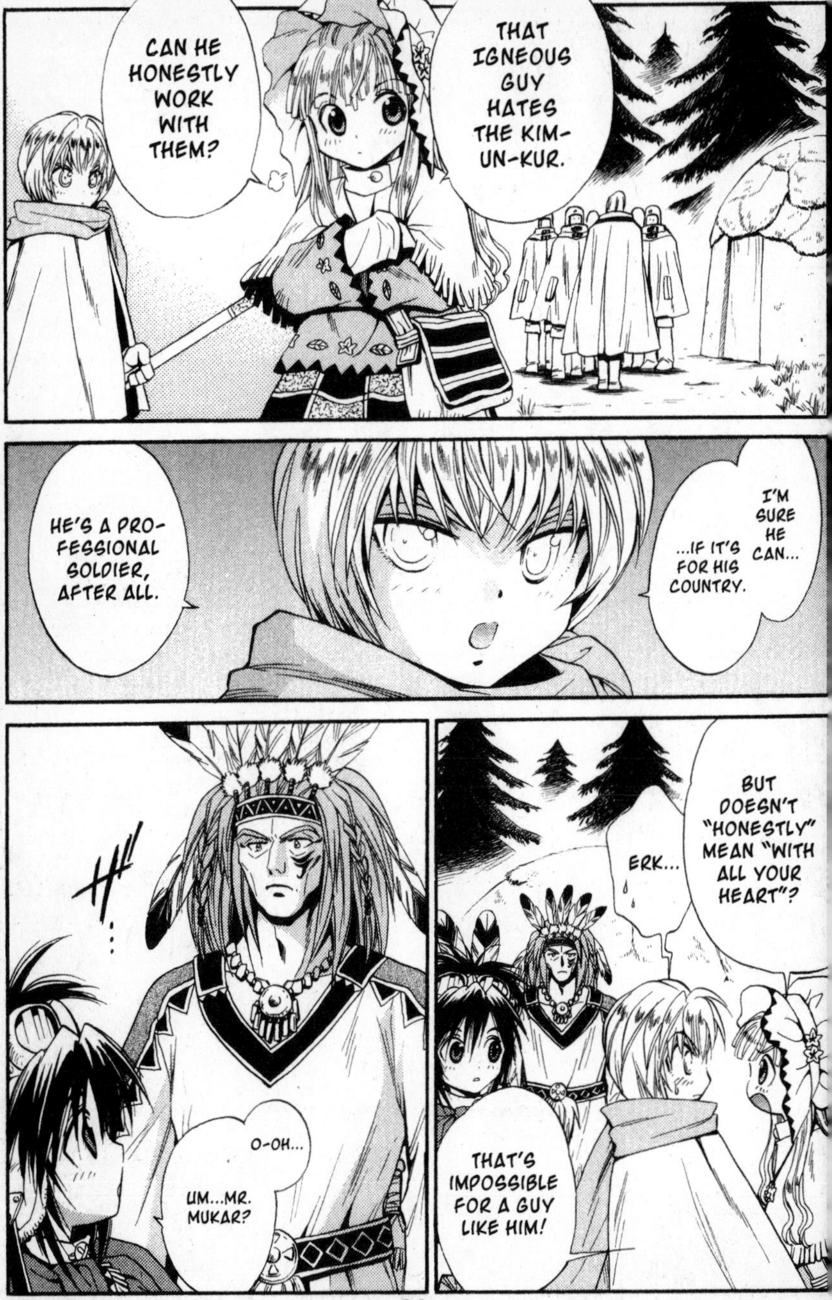
THAT IGNEOUS GUY HATES THE KIM-UN-KUR.
CAN HE HONESTLY WORK WITH THEM?
I'M SURE HE CAN...
...IF IT'S FOR HIS COUNTRY.
HE'S A PRO-FESSIONAL SOLDIER, AFTER ALL.
BUT DOESN'T "HONESTLY" MEAN "WITH ALL YOUR HEART"?
ERK...
THAT'S IMPOSSIBLE FOR A GUY LIKE HIM!
O-OH...
UM...MR. MUKAR?

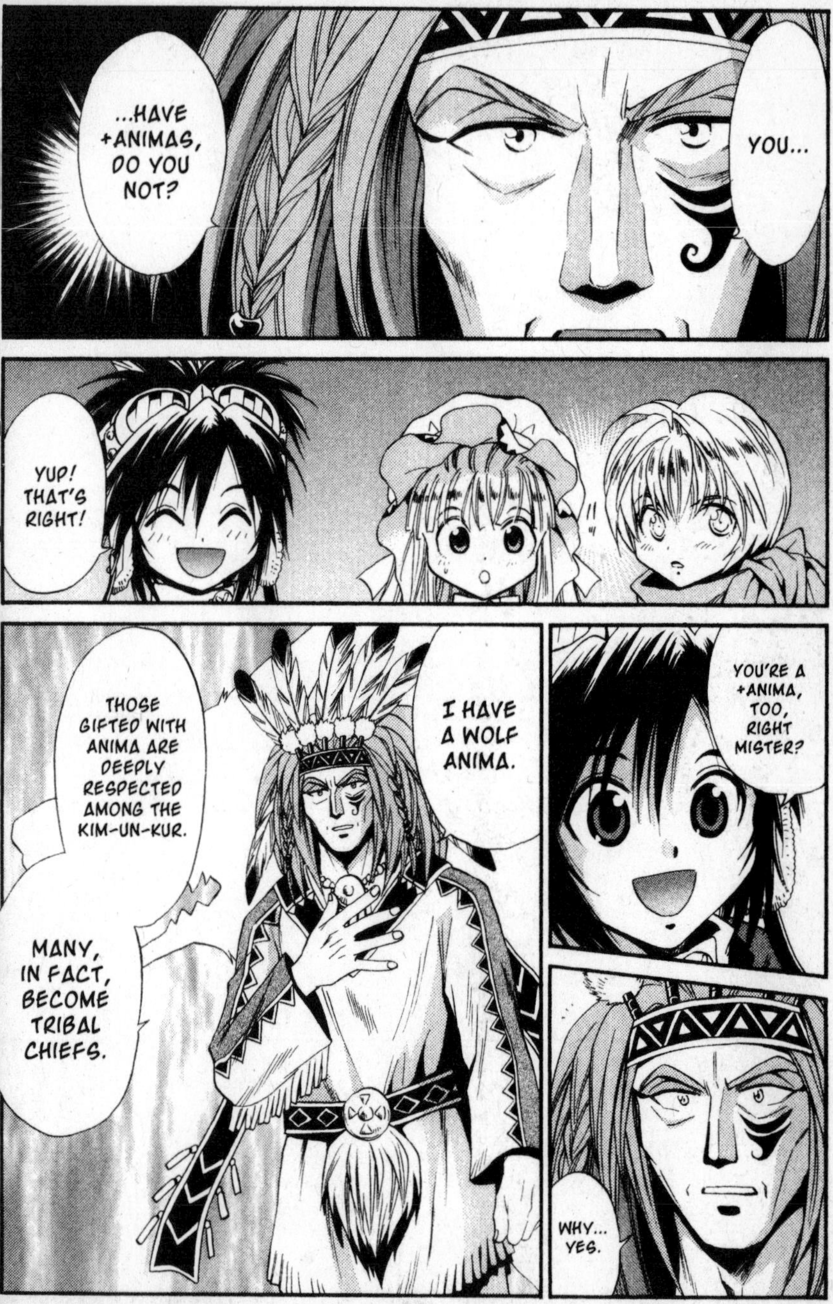
YOU...
...HAVE +ANIMAS, DO YOU NOT?
!!
YUP! THAT'S RIGHT!
YOU'RE A +ANIMA, TOO, RIGHT MISTER?
WHY... YES.
I HAVE A WOLF ANIMA.
THOSE GIFTED WITH ANIMA ARE DEEPLY RESPECTED AMONG THE KIM-UN-KUR.
MANY, IN FACT, BECOME TRIBAL CHIEFS.

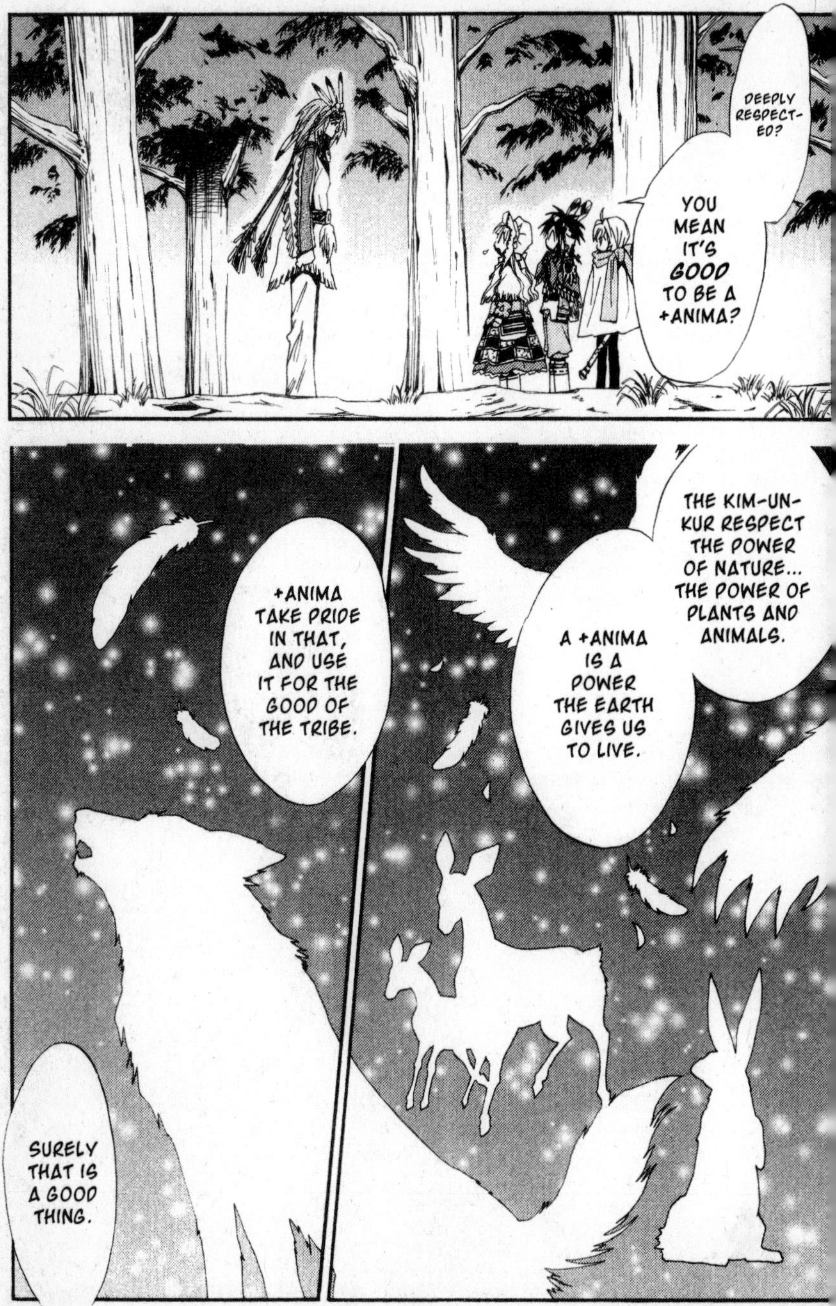
DEEPLY RESPECT-ED?
YOU MEAN IT'S GOOD TO BE A +ANIMA?
THE KIM-UN-KUR RESPECT THE POWER OF NATURE... THE POWER OF PLANTS AND ANIMALS.
A +ANIMA IS A POWER THE EARTH GIVES US TO LIVE.
+ANIMA TAKE PRIDE IN THAT, AND USE IT FOR THE GOOD OF THE TRIBE.
SURELY THAT IS A GOOD THING.

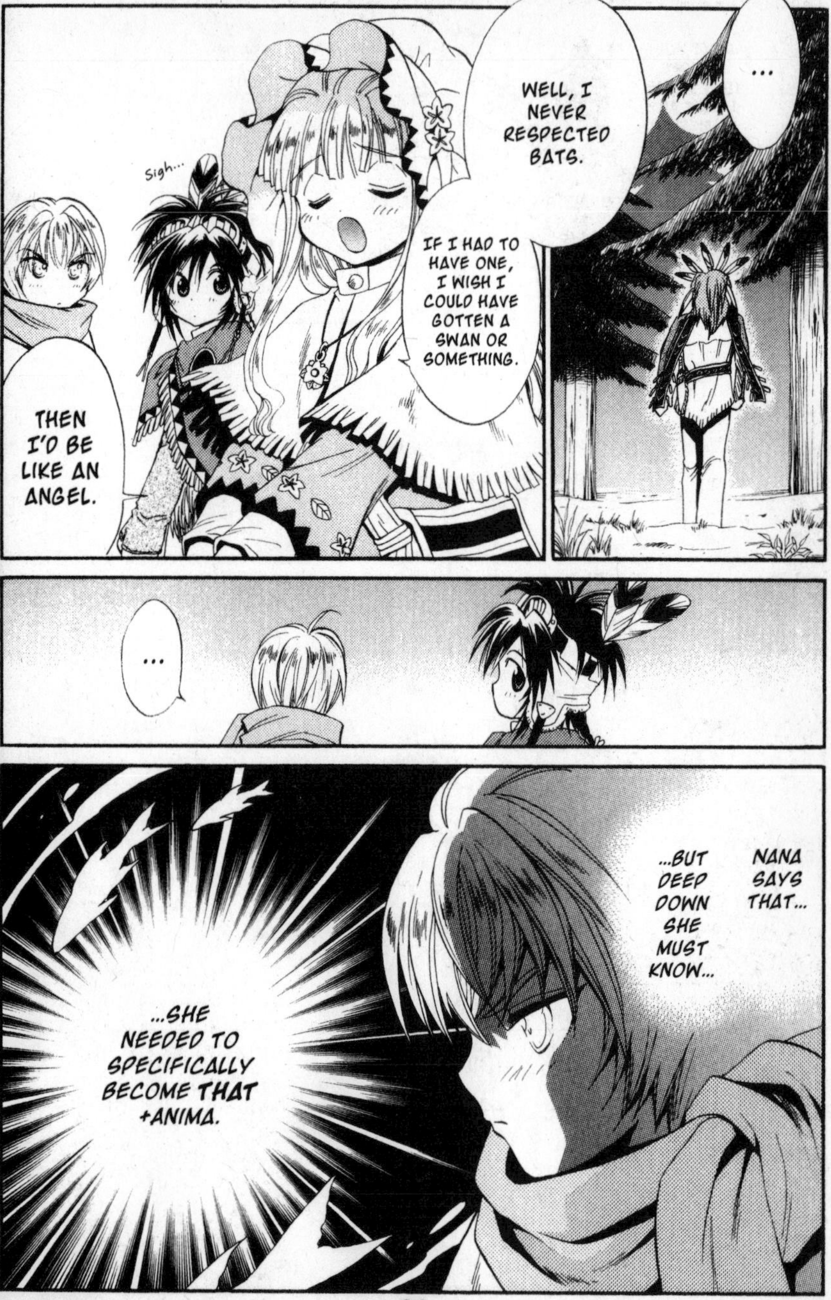
...
WELL, I NEVER RESPECTED BATS.
IF I HAD TO HAVE ONE, I WISH I COULD HAVE GOTTEN A SWAN OR SOMETHING.
Sigh...
THEN I'D BE LIKE AN ANGEL.
...
NANA SAYS THAT...
...BUT DEEP DOWN SHE MUST KNOW...
...SHE NEEDED TO SPECIFICALLY BECOME THAT +ANIMA.

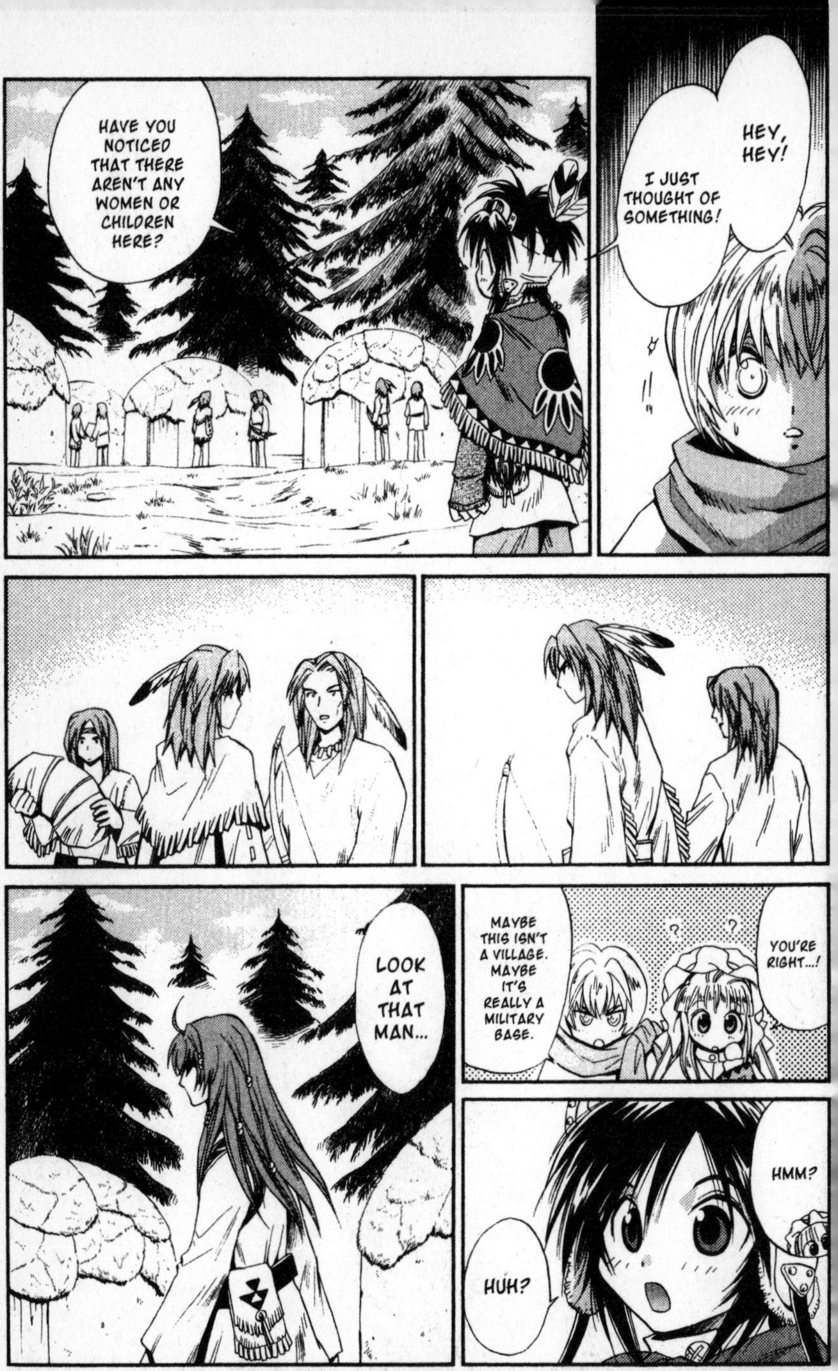
HEY, HEY!
I JUST THOUGHT OF SOMETHING!
HAVE YOU NOTICED THAT THERE AREN'T ANY WOMEN OR CHILDREN HERE?
MAYBE THIS ISN'T A VILLAGE. MAYBE IT'S REALLY A MILITARY BASE.
YOU'RE RIGHT...!
HMM?
HUH?
LOOK AT THAT MAN...

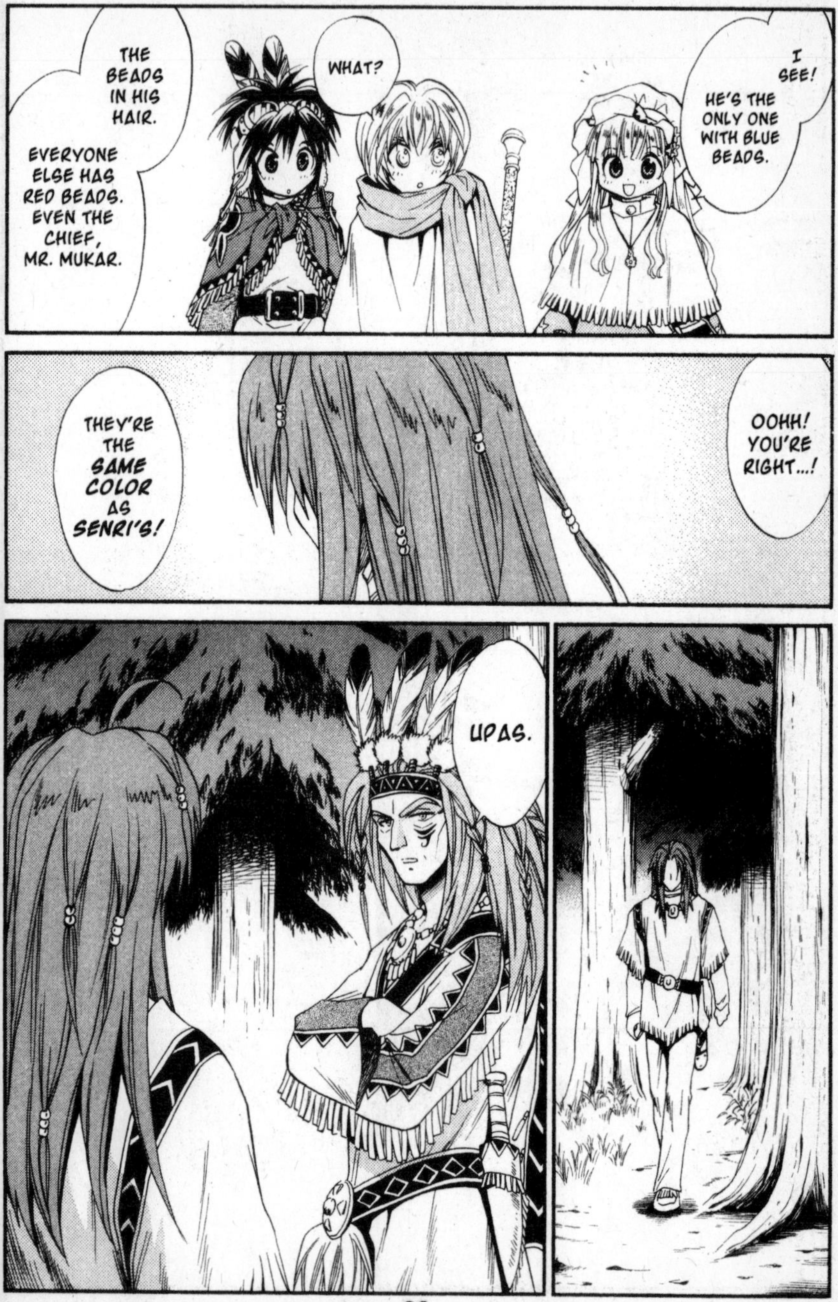
I SEE! HE'S THE ONLY ONE WITH BLUE BEADS.
WHAT?
THE BEADS IN HIS HAIR.
EVERYONE ELSE HAS RED BEADS. EVEN THE CHIEF, MR. MUKAR.
OOHH! YOU'RE RIGHT...!
THEY'RE THE SAME COLOR AS SENRI'S!
UPAS.

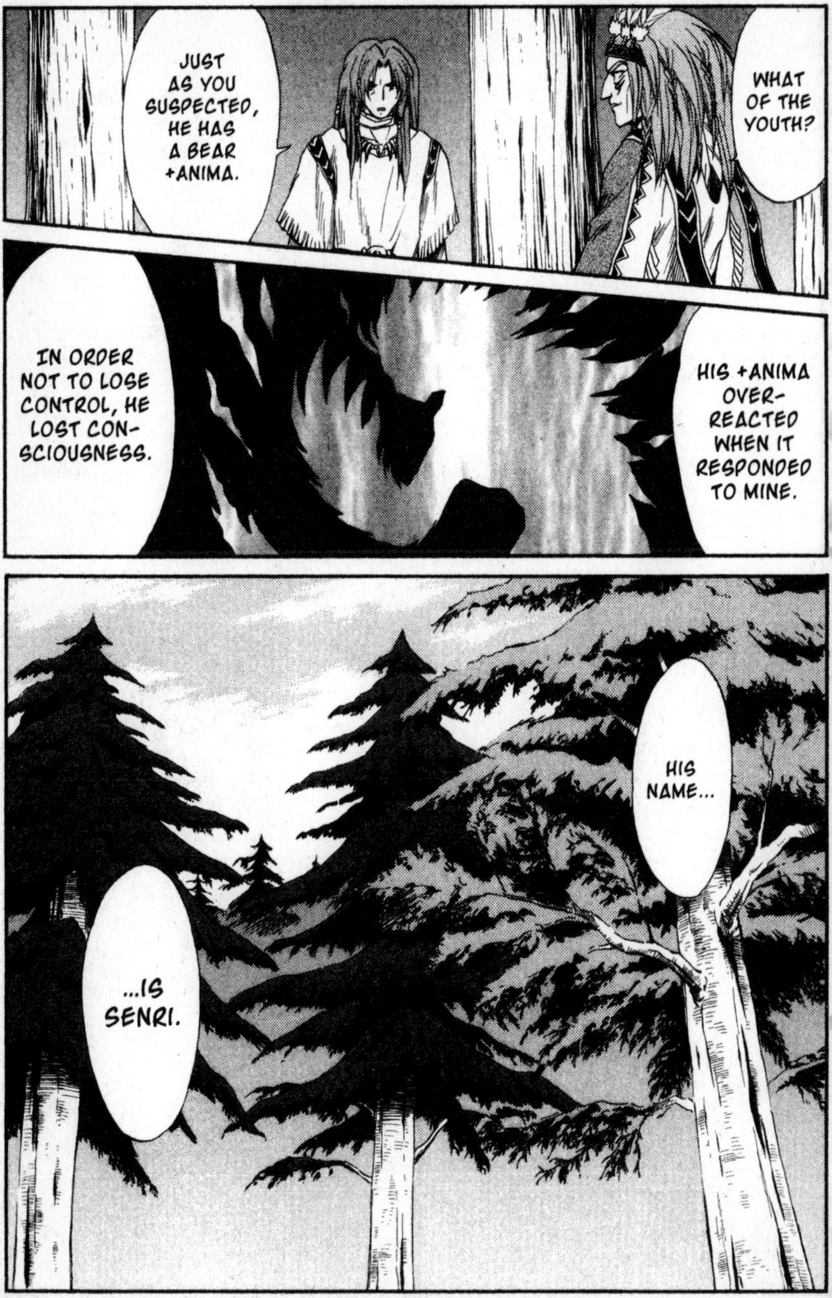
WHAT OF THE YOUTH?
JUST AS YOU SUSPECTED, HE HAS A BEAR +ANIMA.
HIS +ANIMA OVER-REACTED WHEN IT RESPONDED TO MINE.
IN ORDER NOT TO LOSE CONTROL, HE LOST CON-SCIOUSNESS.
HIS NAME...
...IS SENRI.

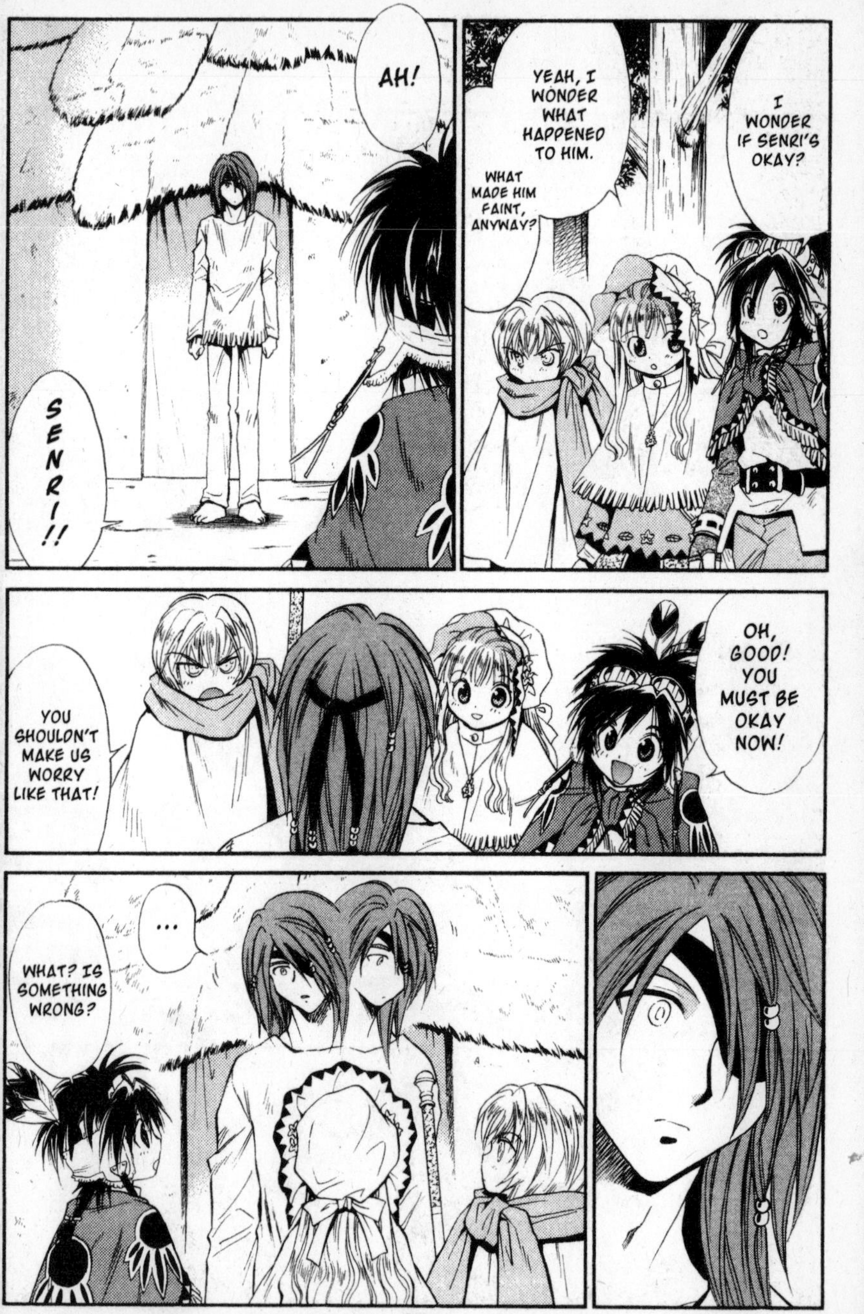
I WONDER IF SENRI'S OKAY?
YEAH, I WONDER WHAT HAPPENED TO HIM.
WHAT MADE HIM FAINT, ANYWAY?
AH!
SENRI!!
OH, GOOD! YOU MUST BE OKAY NOW!
YOU SHOULDN'T MAKE US WORRY LIKE THAT!
...
WHAT? IS SOMETHING WRONG?

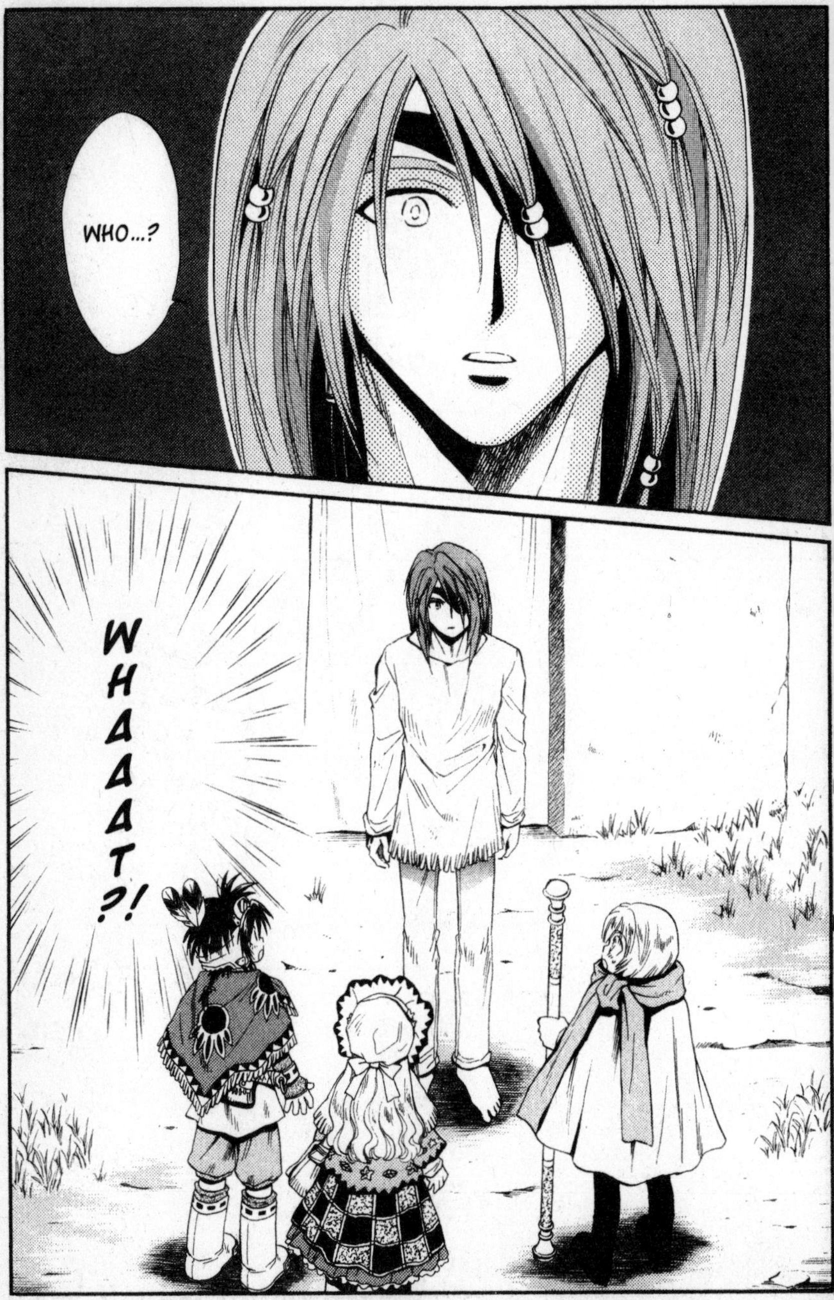
WHO...?
WHAAAAT?!

Staff

+Anima Staff
Mukai (manga artist)
Always uses her favorite wooden mechanical pencil.
Loves coffee.
Assistant T-san, in charge of backgrounds
I love café latte!
Assistant H-san, tone master
I like black tea!
Fuuta, official healer
Long-bodied Corgi--very rowdy.
MAY I GO SMELL THE DOG?!
THE OFFICIAL HEALER IS OVER-WORKED...
Mmm...
Shoot!
OKAY...

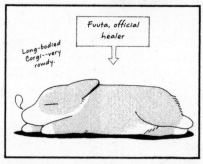

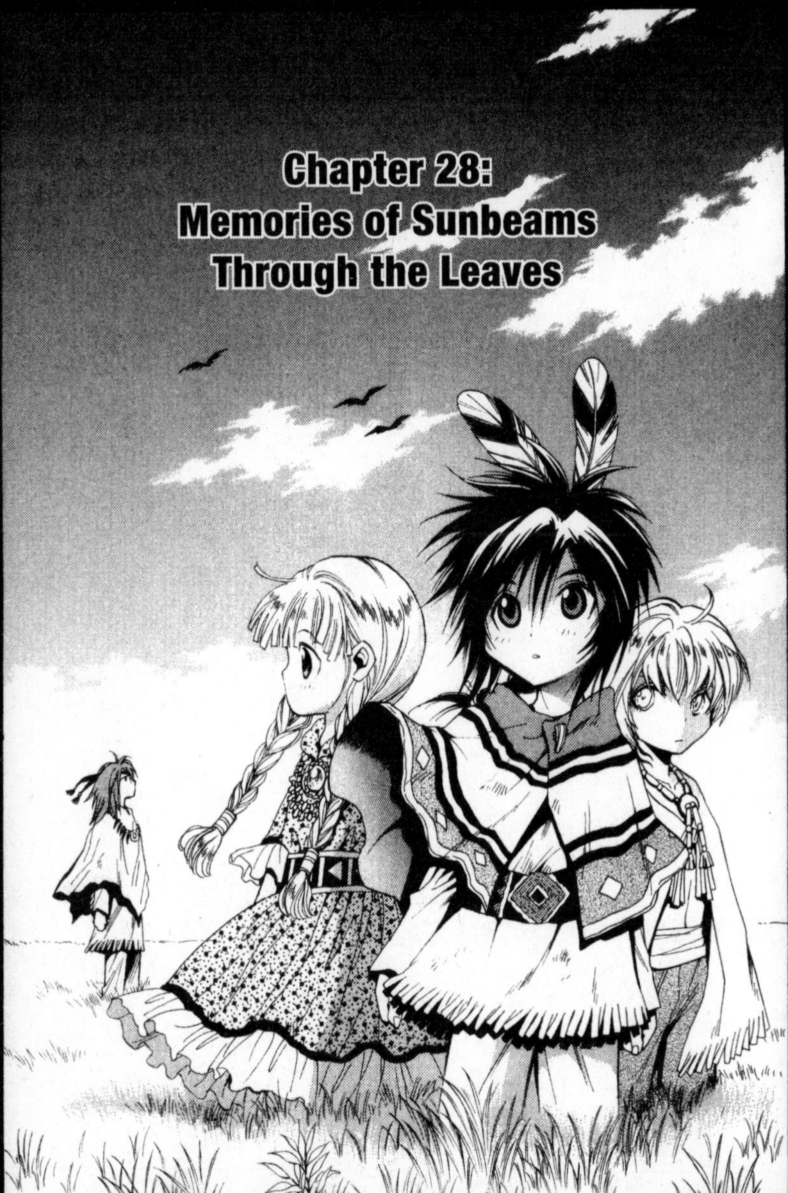
Chapter 28:
Memories of Sunbeams
Through the Leaves

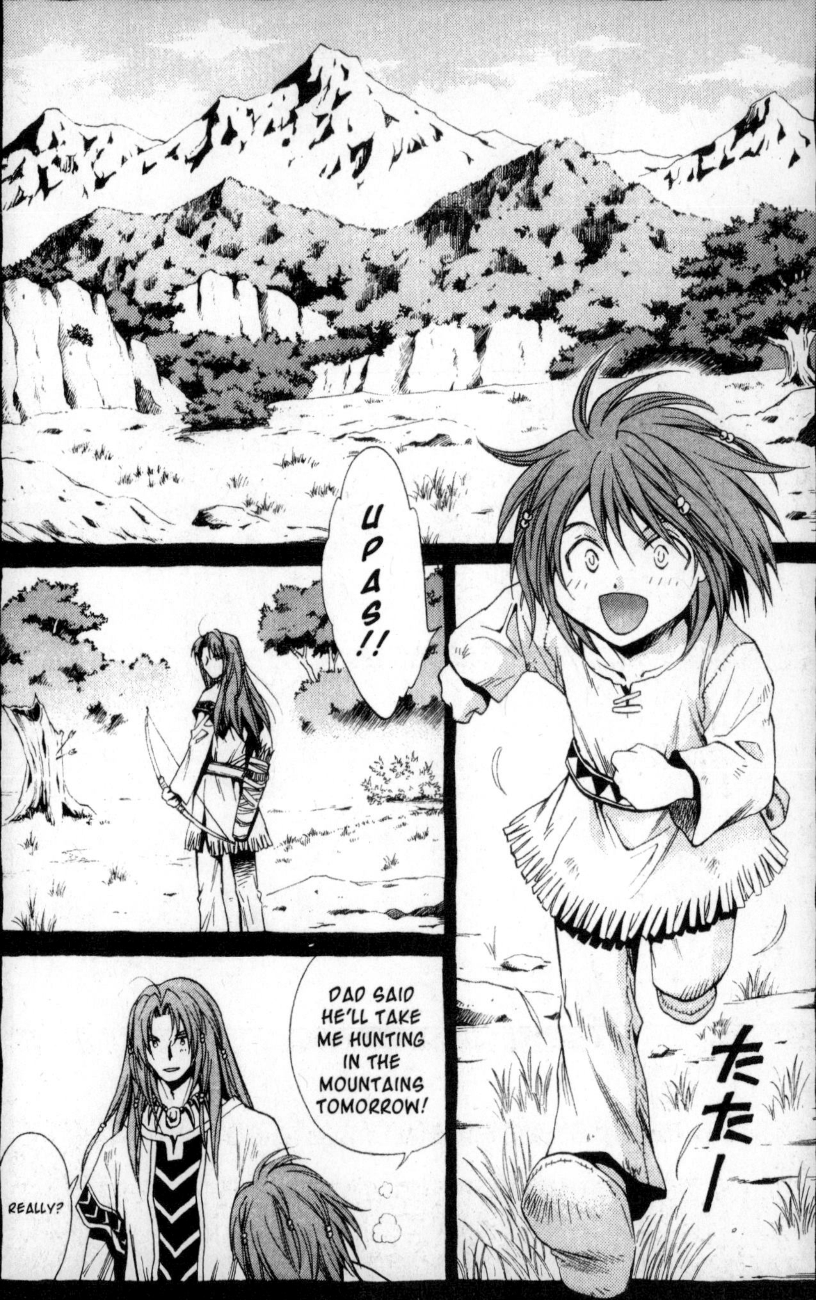
UPAS!!
たたー
DAD SAID HE'LL TAKE ME HUNTING IN THE MOUNTAINS TOMORROW!
REALLY?

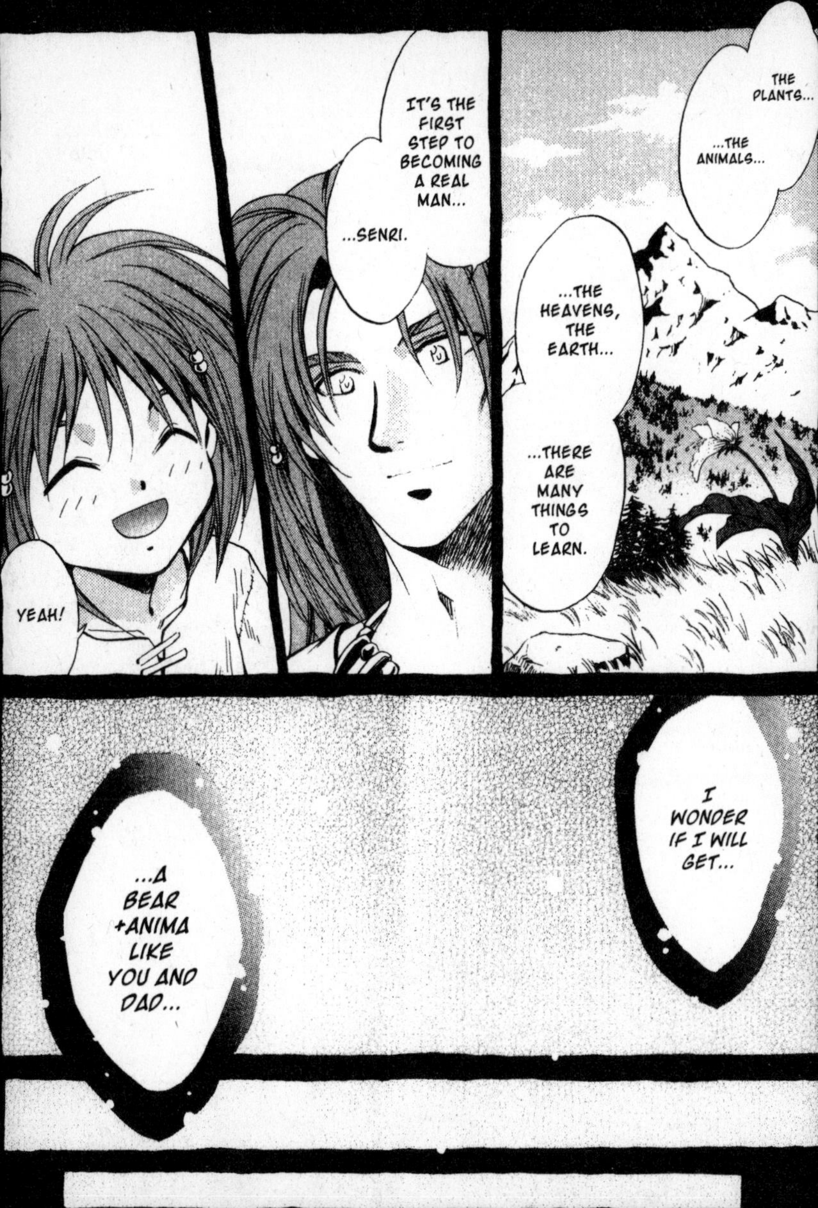
THE PLANTS...
...THE ANIMALS...
...THE HEAVENS, THE EARTH...
...THERE ARE MANY THINGS TO LEARN.
IT'S THE FIRST STEP TO BECOMING A REAL MAN...
...SENRI.
YEAH!
I WONDER IF I WILL GET...
...A BEAR +ANIMA LIKE YOU AND DAD...

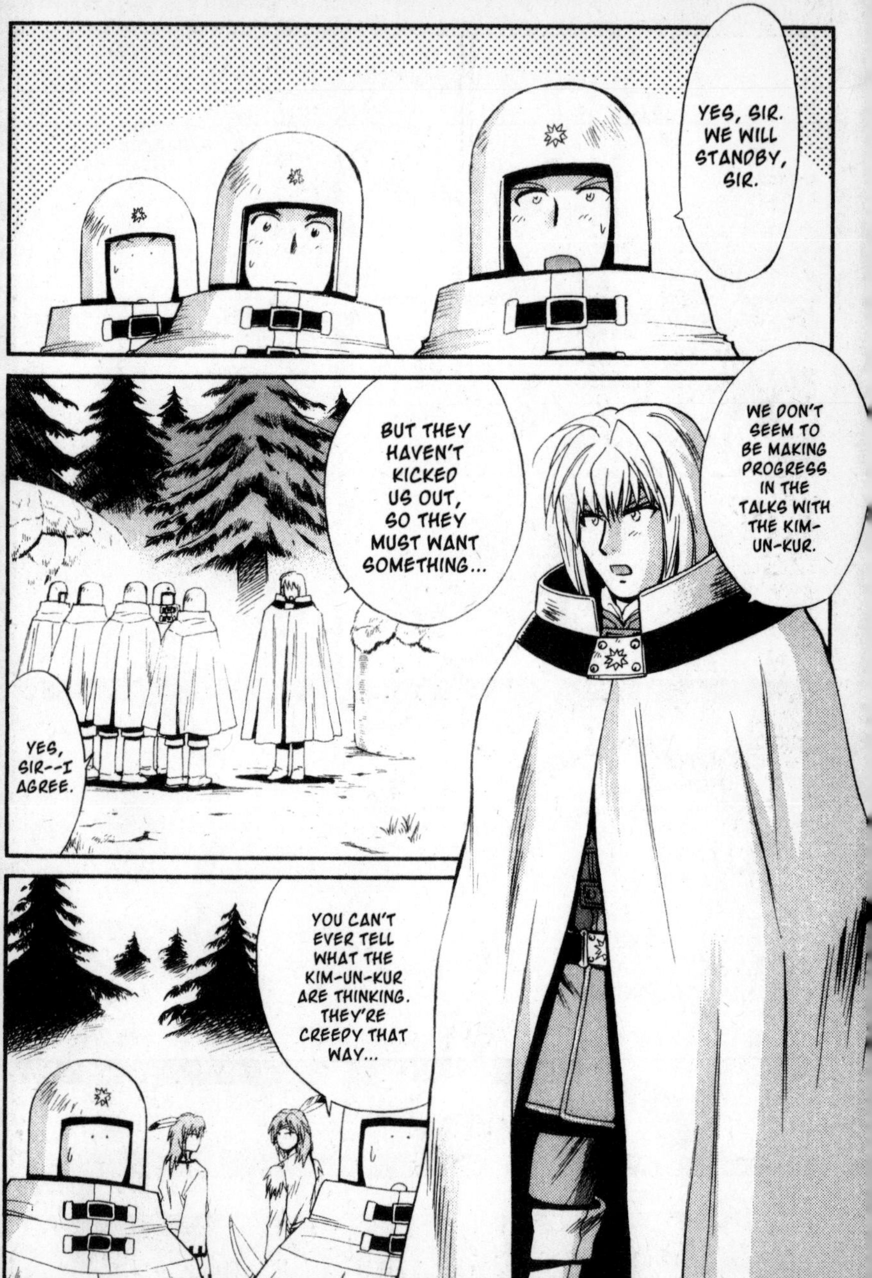
YES, SIR. WE WILL STANDBY, SIR.
WE DON'T SEEM TO BE MAKING PROGRESS IN THE TALKS WITH THE KIM-UN-KUR.
BUT THEY HAVEN'T KICKED US OUT, SO THEY MUST WANT SOMETHING...
YES, SIR--I AGREE.
YOU CAN'T EVER TELL WHAT THE KIM-UN-KUR ARE THINKING. THEY'RE CREEPY THAT WAY...

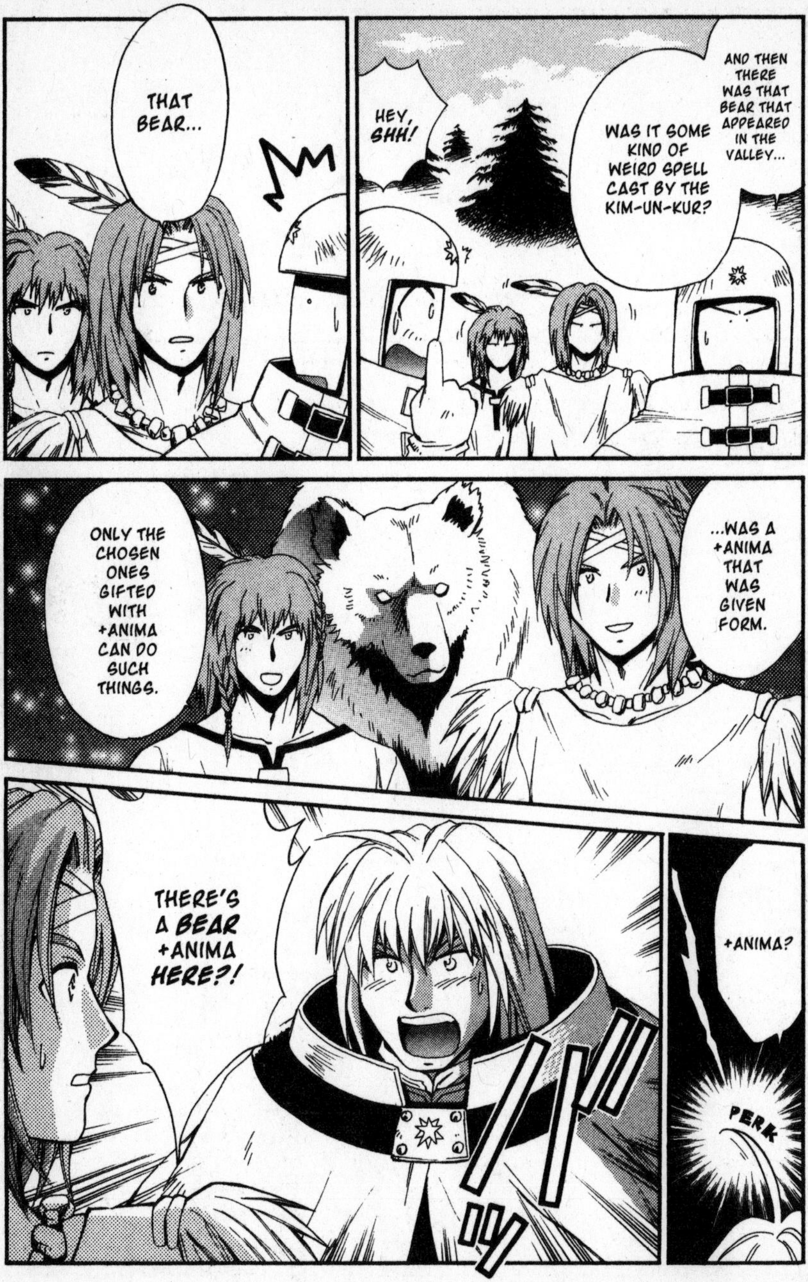
AND THEN THERE WAS THAT BEAR THAT APPEARED IN THE VALLEY...
WAS IT SOME KIND OF WEIRD SPELL CAST BY THE KIM-UN-KUR?
HEY, SHH!
THAT BEAR...
...WAS A +ANIMA THAT WAS GIVEN FORM.
ONLY THE CHOSEN ONES GIFTED WITH +ANIMA CAN DO SUCH THINGS.
+ANIMA?
PERK
THERE'S A BEAR +ANIMA HERE?!

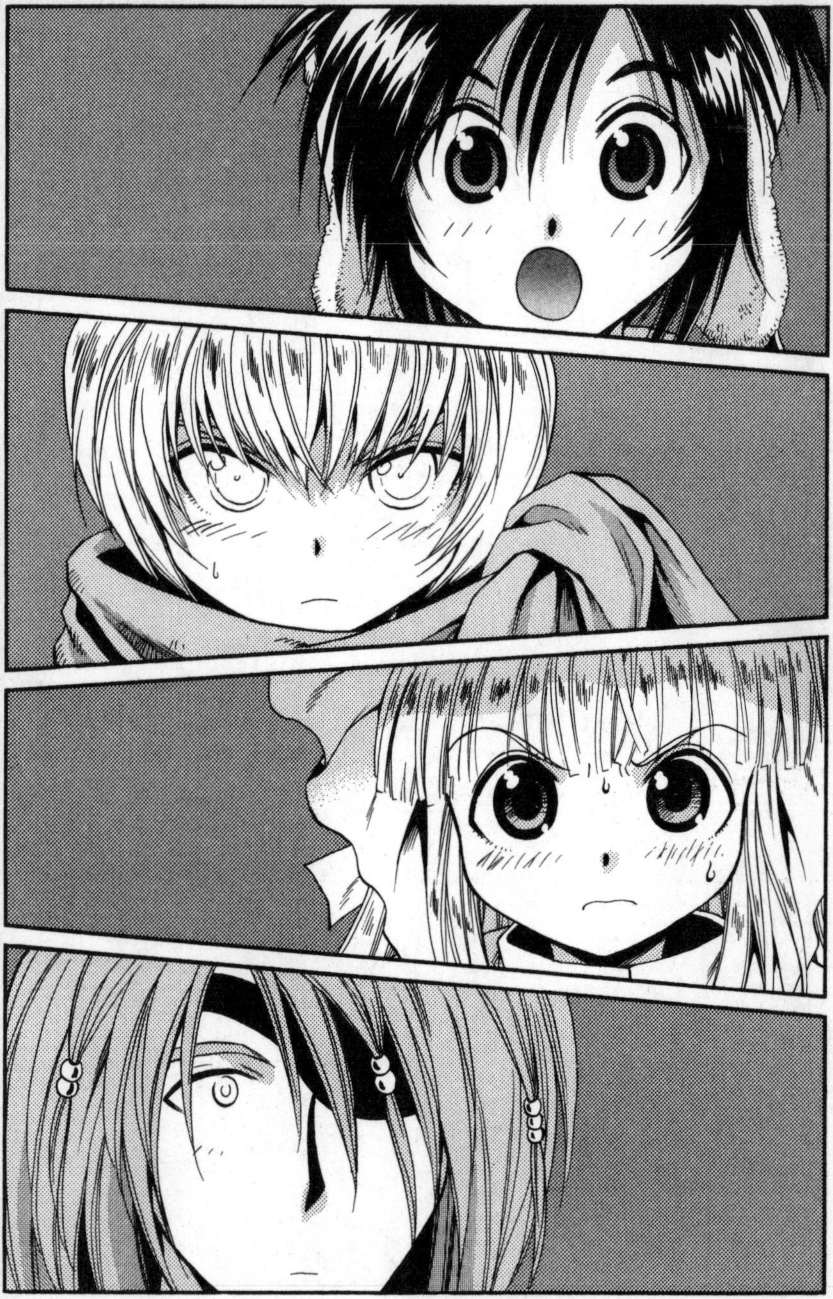

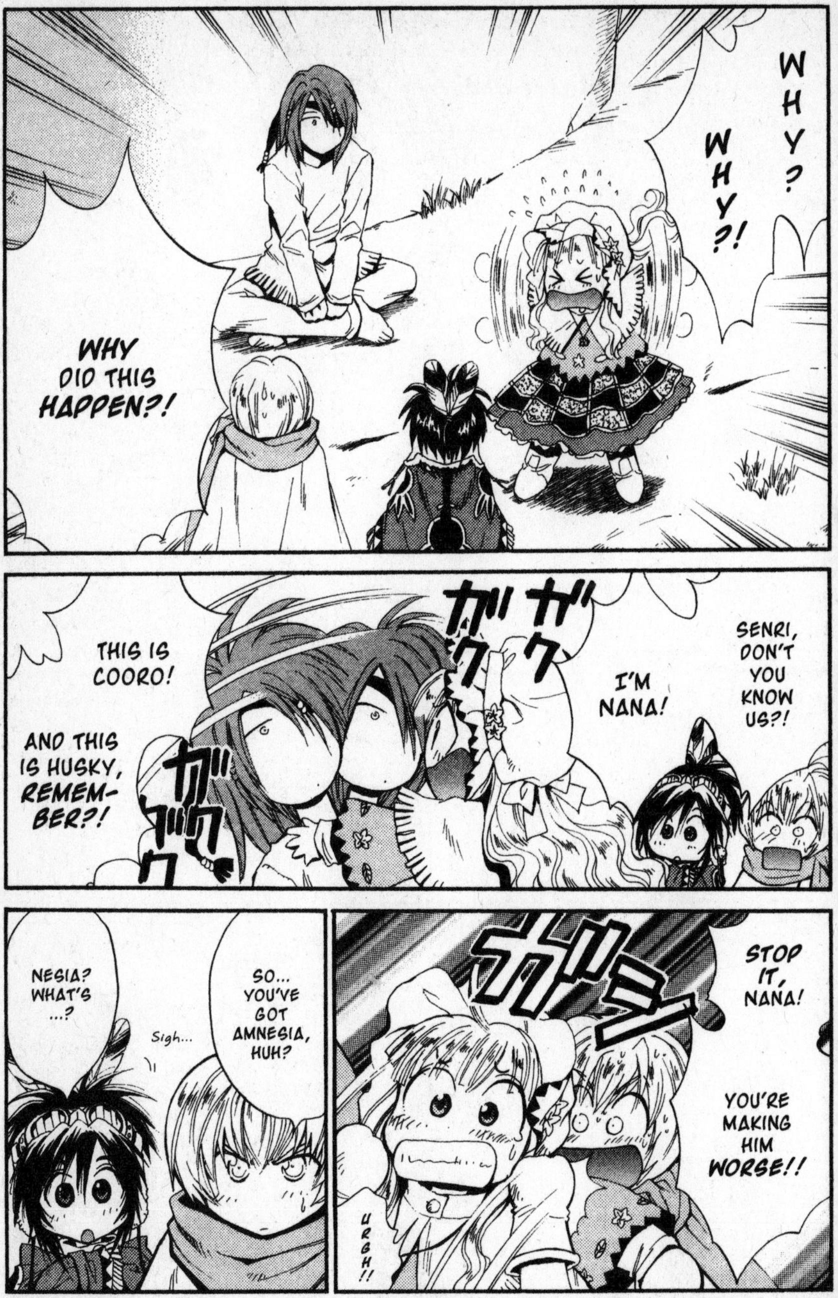

WHY?
WHY?!
WHY DID THIS HAPPEN?!
SENRI, DON'T YOU KNOW US?!
I'M NANA!
ガク
ガク
THIS IS COORO!
AND THIS IS HUSKY, REMEMBER?!
ガク
ガク
STOP IT, NANA!
YOU'RE MAKING HIM WORSE!!
URGH!!
SO... YOU'VE GOT AMNESIA, HUH?
Sigh...
NESIA? WHAT'S ...?

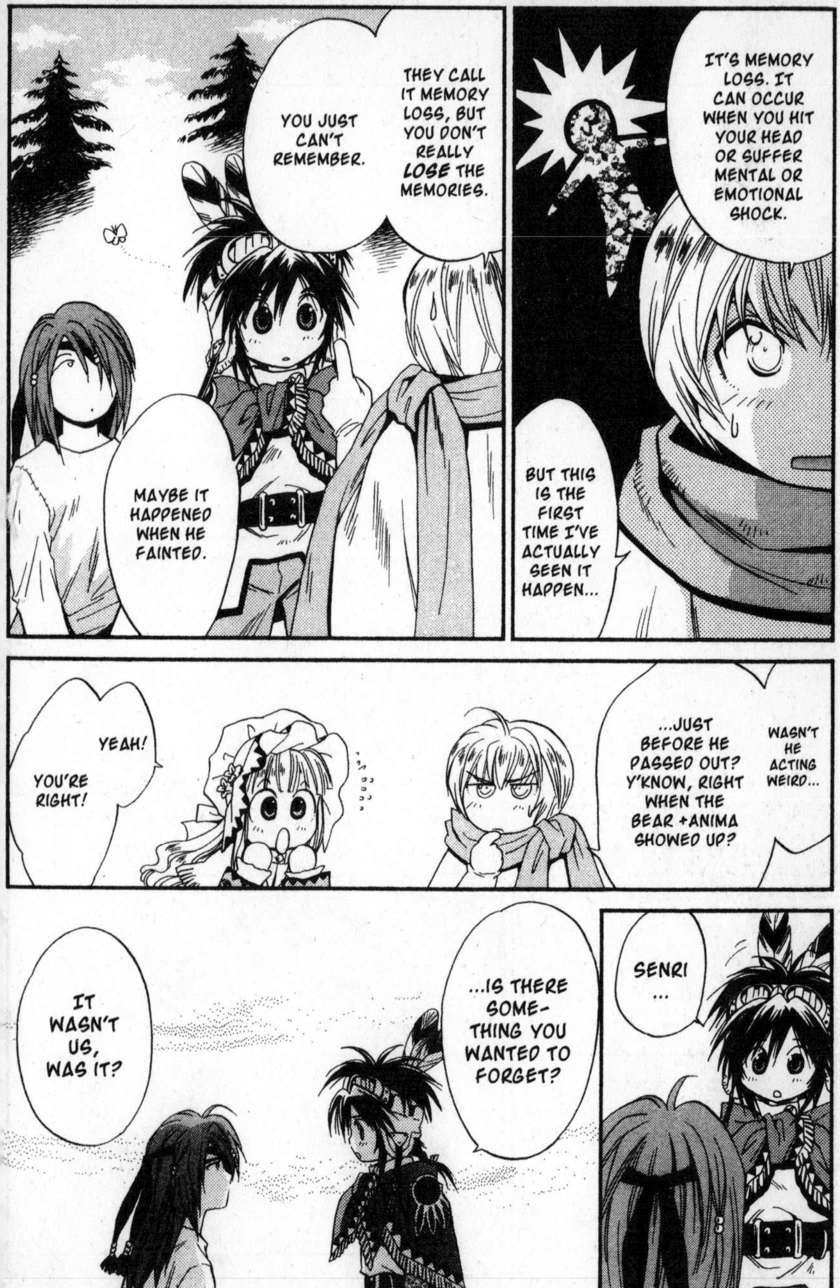
IT'S MEMORY LOSS. IT CAN OCCUR WHEN YOU HIT YOUR HEAD OR SUFFER MENTAL OR EMOTIONAL SHOCK.
BUT THIS IS THE FIRST TIME I'VE ACTUALLY SEEN IT HAPPEN...
THEY CALL IT MEMORY LOSS, BUT YOU DON'T REALLY *LOSE* THE MEMORIES.
YOU JUST CAN'T REMEMBER.
MAYBE IT HAPPENED WHEN HE FAINTED.
WASN'T HE ACTING WEIRD...
...JUST BEFORE HE PASSED OUT? Y'KNOW, RIGHT WHEN THE BEAR +ANIMA SHOWED UP?
YEAH!
YOU'RE RIGHT!
SENRI ...
...IS THERE SOME-THING YOU WANTED TO FORGET?
IT WASN'T US, WAS IT?

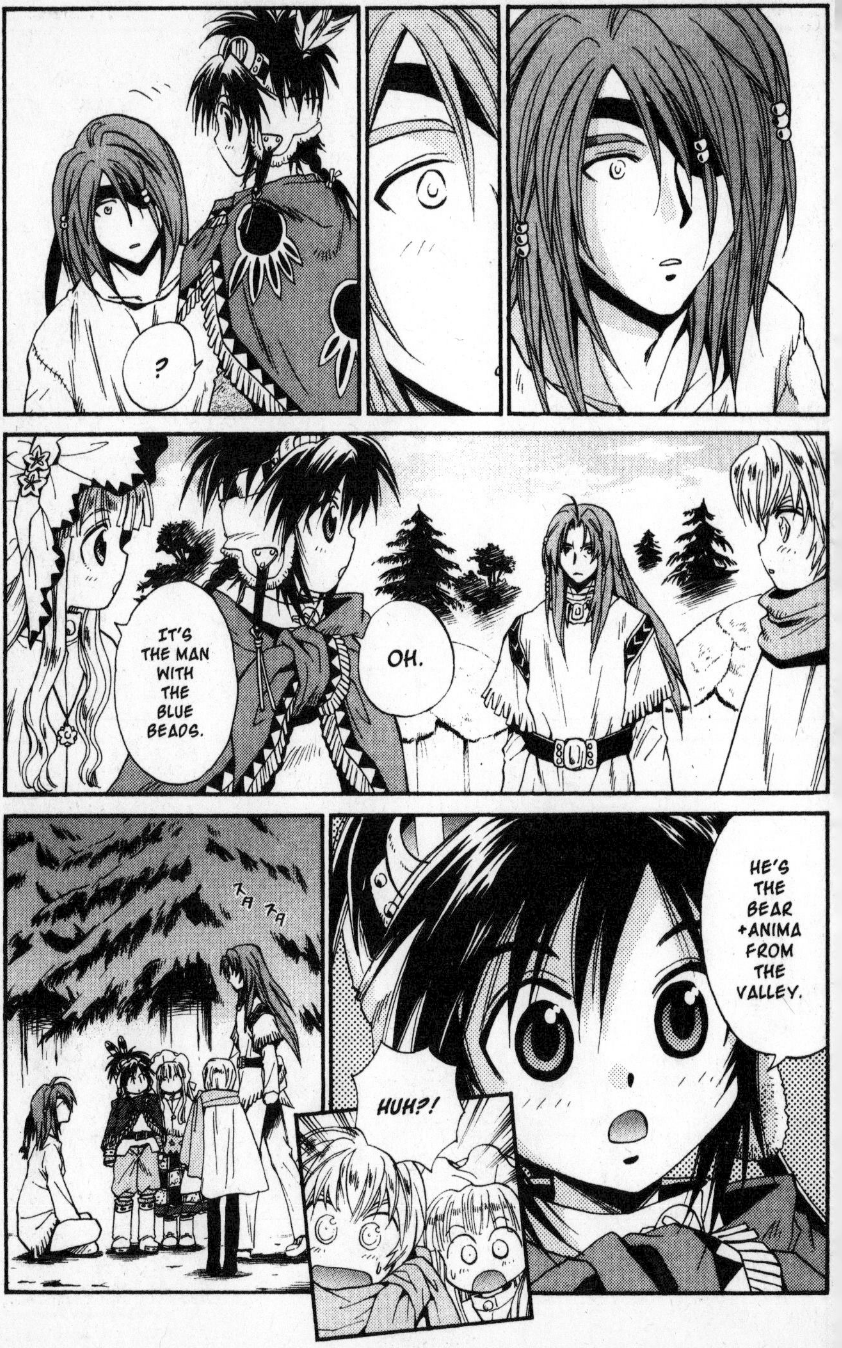
?
OH.
IT'S THE MAN WITH THE BLUE BEADS.
HE'S THE BEAR +ANIMA FROM THE VALLEY.
HUH?!
スタ スタ

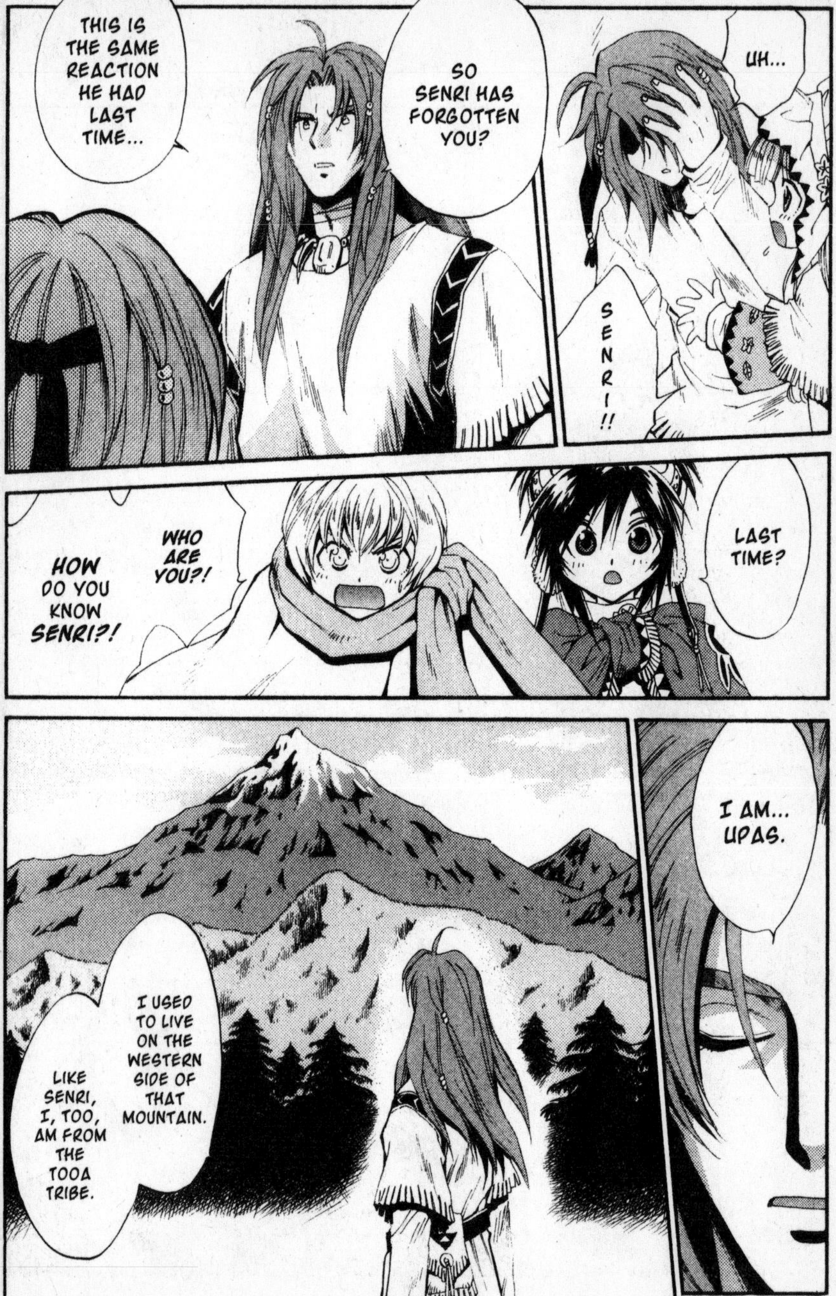
UH...
SENRI!!
SO SENRI HAS FORGOTTEN YOU?
THIS IS THE SAME REACTION HE HAD LAST TIME...
LAST TIME?
WHO ARE YOU?!
HOW DO YOU KNOW SENRI?!
I AM... UPAS.
I USED TO LIVE ON THE WESTERN SIDE OF THAT MOUNTAIN.
LIKE SENRI, I, TOO, AM FROM THE TOOA TRIBE.

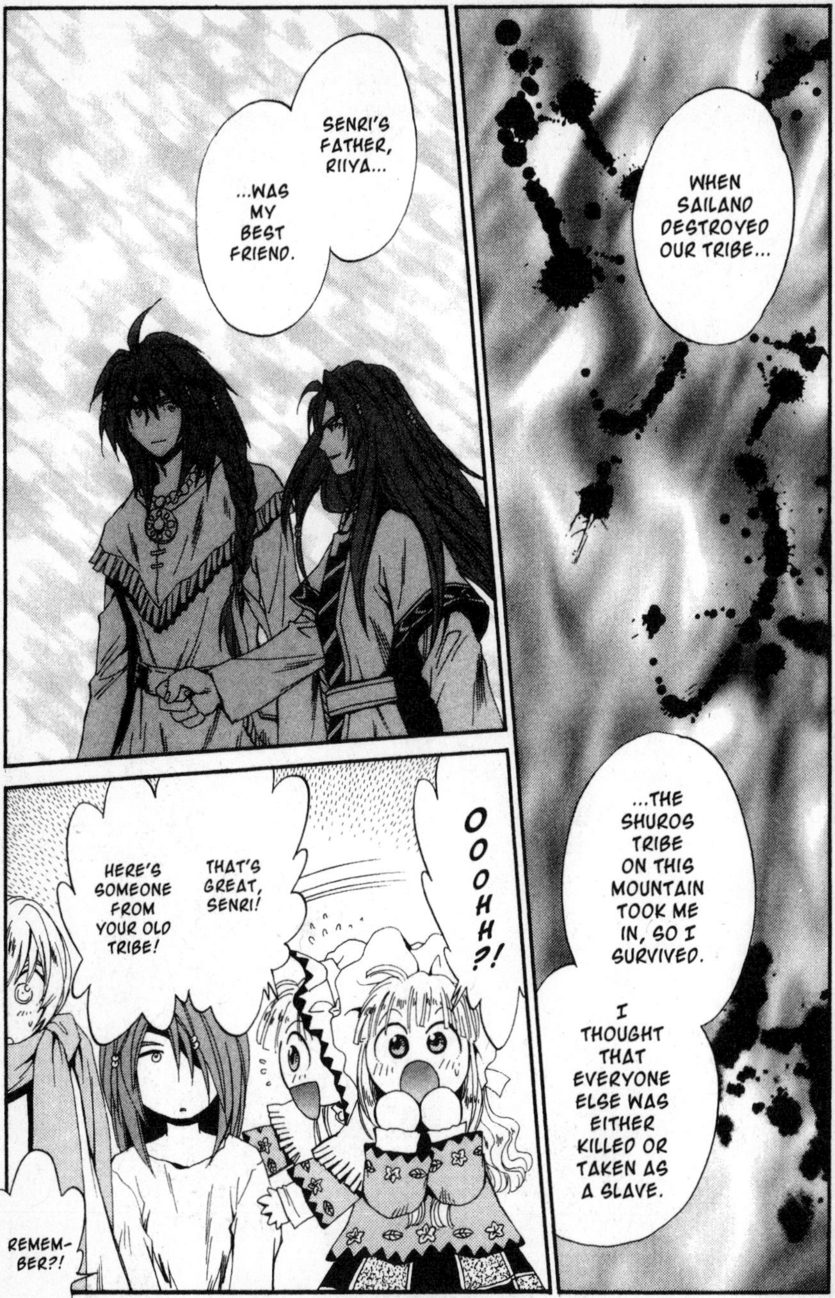
WHEN SAILAND DESTROYED OUR TRIBE...
...THE SHUROS TRIBE ON THIS MOUNTAIN TOOK ME IN, SO I SURVIVED.
I THOUGHT THAT EVERYONE ELSE WAS EITHER KILLED OR TAKEN AS A SLAVE.
SENRI'S FATHER, RIIYA...
...WAS MY BEST FRIEND.
OOOOHH?!
THAT'S GREAT, SENRI!
HERE'S SOMEONE FROM YOUR OLD TRIBE!
REMEMBER?!

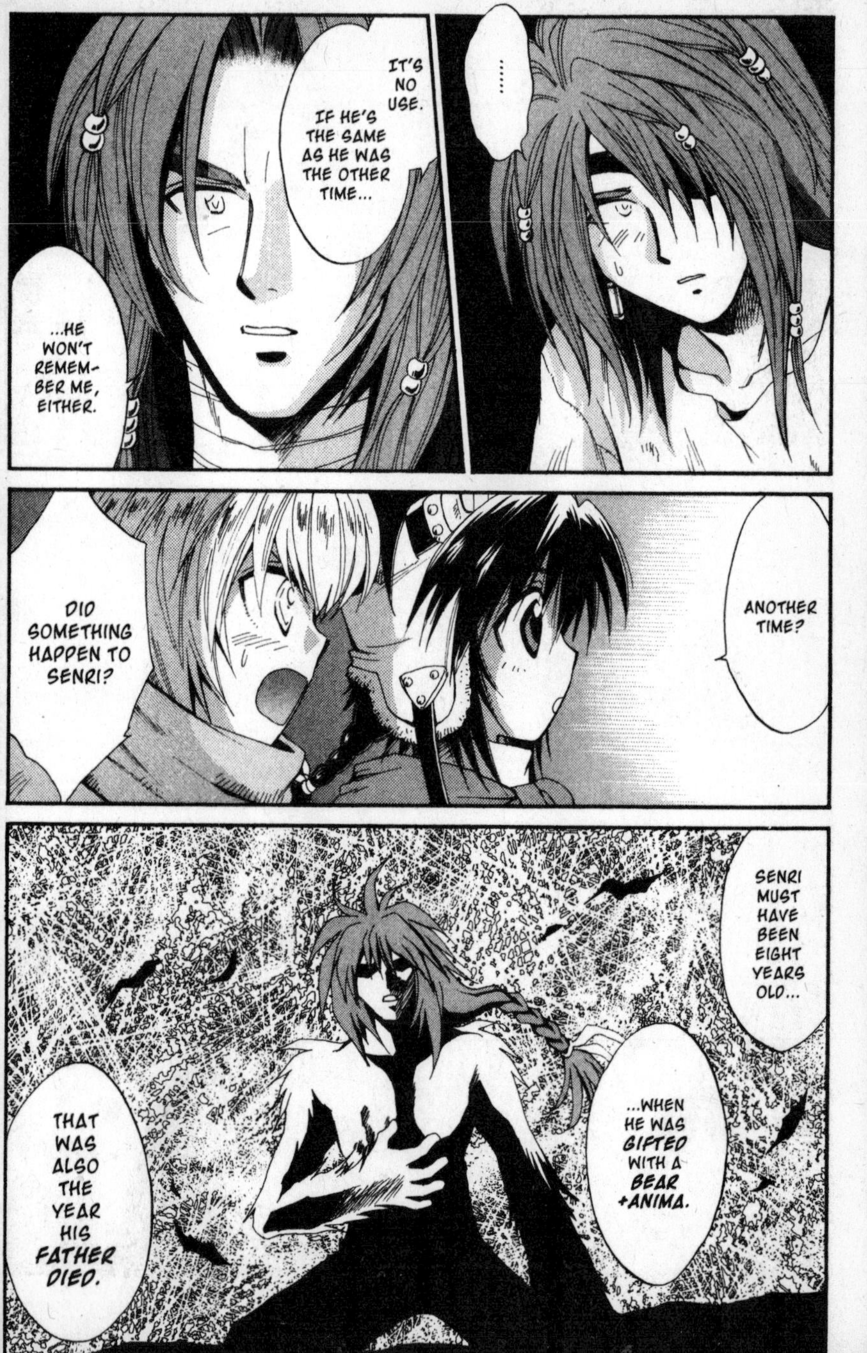
......
IT'S NO USE.
IF HE'S THE SAME AS HE WAS THE OTHER TIME...
...HE WON'T REMEMBER ME, EITHER.
ANOTHER TIME?
DID SOMETHING HAPPEN TO SENRI?
SENRI MUST HAVE BEEN EIGHT YEARS OLD...
...WHEN HE WAS GIFTED WITH A BEAR +ANIMA.
THAT WAS ALSO THE YEAR HIS FATHER DIED.

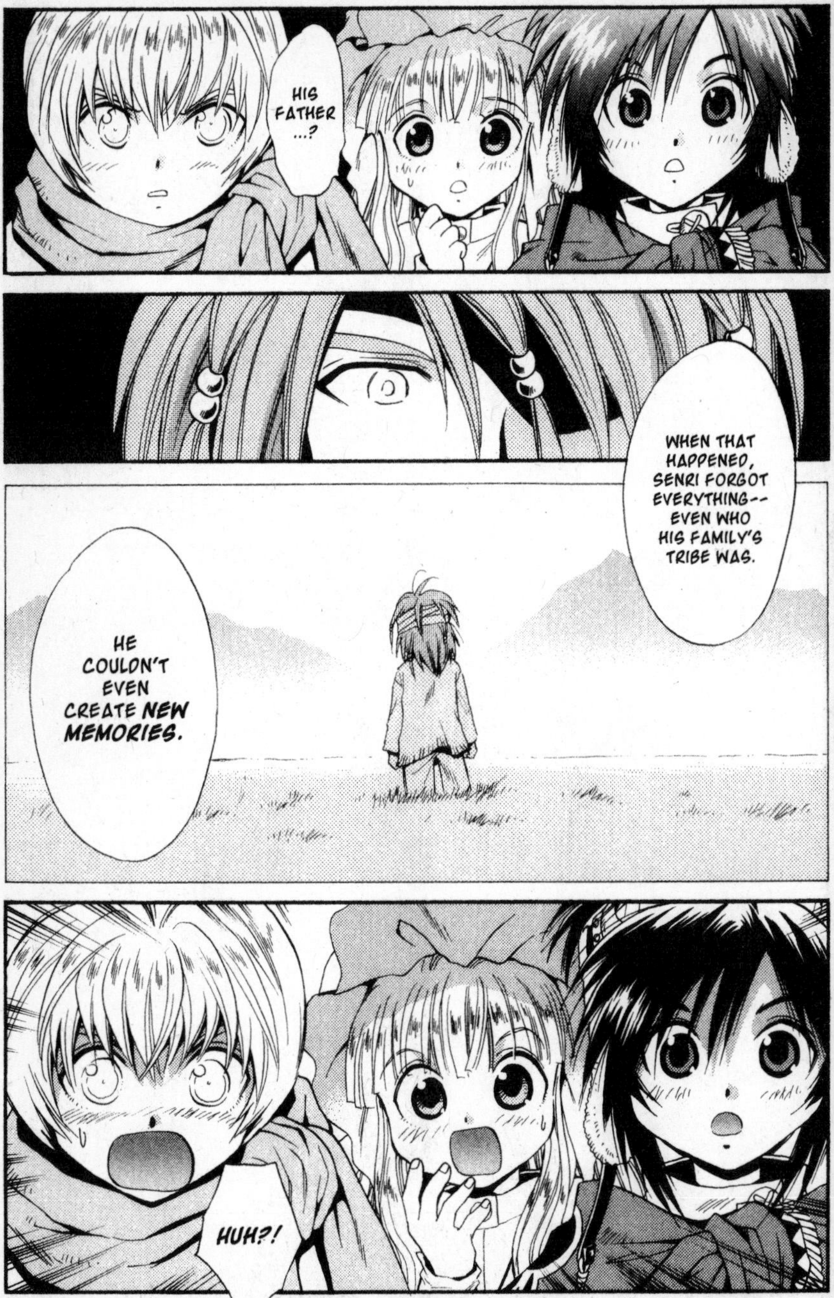
HIS FATHER ...?
WHEN THAT HAPPENED, SENRI FORGOT EVERYTHING--EVEN WHO HIS FAMILY'S TRIBE WAS.
HE COULDN'T EVEN CREATE **NEW MEMORIES.**
HUH?!

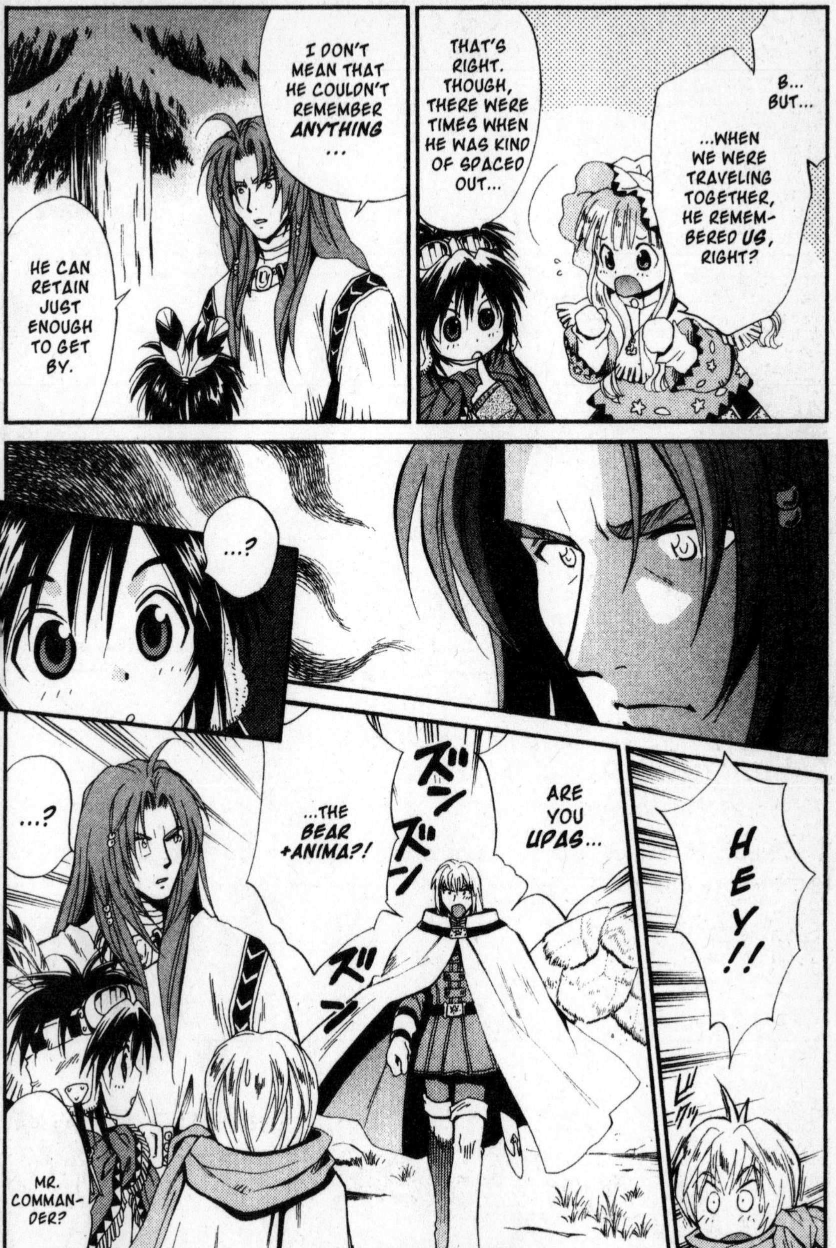
B... BUT...
...WHEN WE WERE TRAVELING TOGETHER, HE REMEMBERED US, RIGHT?
THAT'S RIGHT. THOUGH, THERE WERE TIMES WHEN HE WAS KIND OF SPACED OUT...
I DON'T MEAN THAT HE COULDN'T REMEMBER ANYTHING...
HE CAN RETAIN JUST ENOUGH TO GET BY.
...?
HEY!!
ARE YOU UPAS...
...THE BEAR +ANIMA?!
ズン
ズン
ズン
...?
MR. COMMANDER?

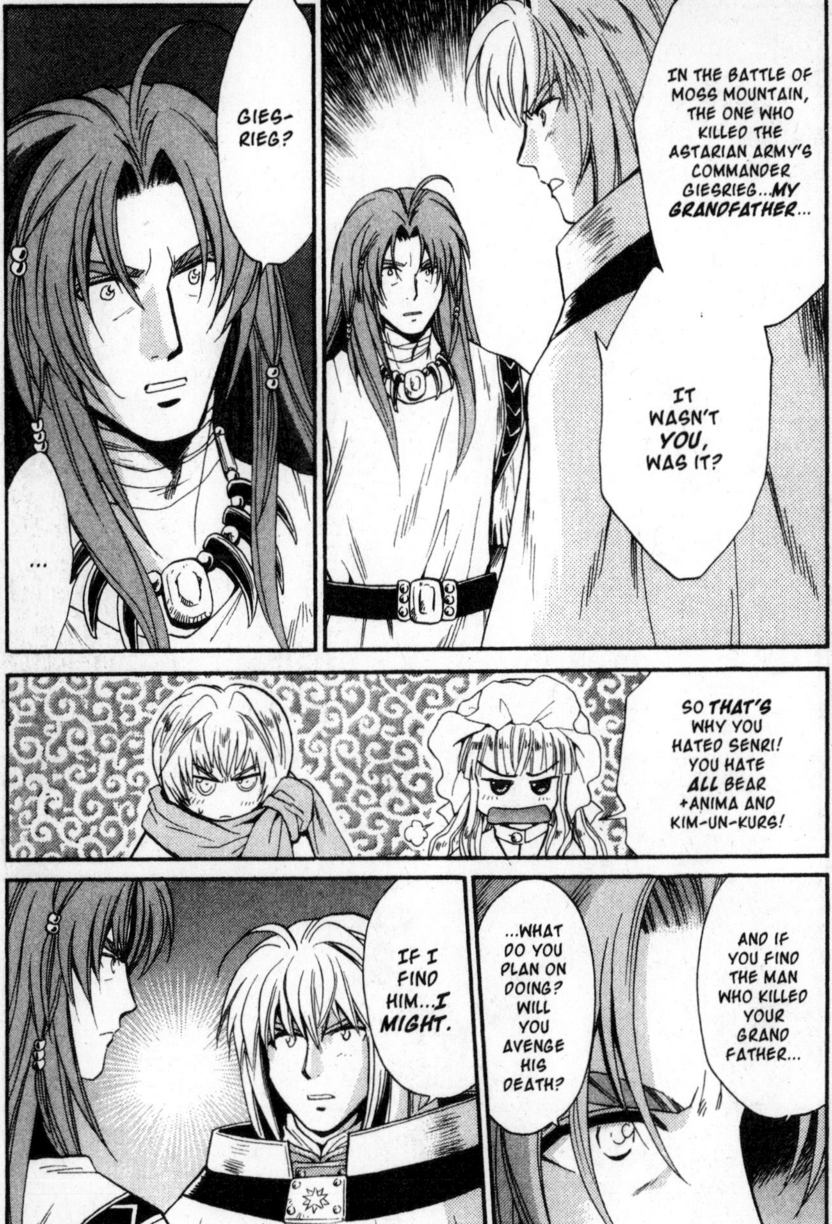
IN THE BATTLE OF MOSS MOUNTAIN, THE ONE WHO KILLED THE ASTARIAN ARMY'S COMMANDER GIESRIEG...MY GRANDFATHER...
IT WASN'T YOU, WAS IT?
GIES-RIEG?
...
SO THAT'S WHY YOU HATED SENRI! YOU HATE ALL BEAR +ANIMA AND KIM-UN-KURS!
AND IF YOU FIND THE MAN WHO KILLED YOUR GRAND FATHER...
...WHAT DO YOU PLAN ON DOING? WILL YOU AVENGE HIS DEATH?
IF I FIND HIM...I MIGHT.

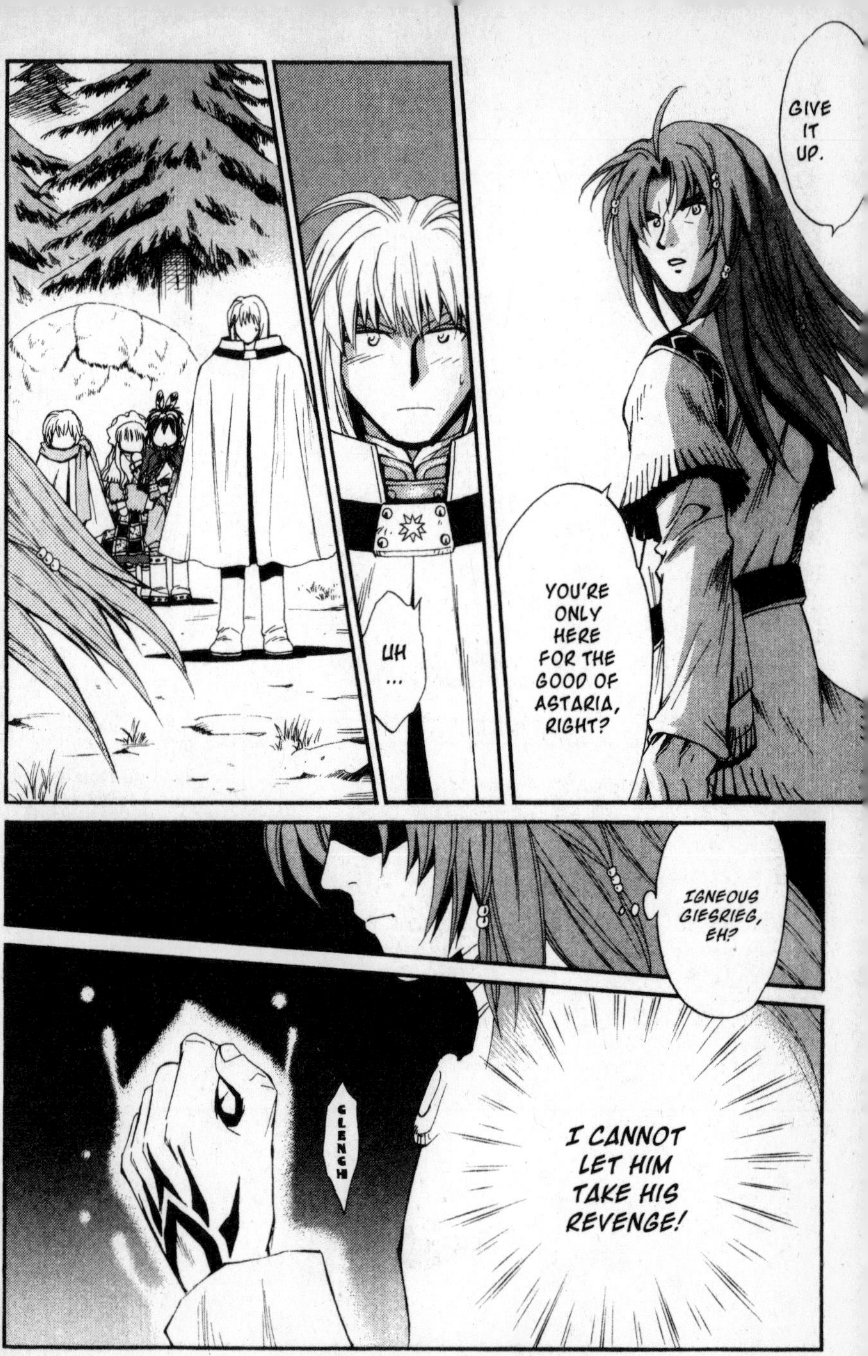
GIVE IT UP.
YOU'RE ONLY HERE FOR THE GOOD OF ASTARIA, RIGHT?
UH ...
IGNEOUS GIESRIEG, EH?
I CANNOT LET HIM TAKE HIS REVENGE!
CLENCH

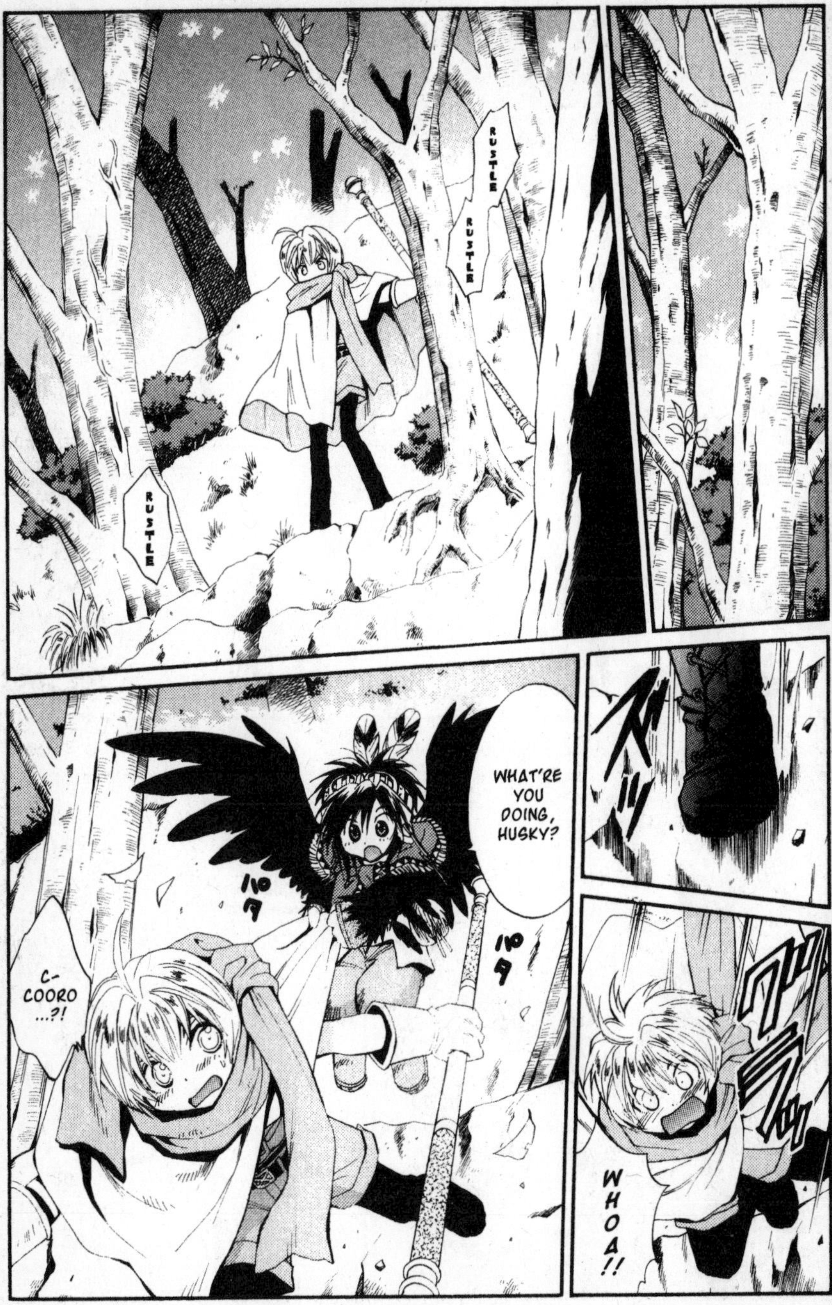
RUSTLE
RUSTLE
RUSTLE
WHOA!!
WHAT'RE YOU DOING, HUSKY?
C-COORO ...?!

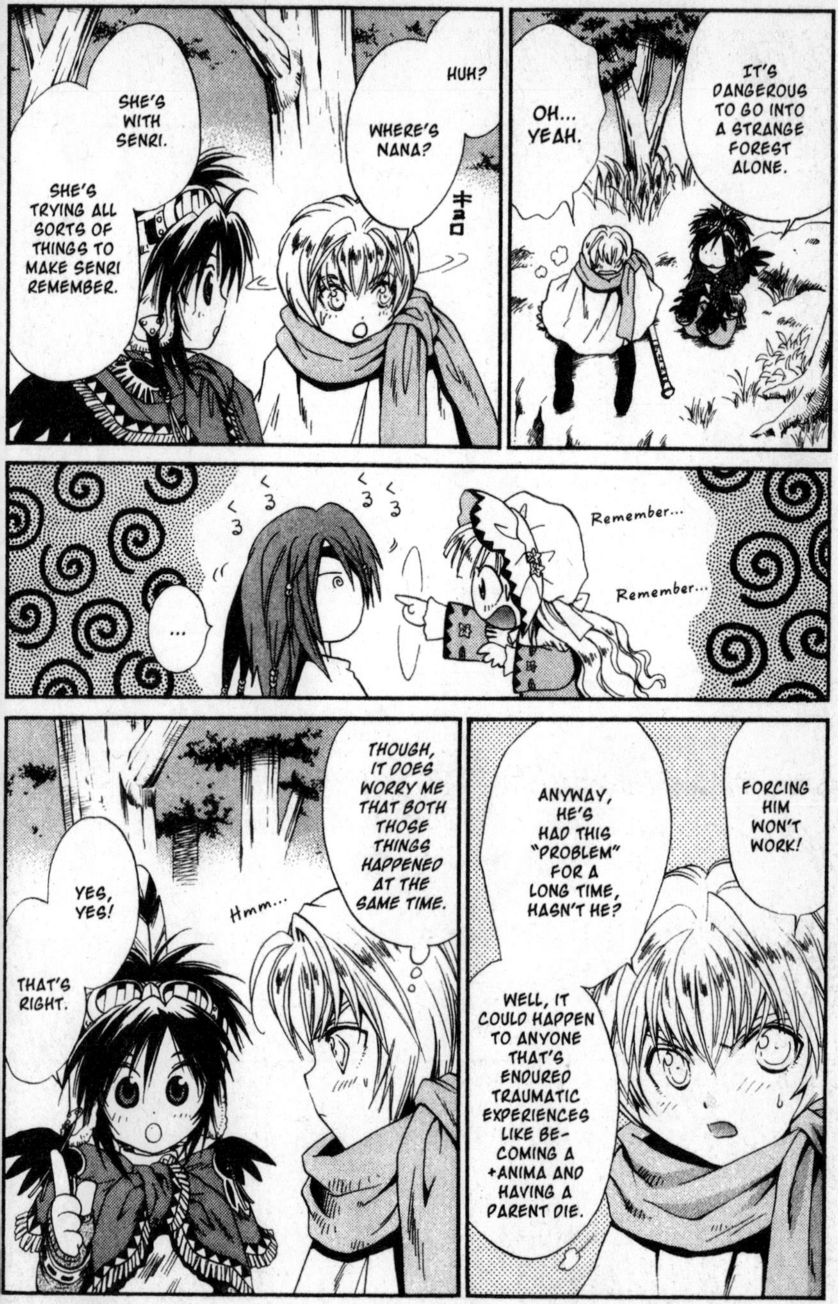

IT'S DANGEROUS TO GO INTO A STRANGE FOREST ALONE.
OH... YEAH.
HUH?
WHERE'S NANA?
キョロ
SHE'S WITH SENRI.
SHE'S TRYING ALL SORTS OF THINGS TO MAKE SENRI REMEMBER.
Remember...
Remember...
...
FORCING HIM WON'T WORK!
ANYWAY, HE'S HAD THIS "PROBLEM" FOR A LONG TIME, HASN'T HE?
WELL, IT COULD HAPPEN TO ANYONE THAT'S ENDURED TRAUMATIC EXPERIENCES LIKE BE-COMING A +ANIMA AND HAVING A PARENT DIE.
THOUGH, IT DOES WORRY ME THAT BOTH THOSE THINGS HAPPENED AT THE SAME TIME.
Hmm...
YES, YES!
THAT'S RIGHT.

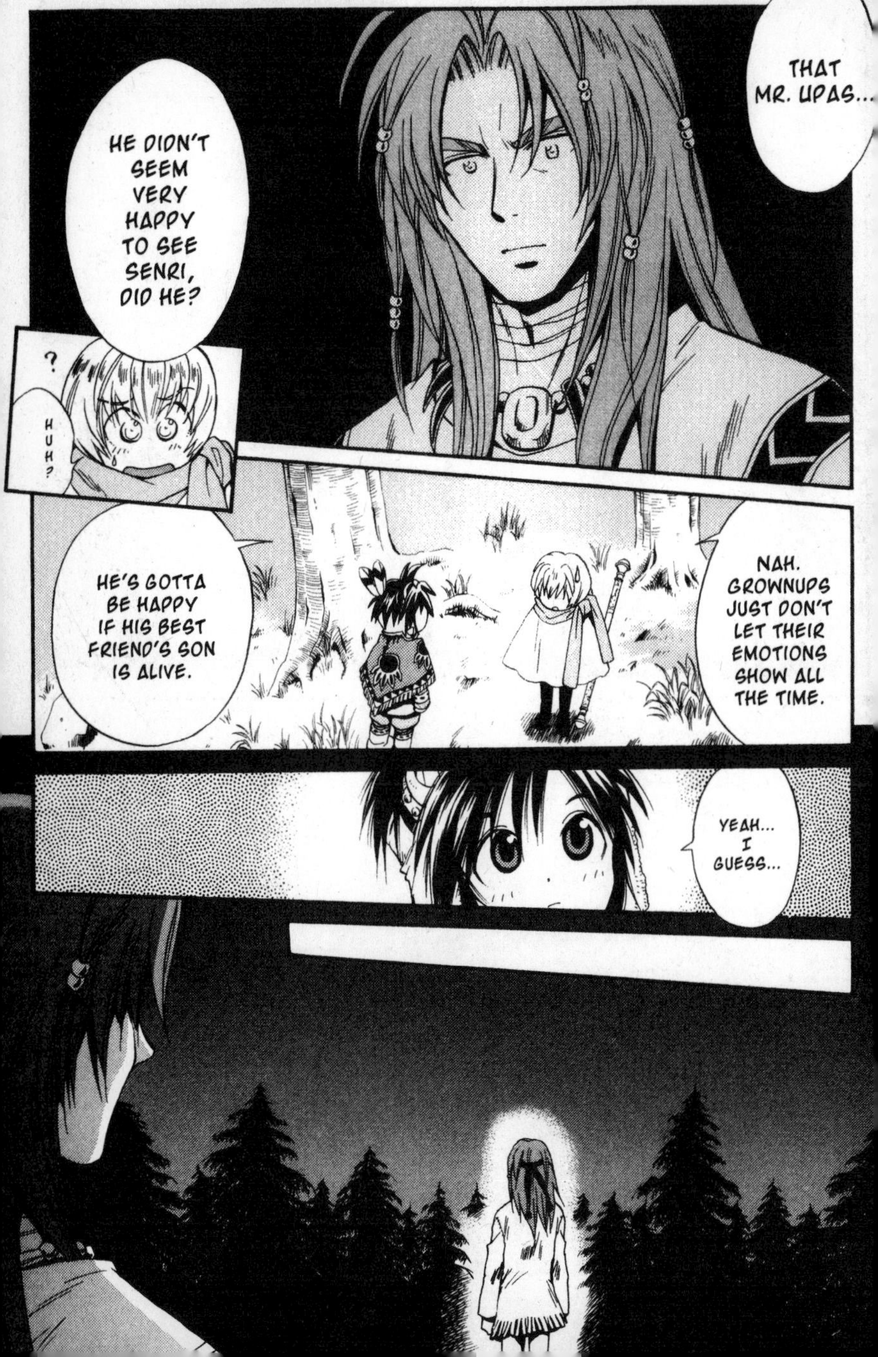
THAT MR. UPAS...
HE DIDN'T SEEM VERY HAPPY TO SEE SENRI, DID HE?
?
HUH?
NAH. GROWNUPS JUST DON'T LET THEIR EMOTIONS SHOW ALL THE TIME.
HE'S GOTTA BE HAPPY IF HIS BEST FRIEND'S SON IS ALIVE.
YEAH... I GUESS...

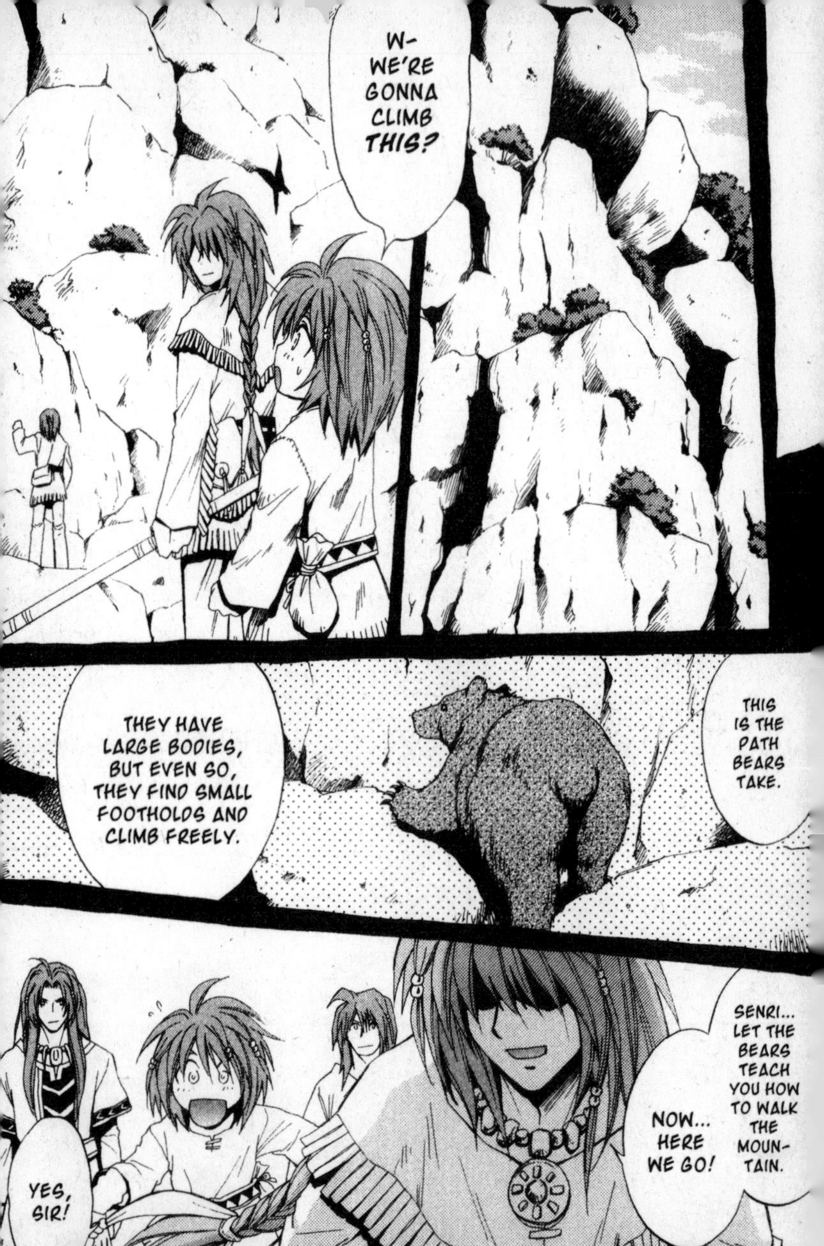
W- WE'RE GONNA CLIMB THIS?
THIS IS THE PATH BEARS TAKE.
THEY HAVE LARGE BODIES, BUT EVEN SO, THEY FIND SMALL FOOTHOLDS AND CLIMB FREELY.
SENRI... LET THE BEARS TEACH YOU HOW TO WALK THE MOUNTAIN.
NOW... HERE WE GO!
YES, SIR!

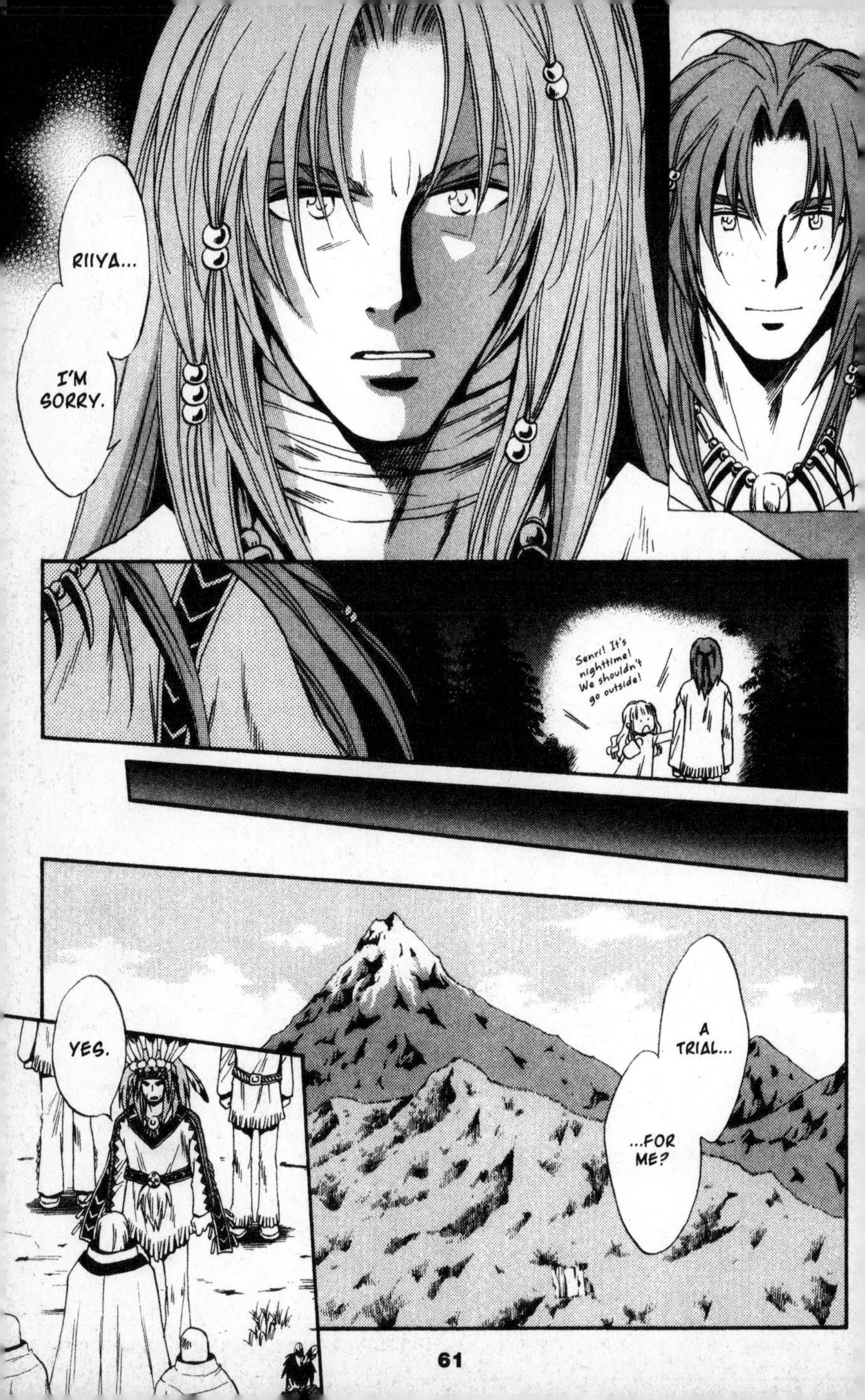
RIIYA...
I'M SORRY.
Senri! It's nighttime! We shouldn't go outside!
A TRIAL...
...FOR ME?
YES.

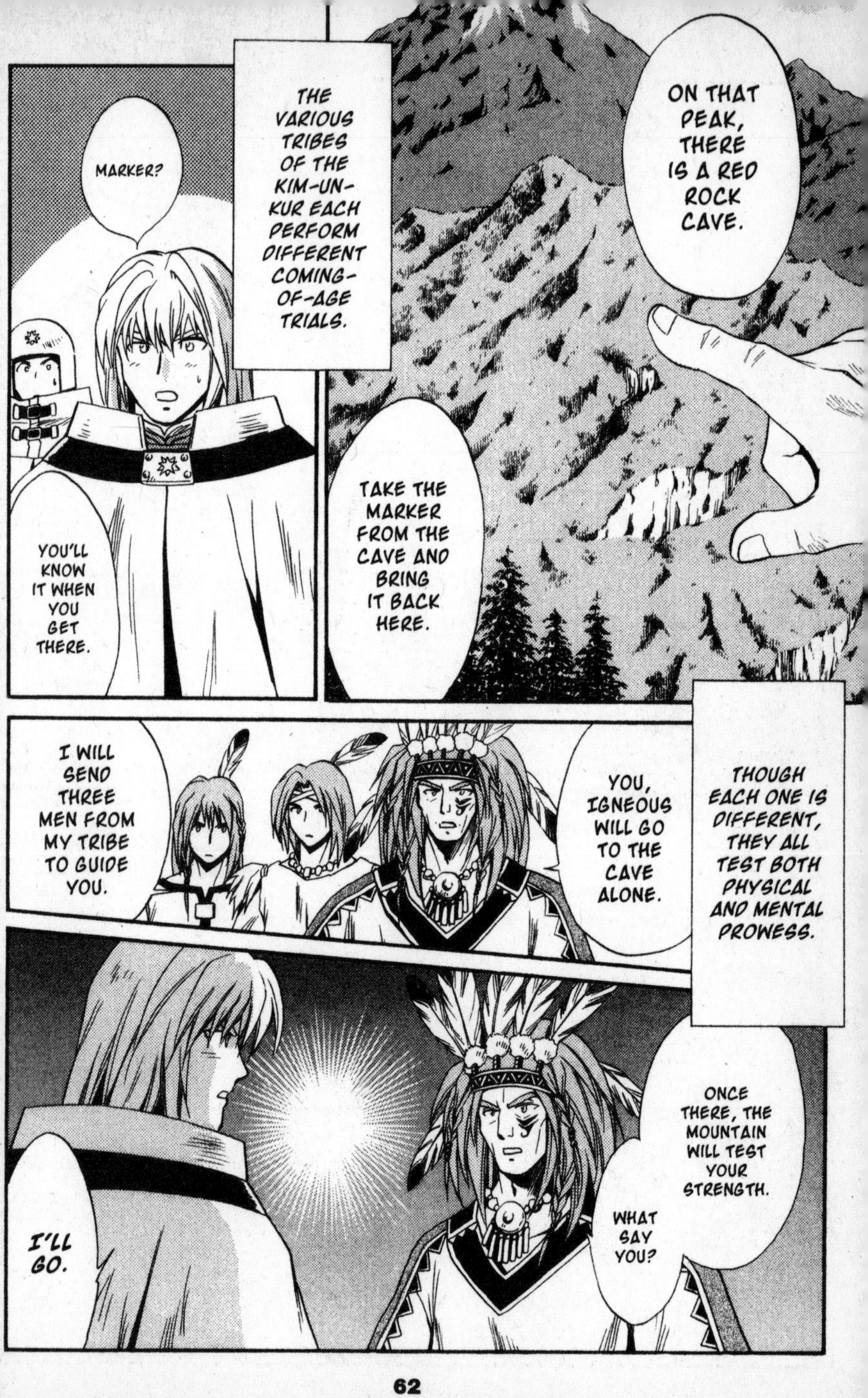
ON THAT PEAK, THERE IS A RED ROCK CAVE.
TAKE THE MARKER FROM THE CAVE AND BRING IT BACK HERE.
THE VARIOUS TRIBES OF THE KIM-UN-KUR EACH PERFORM DIFFERENT COMING-OF-AGE TRIALS.
MARKER?
YOU'LL KNOW IT WHEN YOU GET THERE.
THOUGH EACH ONE IS DIFFERENT, THEY ALL TEST BOTH PHYSICAL AND MENTAL PROWESS.
YOU, IGNEOUS WILL GO TO THE CAVE ALONE.
I WILL SEND THREE MEN FROM MY TRIBE TO GUIDE YOU.
ONCE THERE, THE MOUNTAIN WILL TEST YOUR STRENGTH.
WHAT SAY YOU?
I'LL GO.

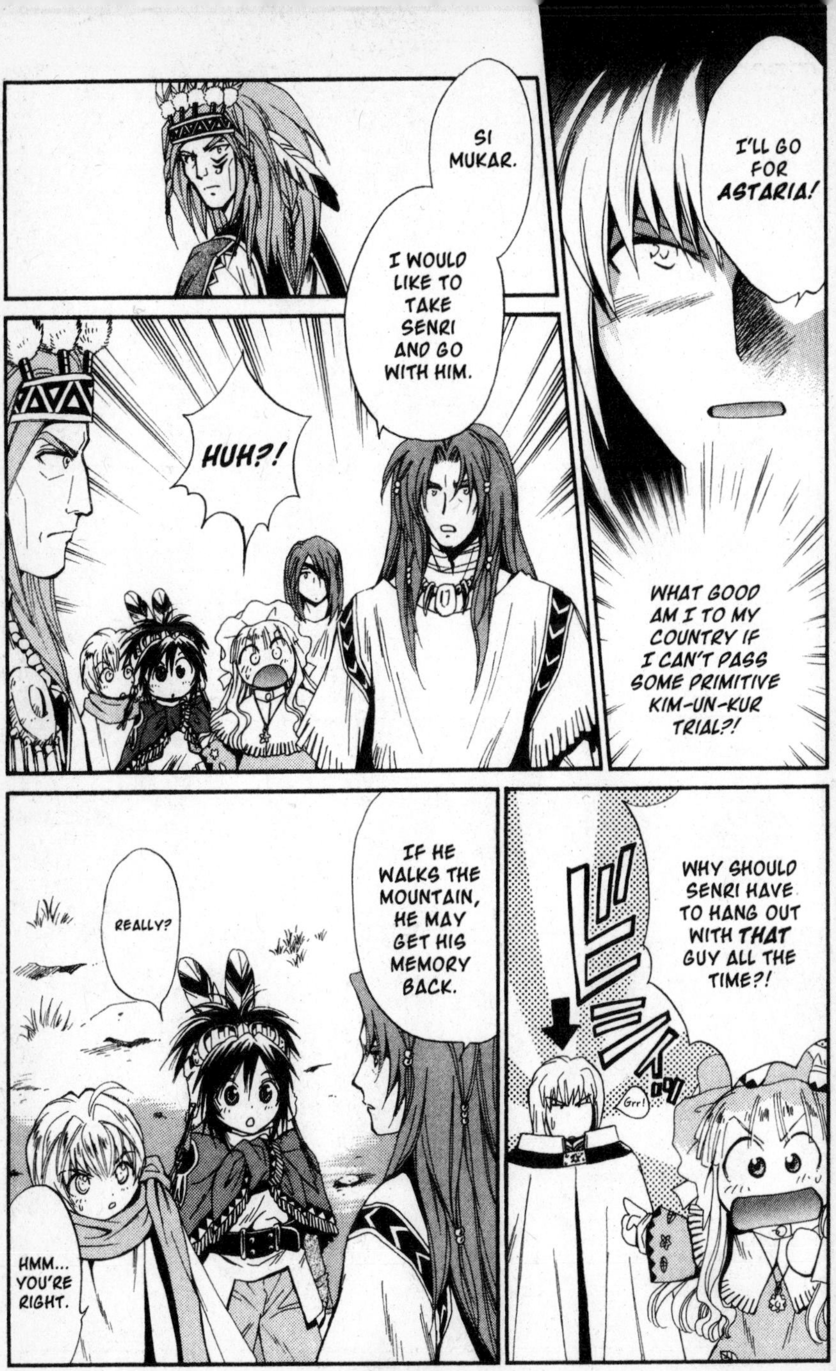
I'LL GO FOR **ASTARIA!**
WHAT GOOD AM I TO MY COUNTRY IF I CAN'T PASS SOME PRIMITIVE KIM-UN-KUR TRIAL?!
SI MUKAR.
I WOULD LIKE TO TAKE SENRI AND GO WITH HIM.
HUH?!
WHY SHOULD SENRI HAVE TO HANG OUT WITH **THAT** GUY ALL THE TIME?!
Grr!
IF HE WALKS THE MOUNTAIN, HE MAY GET HIS MEMORY BACK.
REALLY?
HMM... YOU'RE RIGHT.

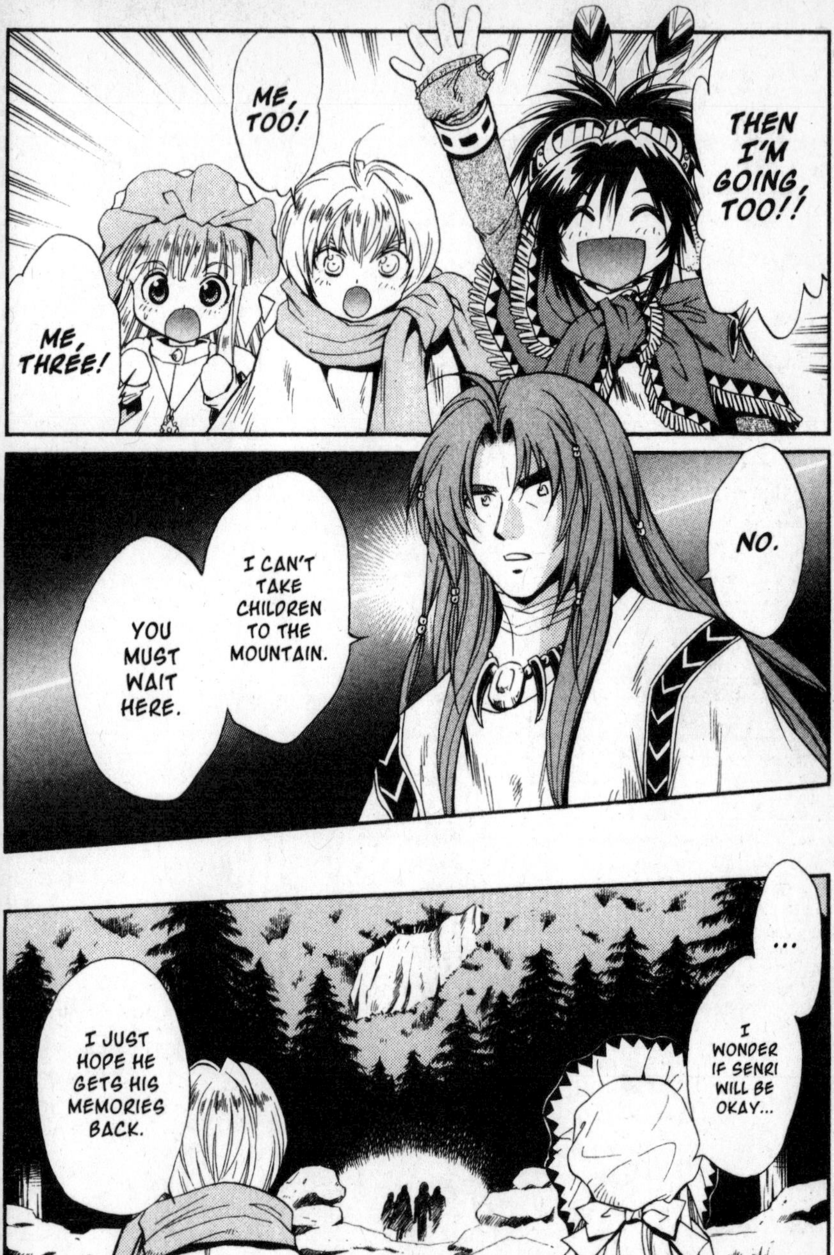
THEN I'M GOING, TOO!!
ME, TOO!
ME, THREE!
NO.
I CAN'T TAKE CHILDREN TO THE MOUNTAIN.
YOU MUST WAIT HERE.
...
I WONDER IF SENRI WILL BE OKAY...
I JUST HOPE HE GETS HIS MEMORIES BACK.

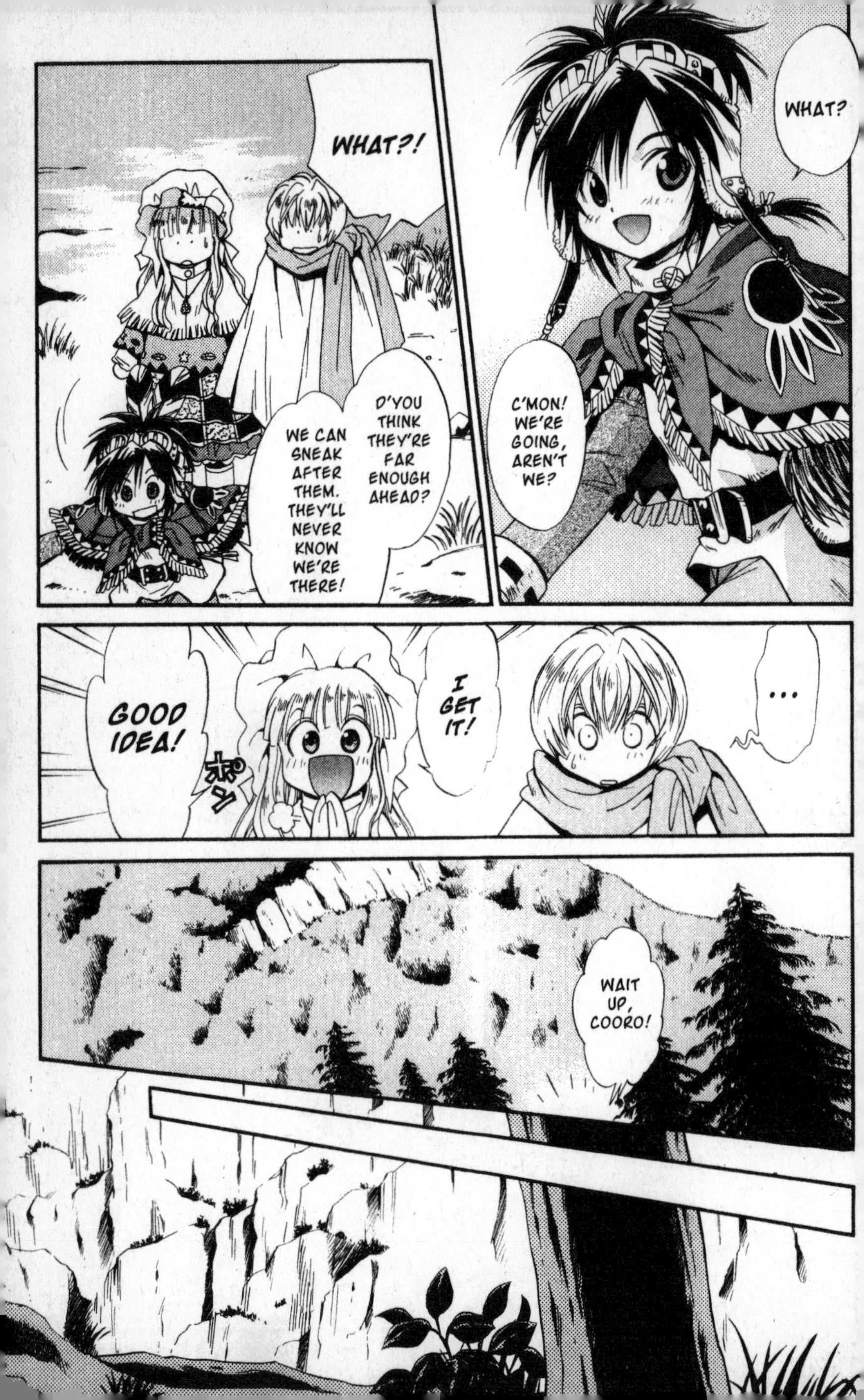
WHAT?
C'MON! WE'RE GOING, AREN'T WE?
WHAT?!
D'YOU THINK THEY'RE FAR ENOUGH AHEAD?
WE CAN SNEAK AFTER THEM. THEY'LL NEVER KNOW WE'RE THERE!
...
I GET IT!
GOOD IDEA!
ポン
WAIT UP, COORO!

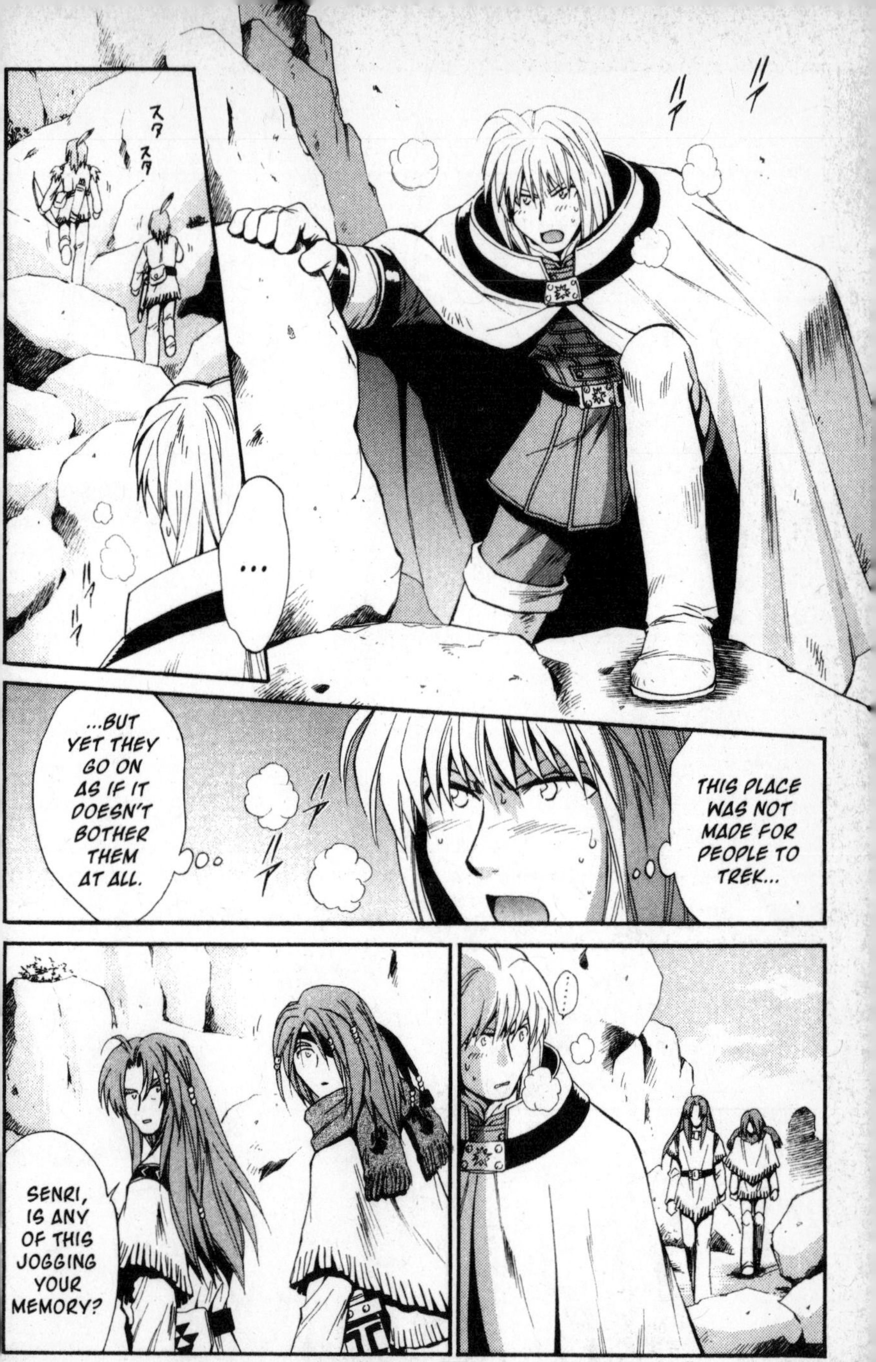
ハァ ハァ
スタ スタ
...
ハァ ハァ
THIS PLACE WAS NOT MADE FOR PEOPLE TO TREK...
...BUT YET THEY GO ON AS IF IT DOESN'T BOTHER THEM AT ALL.
ハァ ハァ
...
SENRI, IS ANY OF THIS JOGGING YOUR MEMORY?

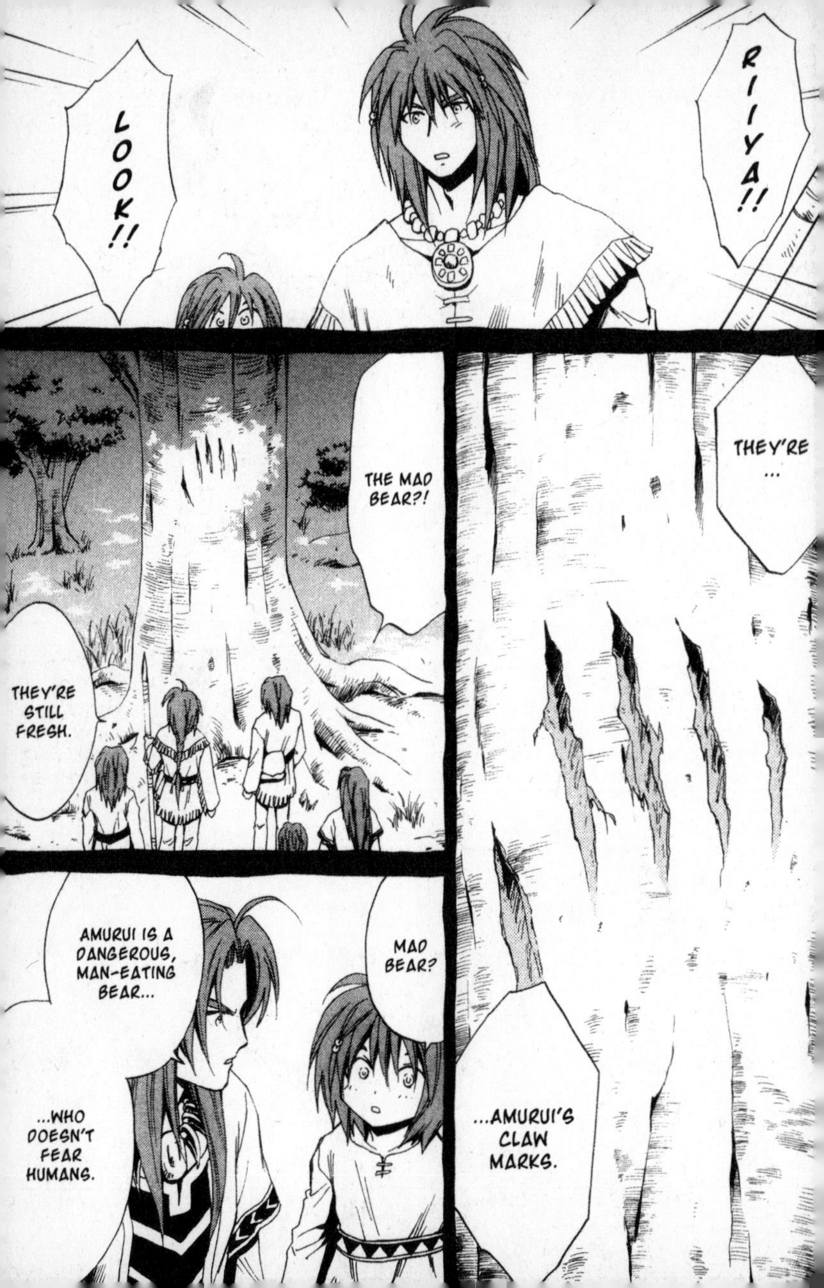
RIIYA!!
LOOK!!
THEY'RE ...
...AMURUI'S CLAW MARKS.
THE MAD BEAR?!
THEY'RE STILL FRESH.
MAD BEAR?
AMURUI IS A DANGEROUS, MAN-EATING BEAR...
...WHO DOESN'T FEAR HUMANS.

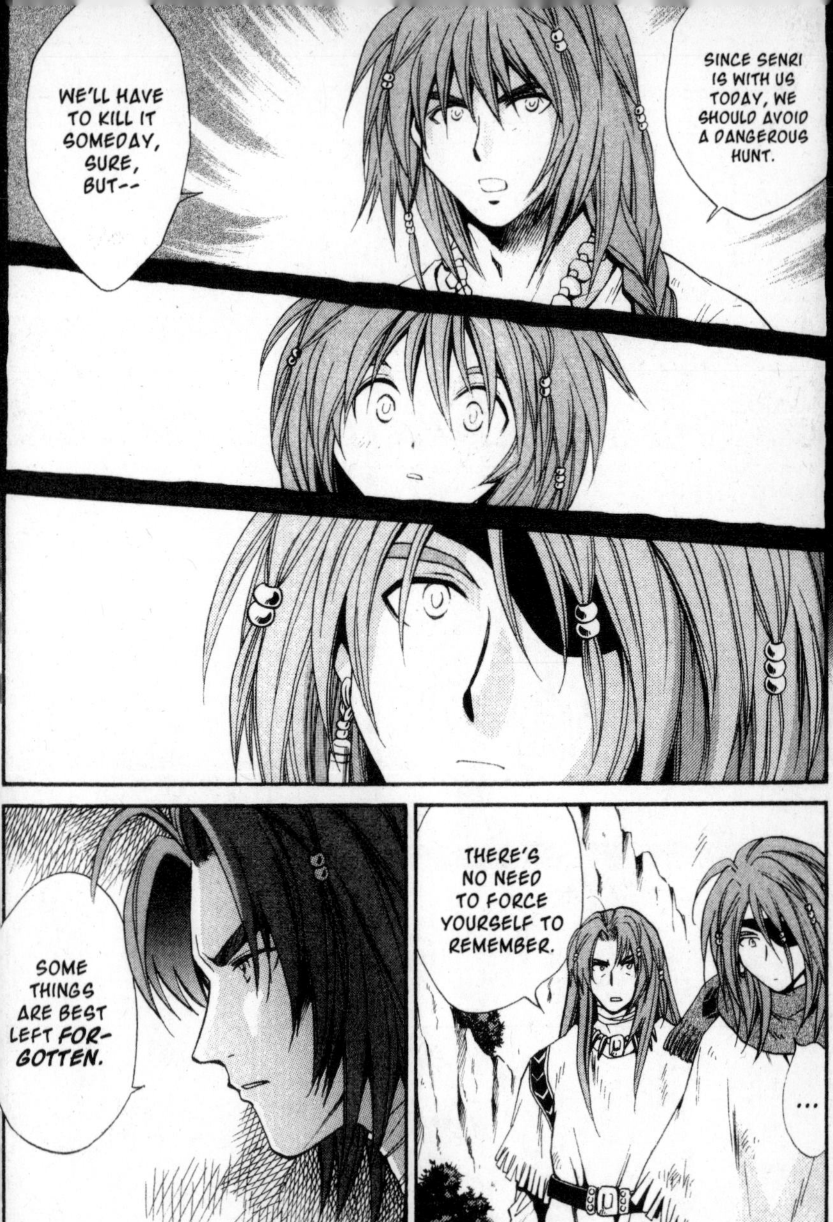
SINCE SENRI IS WITH US TODAY, WE SHOULD AVOID A DANGEROUS HUNT.
WE'LL HAVE TO KILL IT SOMEDAY, SURE, BUT--
THERE'S NO NEED TO FORCE YOURSELF TO REMEMBER.
...
SOME THINGS ARE BEST LEFT *FOR-GOTTEN.*

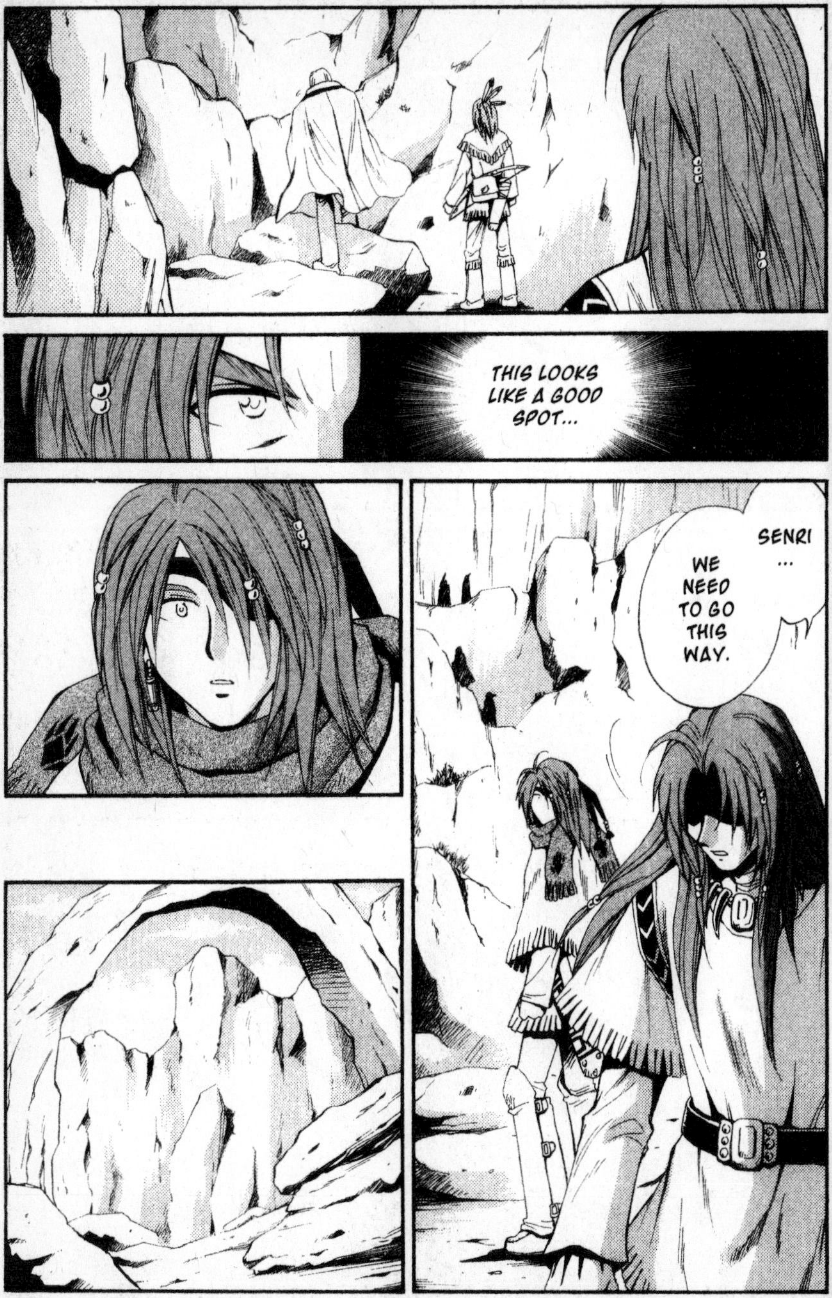
THIS LOOKS LIKE A GOOD SPOT...
SENRI ...
WE NEED TO GO THIS WAY.

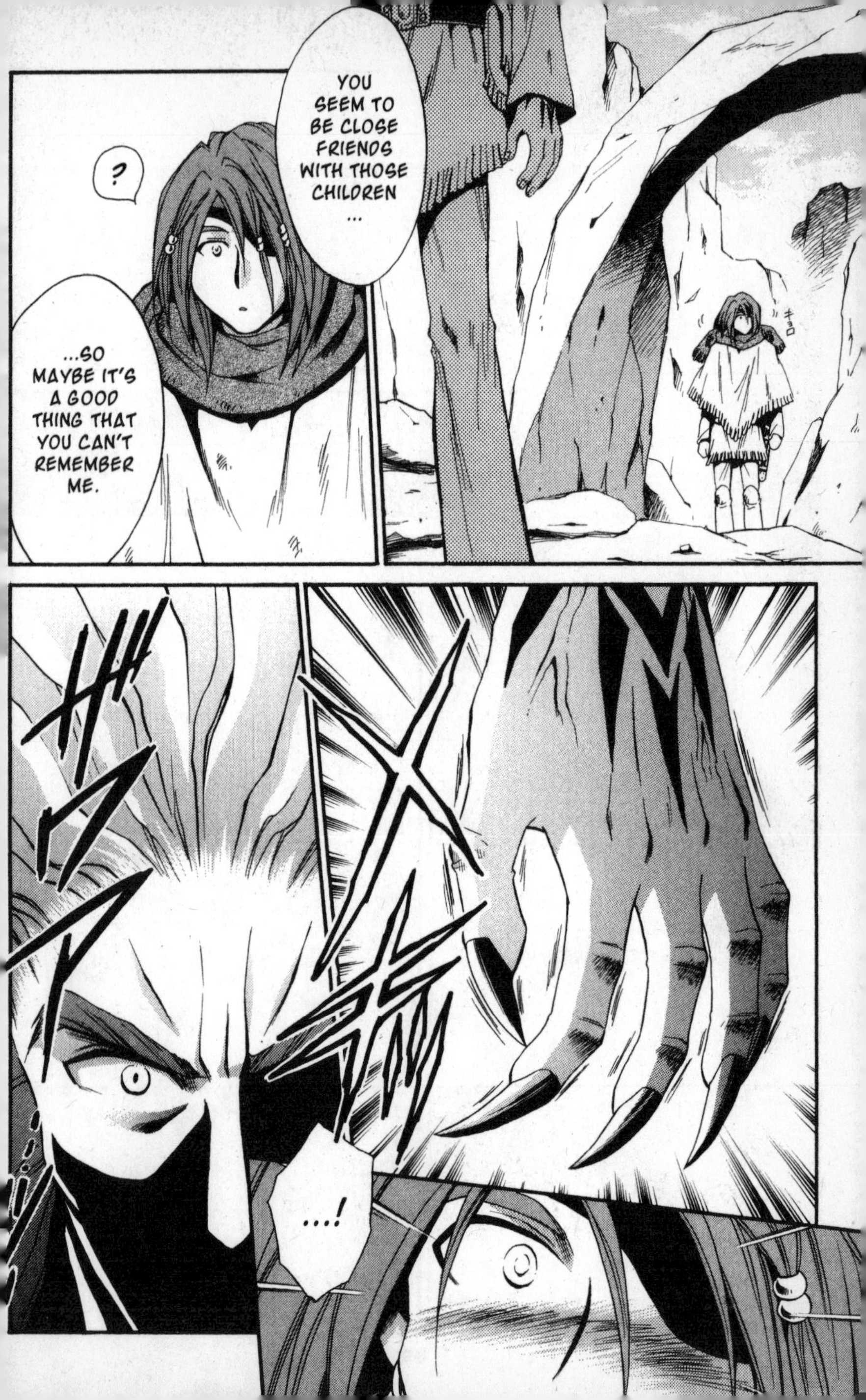
キョロ
YOU SEEM TO BE CLOSE FRIENDS WITH THOSE CHILDREN ...
?
...SO MAYBE IT'S A GOOD THING THAT YOU CAN'T REMEMBER ME.
...!

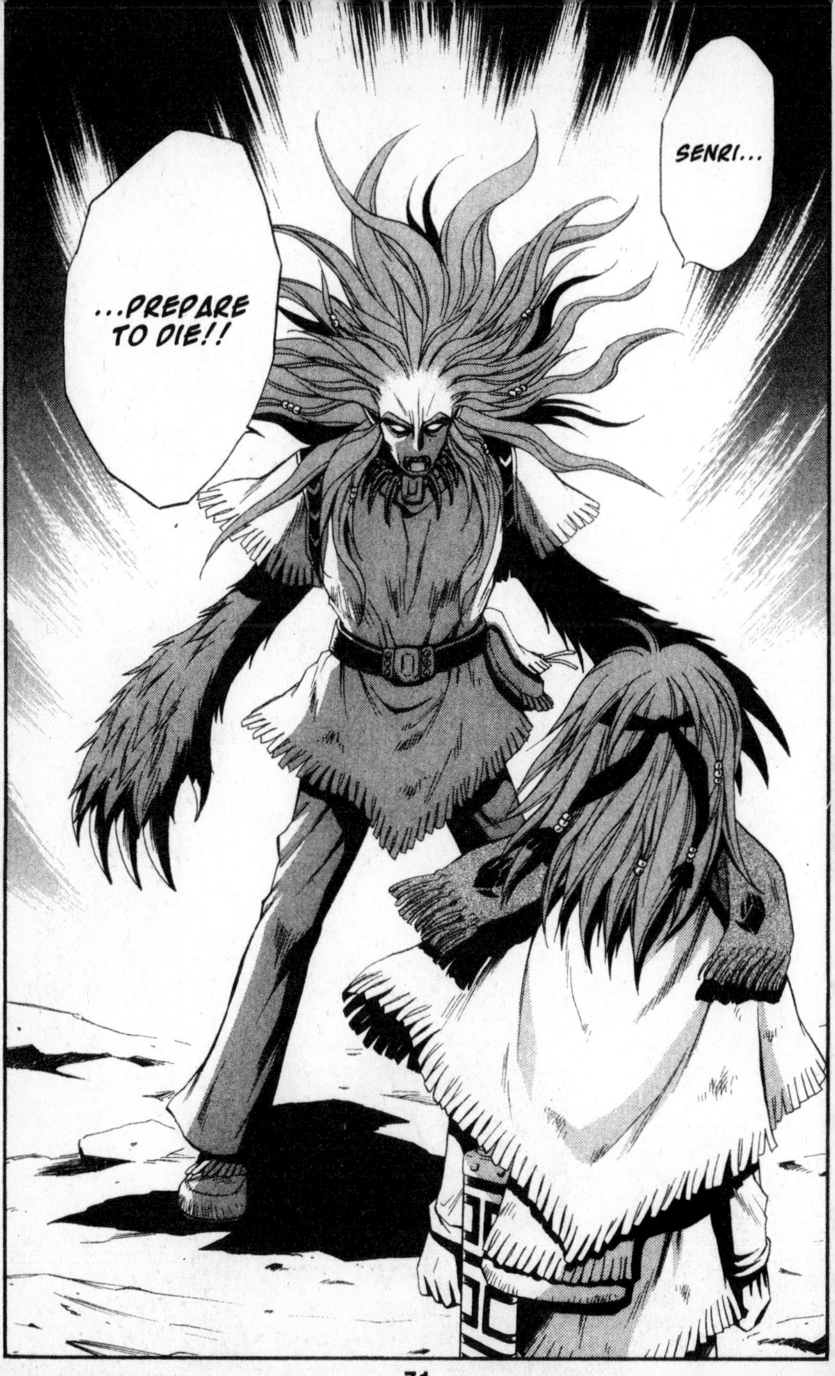
SENRI...
...PREPARE TO DIE!!

Song

WHEN COORO SINGS...
...IT'S ALWAYS THE SAME.
Honey, honey, taking a bath, taking a bath...
Gasp!
NOW THAT YOU MENTION IT...
Well, then...
IT'S ABOUT TIME FOR SOME SNACKS!
YAY! ♡
(Chocolate!)
CHOCOLATE, CHOCOLATE...
CHOCO-CHOCO, CHOCO-CHOCO CHOCOLATE!
Gasp!
Same level as Cooro.

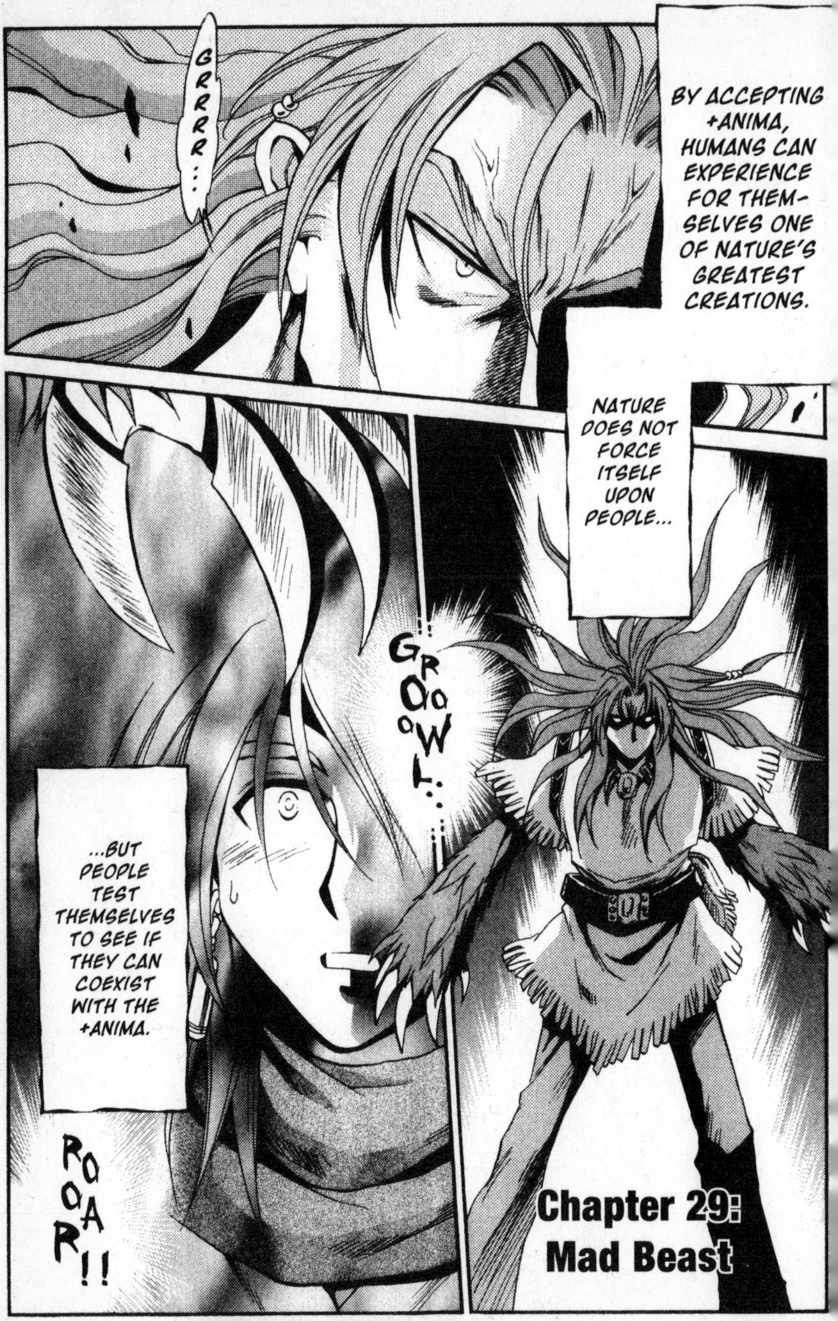
BY ACCEPTING +ANIMA, HUMANS CAN EXPERIENCE FOR THEMSELVES ONE OF NATURE'S GREATEST CREATIONS.
GRRRR...
NATURE DOES NOT FORCE ITSELF UPON PEOPLE...
GROOOWL...
...BUT PEOPLE TEST THEMSELVES TO SEE IF THEY CAN COEXIST WITH THE +ANIMA.
ROOAR!!

Chapter 29: Mad Beast

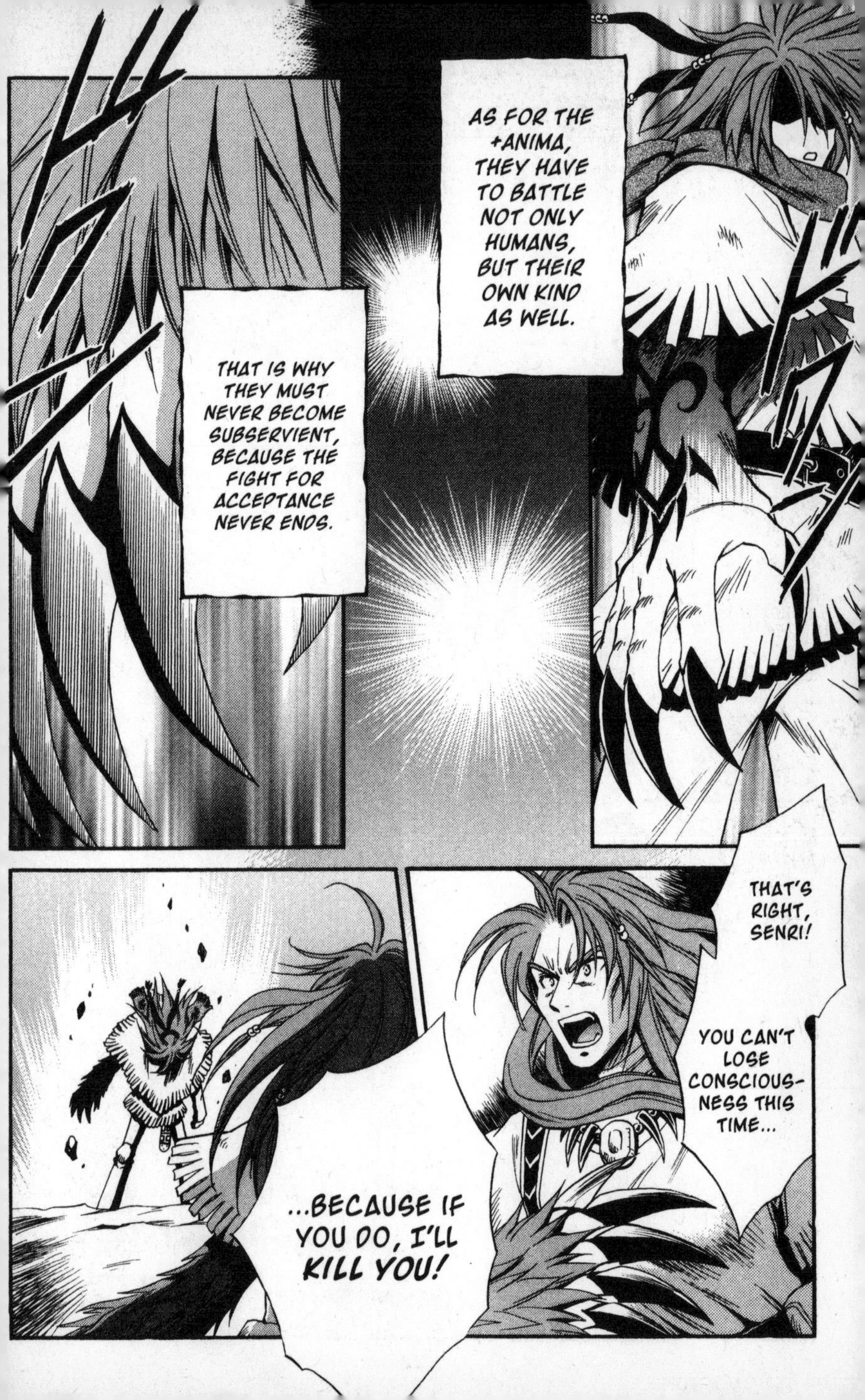
AS FOR THE +ANIMA, THEY HAVE TO BATTLE NOT ONLY HUMANS, BUT THEIR OWN KIND AS WELL.
THAT IS WHY THEY MUST NEVER BECOME SUBSERVIENT, BECAUSE THE FIGHT FOR ACCEPTANCE NEVER ENDS.
THAT'S RIGHT, SENRI!
YOU CAN'T LOSE CONSCIOUS-NESS THIS TIME...
...BECAUSE IF YOU DO, I'LL KILL YOU!

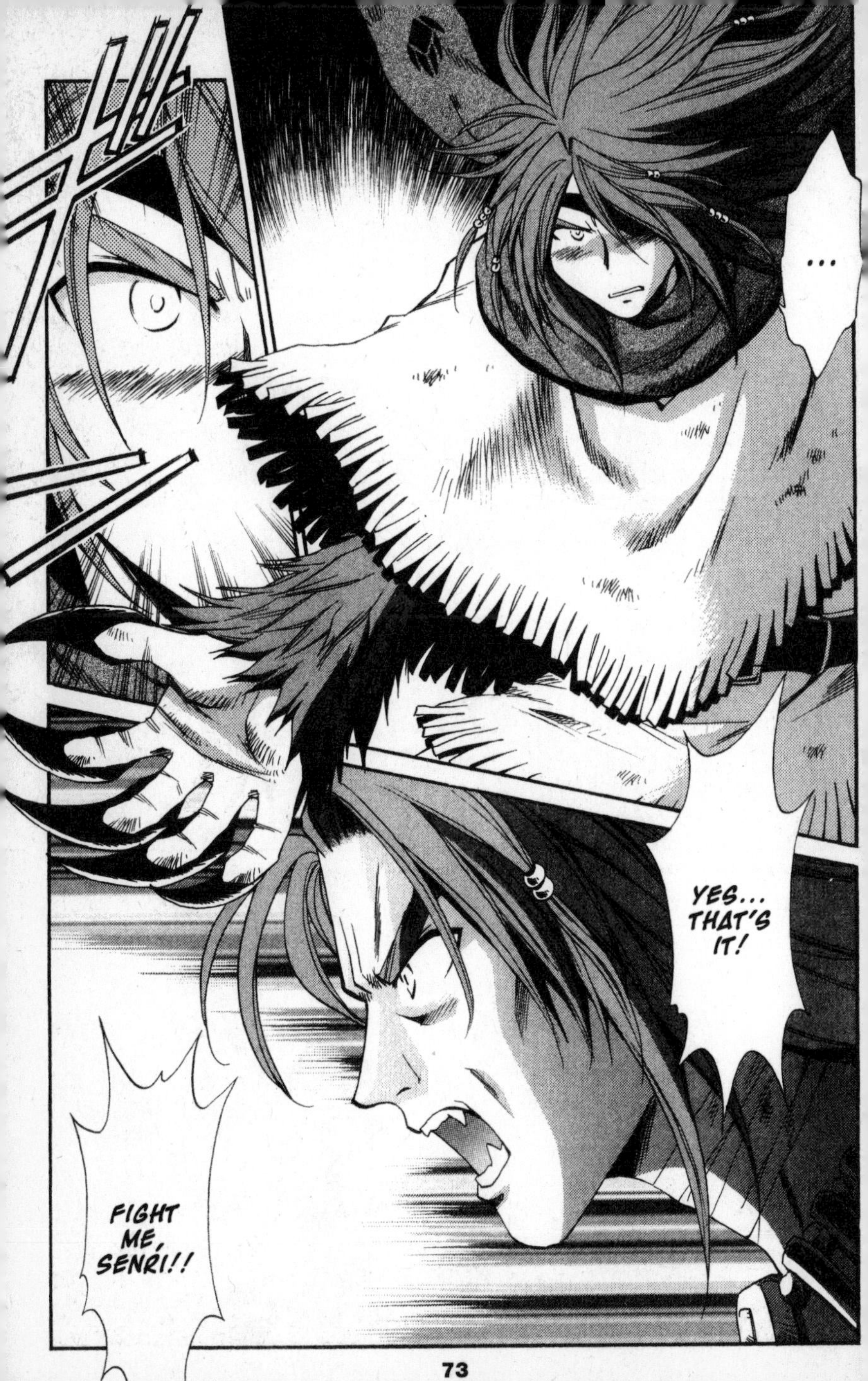
...
YES... THAT'S IT!
FIGHT ME, SENRI!!

HUH?
ARE WE GOING THE WRONG WAY?
YOU TOLD US TO GO THIS WAY, COORO!
ER, I WAS TRYING TO MAKE SURE MR. UPAS DIDN'T SEE US...AND I GOT CONFUSED.
Heh heh!
WE'VE FALLEN TOO FAR BEHIND THEM, FEATHER-BRAIN!
SIGH... NANA...
...CAN YOU HEAR ANYTHING WITH YOUR BAT EARS?
BAT EARS?! YOU MAKE IT SOUND SO...WELL, ICKY!
HMM...
ROAR
SLASH
IT SOUNDS LIKE SOMEONE'S ON A RAMPAGE...
SENRI!!

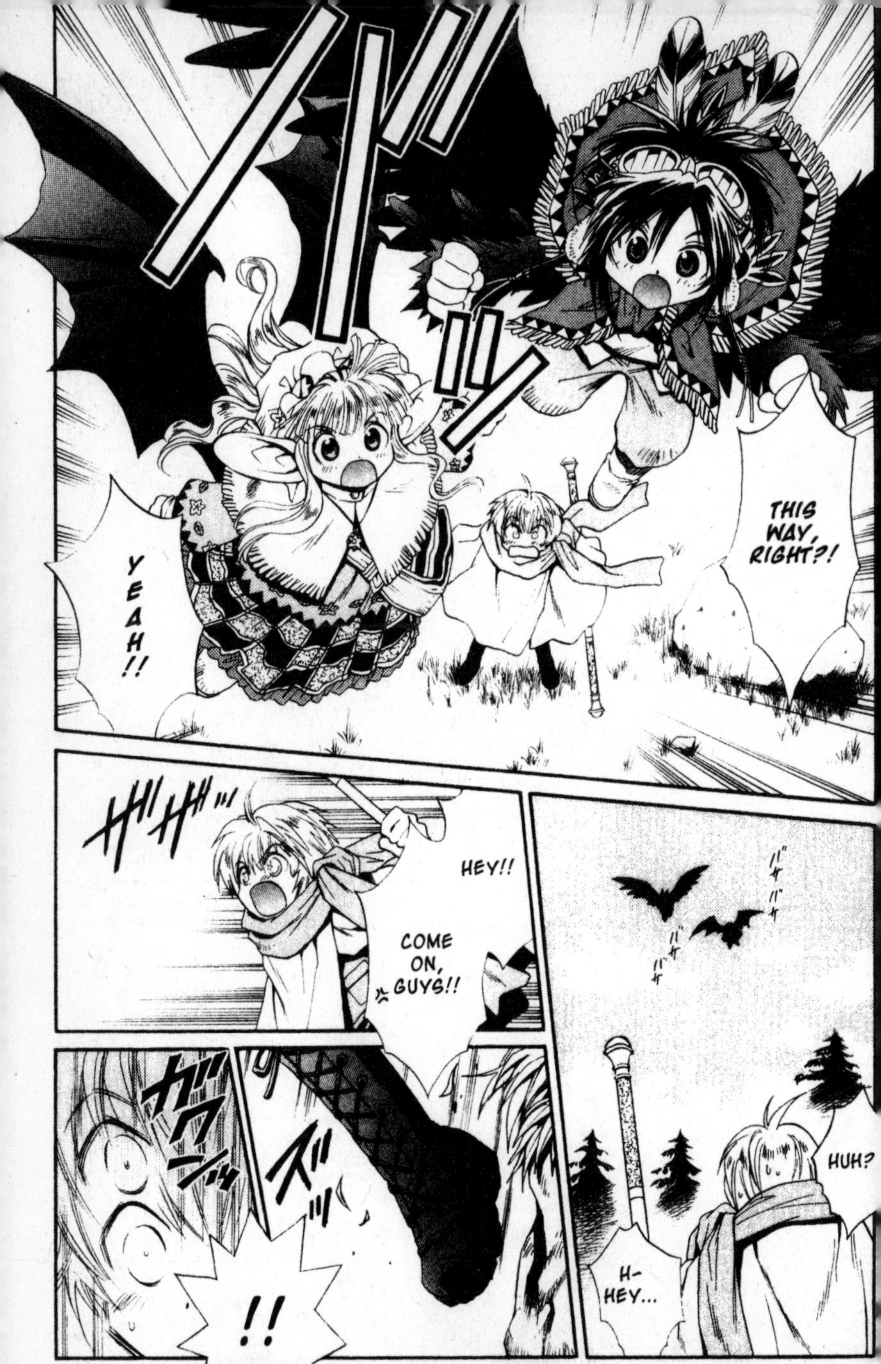
THIS WAY, RIGHT?!
YEAH!!
HUH?
H-HEY...
HEY!!
COME ON, GUYS!!
!!

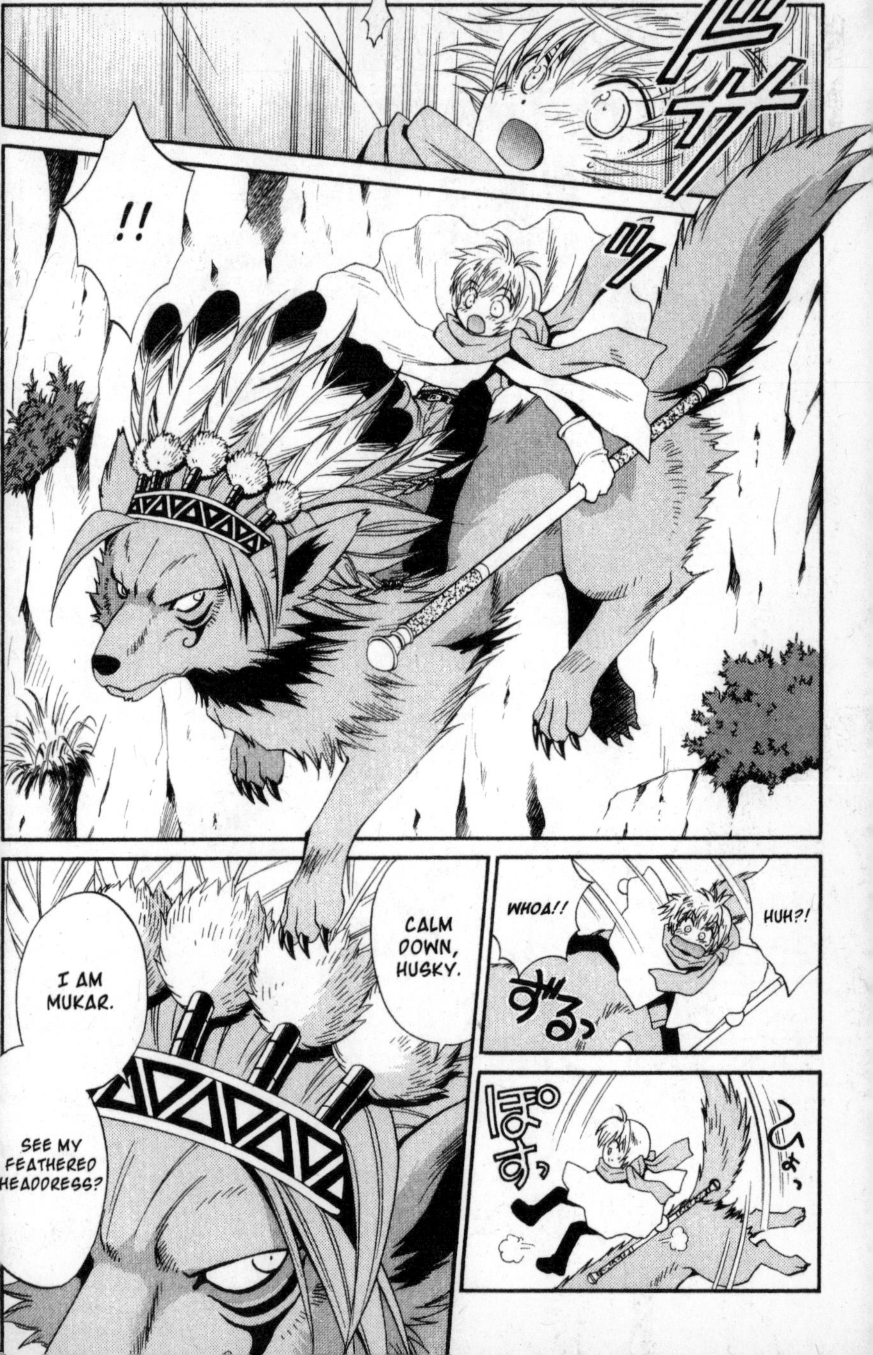

!!
HUH?!
WHOA!!
ずるっ
ひょっ
ぽすっ
CALM DOWN, HUSKY.
I AM MUKAR.
SEE MY FEATHERED HEADDRESS?

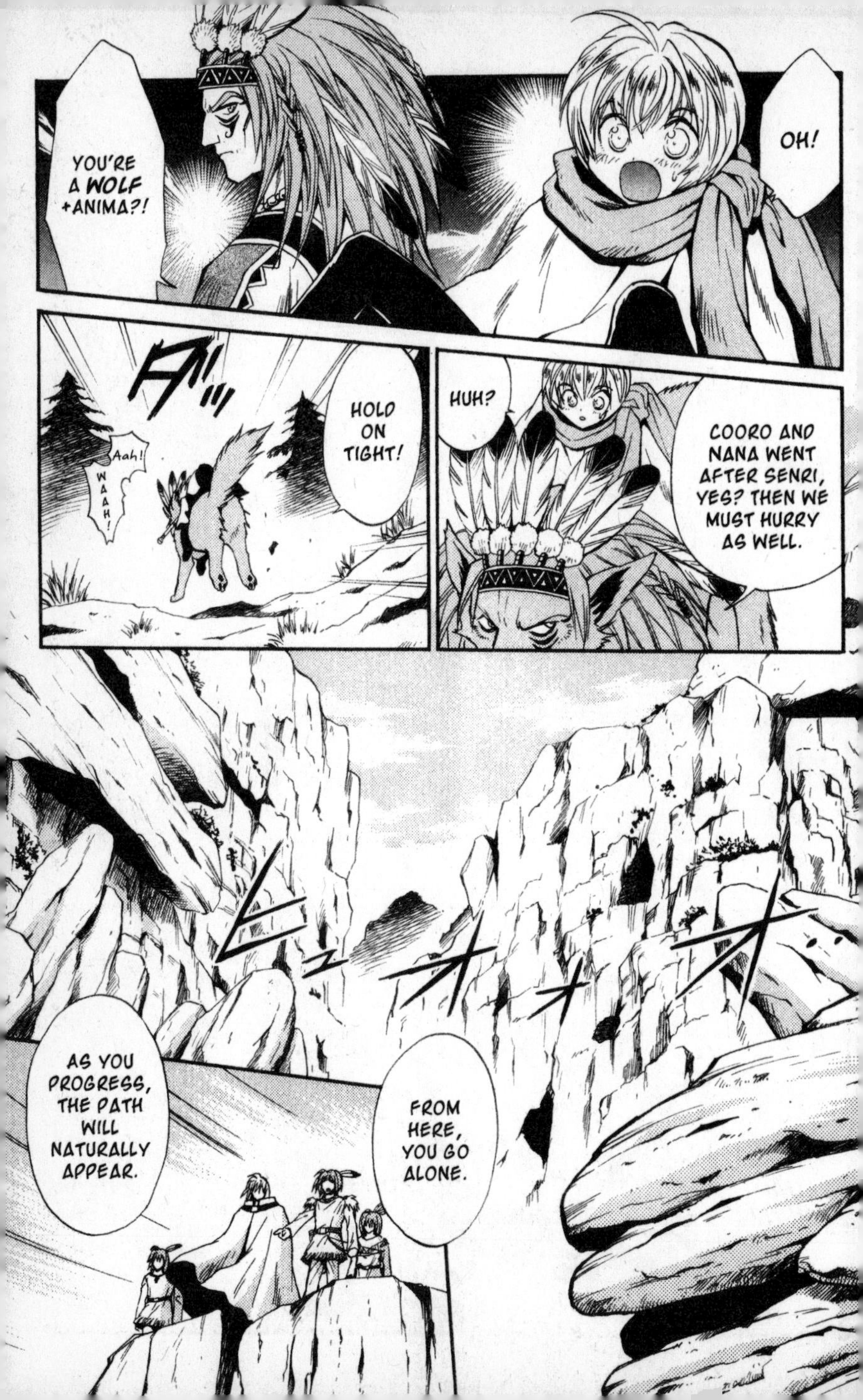
OH!
YOU'RE A WOLF +ANIMA?!
HUH?
COORO AND NANA WENT AFTER SENRI, YES? THEN WE MUST HURRY AS WELL.
HOLD ON TIGHT!
Aah!
WAAAH!
FROM HERE, YOU GO ALONE.
AS YOU PROGRESS, THE PATH WILL NATURALLY APPEAR.

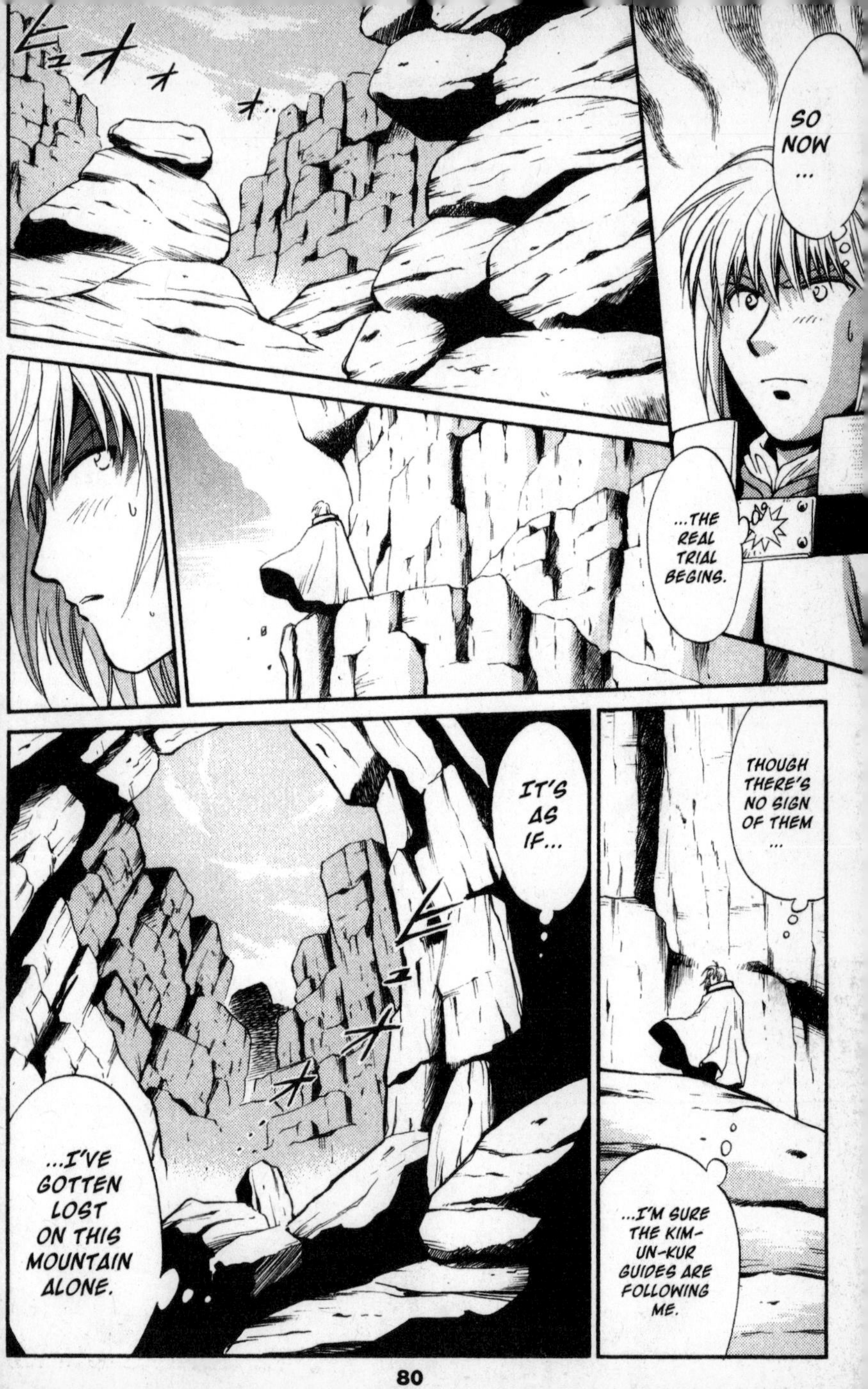
SO NOW ...
...THE REAL TRIAL BEGINS.
THOUGH THERE'S NO SIGN OF THEM ...
...I'M SURE THE KIM-UN-KUR GUIDES ARE FOLLOWING ME.
IT'S AS IF...
...I'VE GOTTEN LOST ON THIS MOUNTAIN ALONE.

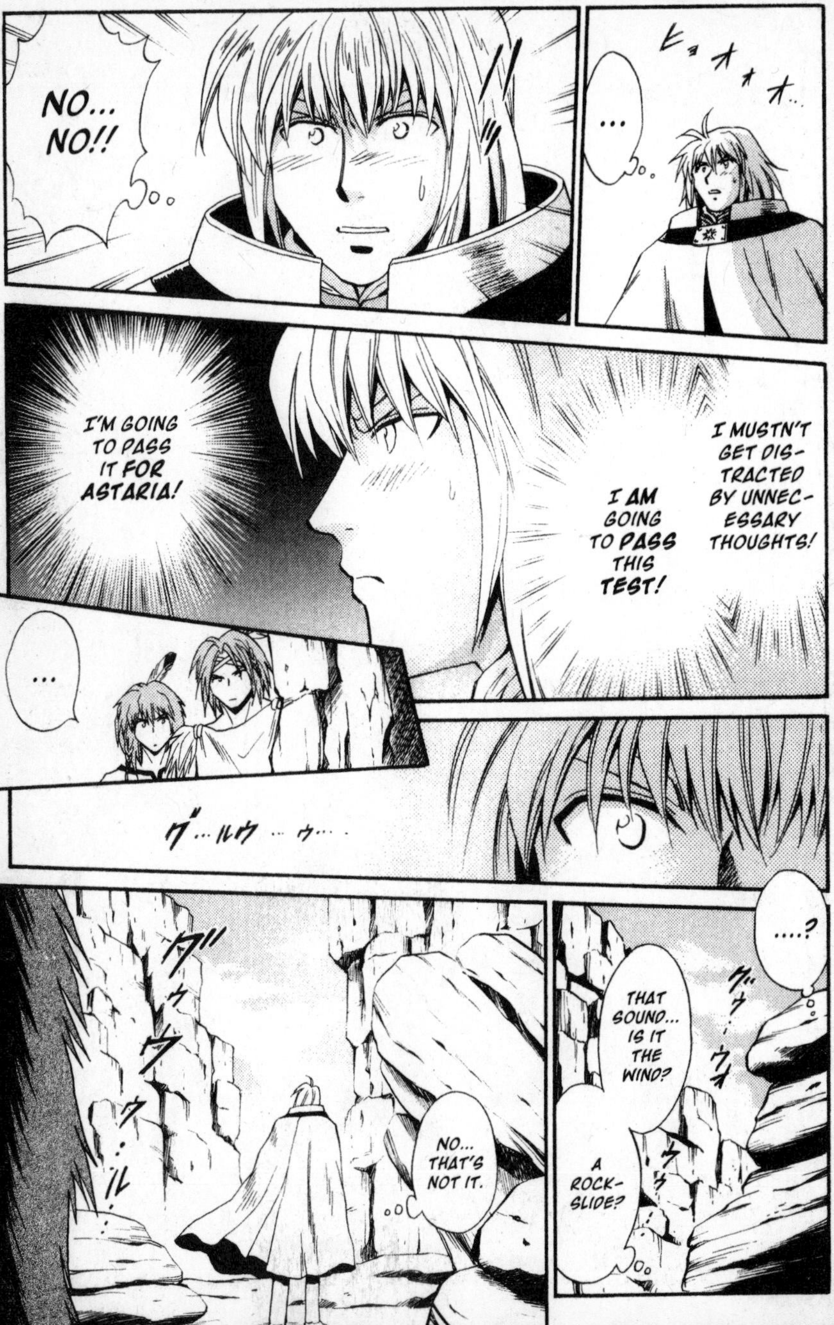

ヒョオオオ…
...
NO... NO!!
I MUSTN'T GET DIS-TRACTED BY UNNEC-ESSARY THOUGHTS!
I AM GOING TO PASS THIS TEST!
I'M GOING TO PASS IT FOR ASTARIA!
...
グ…ルウ…ウ…
....?
THAT SOUND... IS IT THE WIND?
A ROCK-SLIDE?
NO... THAT'S NOT IT.

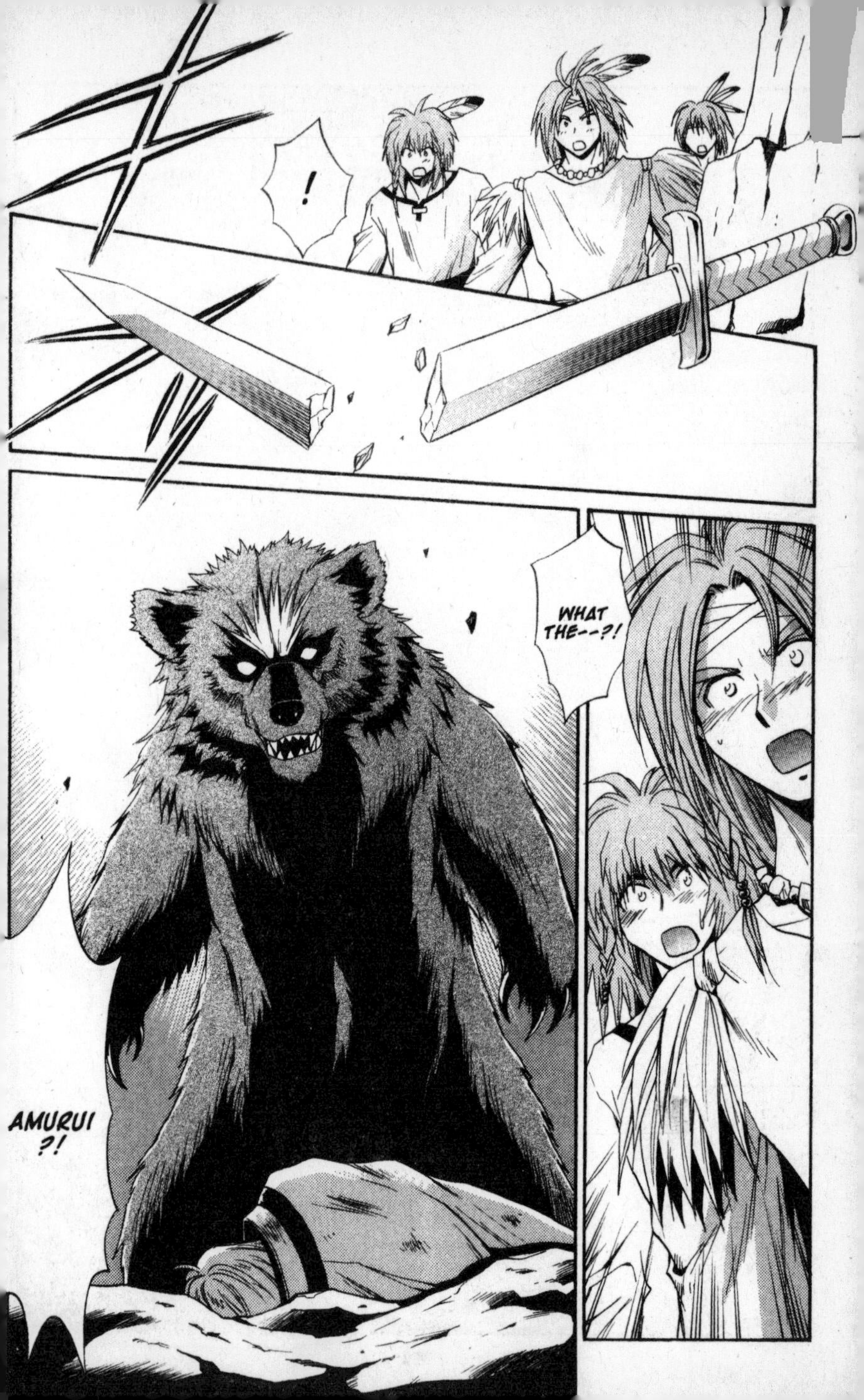
!
WHAT THE--?!
AMURUI ?!

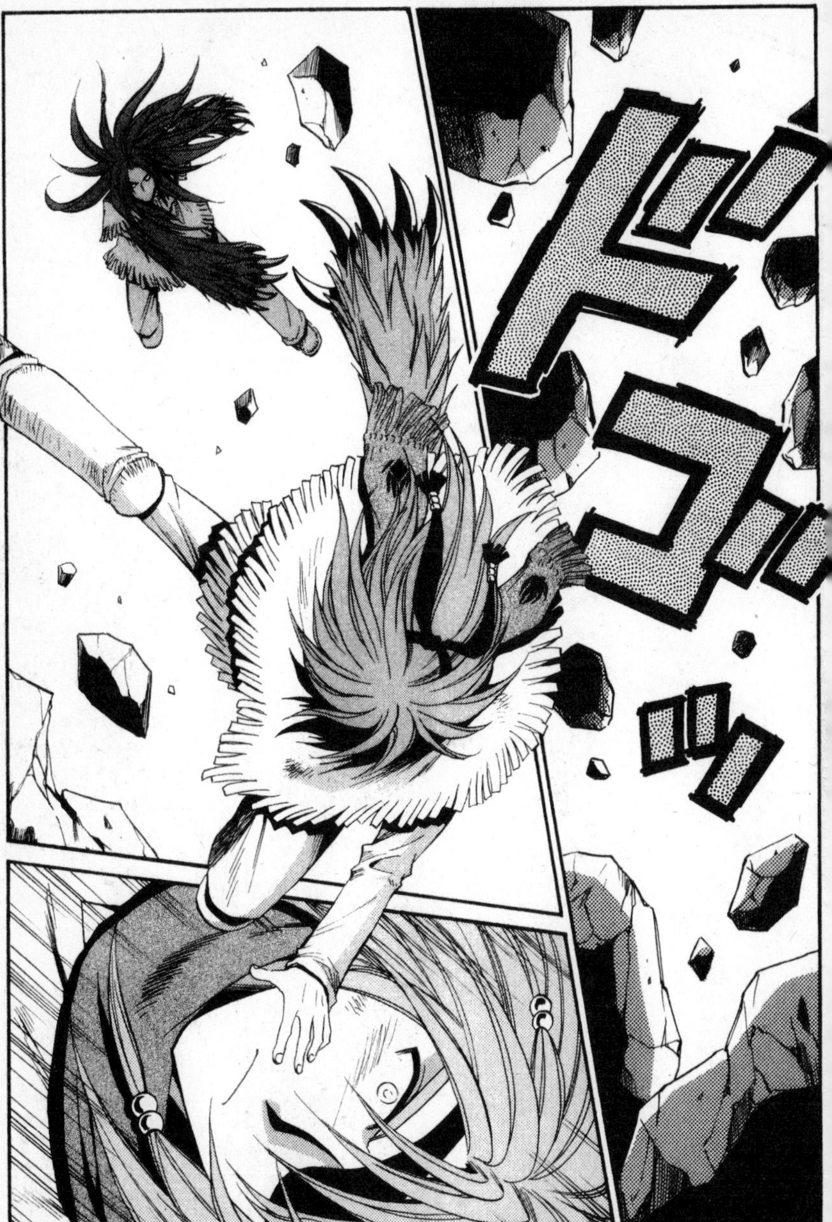
ドゴッ

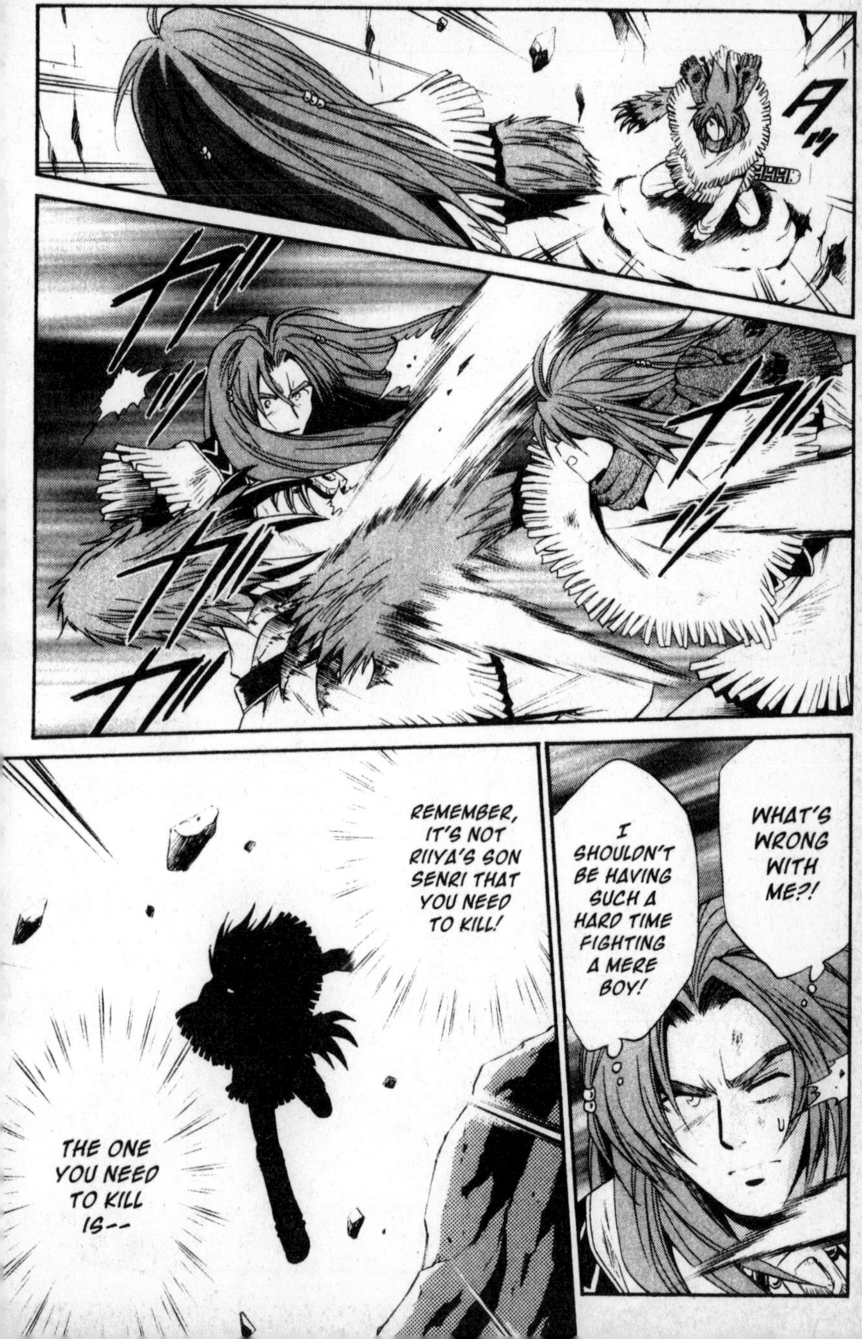
WHAT'S WRONG WITH ME?!
I SHOULDN'T BE HAVING SUCH A HARD TIME FIGHTING A MERE BOY!
REMEMBER, IT'S NOT RIIYA'S SON SENRI THAT YOU NEED TO KILL!
THE ONE YOU NEED TO KILL IS--

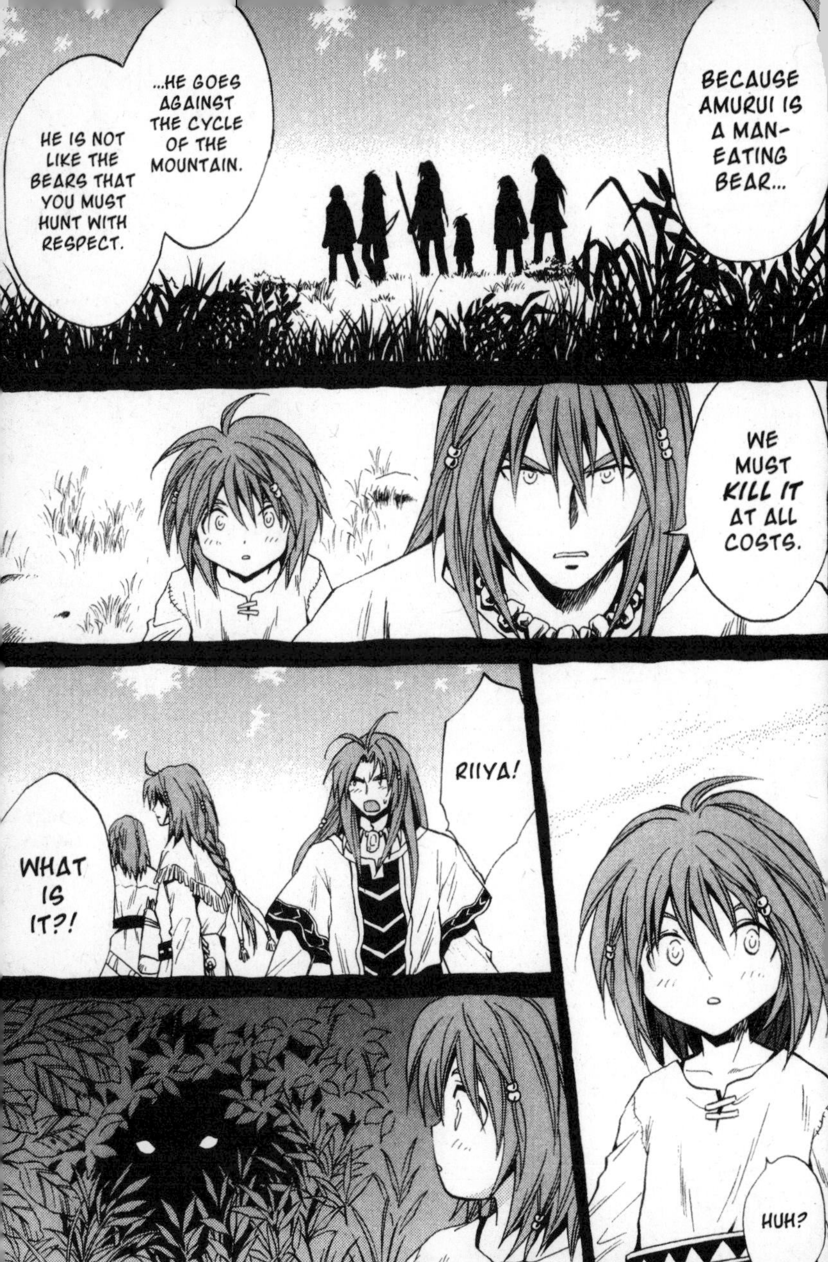
BECAUSE AMURUI IS A MAN-EATING BEAR...
...HE GOES AGAINST THE CYCLE OF THE MOUNTAIN.
HE IS NOT LIKE THE BEARS THAT YOU MUST HUNT WITH RESPECT.
WE MUST KILL IT AT ALL COSTS.
HUH?
RIIYA!
WHAT IS IT?!

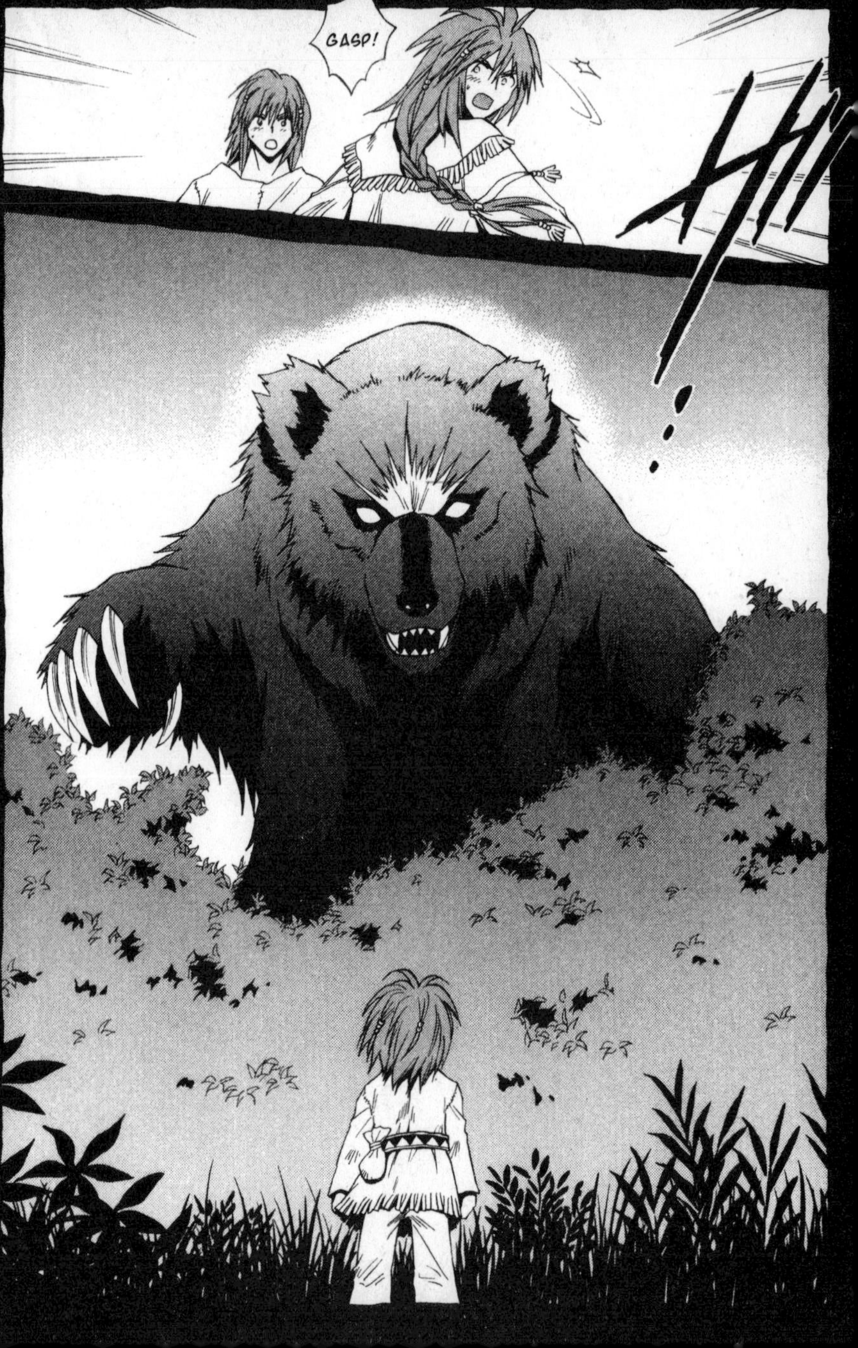
GASP!

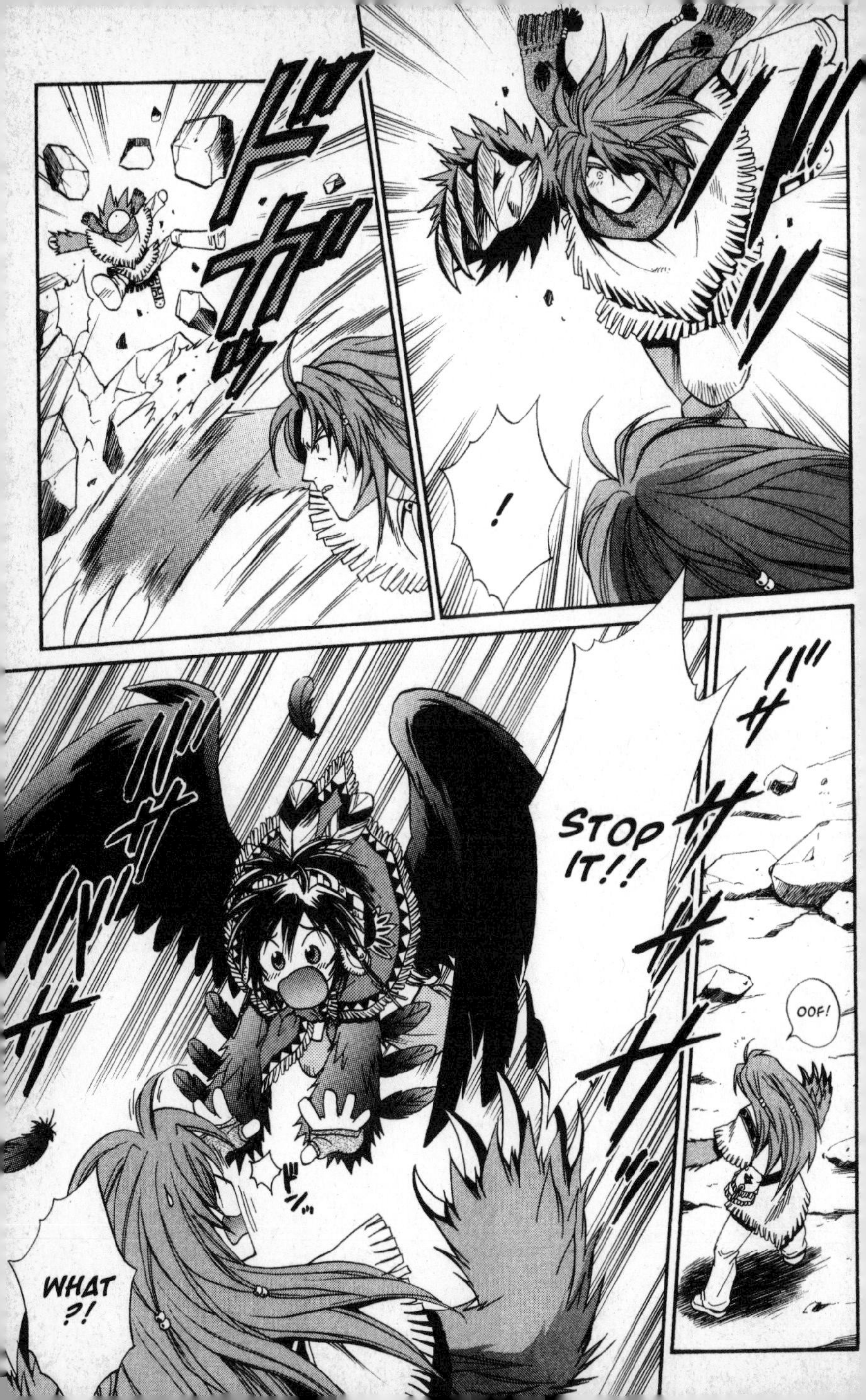
!
STOP IT!!
OOF!
WHAT ?!

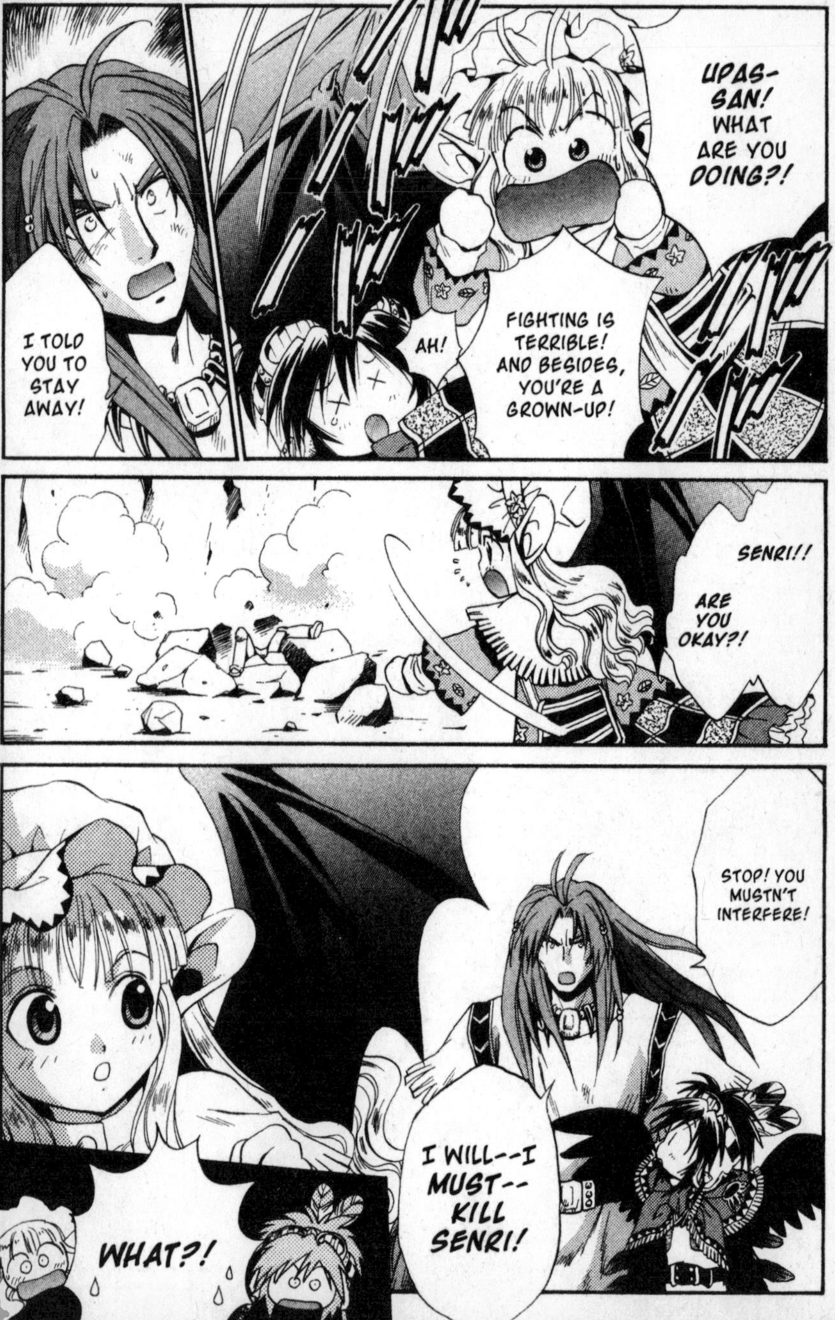
UPAS-SAN! WHAT ARE YOU DOING?!
FIGHTING IS TERRIBLE! AND BESIDES, YOU'RE A GROWN-UP!
AH!
I TOLD YOU TO STAY AWAY!
SENRI!!
ARE YOU OKAY?!
STOP! YOU MUSTN'T INTERFERE!
I WILL--I MUST--KILL SENRI!
WHAT?!

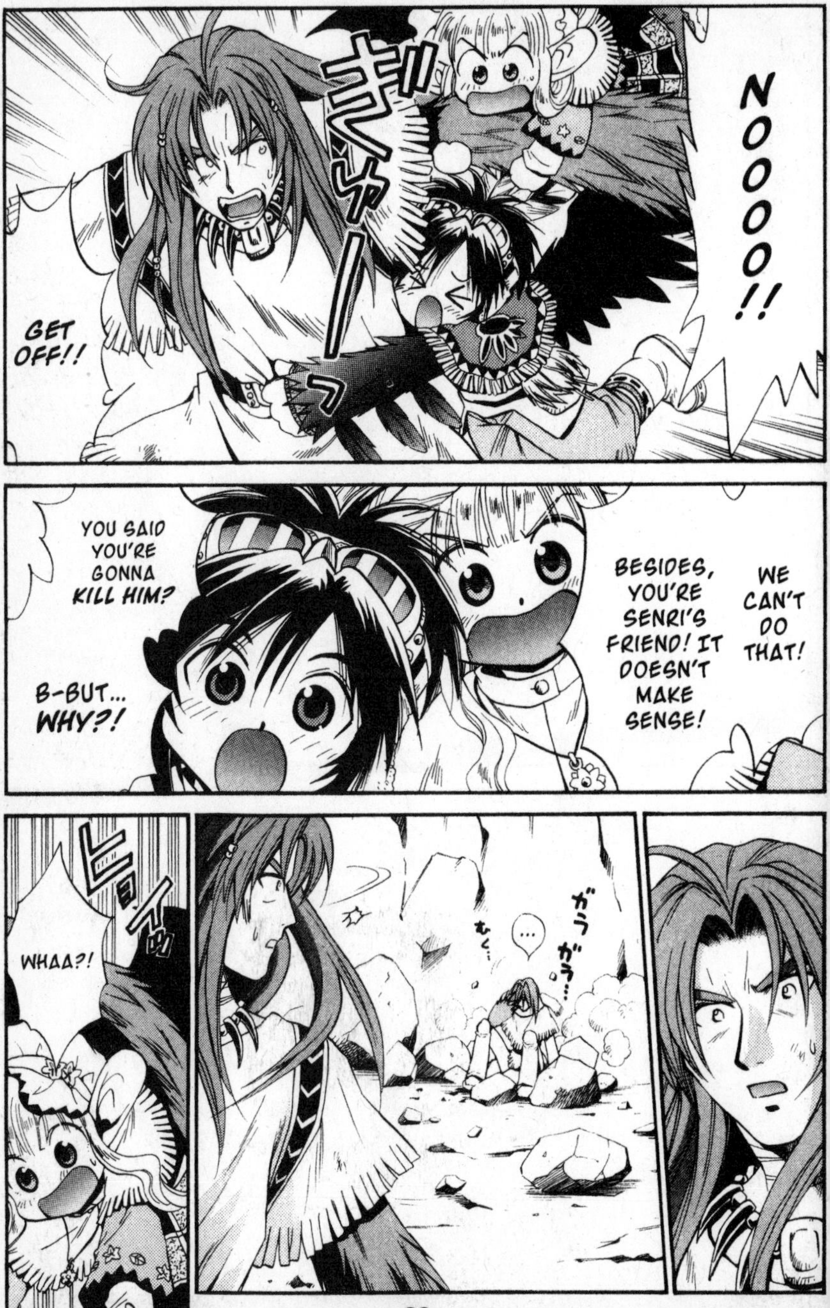
NOOOOO!!
ぎゃーっ
GET OFF!!
WE CAN'T DO THAT!
BESIDES, YOU'RE SENRI'S FRIEND! IT DOESN'T MAKE SENSE!
YOU SAID YOU'RE GONNA KILL HIM?
B-BUT... WHY?!
ガラ ガラ…
…
むく…
ヒョイ
WHAA?!

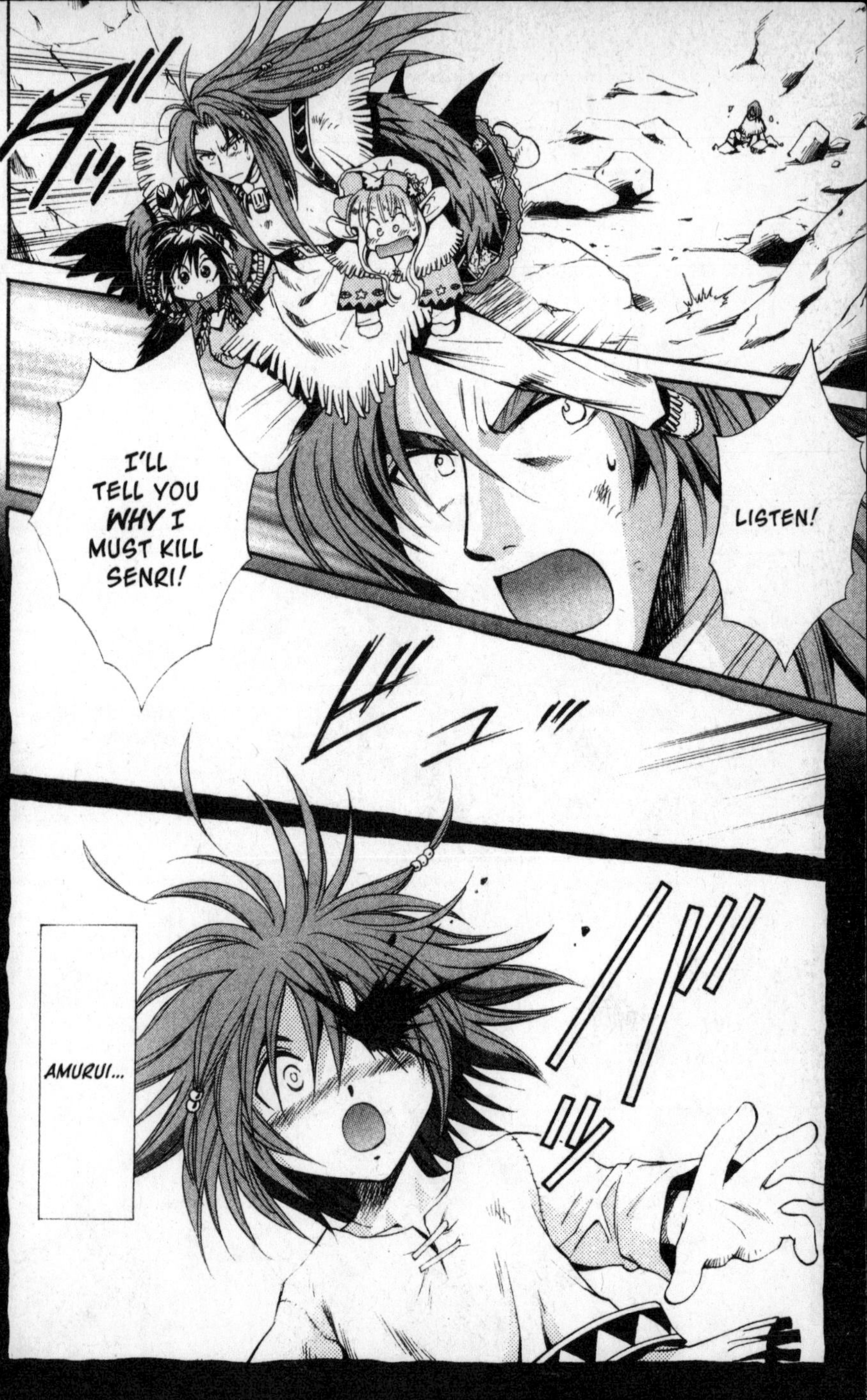
LISTEN!
I'LL TELL YOU WHY I MUST KILL SENRI!
AMURUI...

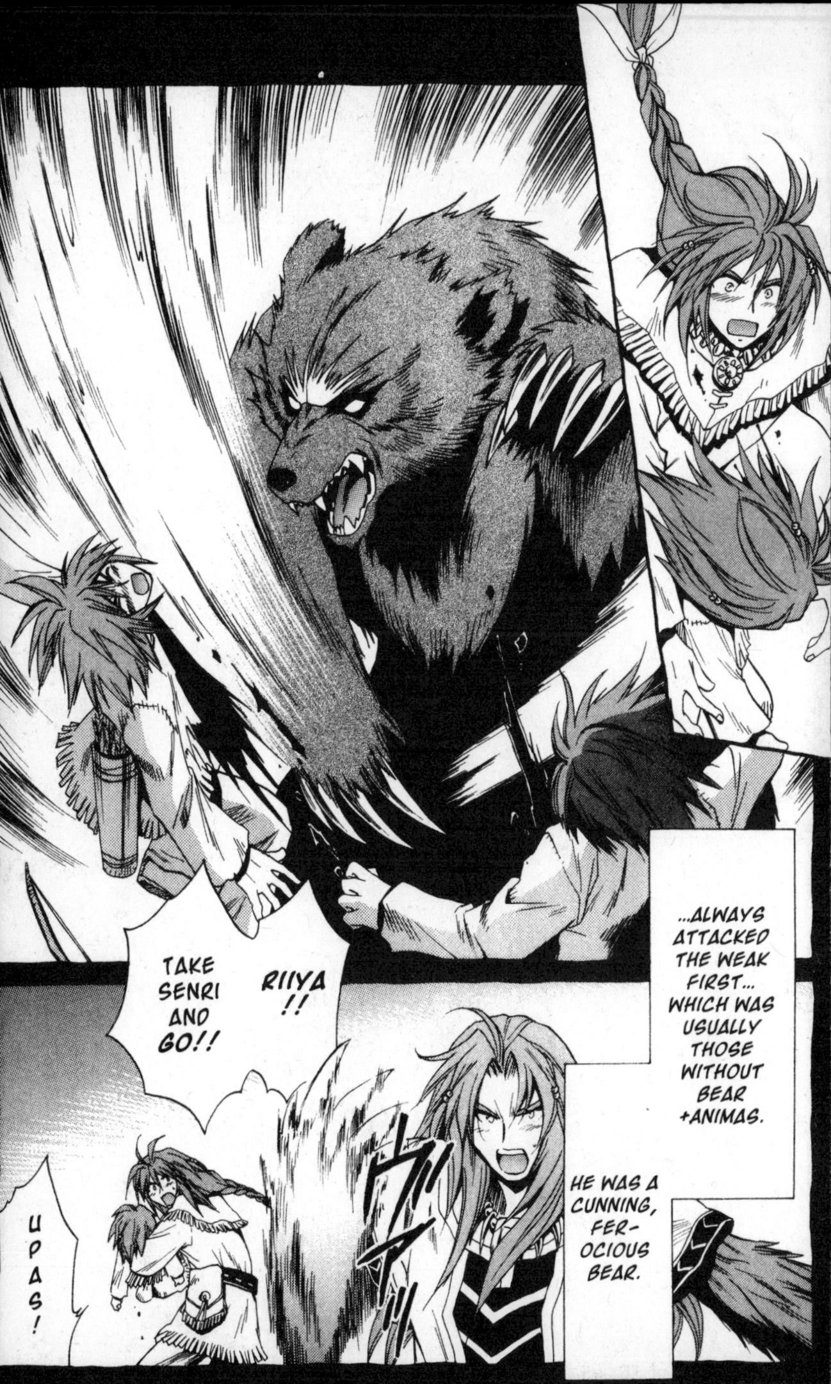
...ALWAYS ATTACKED THE WEAK FIRST... WHICH WAS USUALLY THOSE WITHOUT BEAR +ANIMAS.
HE WAS A CUNNING, FER-OCIOUS BEAR.
RIIYA!!
TAKE SENRI AND GO!!
UPAS!

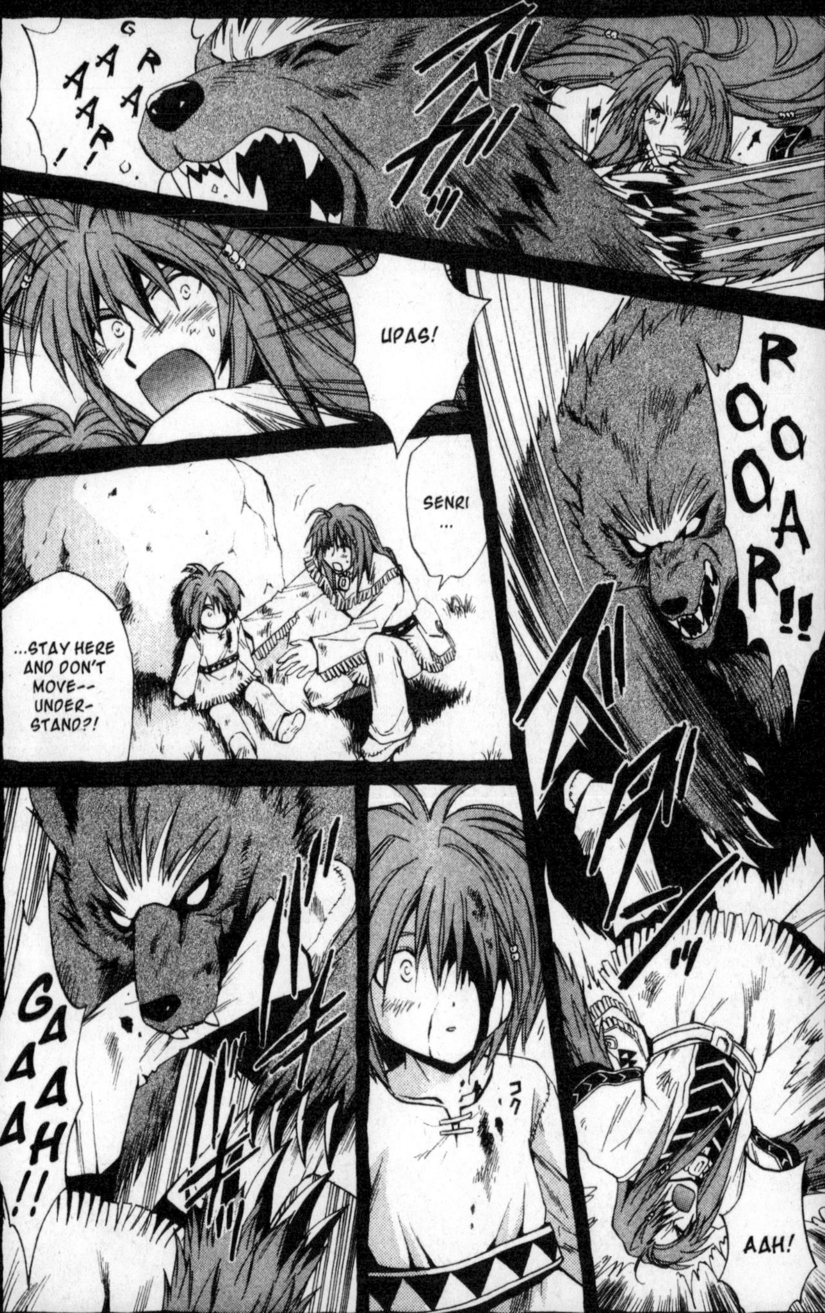
GRAAAAR!!
ROOOAR!!
AAH!
UPAS!
SENRI ...
...STAY HERE AND DON'T MOVE-- UNDER-STAND?!
GAAAAH!!

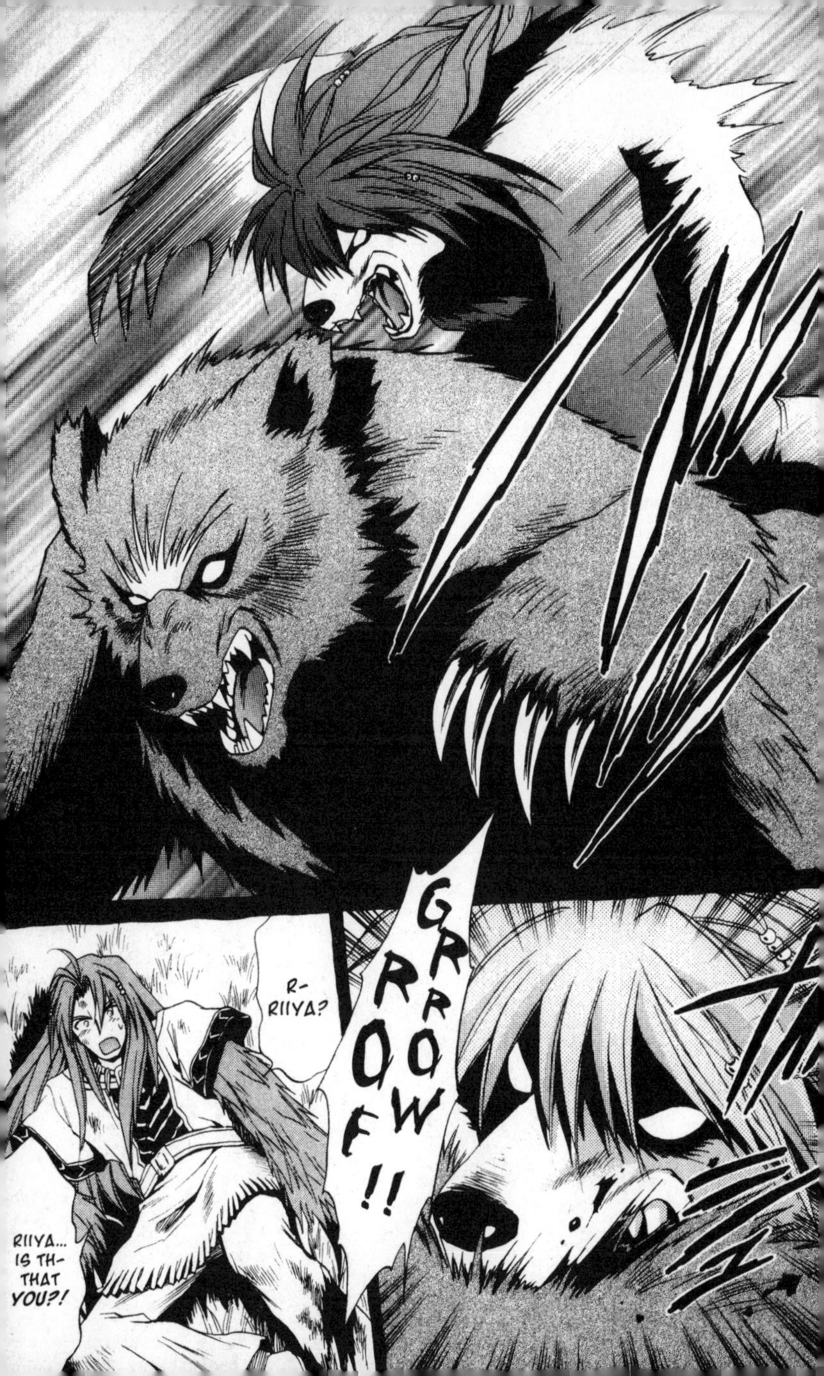
GRROW
ROF!!
R-
RIIYA?
RIIYA...
IS TH-
THAT
YOU?!

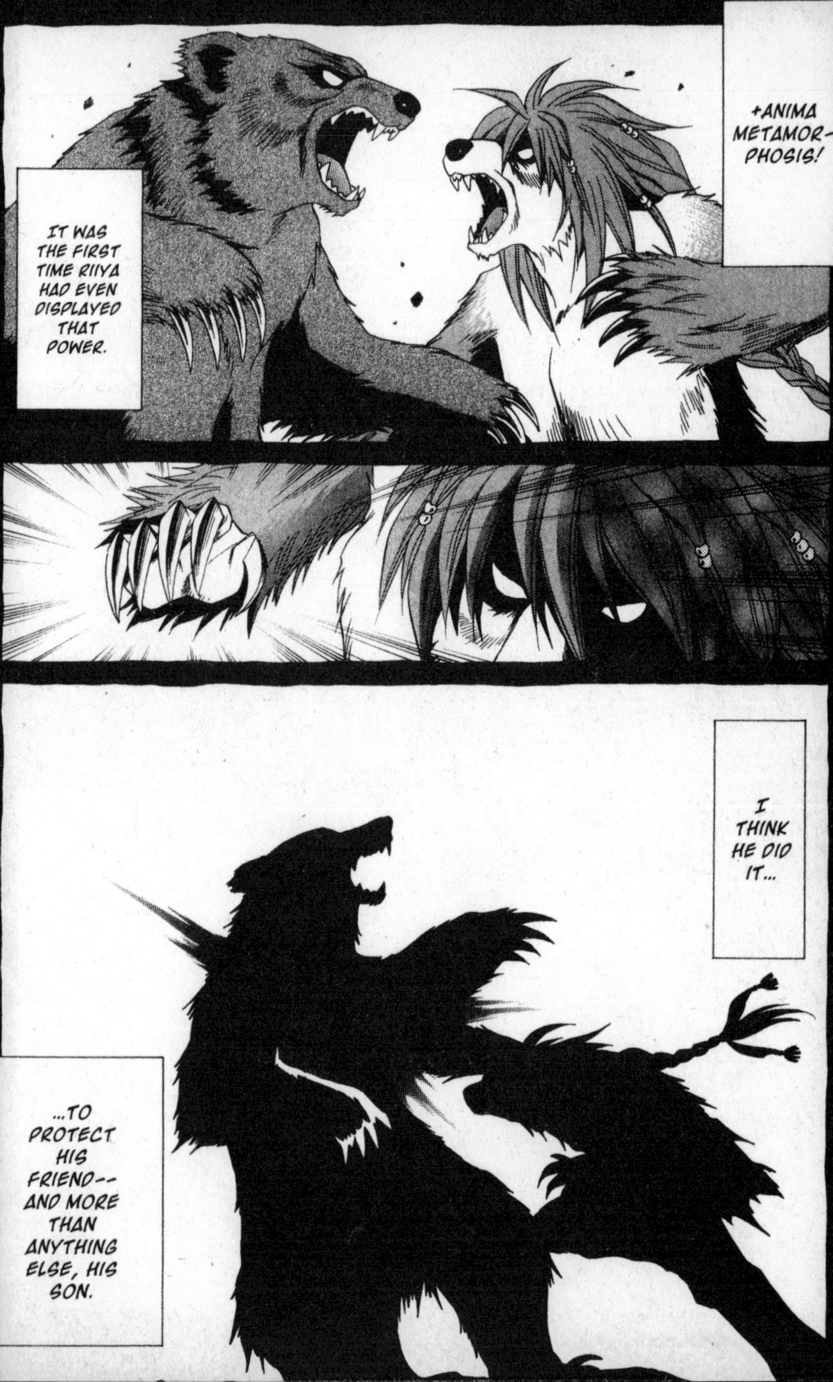
+ANIMA METAMORPHOSIS!
IT WAS THE FIRST TIME RIIYA HAD EVEN DISPLAYED THAT POWER.
I THINK HE DID IT...
...TO PROTECT HIS FRIEND-- AND MORE THAN ANYTHING ELSE, HIS SON.

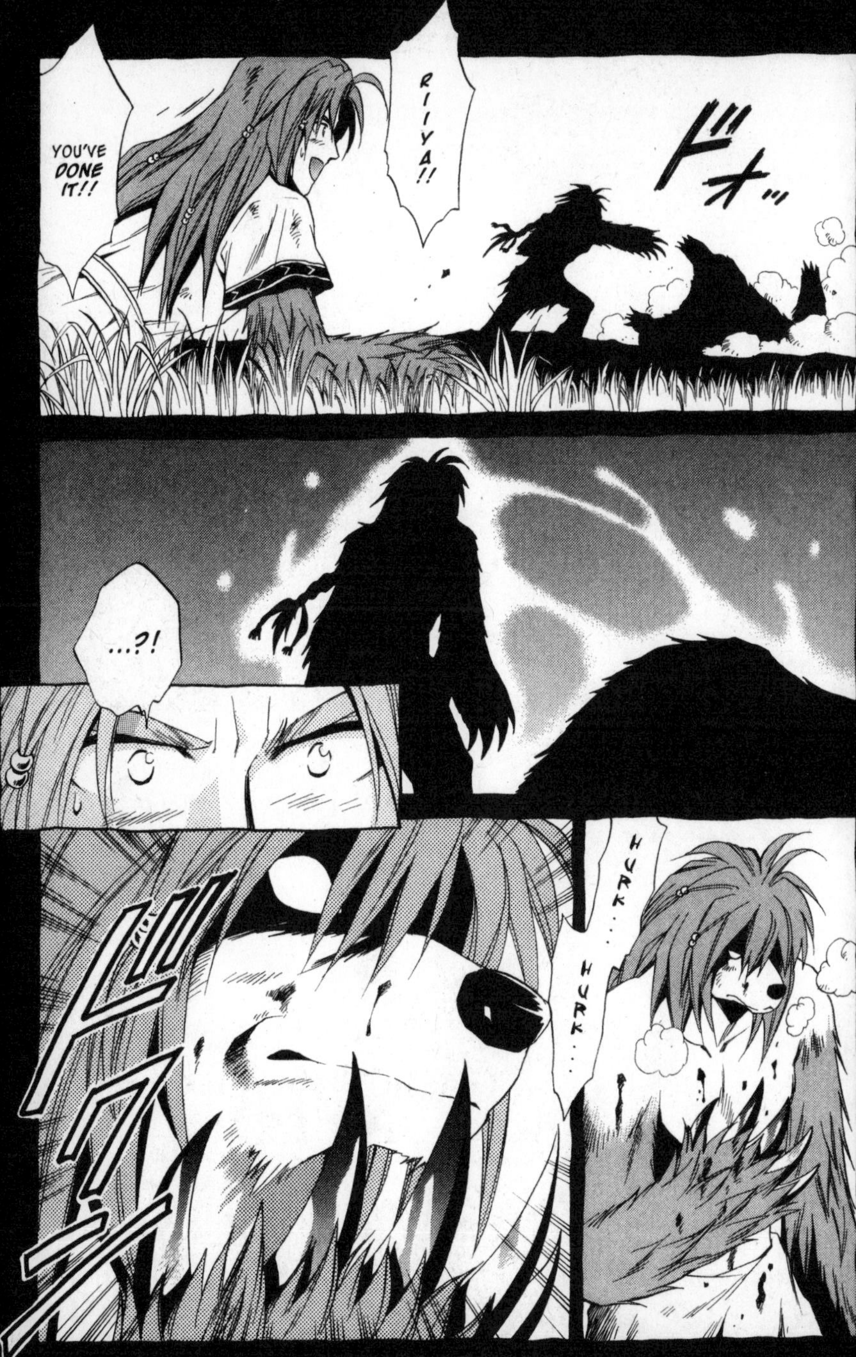
ドォッ
RIIYA!!
YOU'VE DONE IT!!
...?!
HURK... HURK...

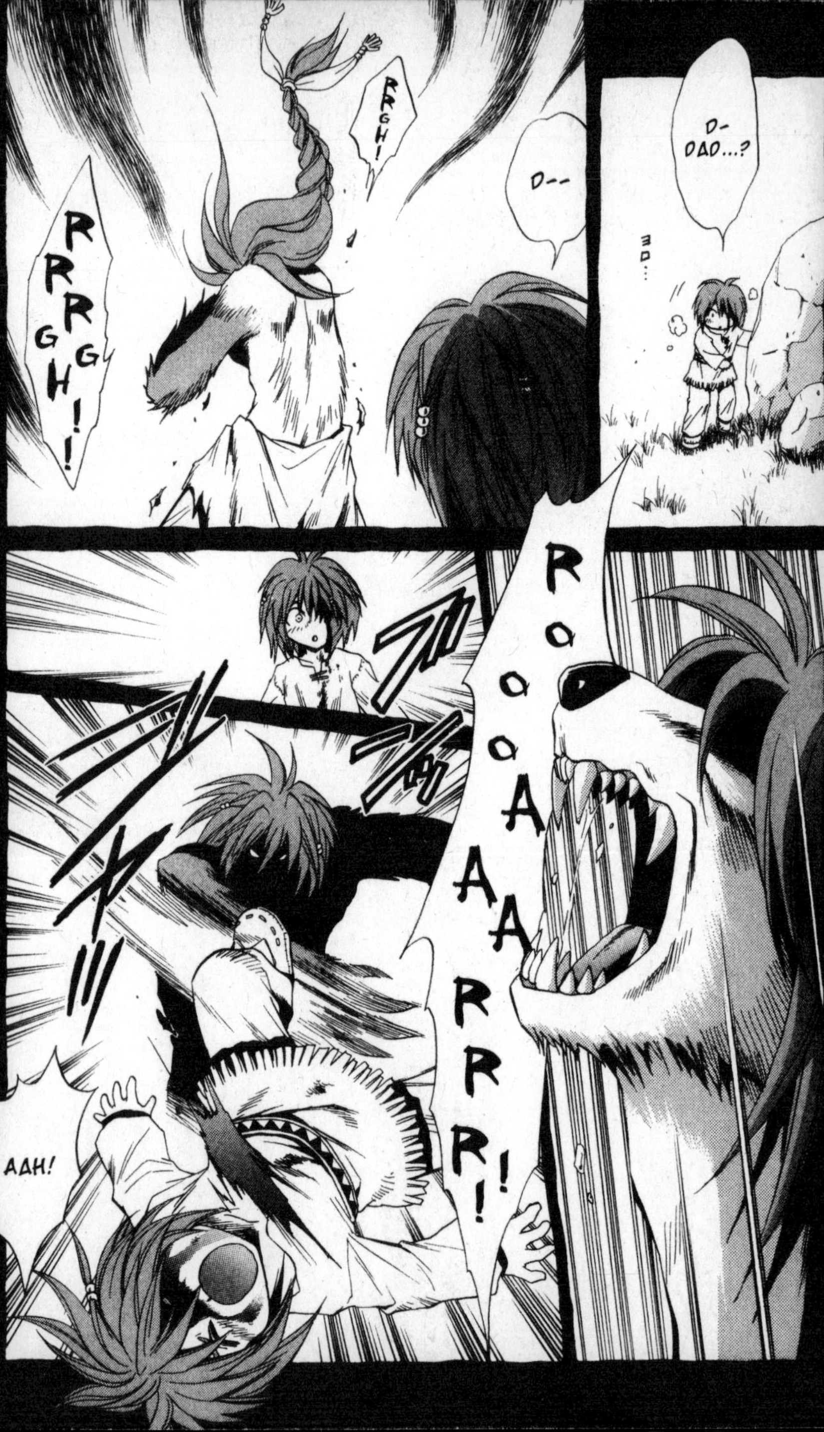

D-DAD...?
ED...
D--
RRGH!
RRRGGH!!!
ROOOAAARRR!!
AAH!

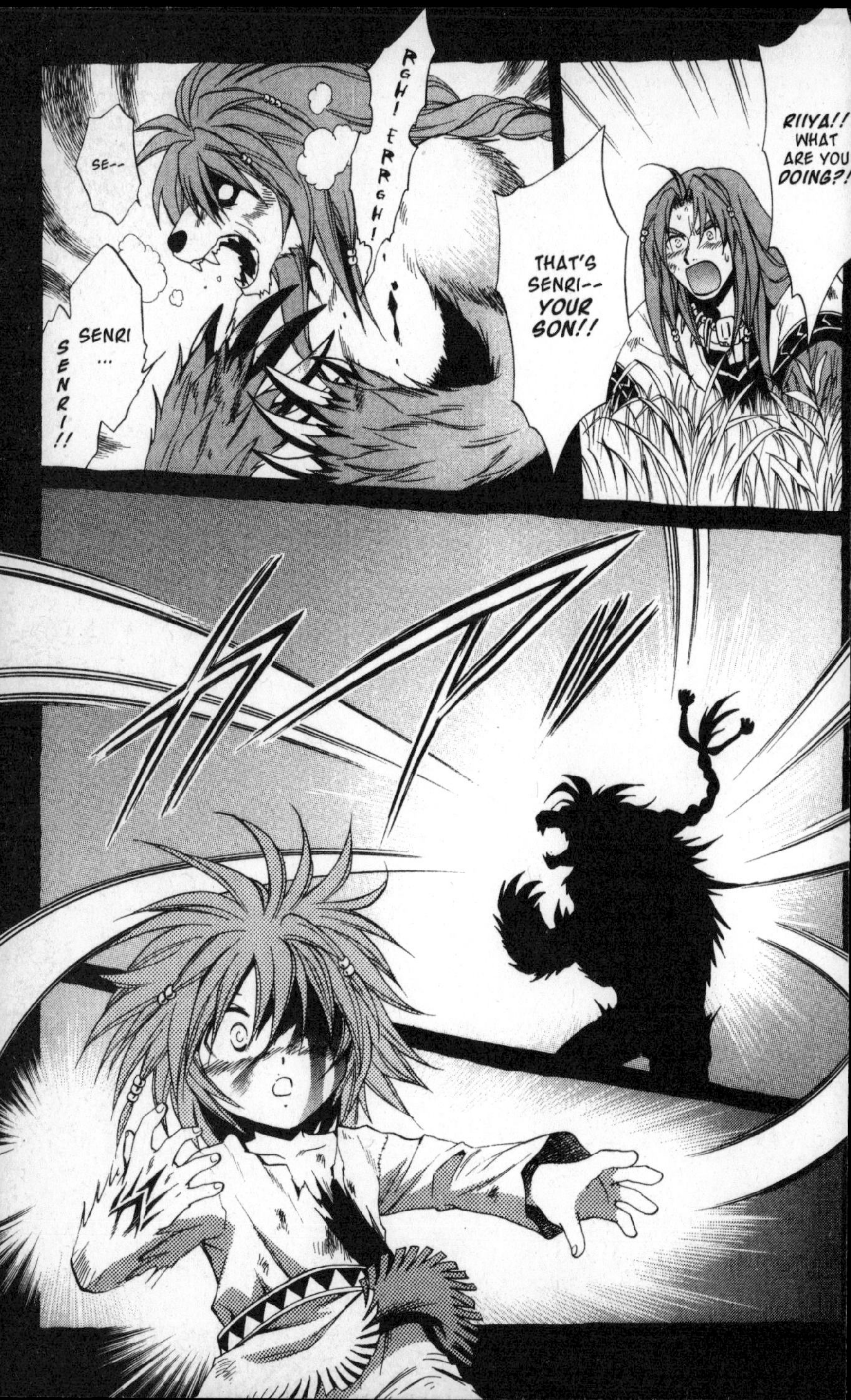
RIIYA!! WHAT ARE YOU DOING?!
THAT'S SENRI-- YOUR SON!!
RGH! ERRGH!
SE--
SENRI ...
SENRI!!

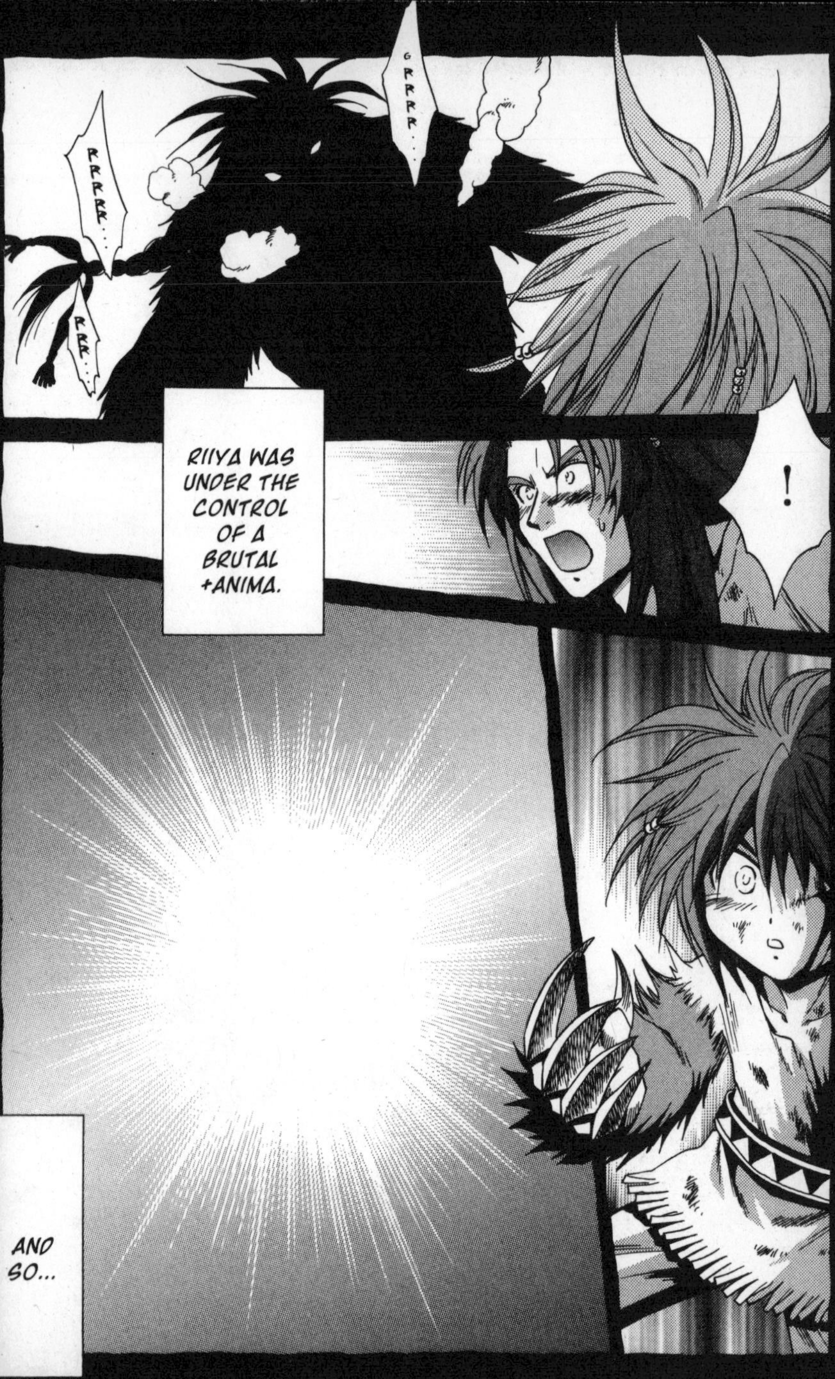
GRRRR...
RRRRR...
RRR...
RIIYA WAS UNDER THE CONTROL OF A BRUTAL +ANIMA.
!
AND SO...

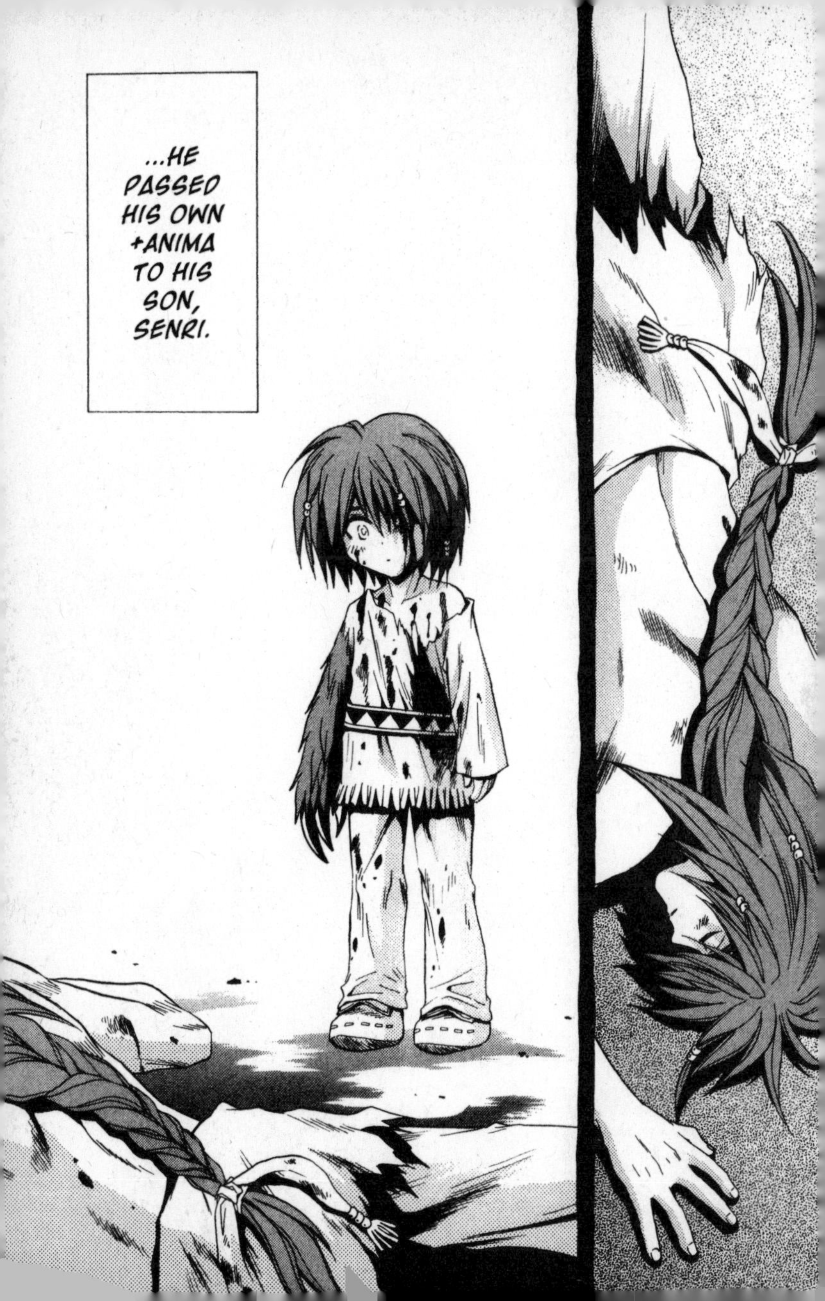
...HE PASSED HIS OWN +ANIMA TO HIS SON, SENRI.

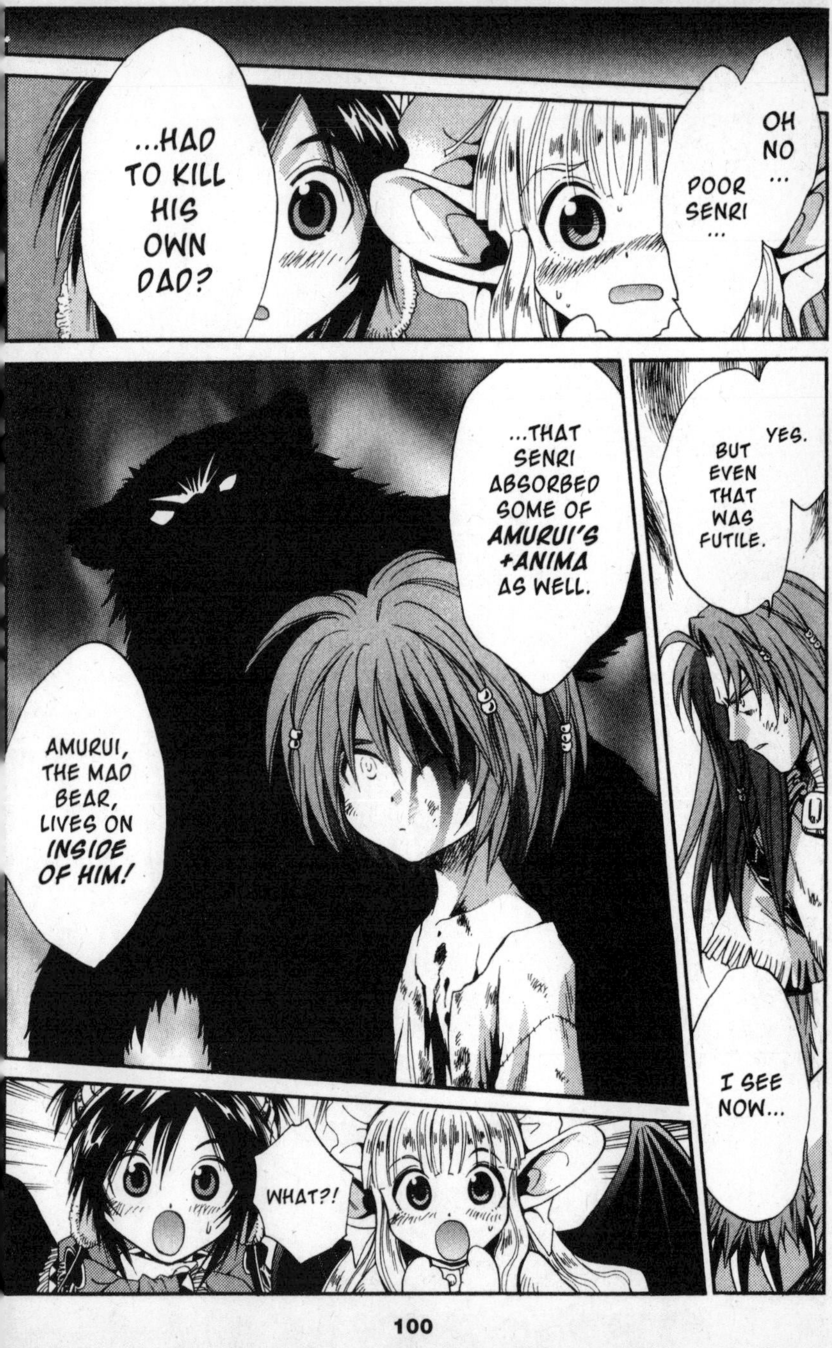
OH NO ... POOR SENRI ...
...HAD TO KILL HIS OWN DAD?
YES. BUT EVEN THAT WAS FUTILE.
I SEE NOW...
...THAT SENRI ABSORBED SOME OF **AMURUI'S +ANIMA** AS WELL.
AMURUI, THE MAD BEAR, LIVES ON ***INSIDE OF HIM!***
WHAT?!

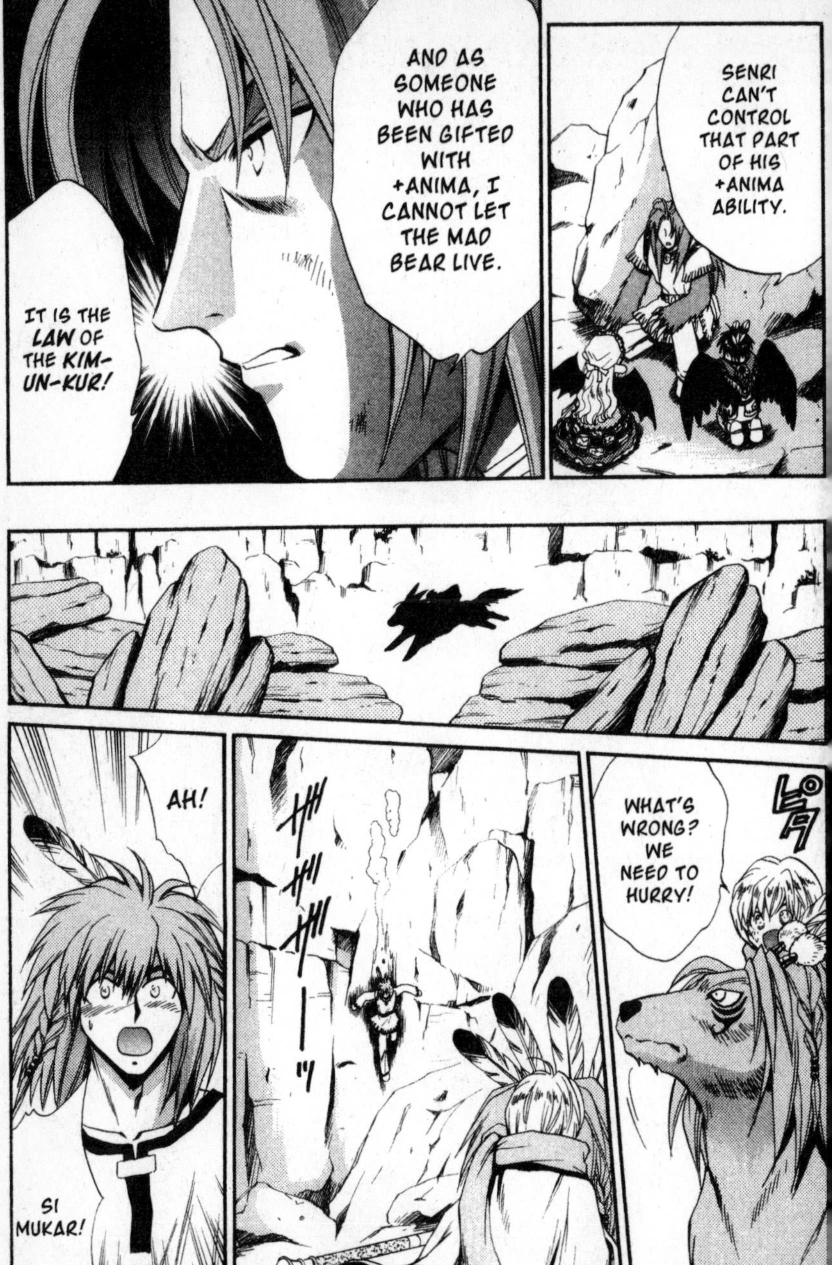

SENRI CAN'T CONTROL THAT PART OF HIS +ANIMA ABILITY.
AND AS SOMEONE WHO HAS BEEN GIFTED WITH +ANIMA, I CANNOT LET THE MAD BEAR LIVE.
IT IS THE LAW OF THE KIM-UN-KUR!
WHAT'S WRONG? WE NEED TO HURRY!
AH!
SI MUKAR!

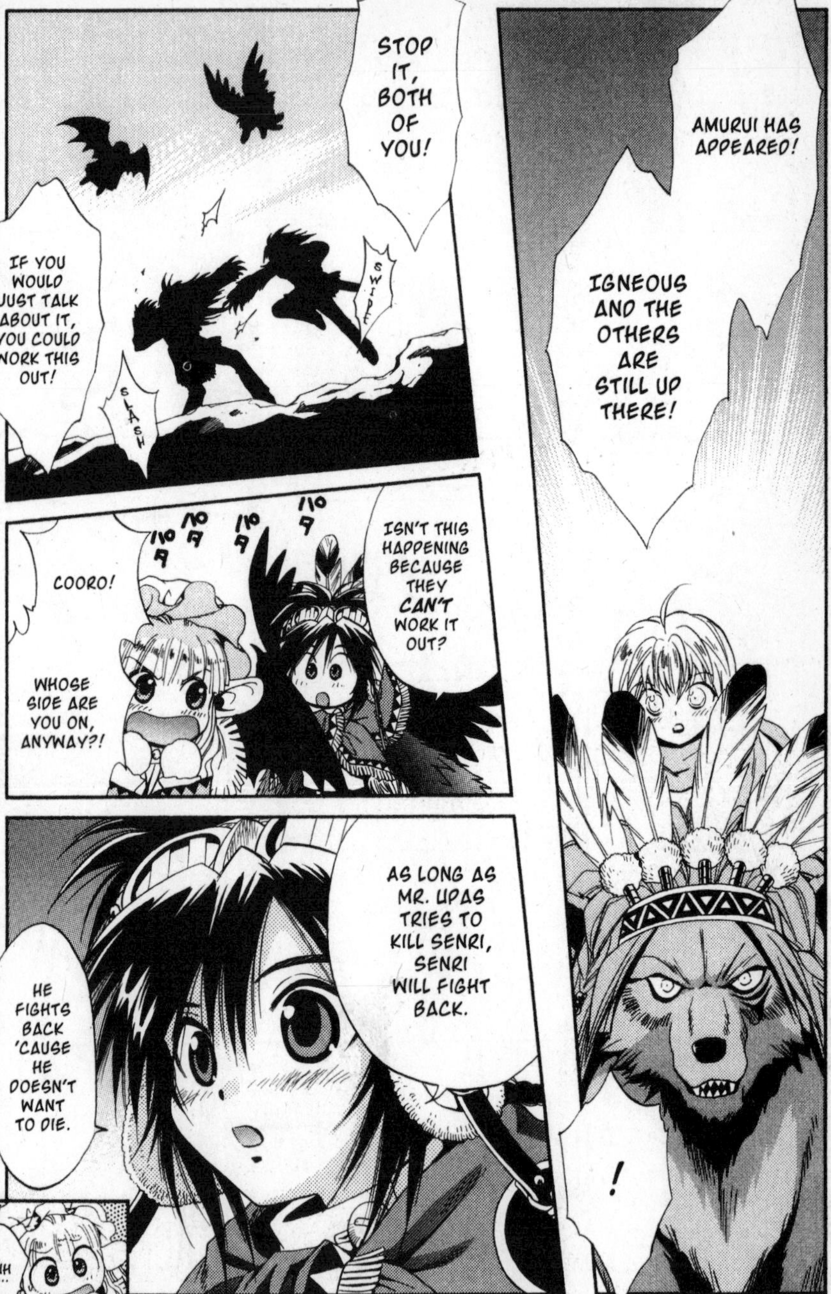

AMURUI HAS APPEARED!
IGNEOUS AND THE OTHERS ARE STILL UP THERE!
!
STOP IT, BOTH OF YOU!
SWIPE
IF YOU WOULD JUST TALK ABOUT IT, YOU COULD WORK THIS OUT!
SLASH
ISN'T THIS HAPPENING BECAUSE THEY *CAN'T* WORK IT OUT?
COORO!
WHOSE SIDE ARE YOU ON, ANYWAY?!
AS LONG AS MR. UPAS TRIES TO KILL SENRI, SENRI WILL FIGHT BACK.
HE FIGHTS BACK 'CAUSE HE DOESN'T WANT TO DIE.
UH...

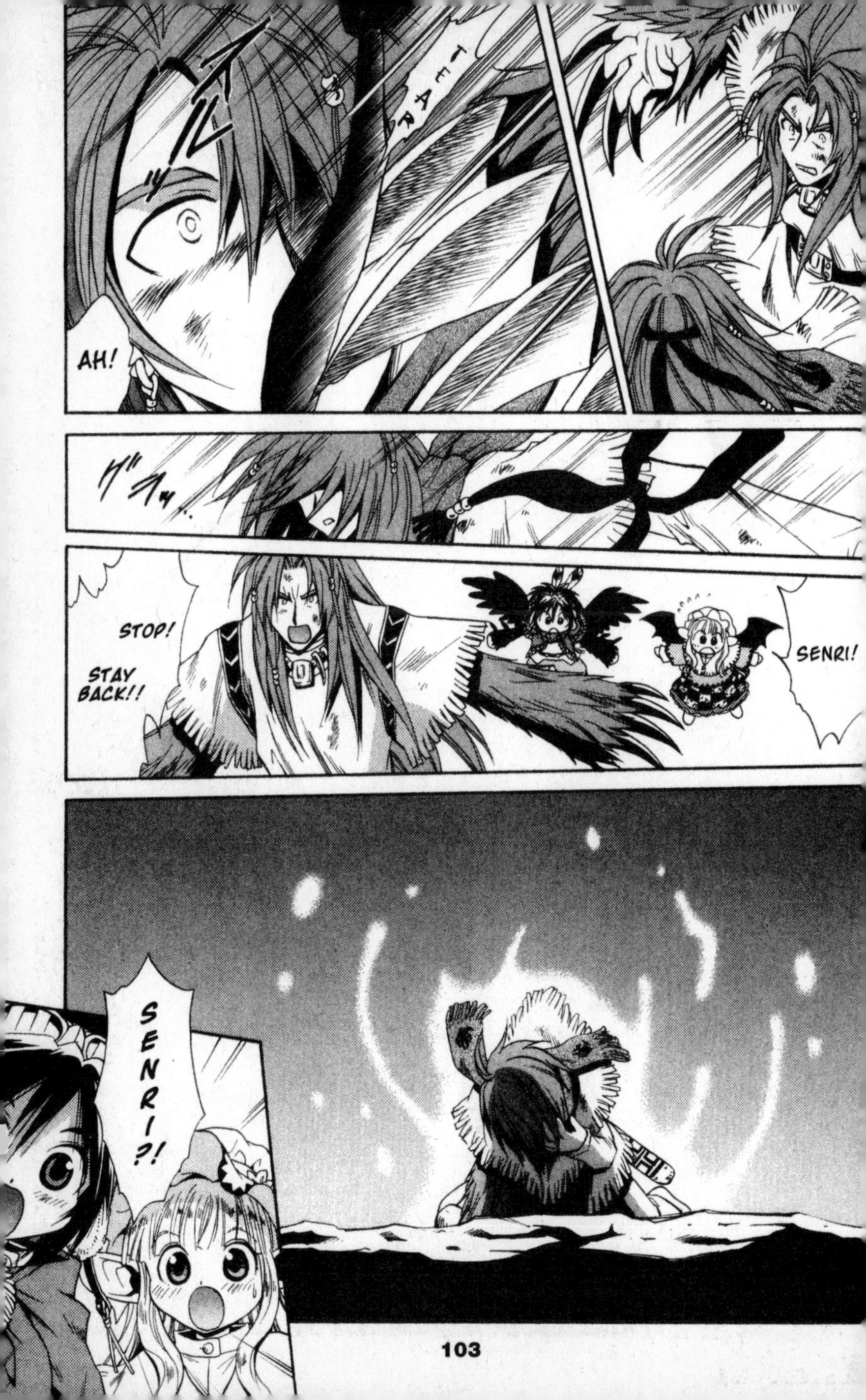
TEAR
AH!
SENRI!
STOP!
STAY BACK!!
SENRI?!

What color?

SOMETIMES, WHEN IT'S PUBLISHED IN GAO MAGAZINE, I CAN HAVE IT PRINTED IN COLORS OTHER THAN BLACK.
Like green or blue.
*The deadline for offset-print books is early.
WE'RE RUNNING SENRI'S STORY ARC.
Gao! (Editor)
THIS IS THE SECOND CHAPTER IN THE ARC. SHOULD WE MAKE IT THE SAME COLOR AS THE FIRST ONE?
SURE!
Gao!
ALL RIGHT, THEN--BEAR COLOR IT IS.
BEAR?!
Gao!
IT'S SENRI, SO THAT WAS THE COLOR FOR THE FIRST CHAPTER.
Brown.
OH... SO YOU DID.

Senri's hair is grey, but most people think of bears as brown.

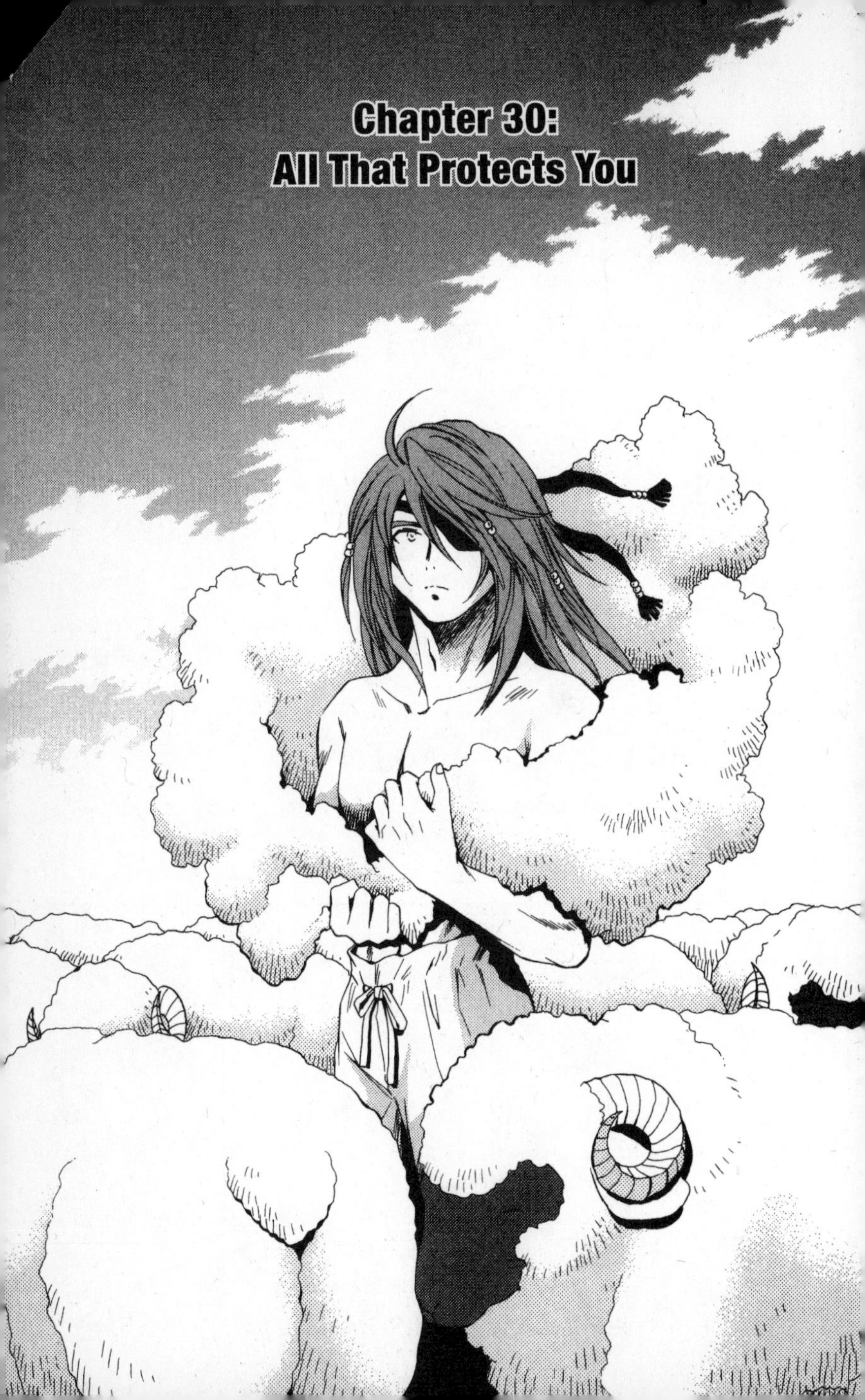
Chapter 30:
All That Protects You

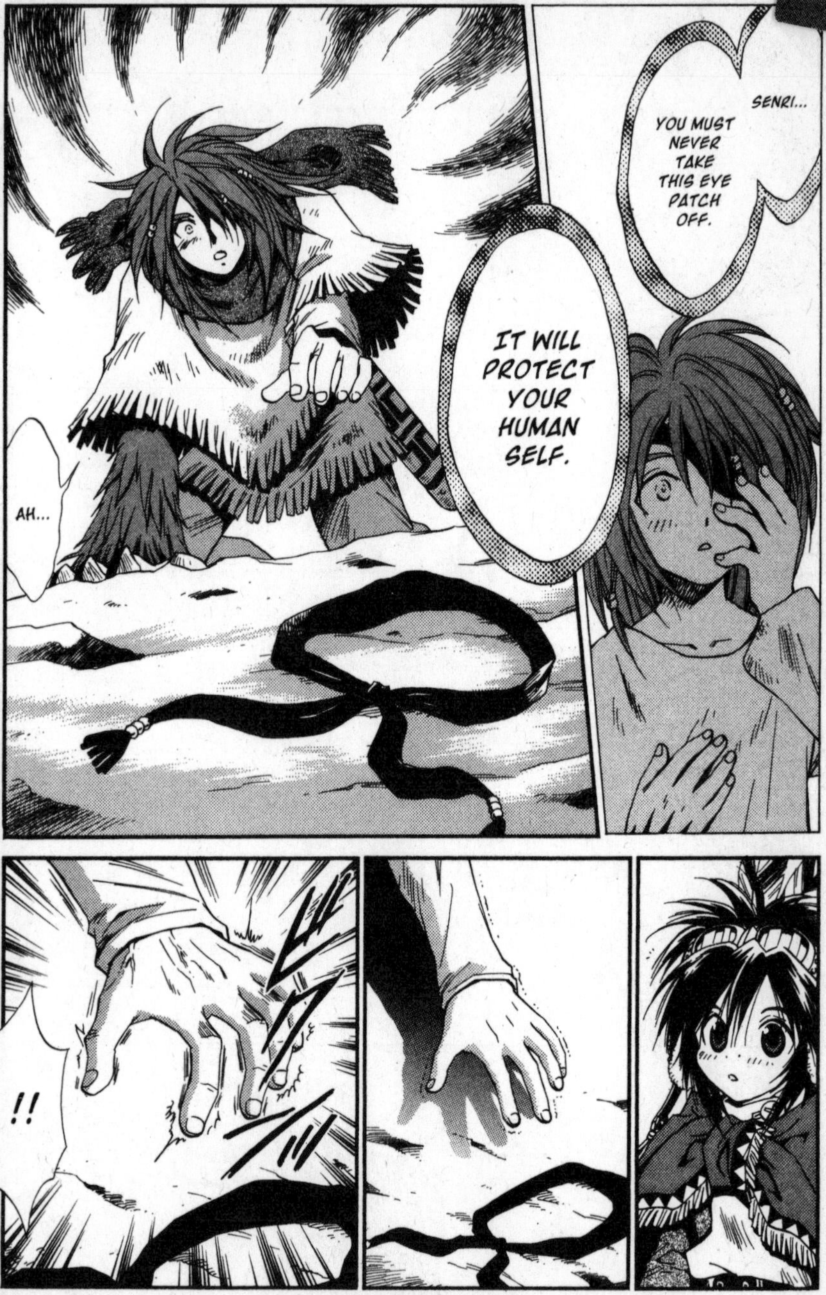
SENRI...
YOU MUST NEVER TAKE THIS EYE PATCH OFF.
IT WILL PROTECT YOUR HUMAN SELF.
AH...
!!

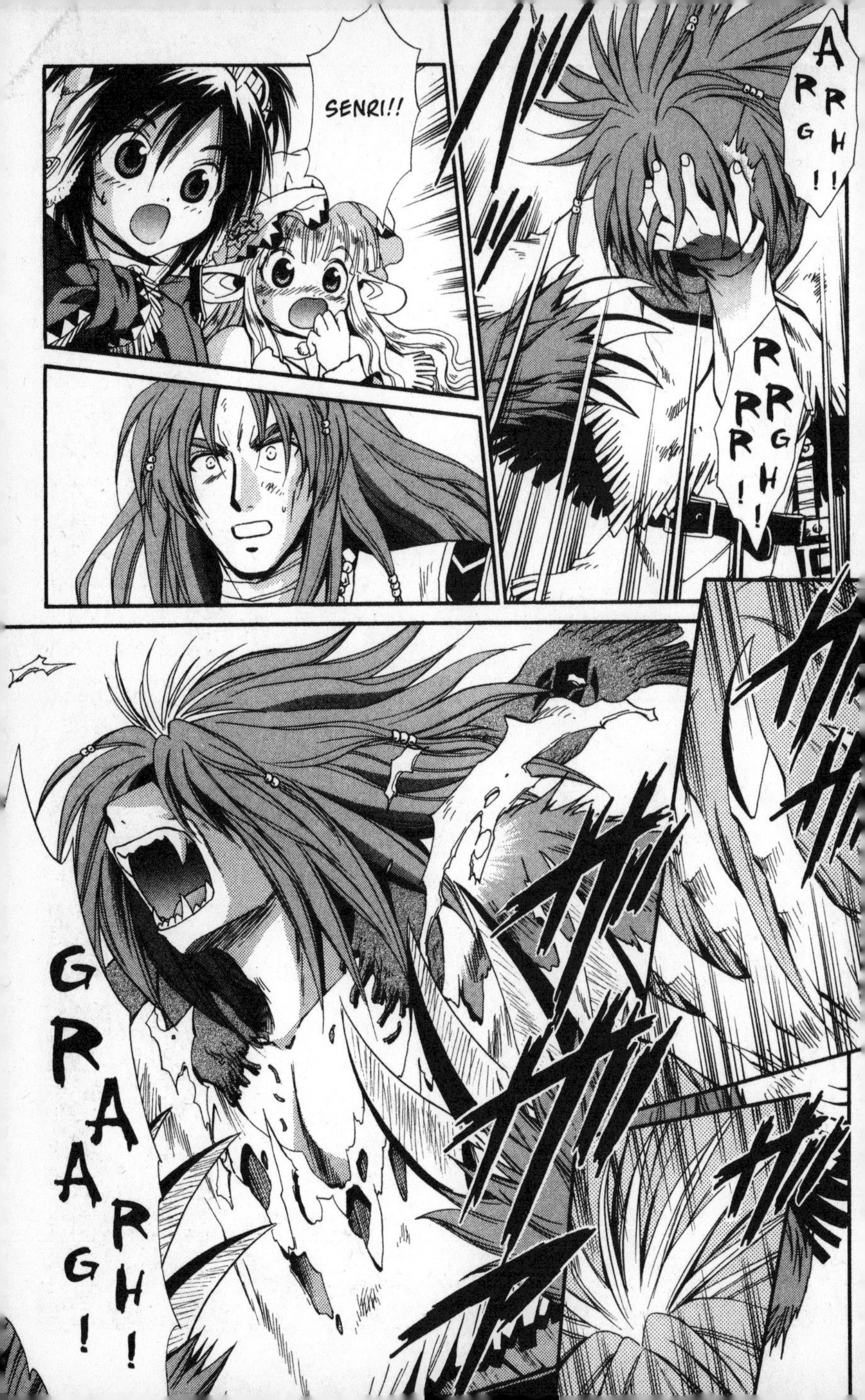
ARRGH!!
RRRRGH!!
SENRI!!
GRAARGH!!

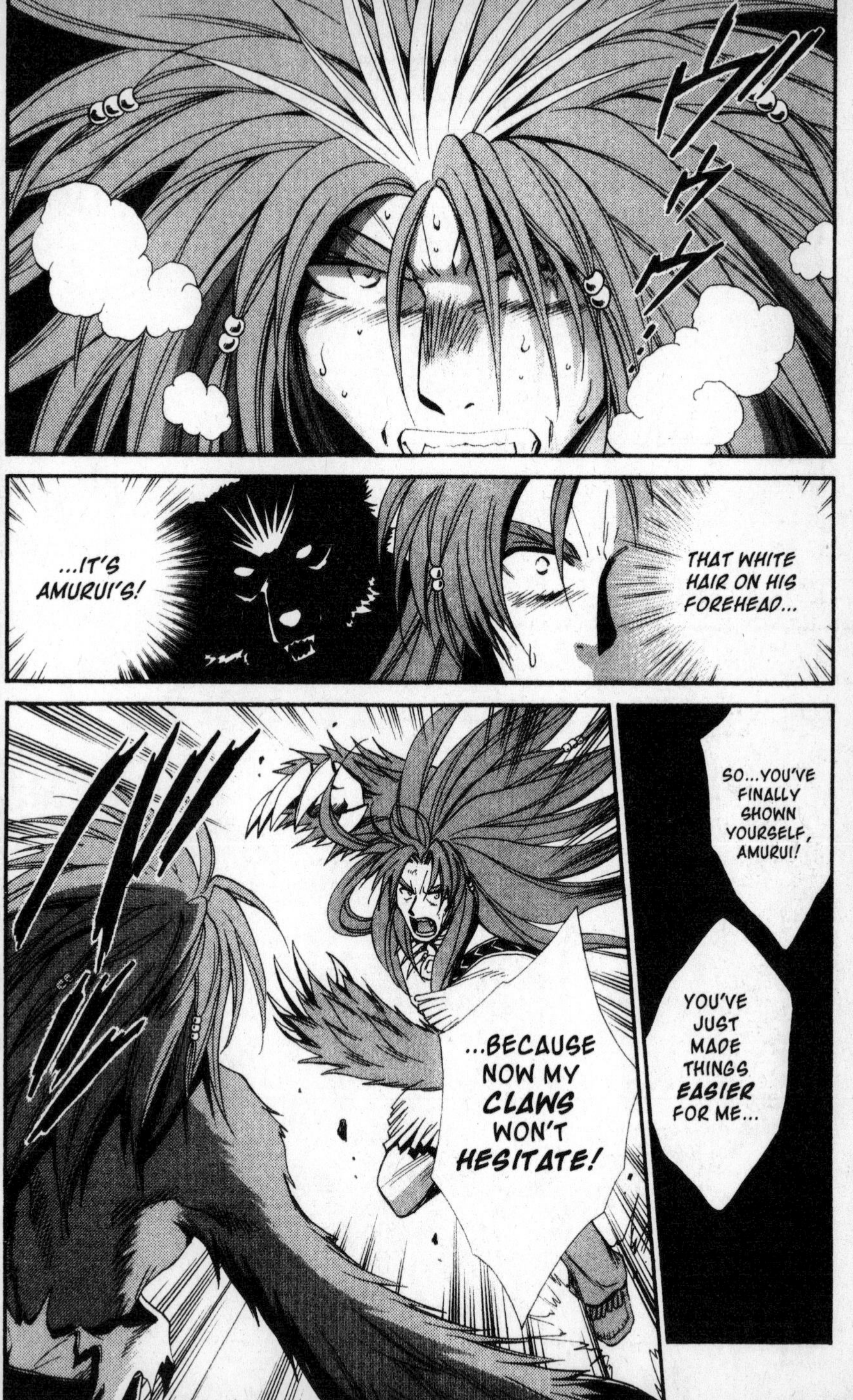
THAT WHITE HAIR ON HIS FOREHEAD...
...IT'S AMURUI'S!
SO...YOU'VE FINALLY SHOWN YOURSELF, AMURUI!
YOU'VE JUST MADE THINGS EASIER FOR ME...
...BECAUSE NOW MY CLAWS WON'T HESITATE!

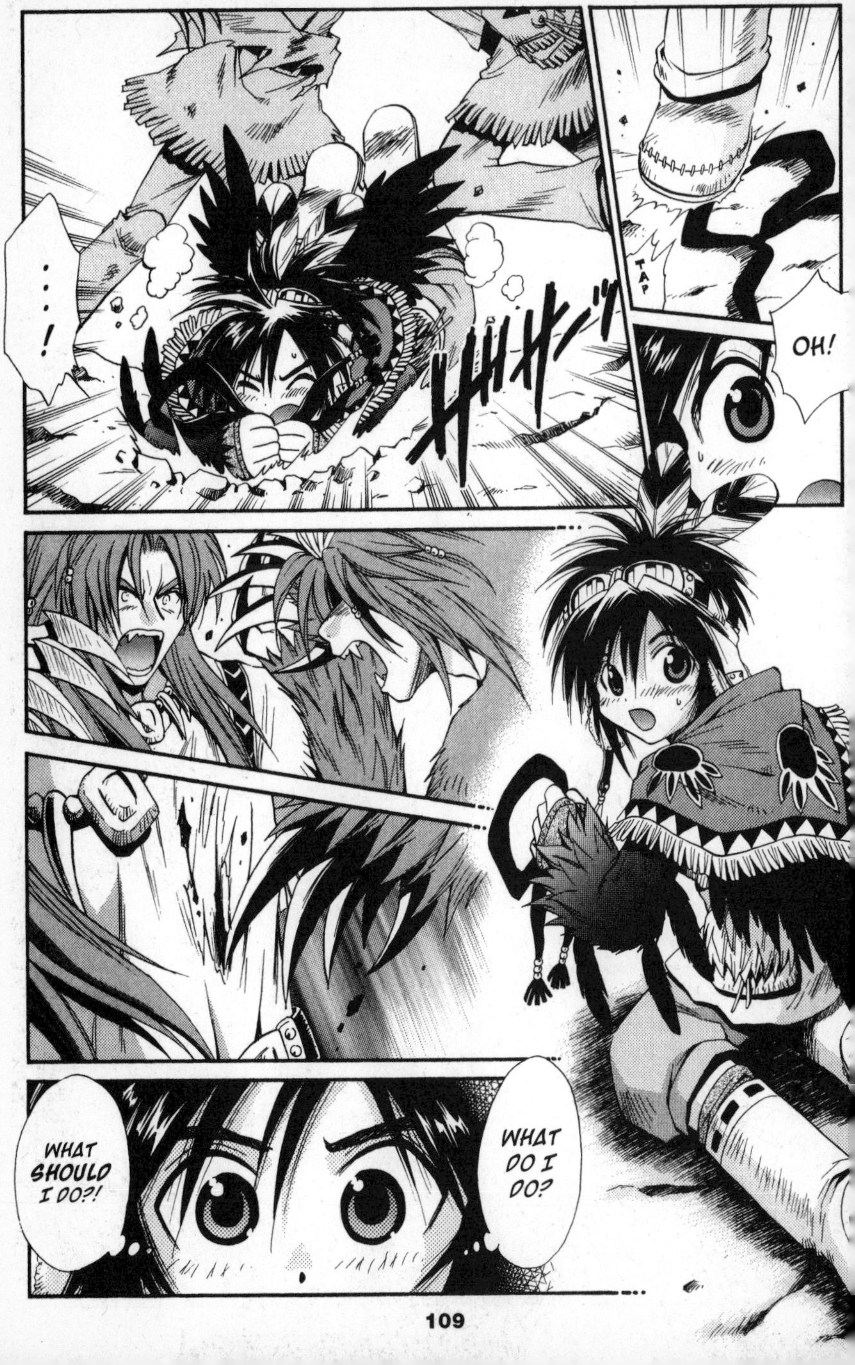
TAP
OH!
...!
WHAT DO I DO?
WHAT SHOULD I DO?!

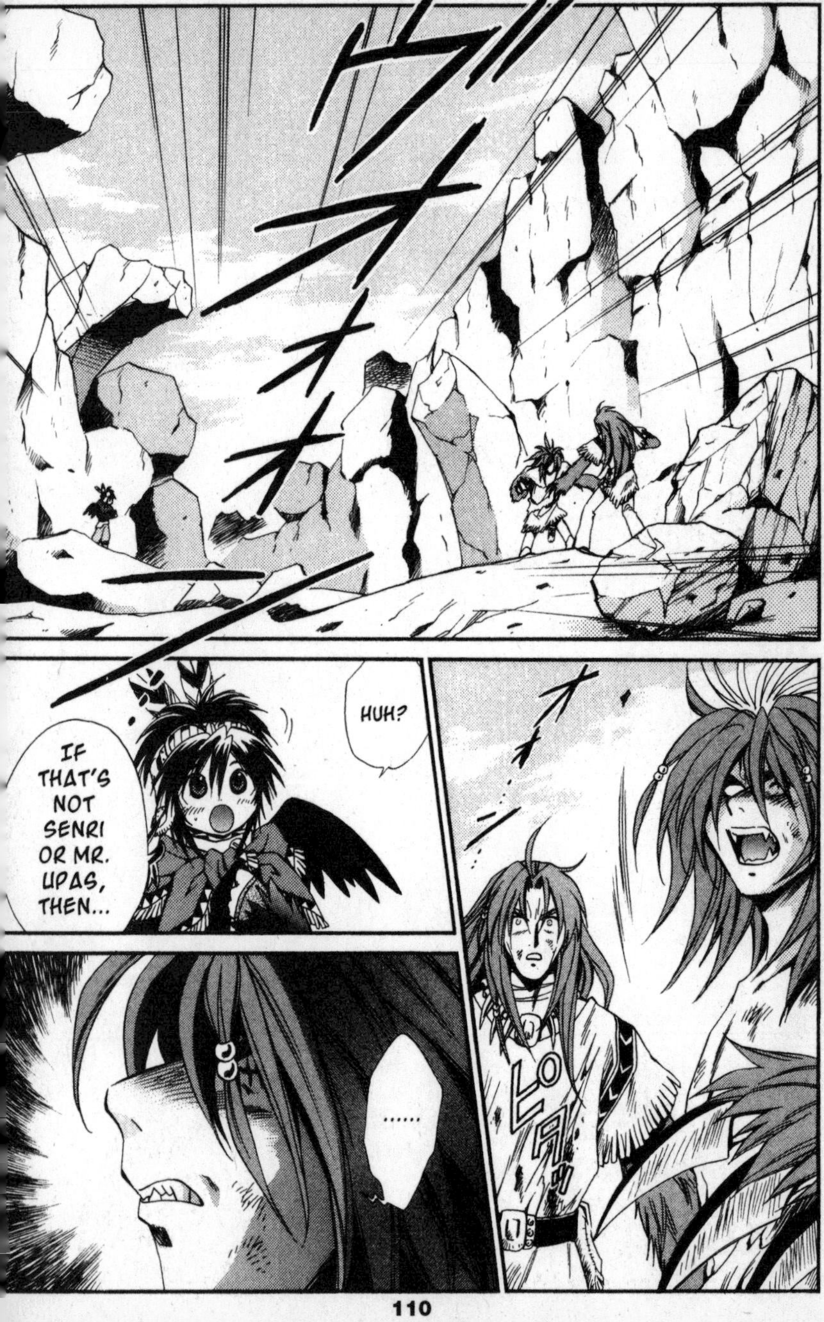
HUH?
IF THAT'S NOT SENRI OR MR. UPAS, THEN...
......

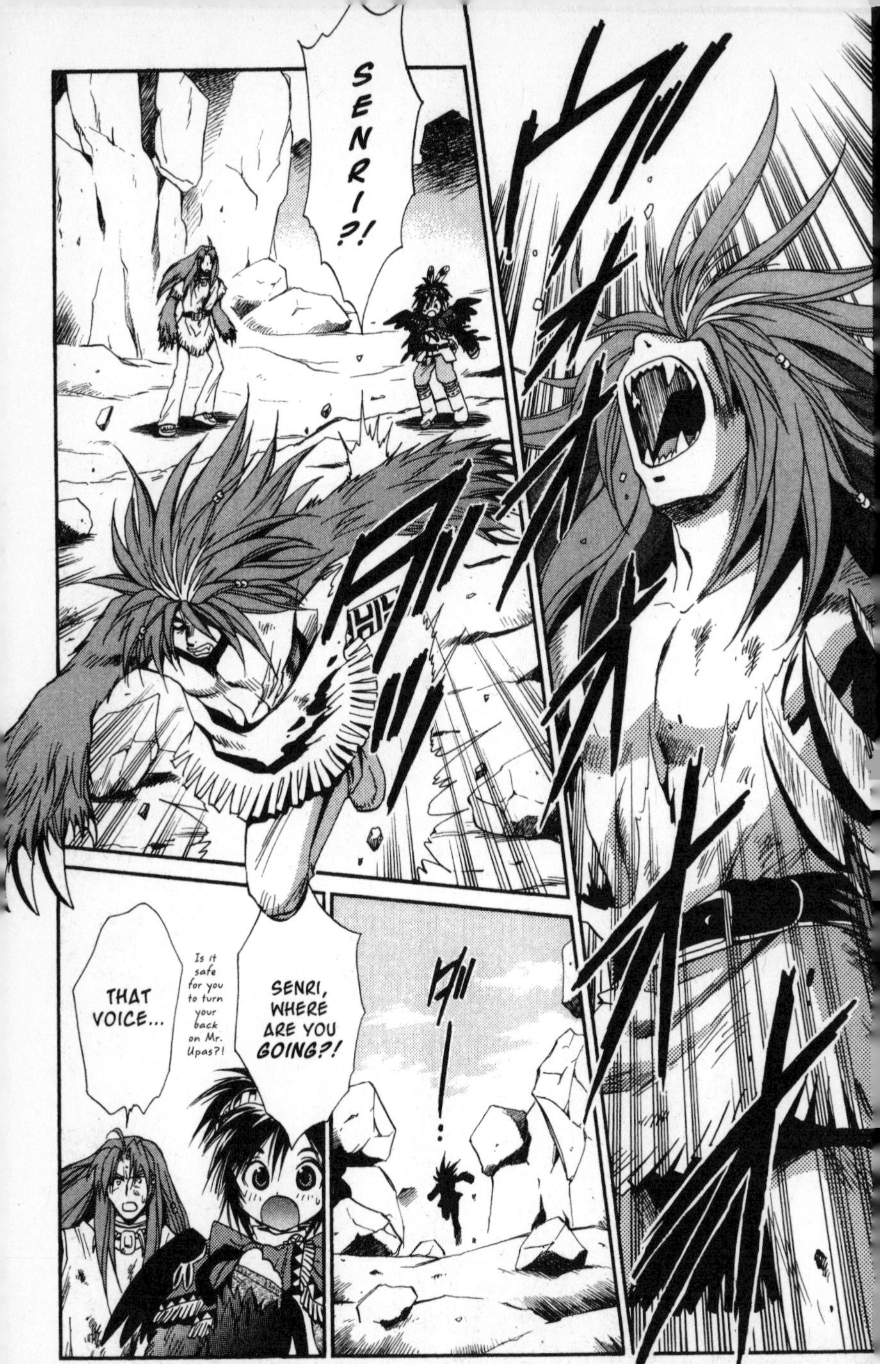
SENRI?!
SENRI, WHERE ARE YOU GOING?!
Is it safe for you to turn your back on Mr. Upas?!
THAT VOICE...

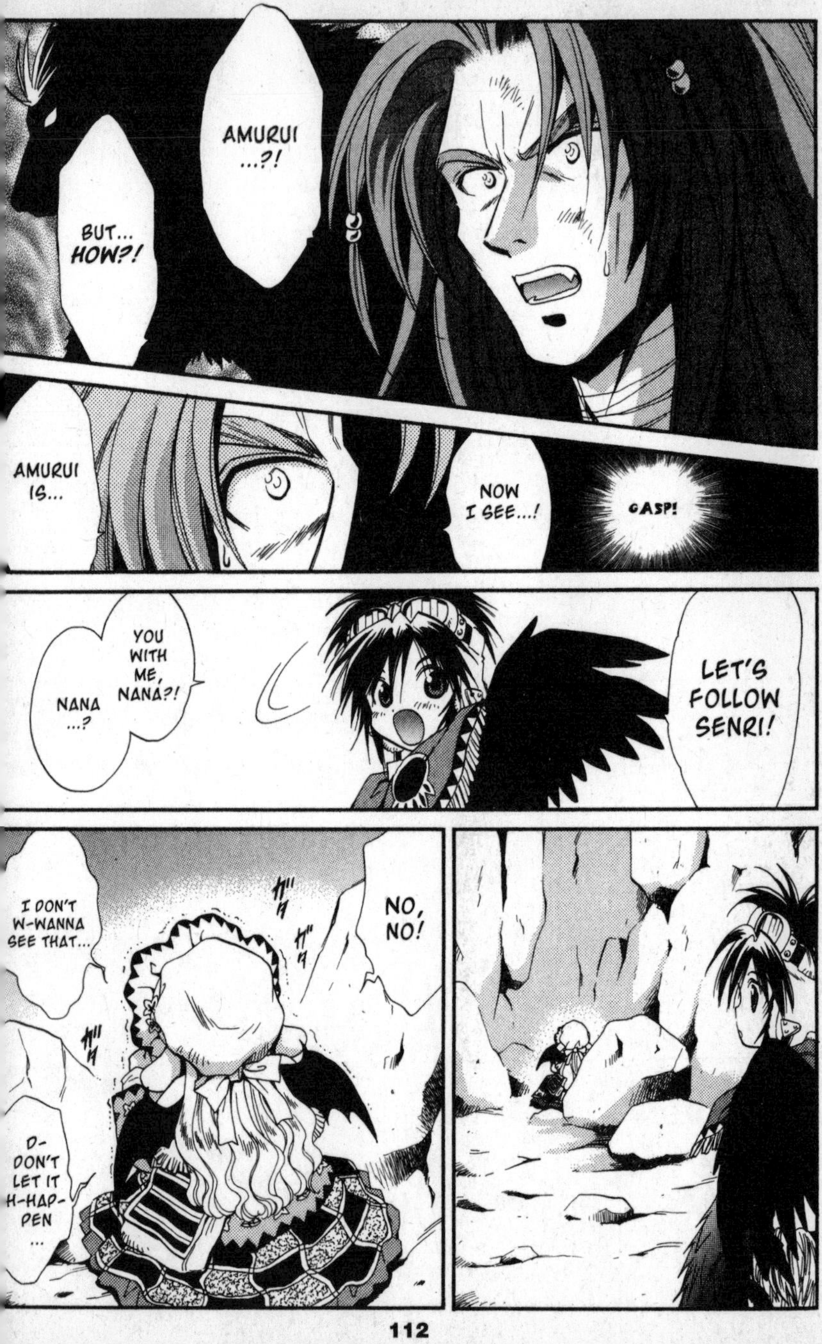
AMURUI ...?!
BUT... HOW?!
GASP!
NOW I SEE...!
AMURUI IS...
LET'S FOLLOW SENRI!
YOU WITH ME, NANA?!
NANA ...?
NO, NO!
I DON'T W-WANNA SEE THAT...
D-DON'T LET IT H-HAPPEN ...

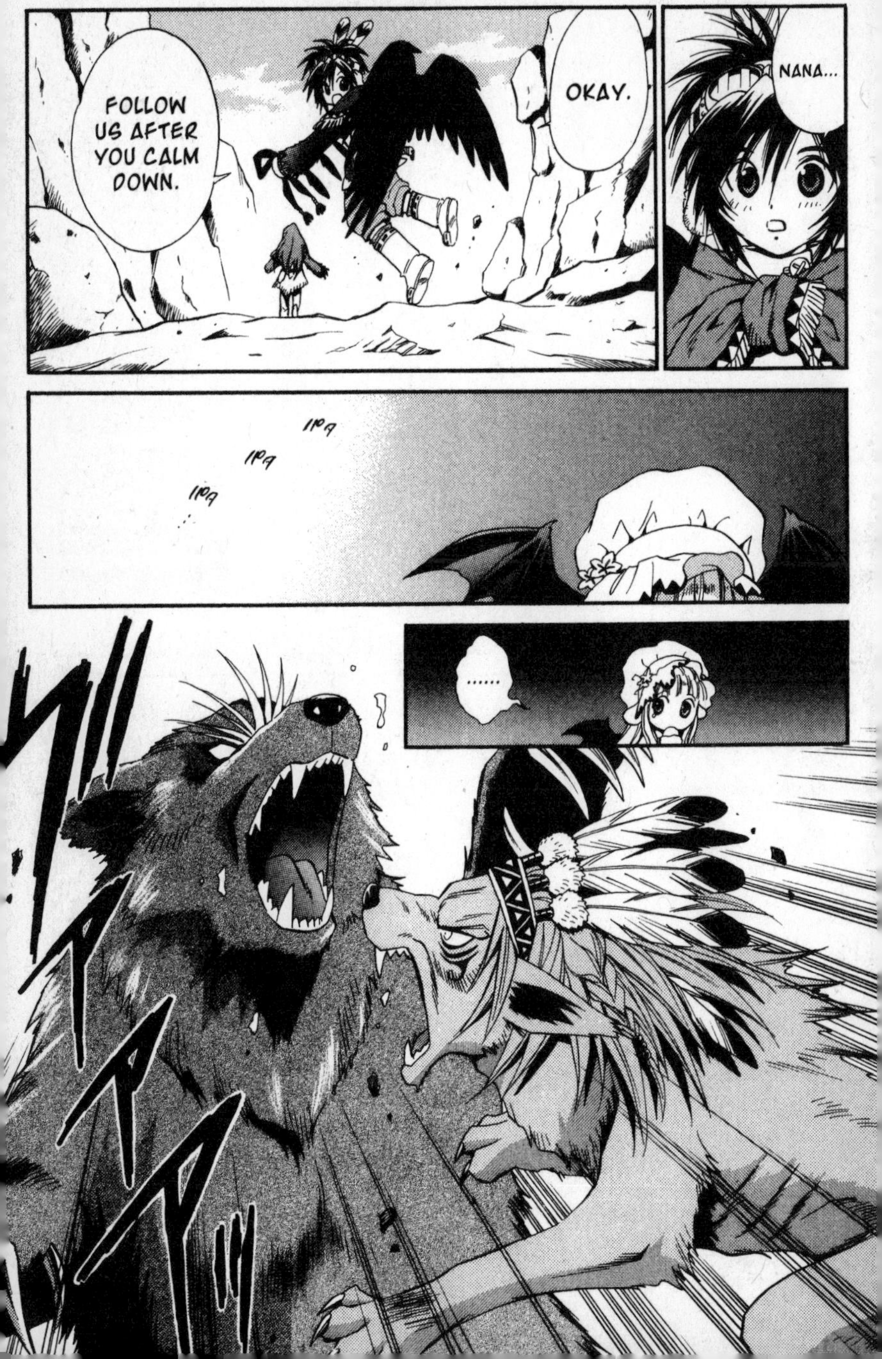
NANA...
OKAY.
FOLLOW US AFTER YOU CALM DOWN.
......

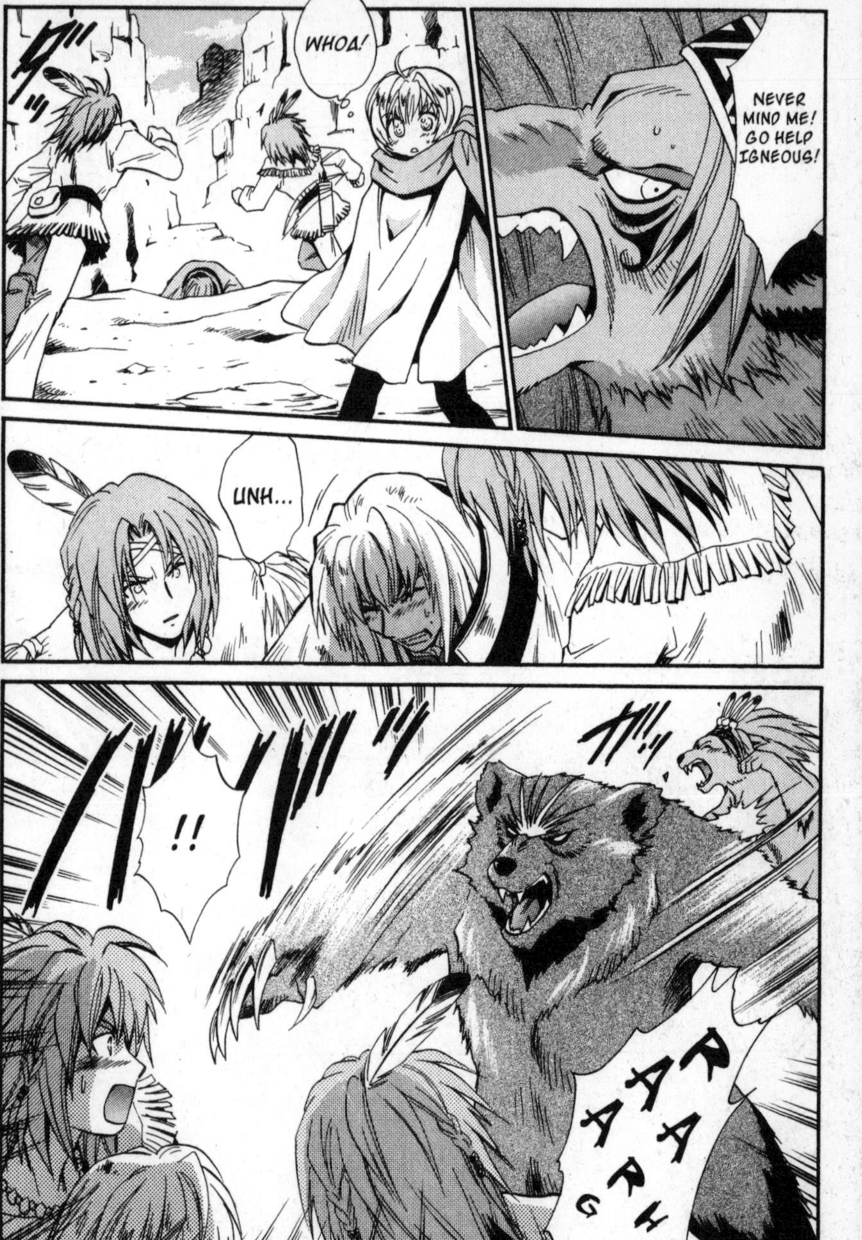
NEVER MIND ME! GO HELP IGNEOUS!
WHOA!
UNH...
!!
RAAARHG!!

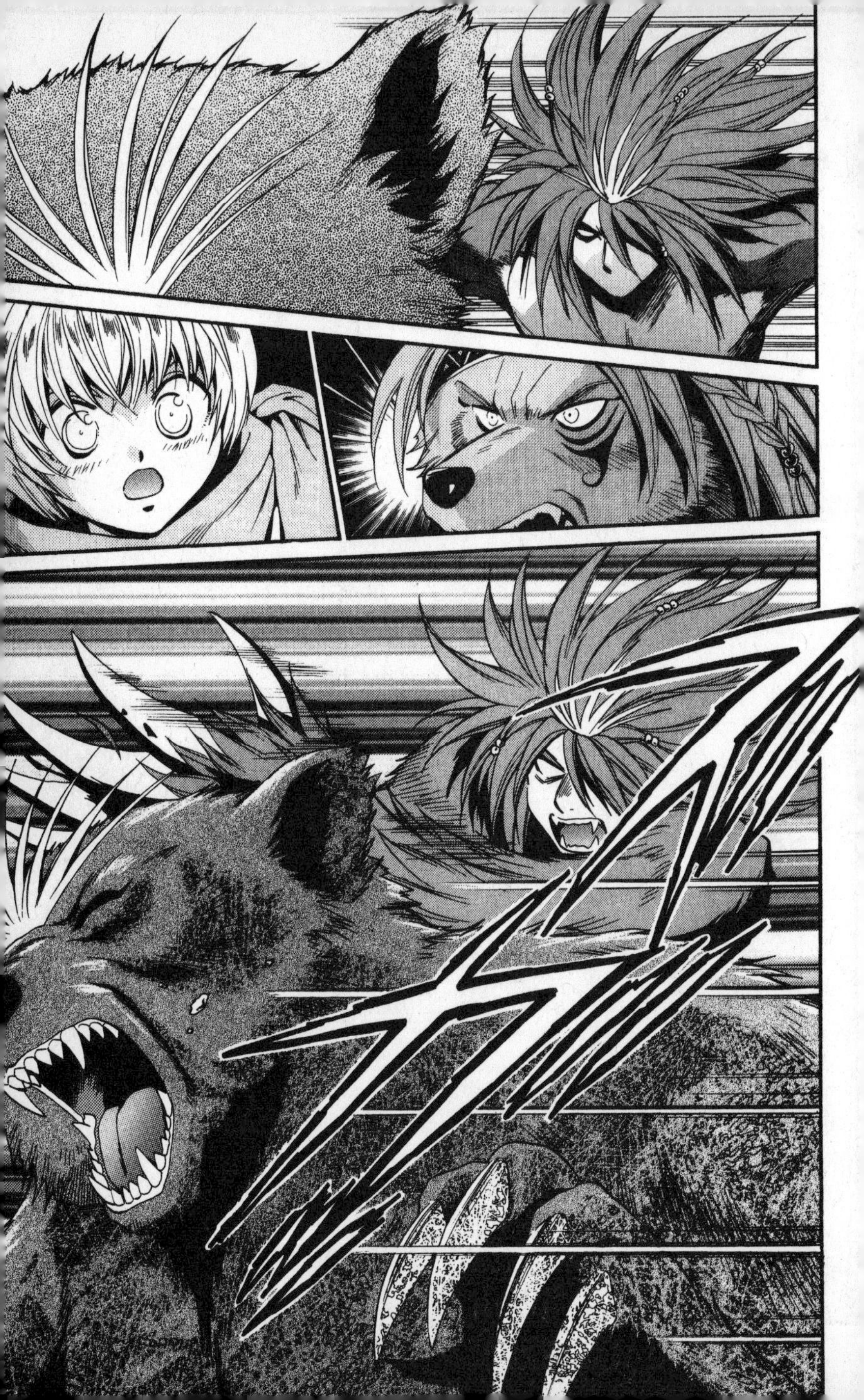

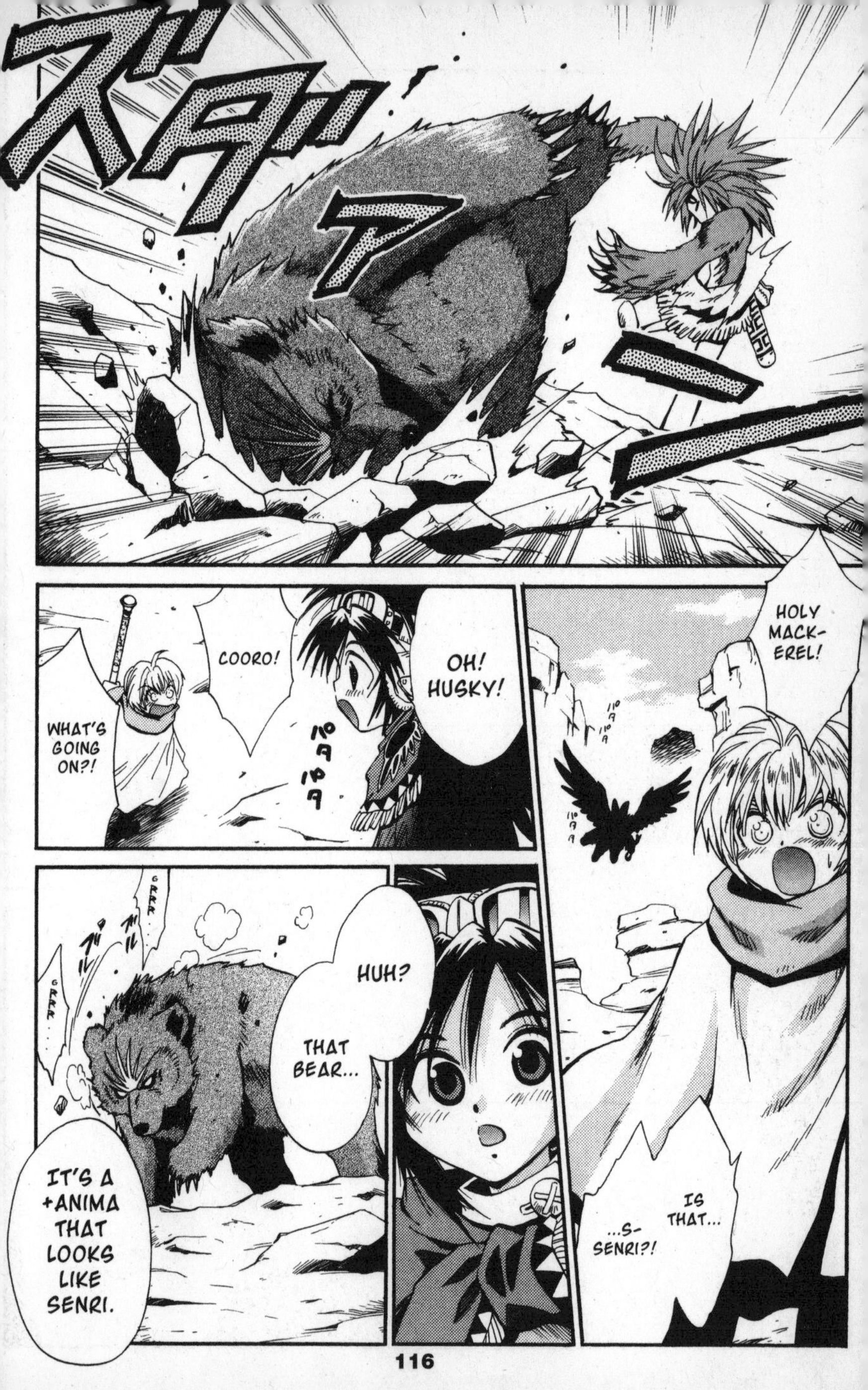
ズダァー
HOLY MACK-EREL!
IS THAT...
...S-SENRI?!
OH! HUSKY!
パタパタ
COORO!
WHAT'S GOING ON?!
HUH?
THAT BEAR...
GRRR
GRRR
IT'S A +ANIMA THAT LOOKS LIKE SENRI.

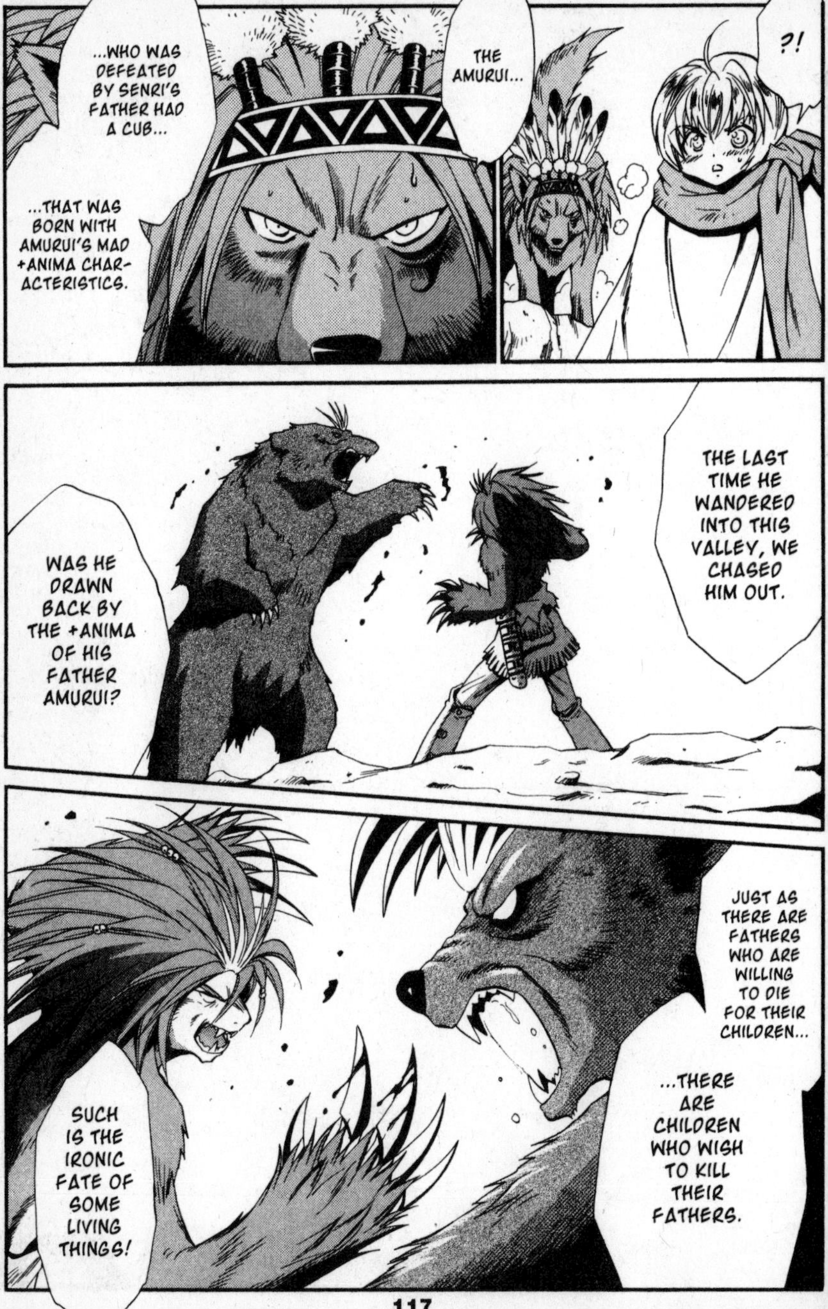
?!
THE AMURUI...
...WHO WAS DEFEATED BY SENRI'S FATHER HAD A CUB...
...THAT WAS BORN WITH AMURUI'S MAD +ANIMA CHAR-ACTERISTICS.
THE LAST TIME HE WANDERED INTO THIS VALLEY, WE CHASED HIM OUT.
WAS HE DRAWN BACK BY THE +ANIMA OF HIS FATHER AMURUI?
JUST AS THERE ARE FATHERS WHO ARE WILLING TO DIE FOR THEIR CHILDREN...
...THERE ARE CHILDREN WHO WISH TO KILL THEIR FATHERS.
SUCH IS THE IRONIC FATE OF SOME LIVING THINGS!

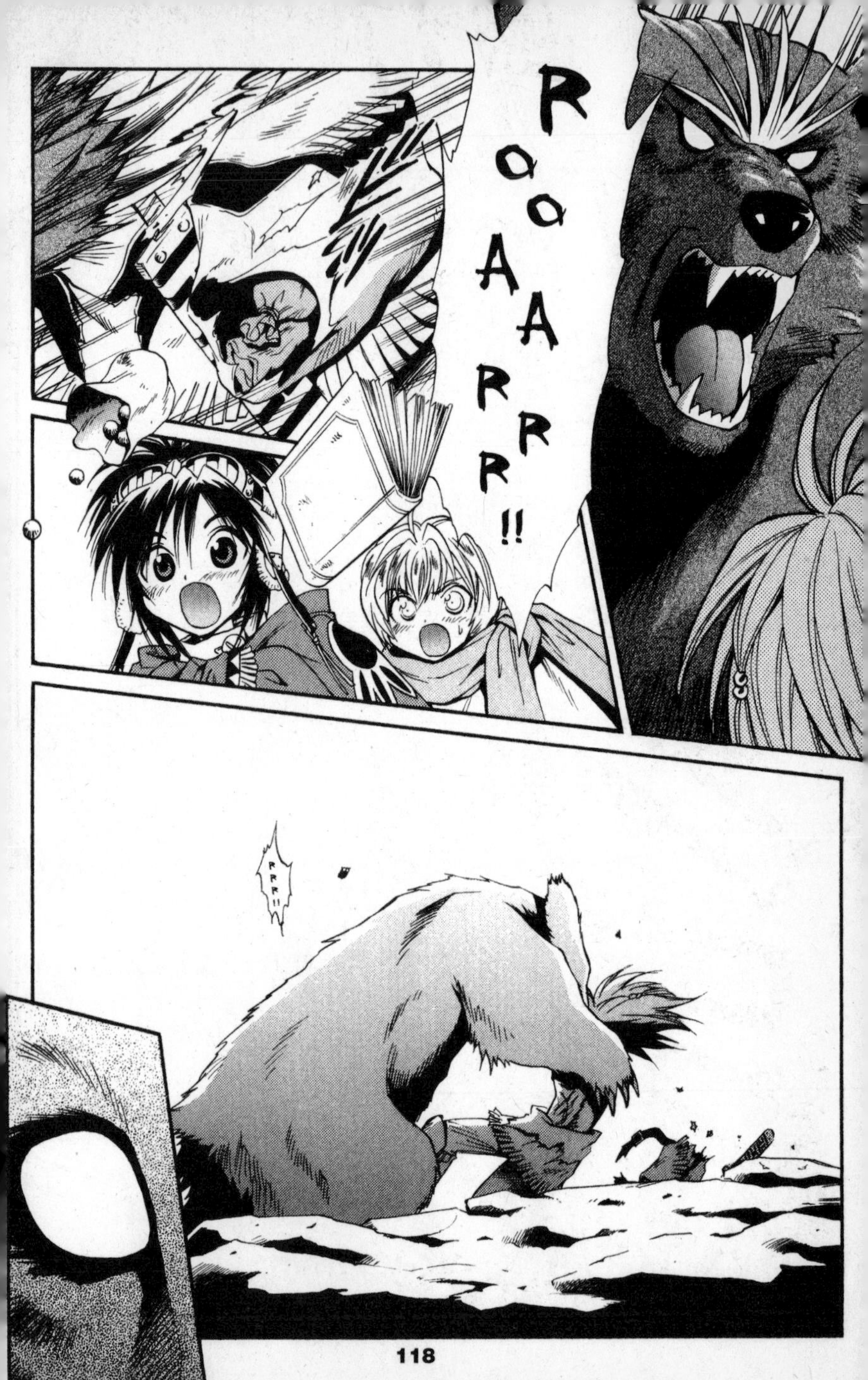
ROOAARRR!!
RRR!!

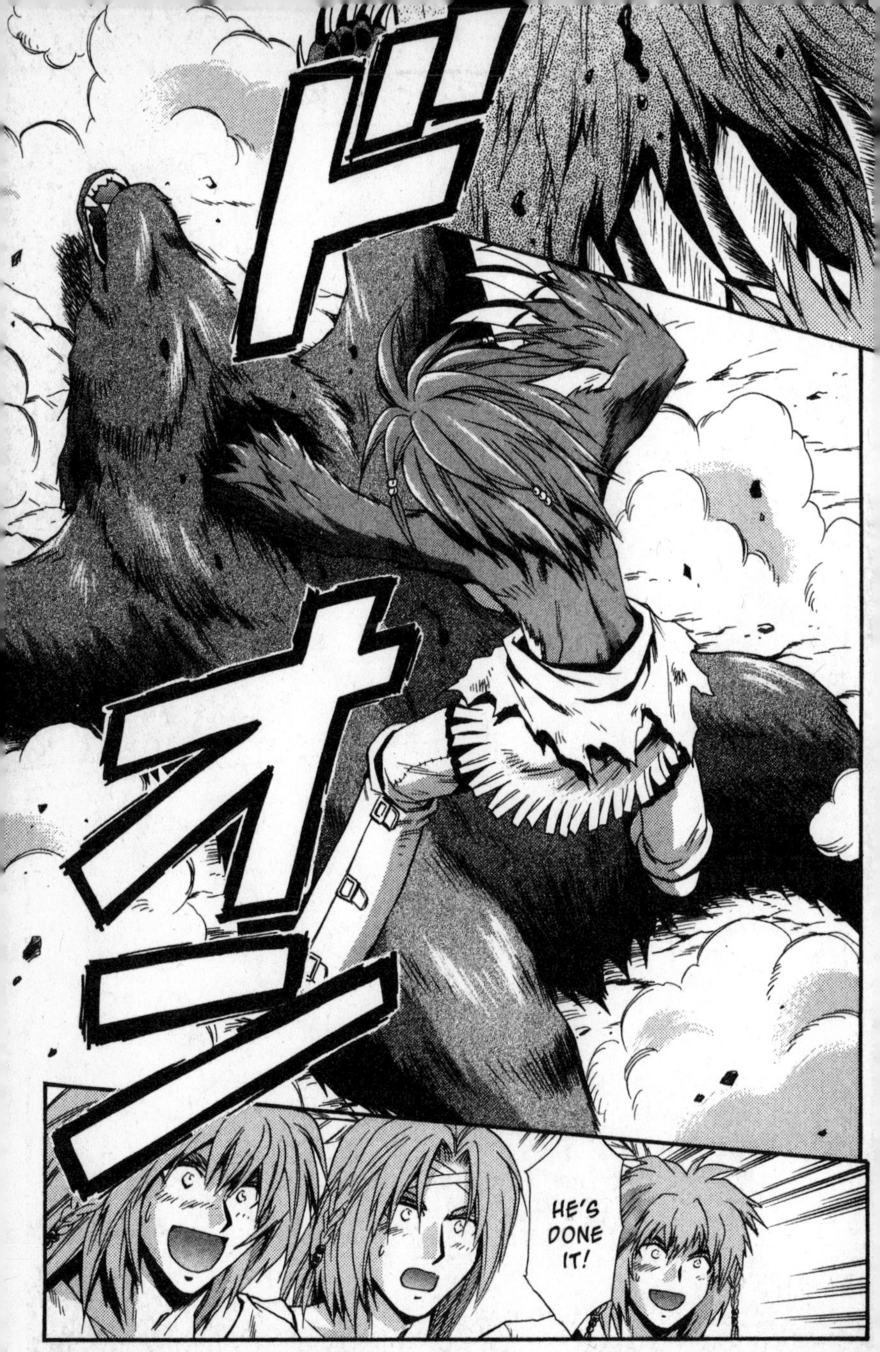
HE'S DONE IT!

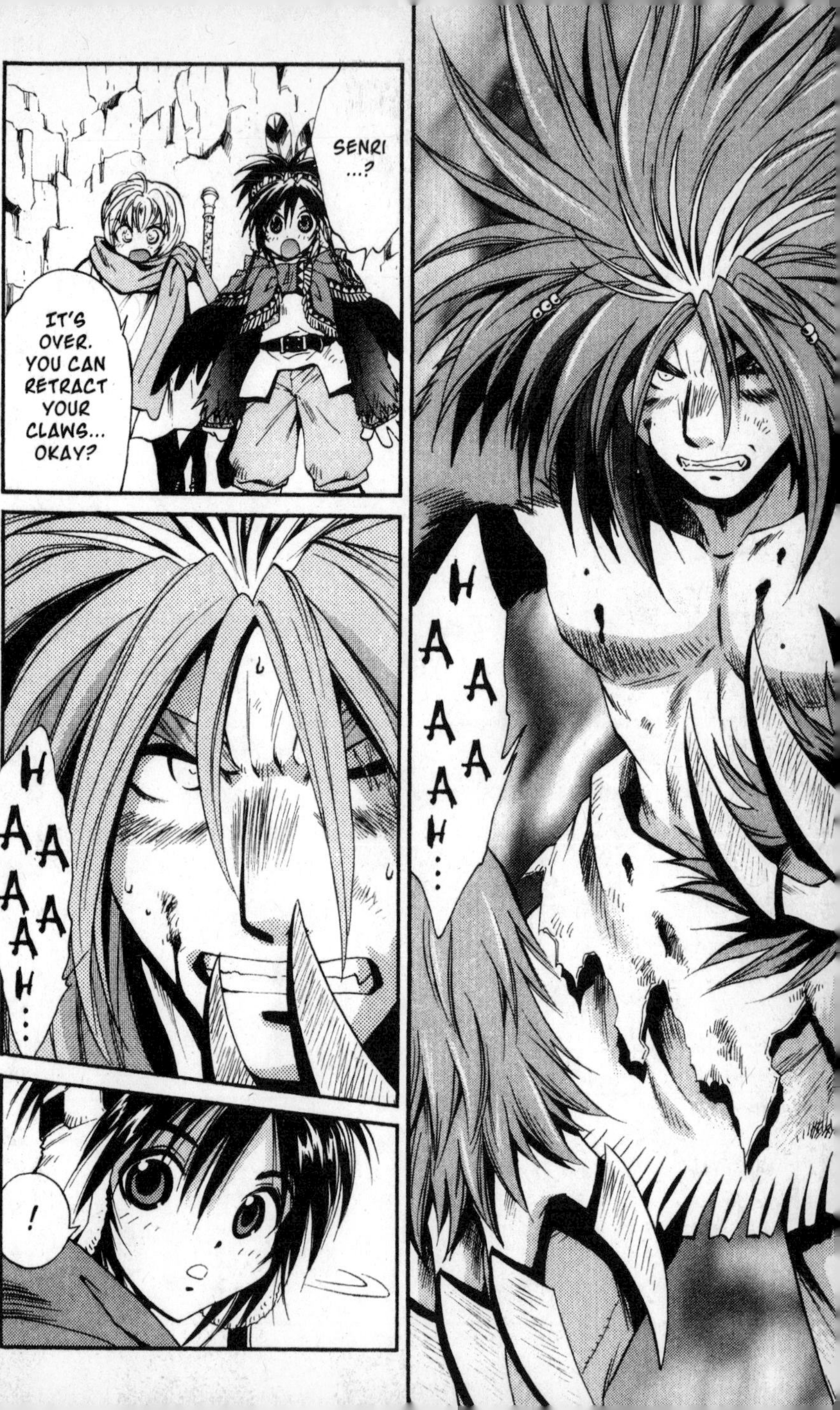
HAAAAAH...
SENRI ...?
IT'S OVER. YOU CAN RETRACT YOUR CLAWS... OKAY?
HAAAAAH...
!

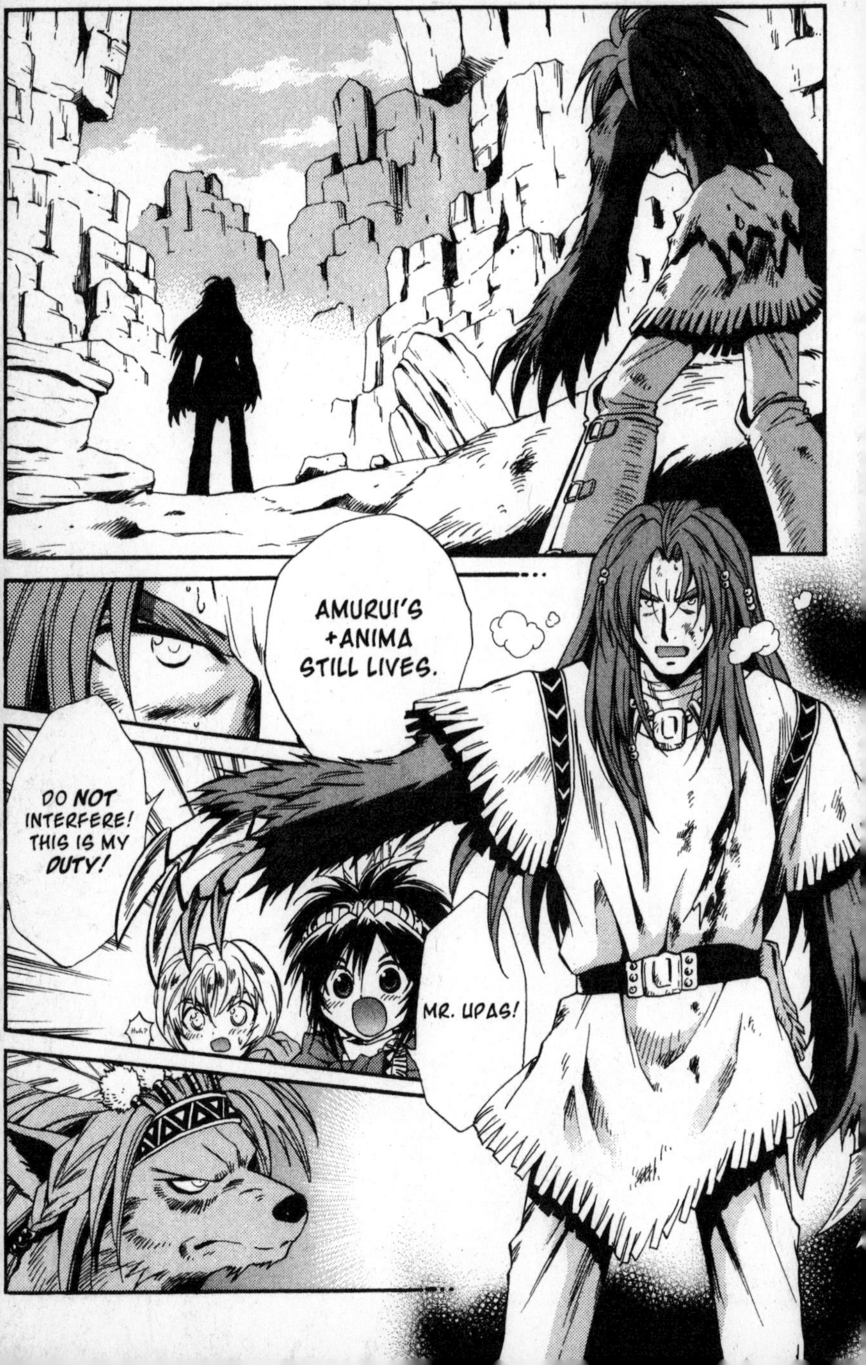
AMURUI'S +ANIMA STILL LIVES.
DO NOT INTERFERE! THIS IS MY DUTY!
MR. UPAS!
Huh?

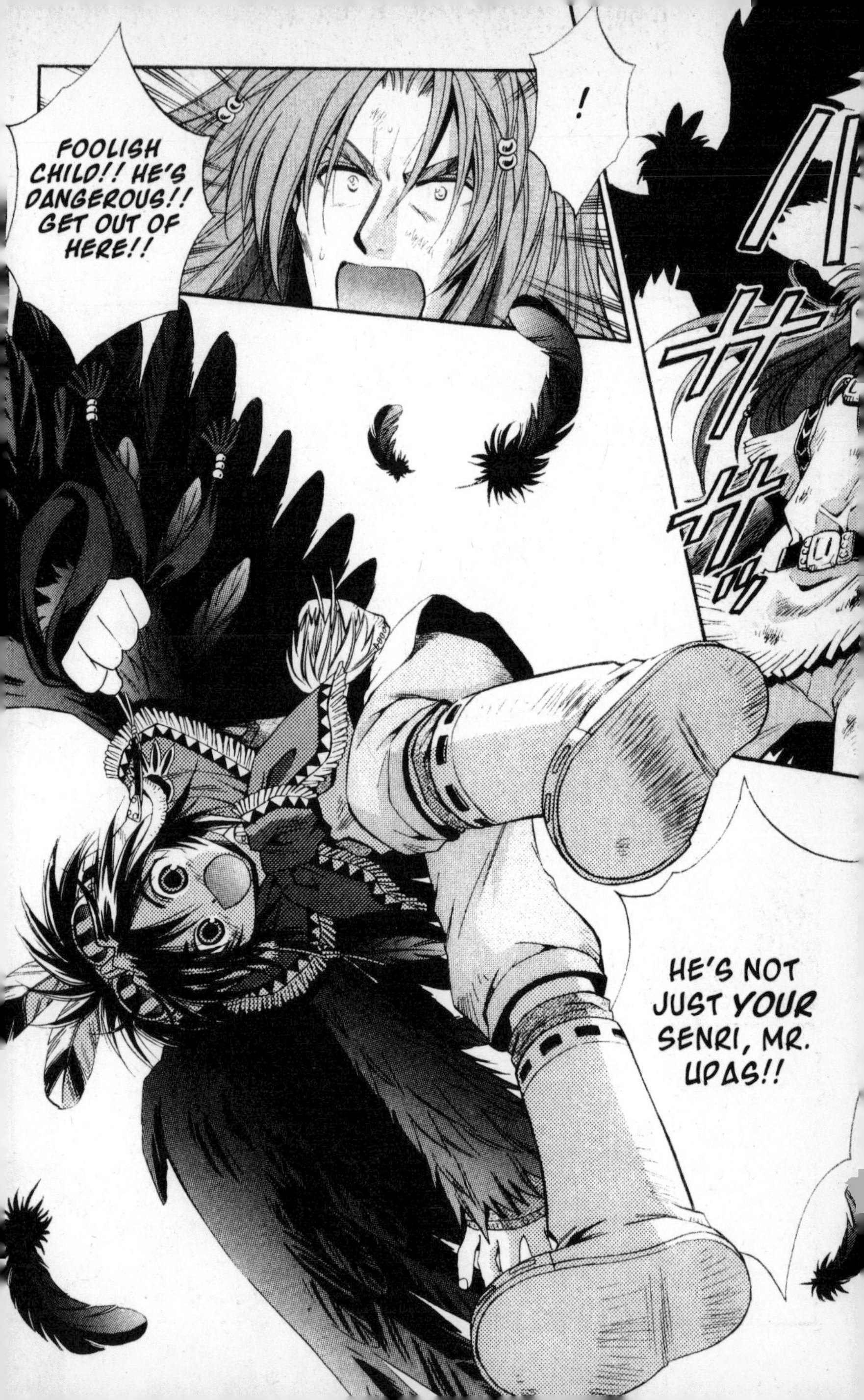
!
ハササッ
FOOLISH CHILD!! HE'S DANGEROUS!! GET OUT OF HERE!!
HE'S NOT JUST YOUR SENRI, MR. UPAS!!

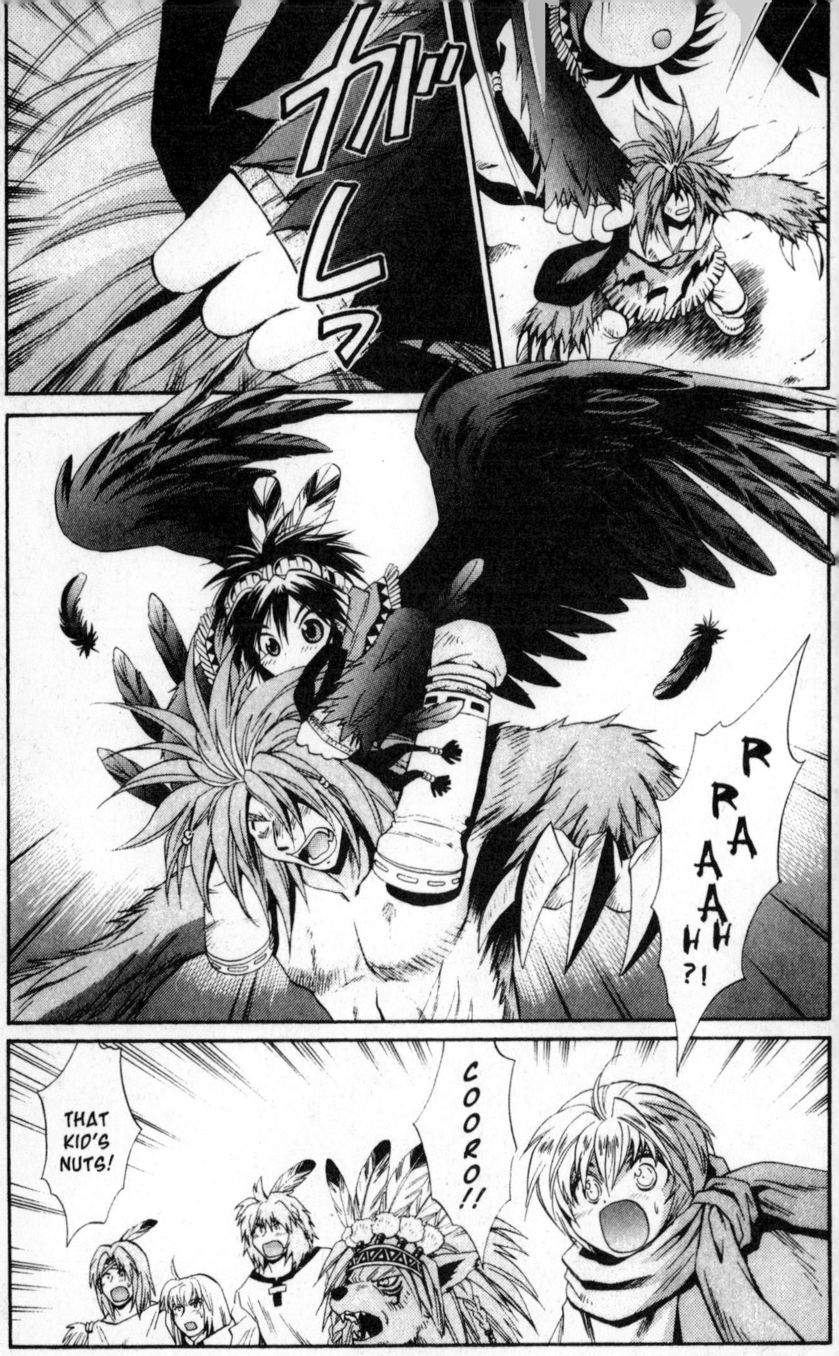
ガしッ
RRAAAAHH?!
COORO!!
THAT KID'S NUTS!

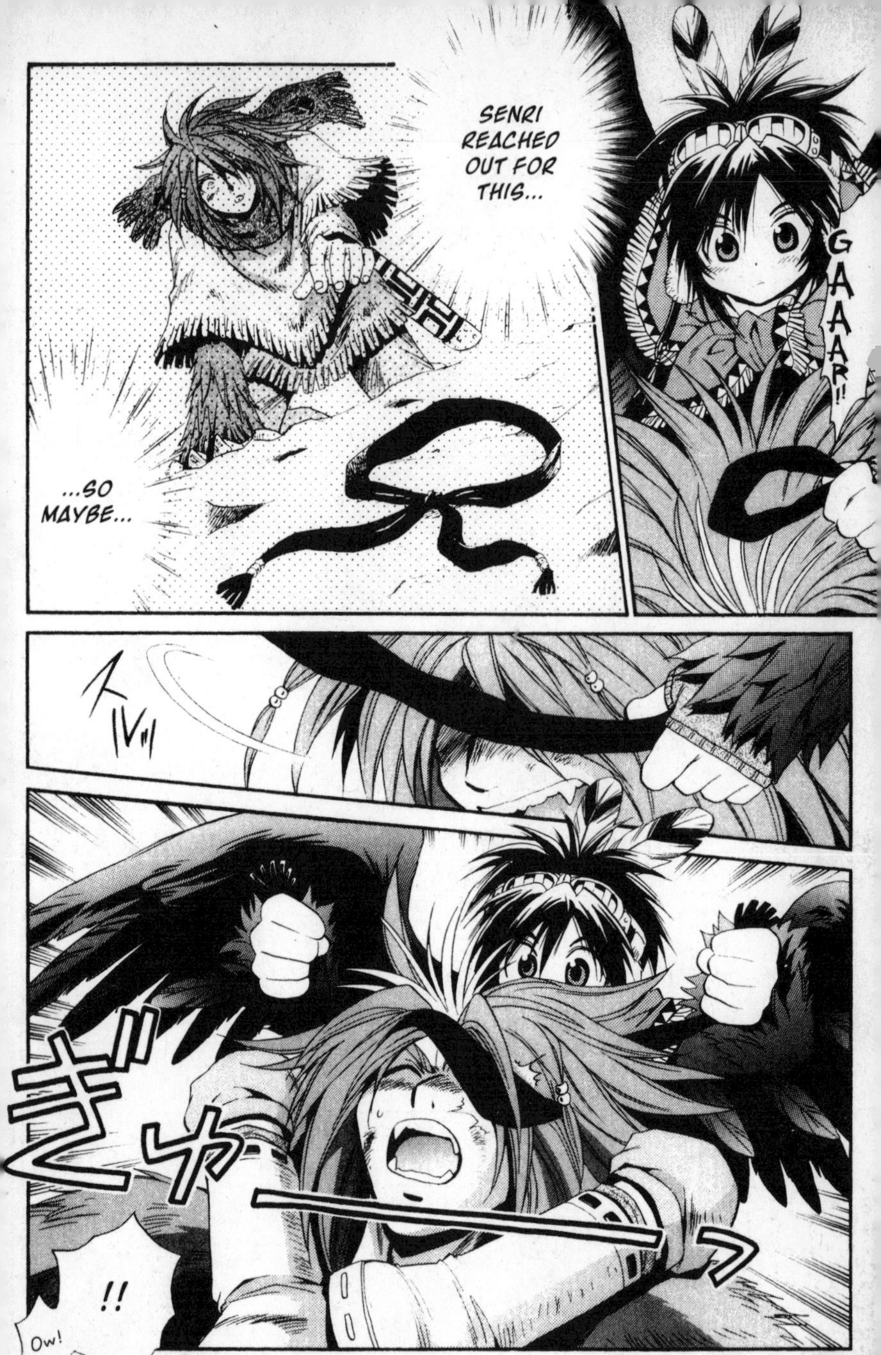
GAAAAR!!
SENRI REACHED OUT FOR THIS...
...SO MAYBE...
!!
Ow!

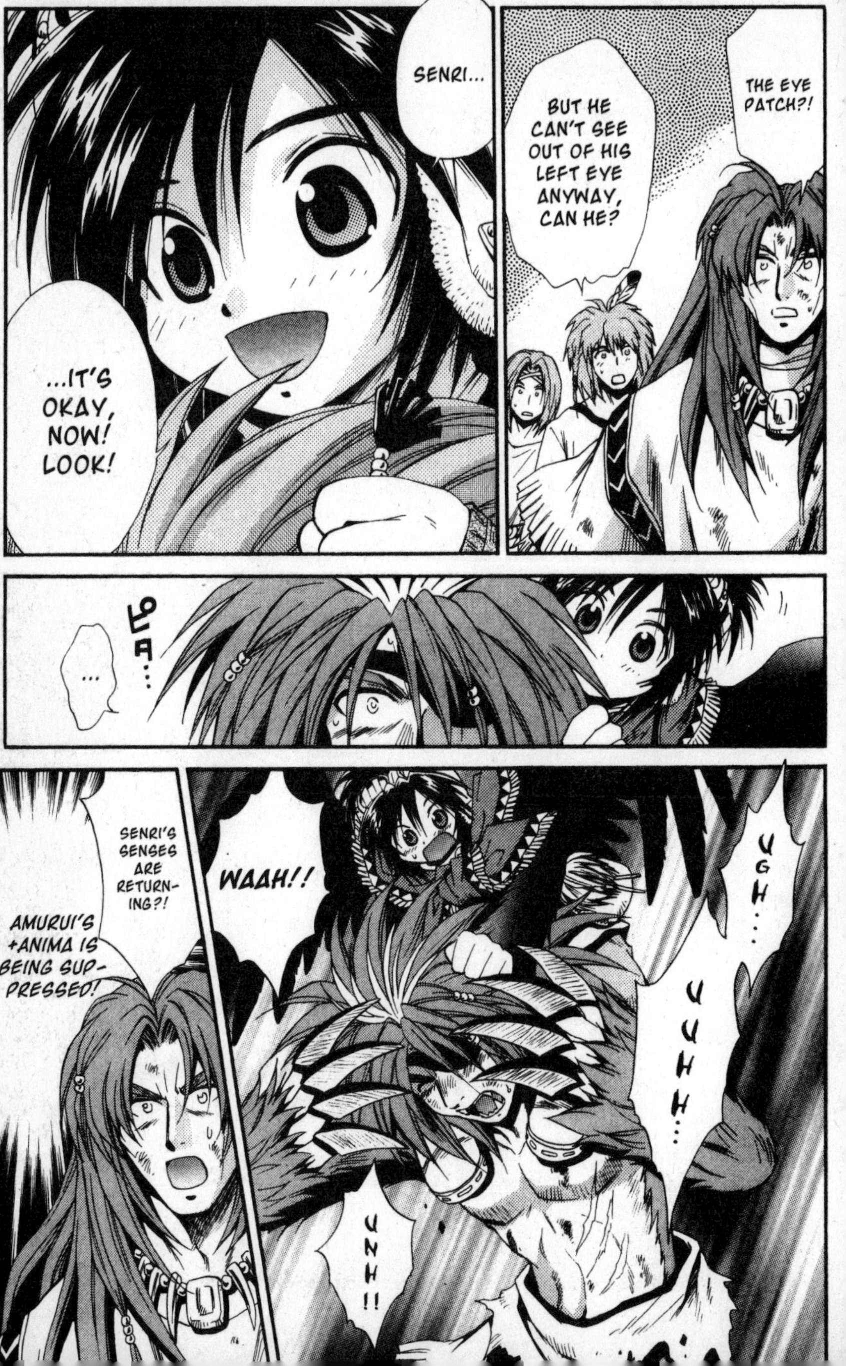
THE EYE PATCH?!
BUT HE CAN'T SEE OUT OF HIS LEFT EYE ANYWAY, CAN HE?
SENRI...
...IT'S OKAY, NOW! LOOK!
ピタ...
...
UGH...
UUHH...
UNH!!
WAAH!!
SENRI'S SENSES ARE RETURNING?!
AMURUI'S +ANIMA IS BEING SUPPRESSED!

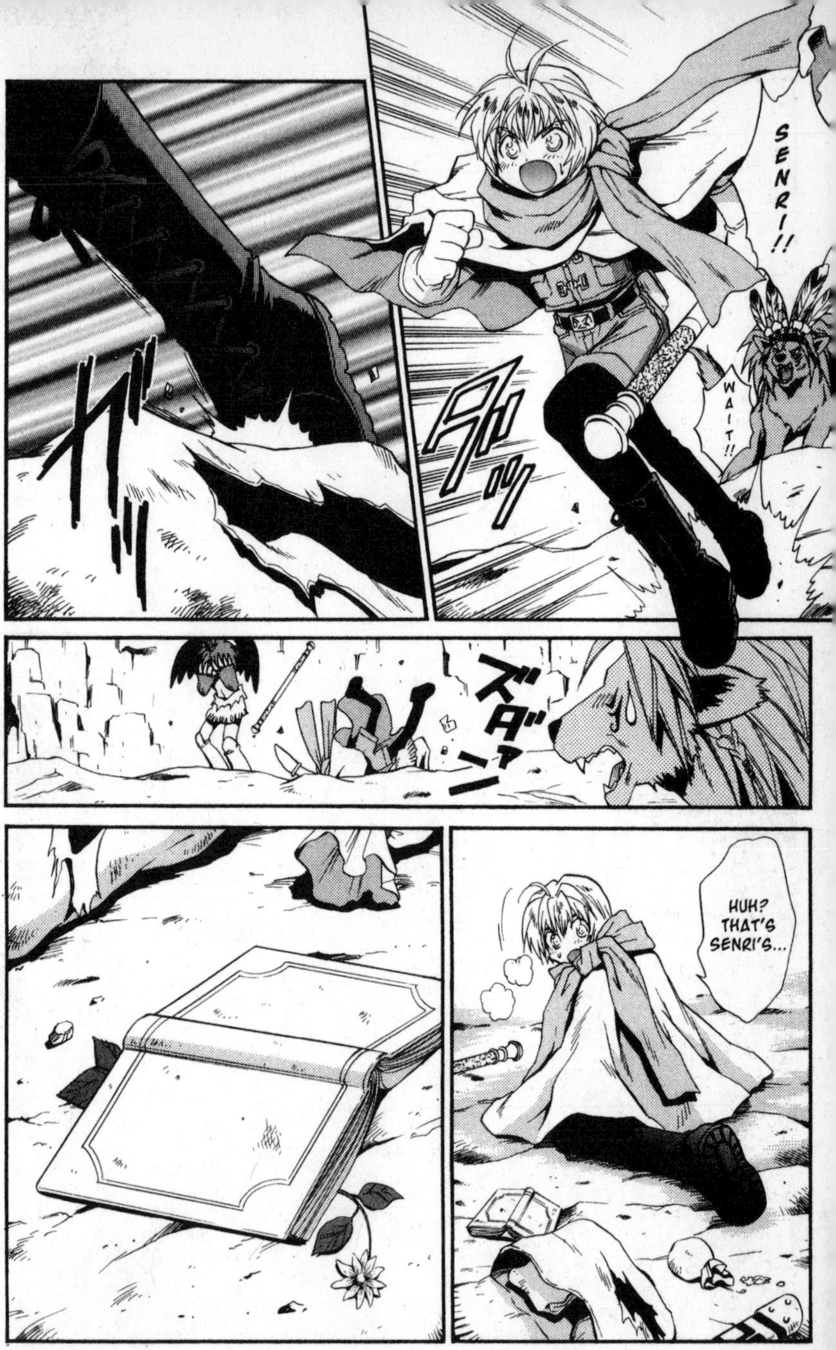
SENRI!!
WAIT!!
ダッ
ズダァーン
HUH? THAT'S SENRI'S...

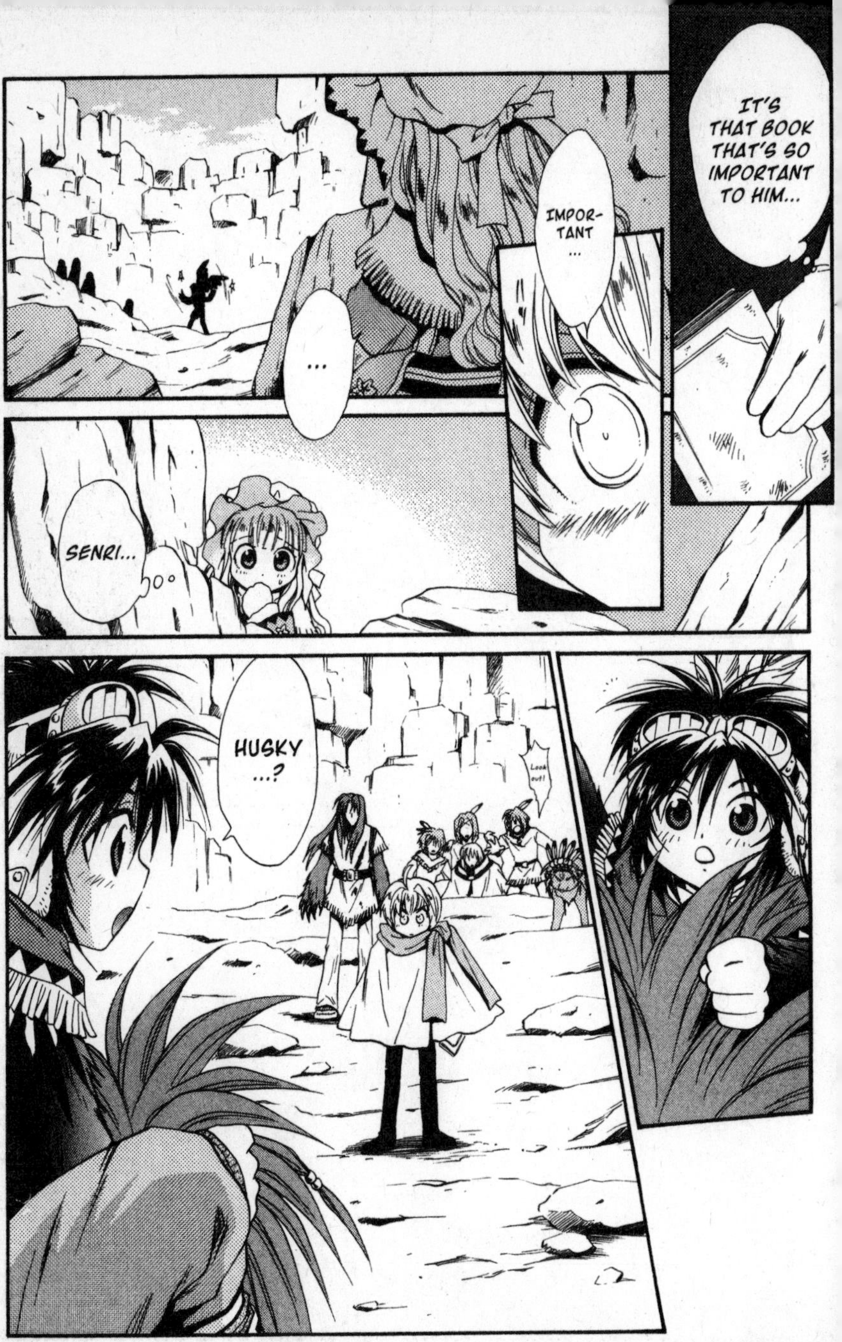
IT'S THAT BOOK THAT'S SO IMPORTANT TO HIM...
IMPORTANT...
...
SENRI...
HUSKY ...?
Look out!

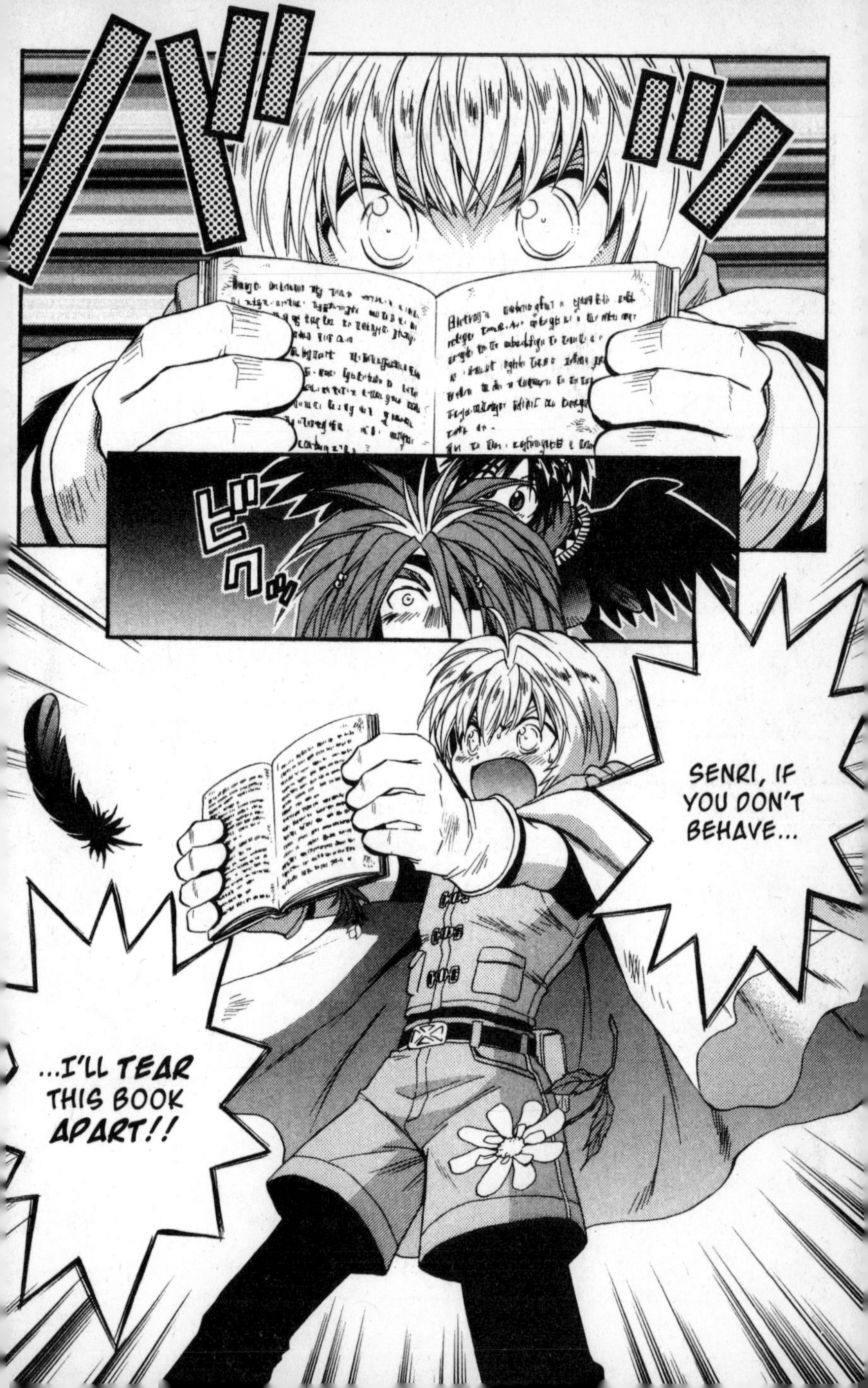
SENRI, IF YOU DON'T BEHAVE...
...I'LL TEAR THIS BOOK APART!!

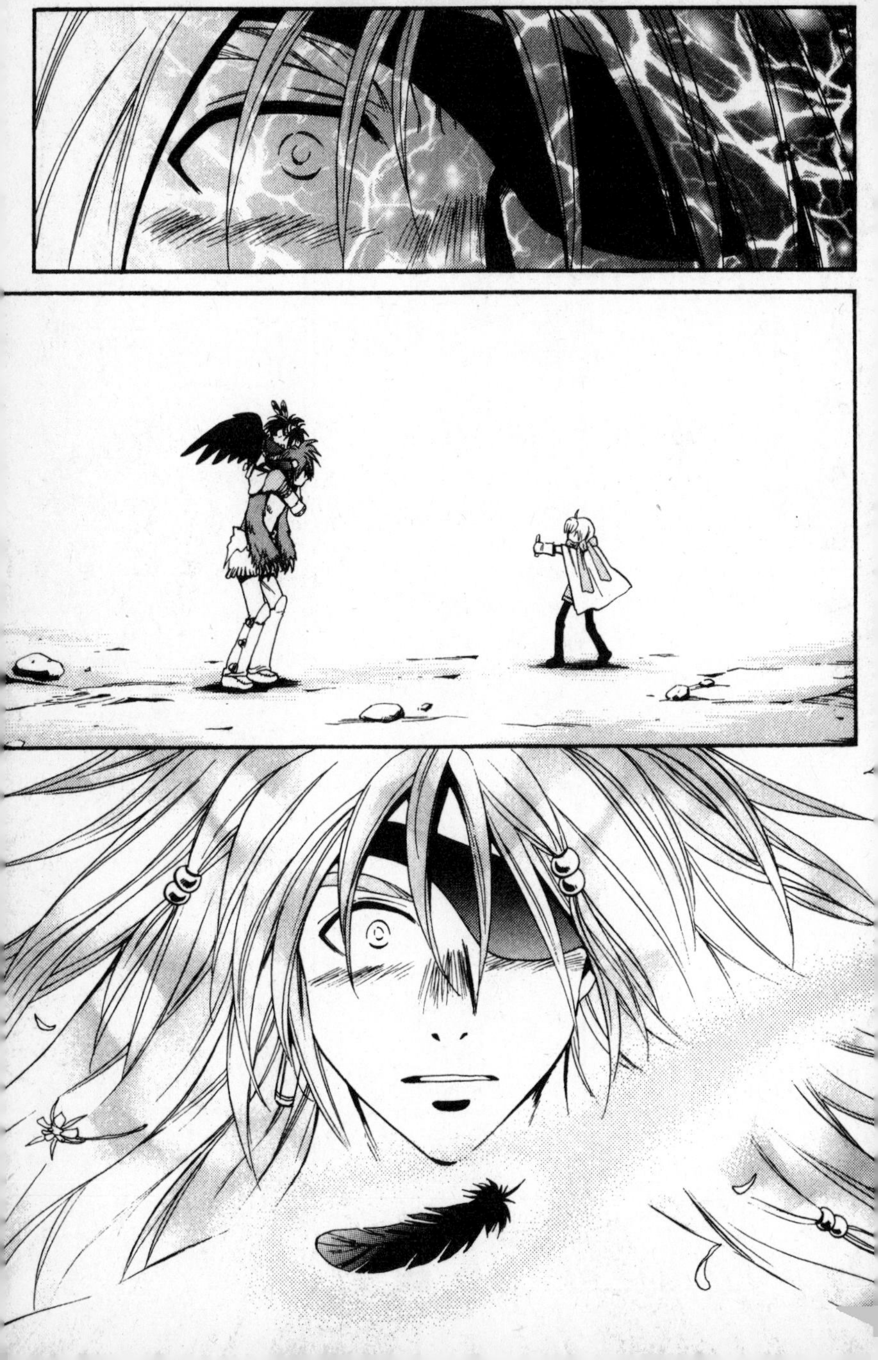

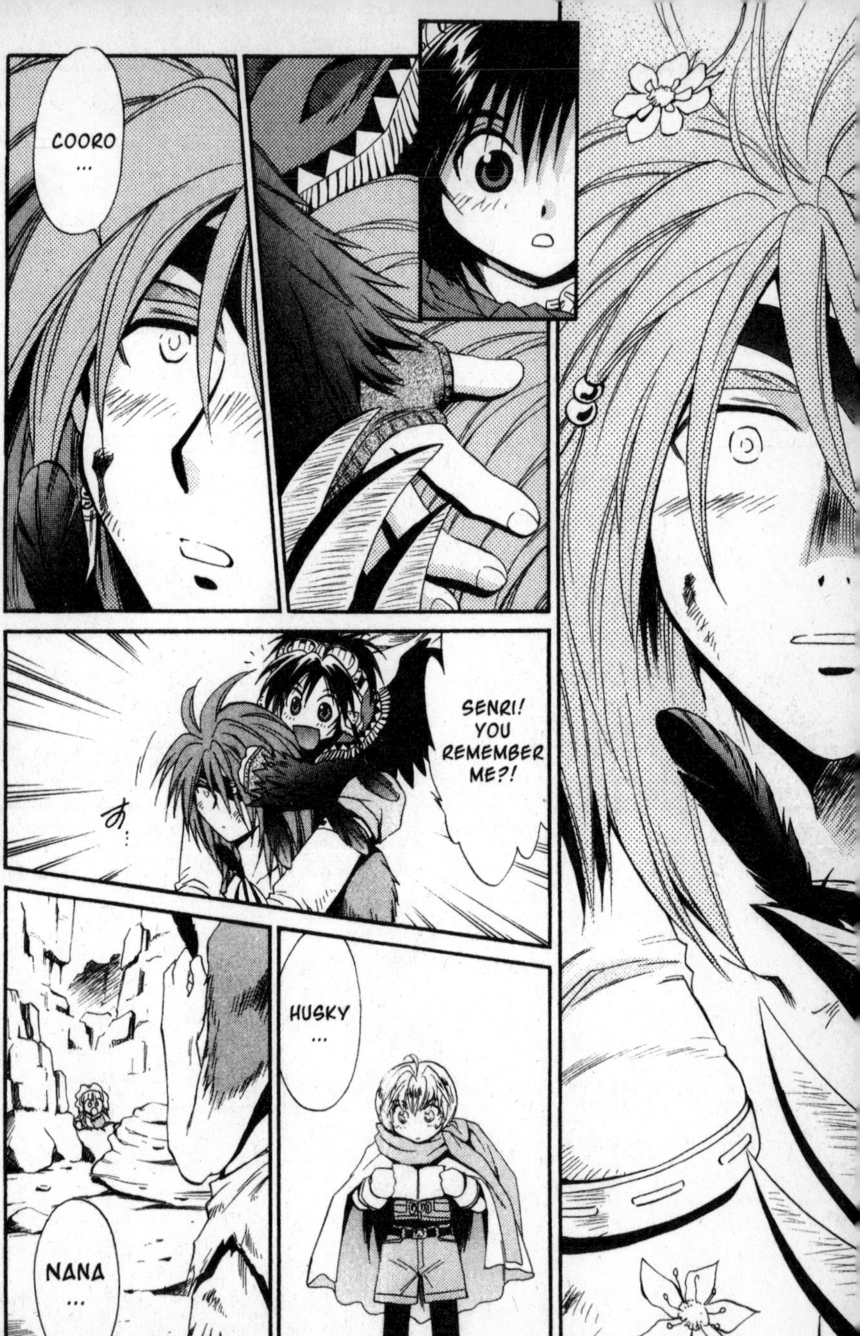
COORO ...
SENRI! YOU REMEMBER ME?!
す…
HUSKY ...
NANA ...

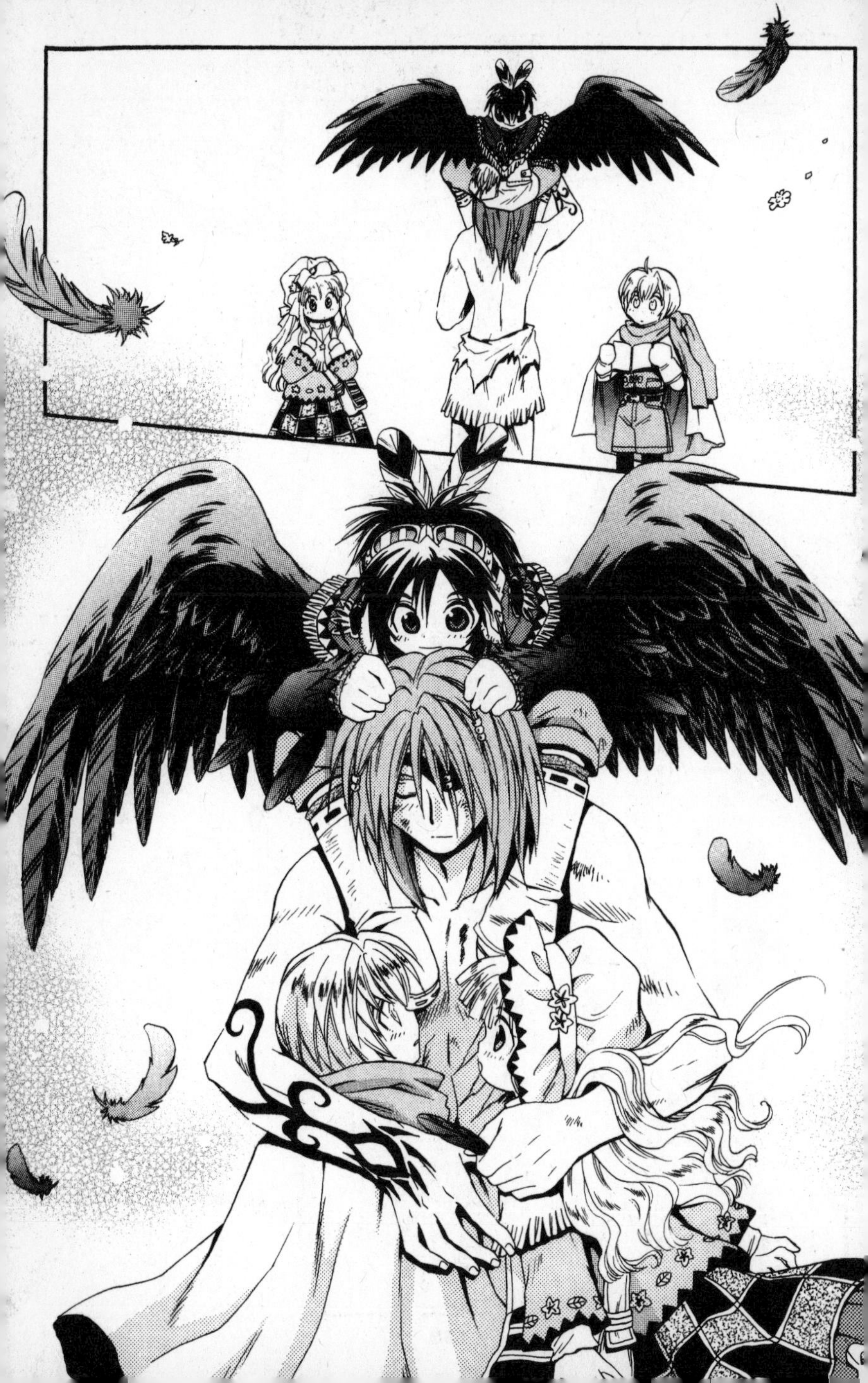

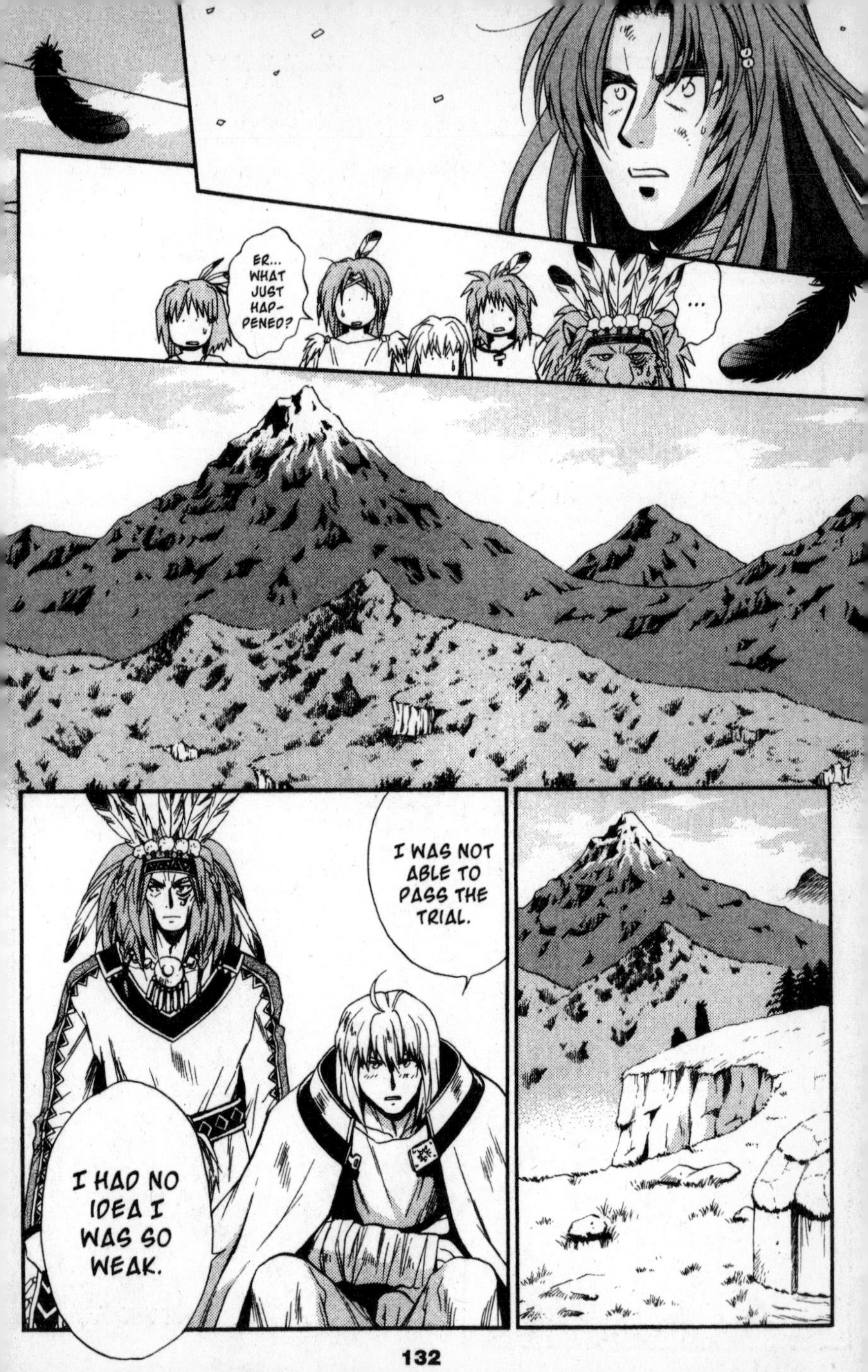
...
ER... WHAT JUST HAPPENED?
I WAS NOT ABLE TO PASS THE TRIAL.
I HAD NO IDEA I WAS SO WEAK.

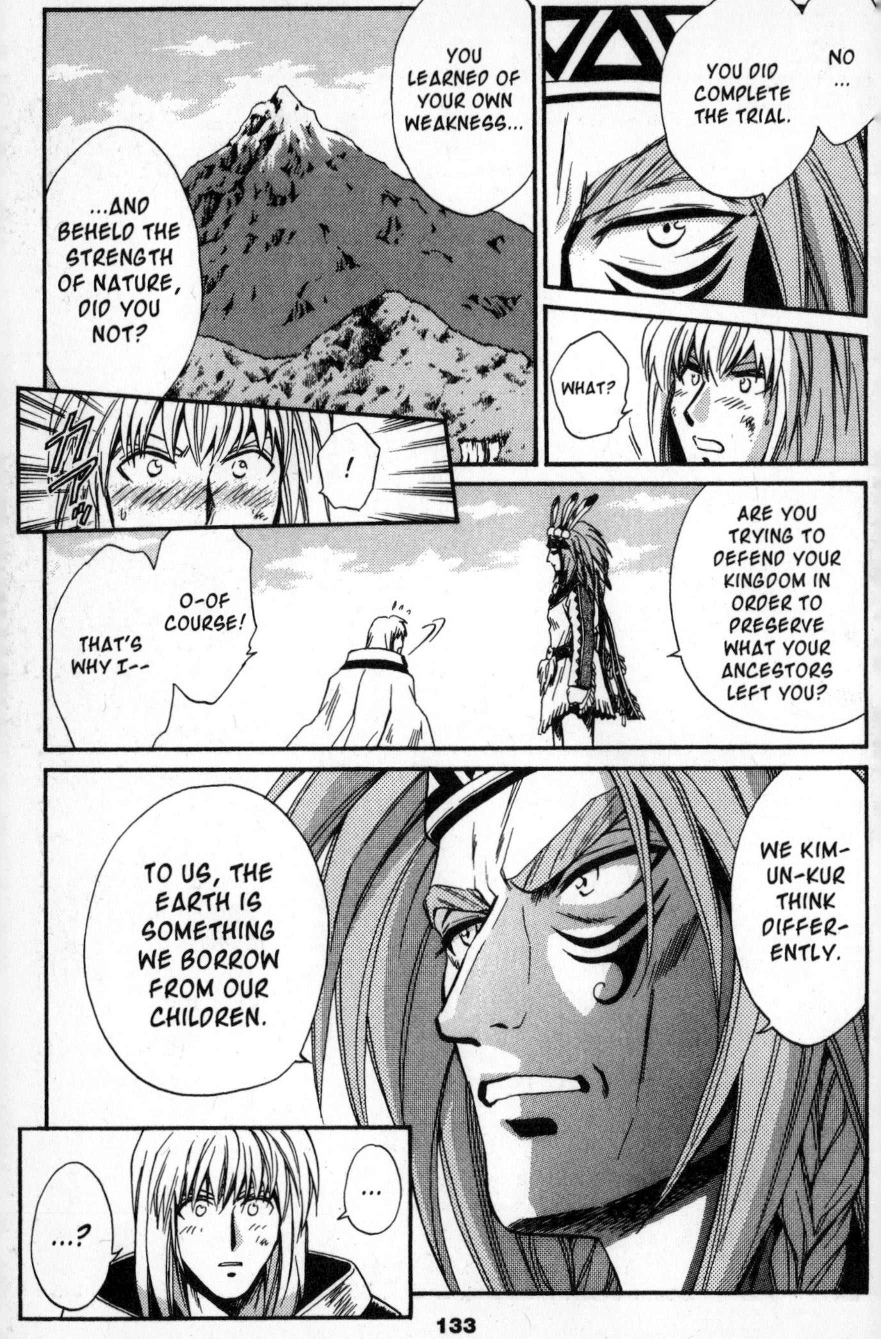
NO ...
YOU DID COMPLETE THE TRIAL.
WHAT?
YOU LEARNED OF YOUR OWN WEAKNESS...
...AND BEHELD THE STRENGTH OF NATURE, DID YOU NOT?
!
ARE YOU TRYING TO DEFEND YOUR KINGDOM IN ORDER TO PRESERVE WHAT YOUR ANCESTORS LEFT YOU?
O-OF COURSE!
THAT'S WHY I--
WE KIM-UN-KUR THINK DIFFER-ENTLY.
TO US, THE EARTH IS SOMETHING WE BORROW FROM OUR CHILDREN.
...
...?

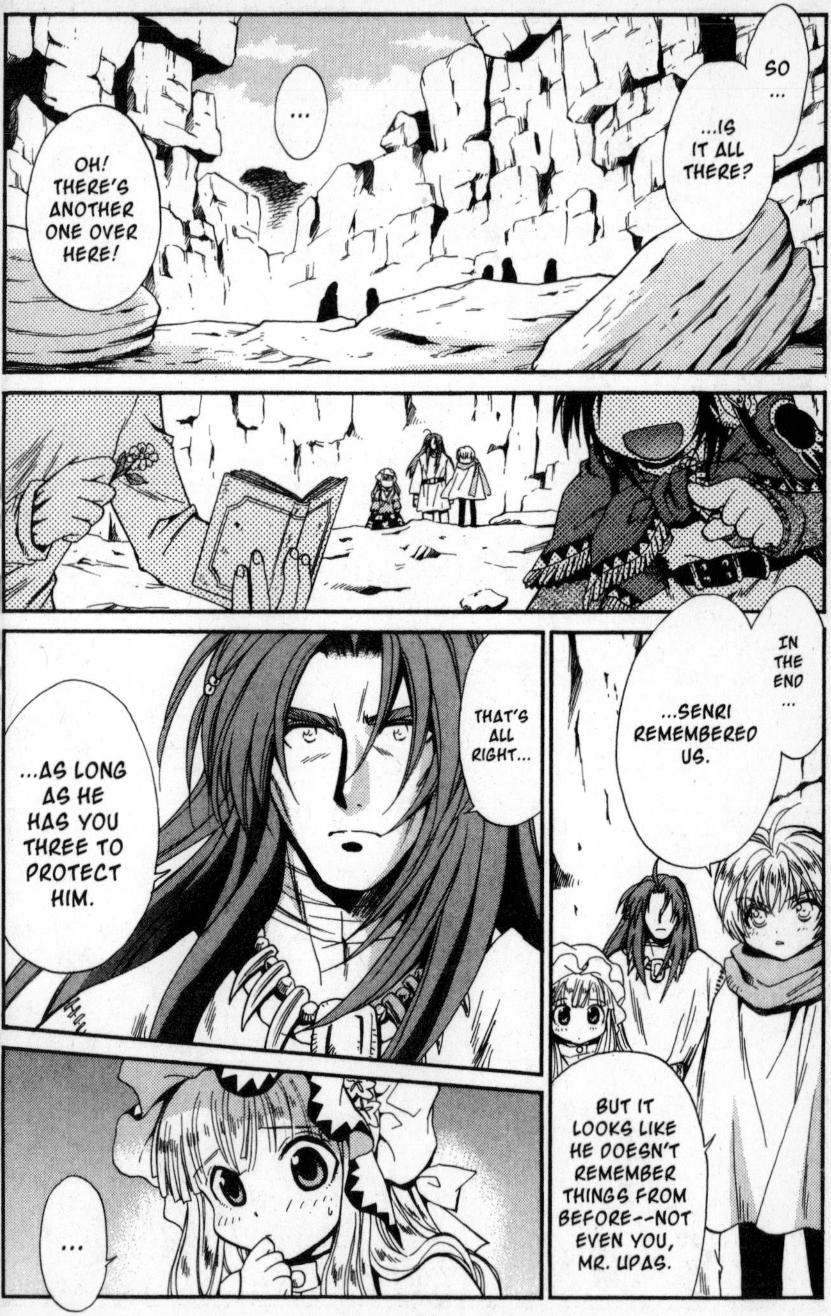
SO ...
...IS IT ALL THERE?
...
OH! THERE'S ANOTHER ONE OVER HERE!
IN THE END ...
...SENRI REMEMBERED US.
BUT IT LOOKS LIKE HE DOESN'T REMEMBER THINGS FROM BEFORE--NOT EVEN YOU, MR. UPAS.
THAT'S ALL RIGHT...
...AS LONG AS HE HAS YOU THREE TO PROTECT HIM.
...

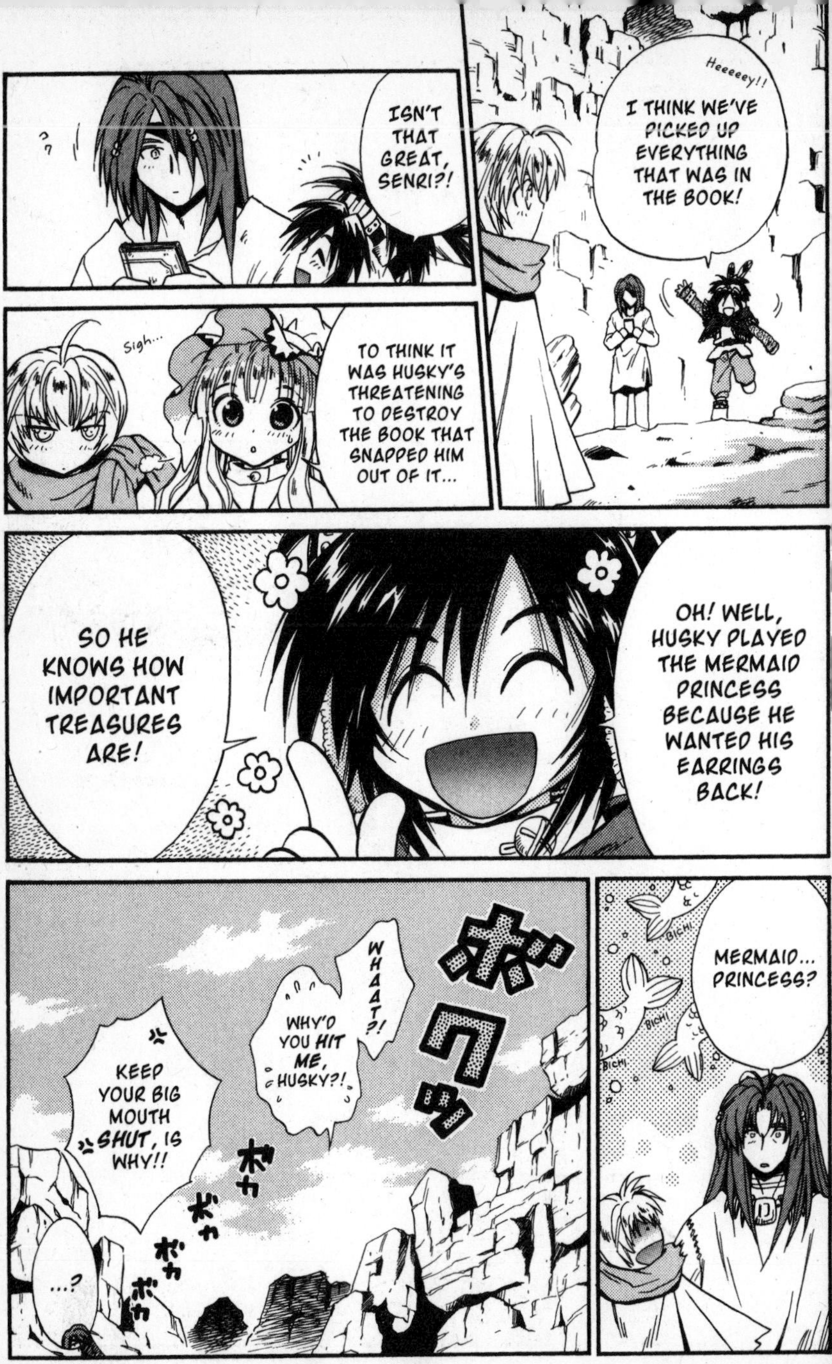
Heeeeey!!
I THINK WE'VE PICKED UP EVERYTHING THAT WAS IN THE BOOK!
ISN'T THAT GREAT, SENRI?!
Sigh...
TO THINK IT WAS HUSKY'S THREATENING TO DESTROY THE BOOK THAT SNAPPED HIM OUT OF IT...
OH! WELL, HUSKY PLAYED THE MERMAID PRINCESS BECAUSE HE WANTED HIS EARRINGS BACK!
SO HE KNOWS HOW IMPORTANT TREASURES ARE!
BICHI
BICHI
BICHI
MERMAID... PRINCESS?
ボカッ
WHAAAT?!
WHY'D YOU HIT ME, HUSKY?!
KEEP YOUR BIG MOUTH SHUT, IS WHY!!
ボカ
ボカ
ボカ
ボカ
...?

Chapter 31: Beyond the Mountains

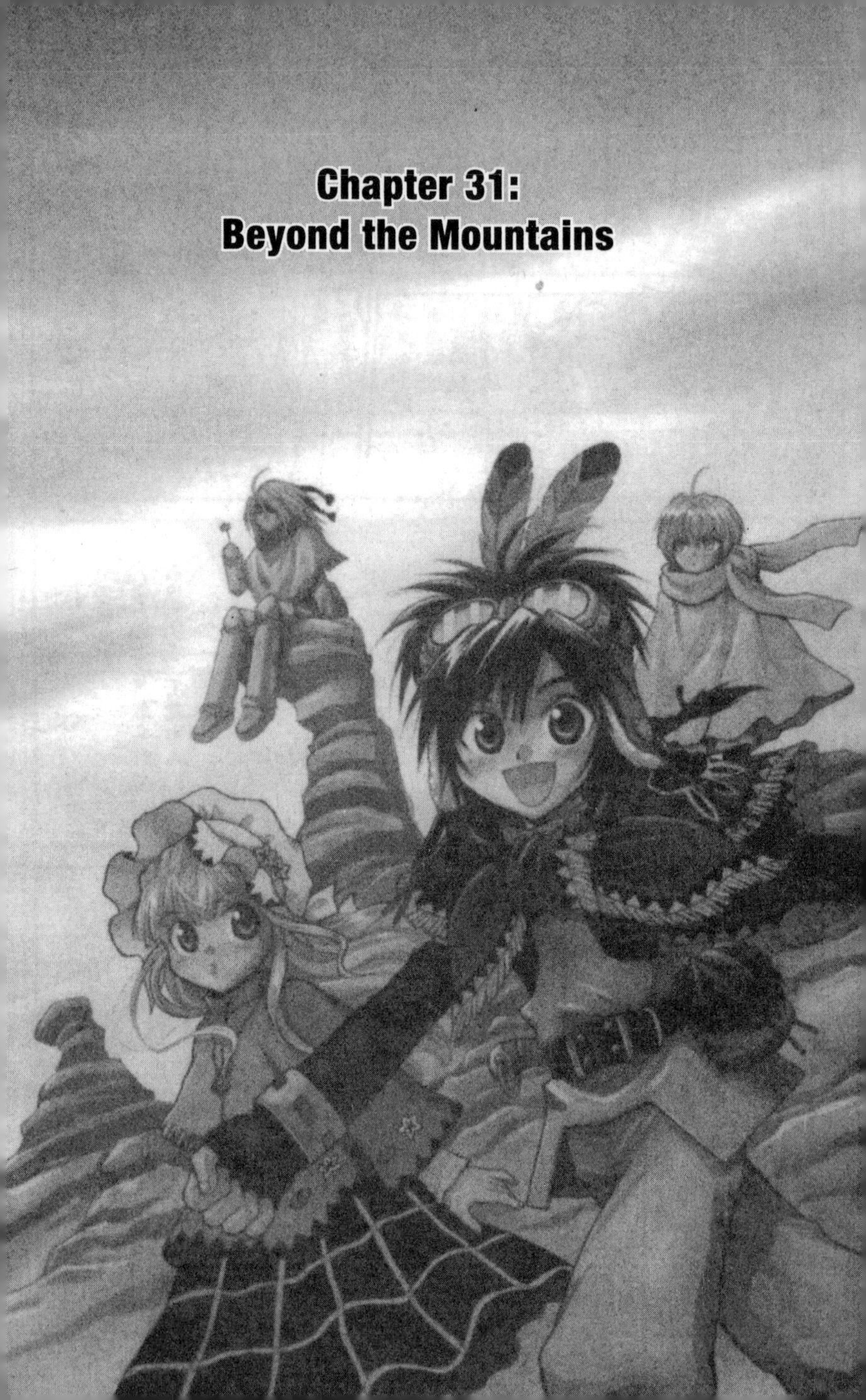

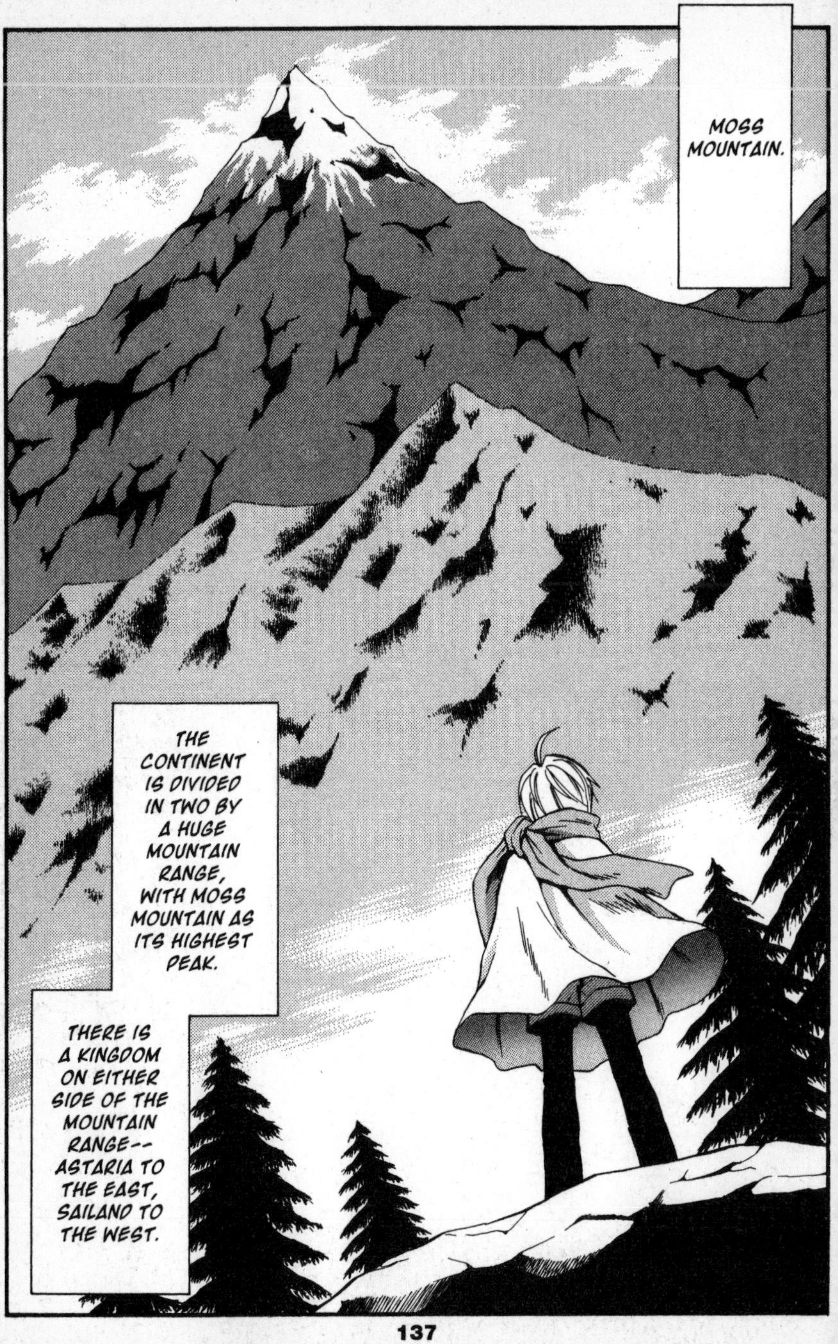
MOSS MOUNTAIN.
THE CONTINENT IS DIVIDED IN TWO BY A HUGE MOUNTAIN RANGE, WITH MOSS MOUNTAIN AS ITS HIGHEST PEAK.
THERE IS A KINGDOM ON EITHER SIDE OF THE MOUNTAIN RANGE-- ASTARIA TO THE EAST, SAILAND TO THE WEST.

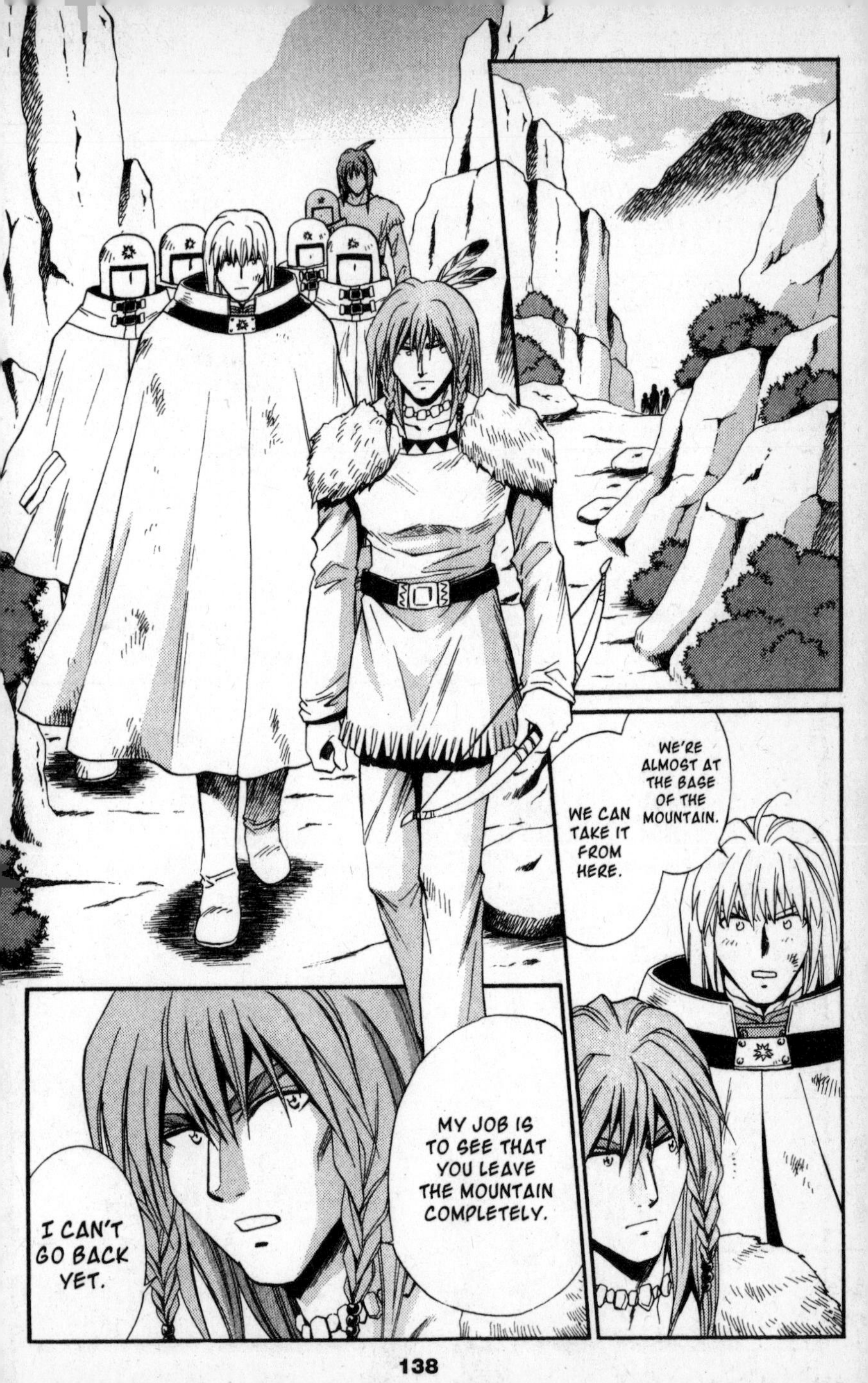
WE'RE ALMOST AT THE BASE OF THE MOUNTAIN.
WE CAN TAKE IT FROM HERE.
MY JOB IS TO SEE THAT YOU LEAVE THE MOUNTAIN COMPLETELY.
I CAN'T GO BACK YET.

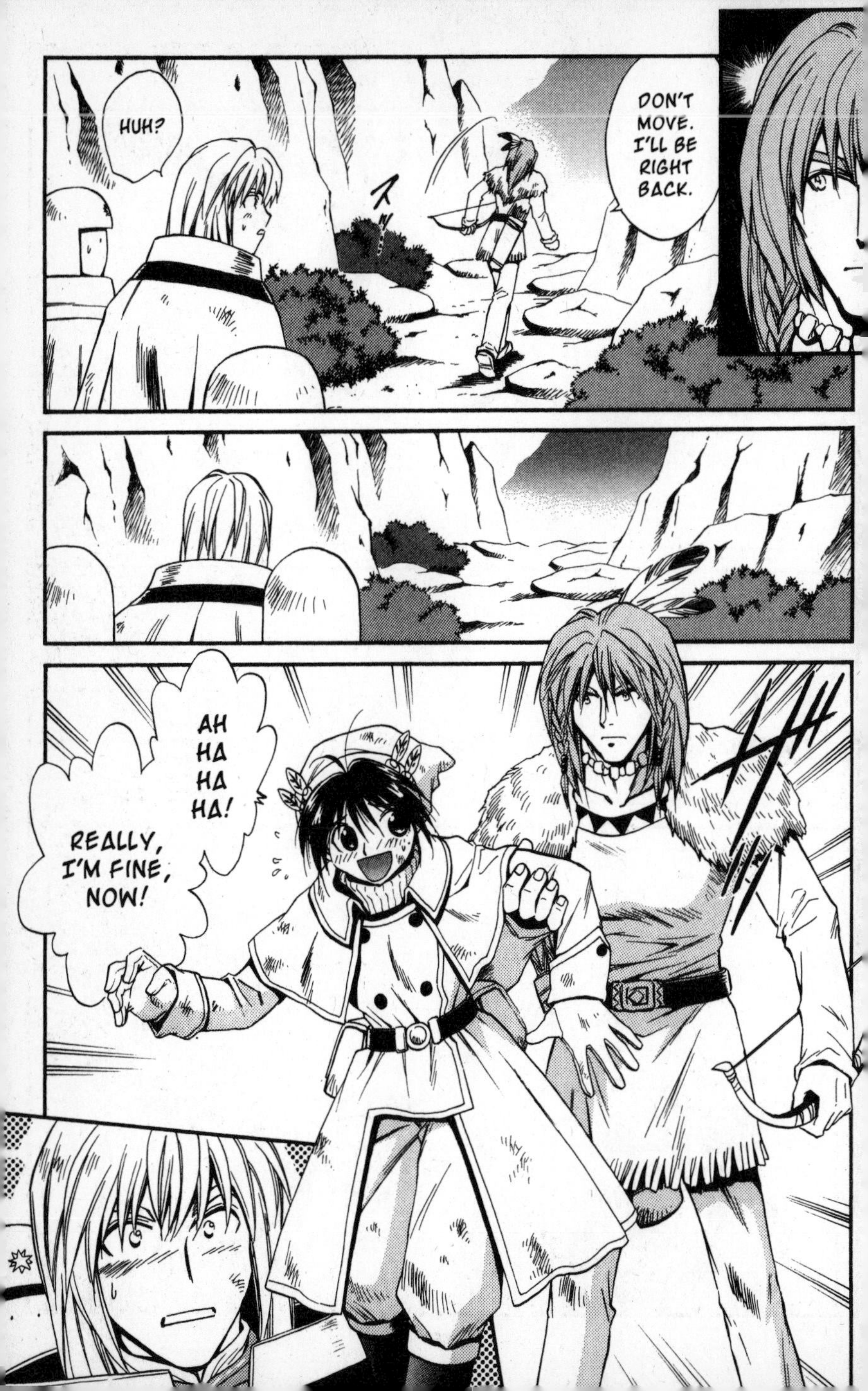
DON'T MOVE. I'LL BE RIGHT BACK.
HUH?
AH HA HA HA!
REALLY, I'M FINE, NOW!

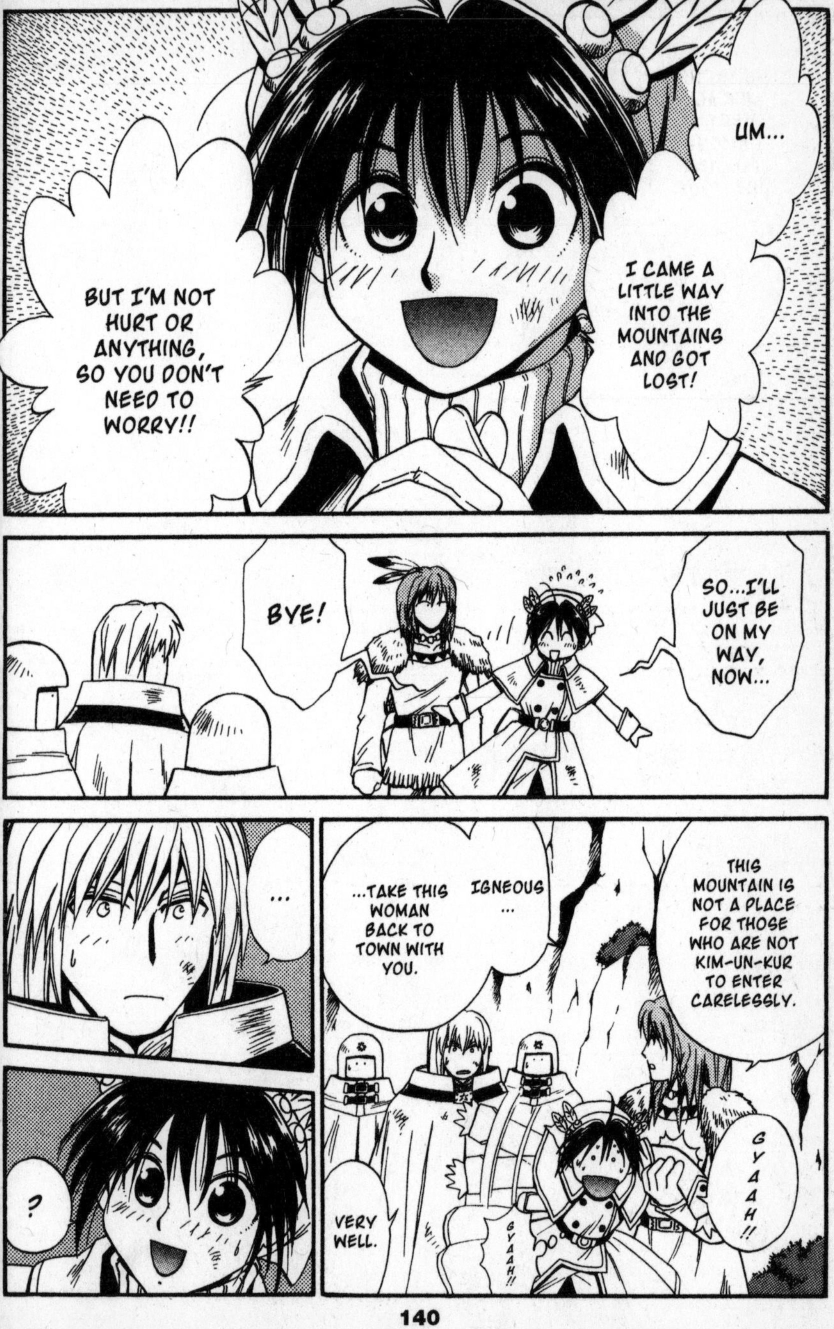
UM...
I CAME A LITTLE WAY INTO THE MOUNTAINS AND GOT LOST!
BUT I'M NOT HURT OR ANYTHING, SO YOU DON'T NEED TO WORRY!!
SO...I'LL JUST BE ON MY WAY, NOW...
BYE!
THIS MOUNTAIN IS NOT A PLACE FOR THOSE WHO ARE NOT KIM-UN-KUR TO ENTER CARELESSLY.
IGNEOUS ...
...TAKE THIS WOMAN BACK TO TOWN WITH YOU.
GYAAH!!
GYAAH!!
VERY WELL.
...
?

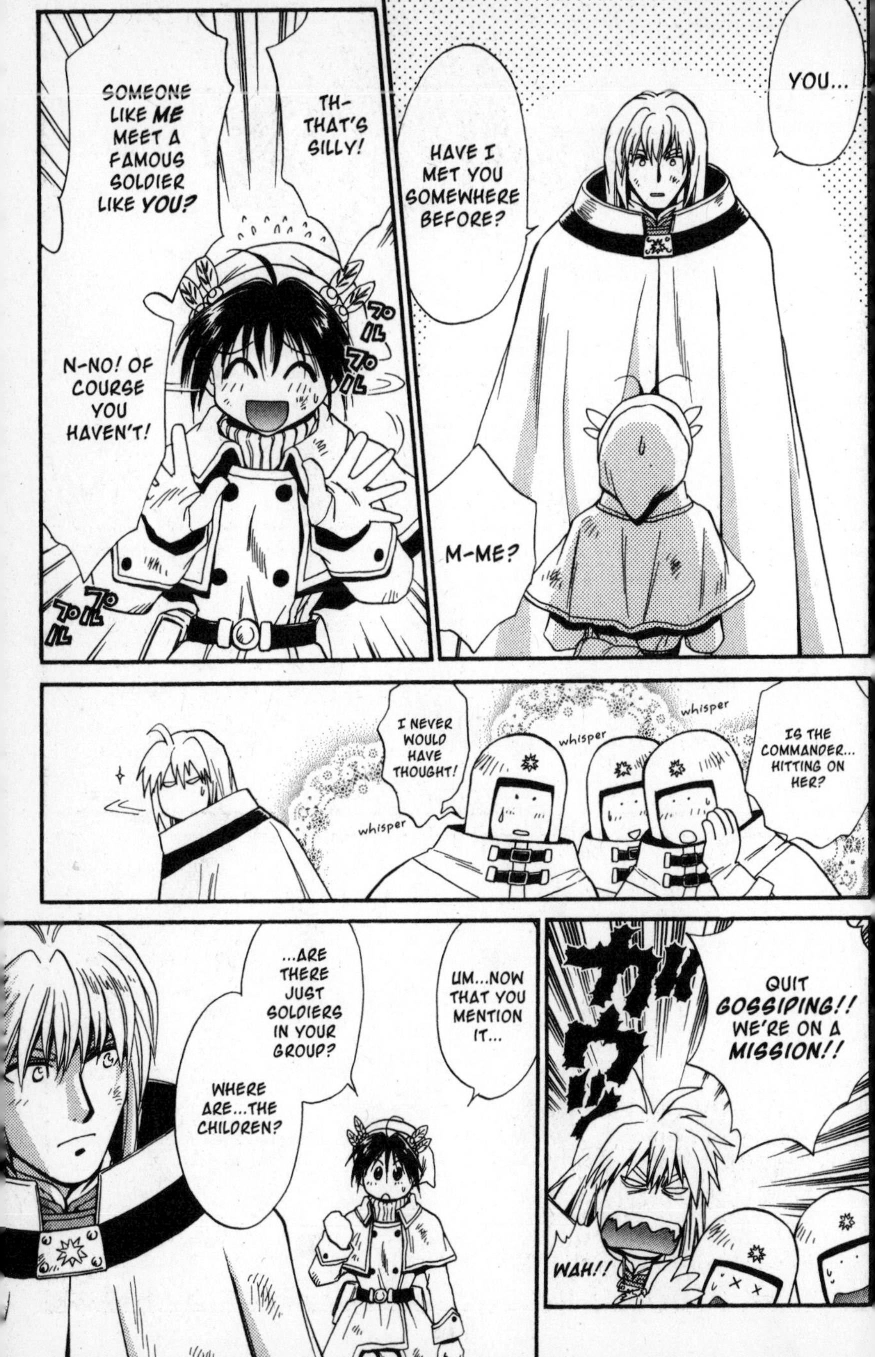
YOU...
HAVE I MET YOU SOMEWHERE BEFORE?
M-ME?
TH-THAT'S SILLY!
SOMEONE LIKE ME MEET A FAMOUS SOLDIER LIKE YOU?
N-NO! OF COURSE YOU HAVEN'T!
IS THE COMMANDER... HITTING ON HER?
whisper
whisper
I NEVER WOULD HAVE THOUGHT!
whisper
QUIT GOSSIPING!! WE'RE ON A MISSION!!
WAH!!
UM...NOW THAT YOU MENTION IT...
...ARE THERE JUST SOLDIERS IN YOUR GROUP?
WHERE ARE...THE CHILDREN?

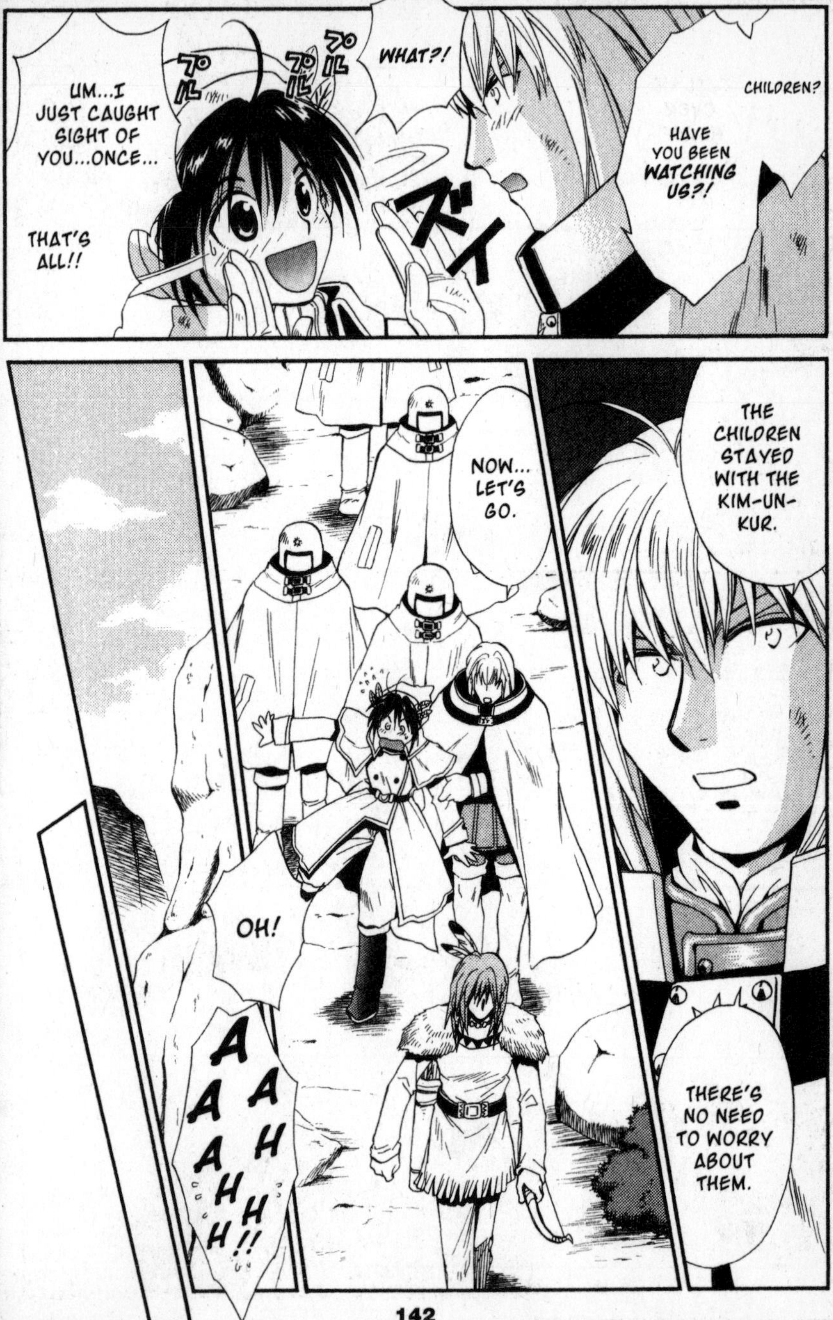
CHILDREN?
HAVE YOU BEEN WATCHING US?!
WHAT?!
プルプル
ズイ
UM...I JUST CAUGHT SIGHT OF YOU...ONCE...
THAT'S ALL!!
THE CHILDREN STAYED WITH THE KIM-UN-KUR.
THERE'S NO NEED TO WORRY ABOUT THEM.
NOW... LET'S GO.
OH!
AAAAHHHH!!

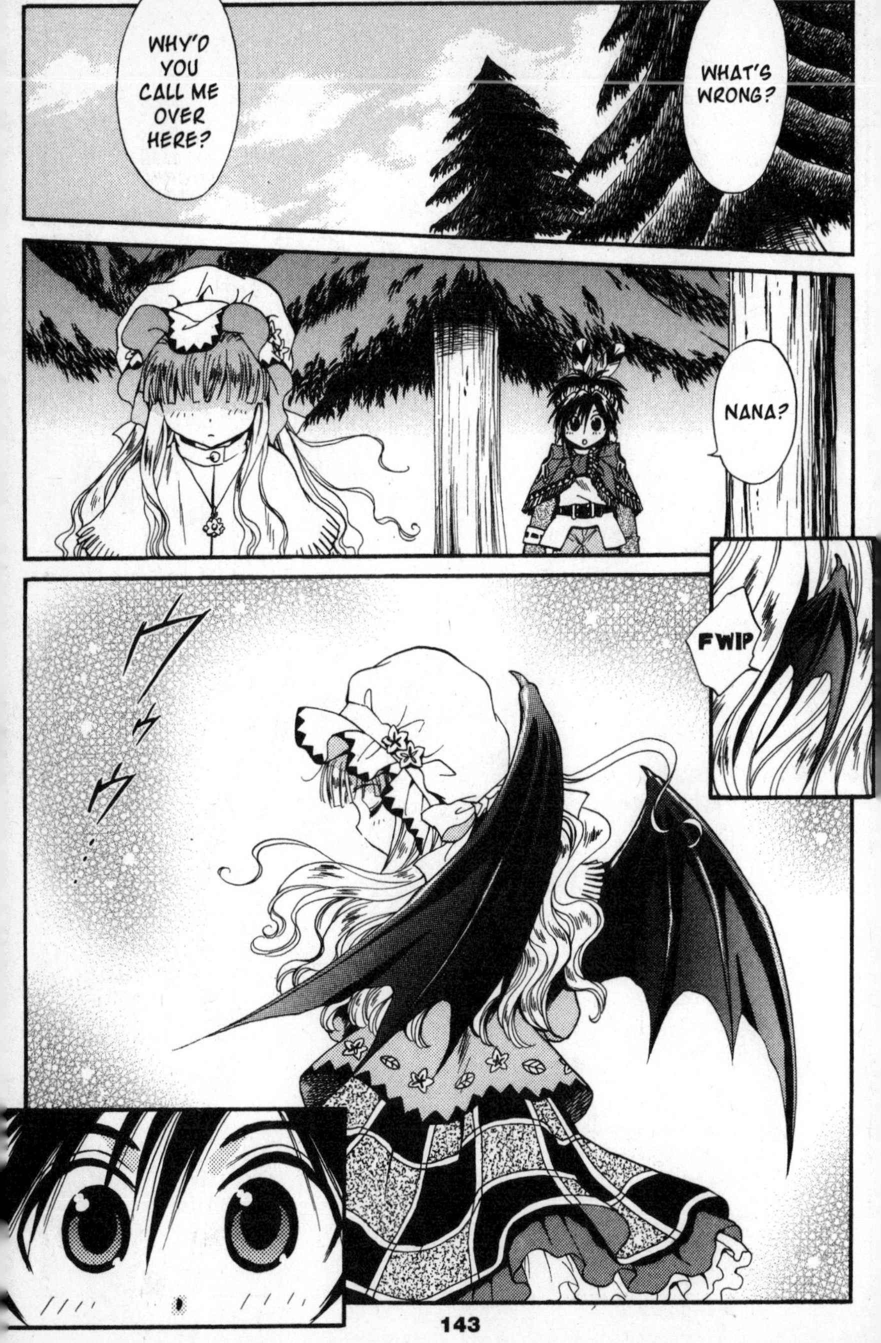
WHAT'S WRONG?
WHY'D YOU CALL ME OVER HERE?
NANA?
FWIP

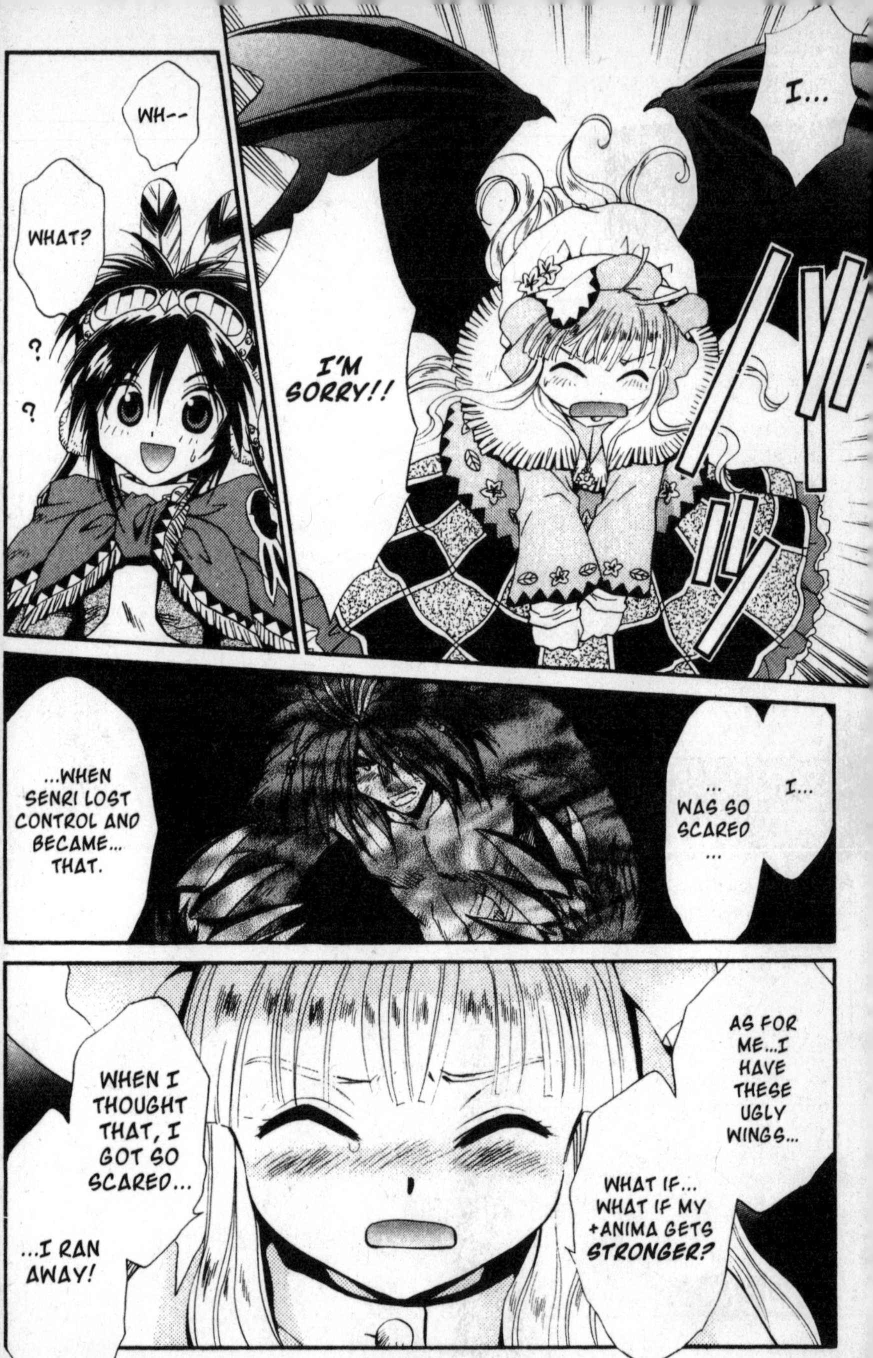
I...
I'M SORRY!!
WH--
WHAT?
? ?
I...
... WAS SO SCARED ...
...WHEN SENRI LOST CONTROL AND BECAME... THAT.
AS FOR ME...I HAVE THESE UGLY WINGS...
WHAT IF... WHAT IF MY +ANIMA GETS STRONGER?
WHEN I THOUGHT THAT, I GOT SO SCARED...
...I RAN AWAY!

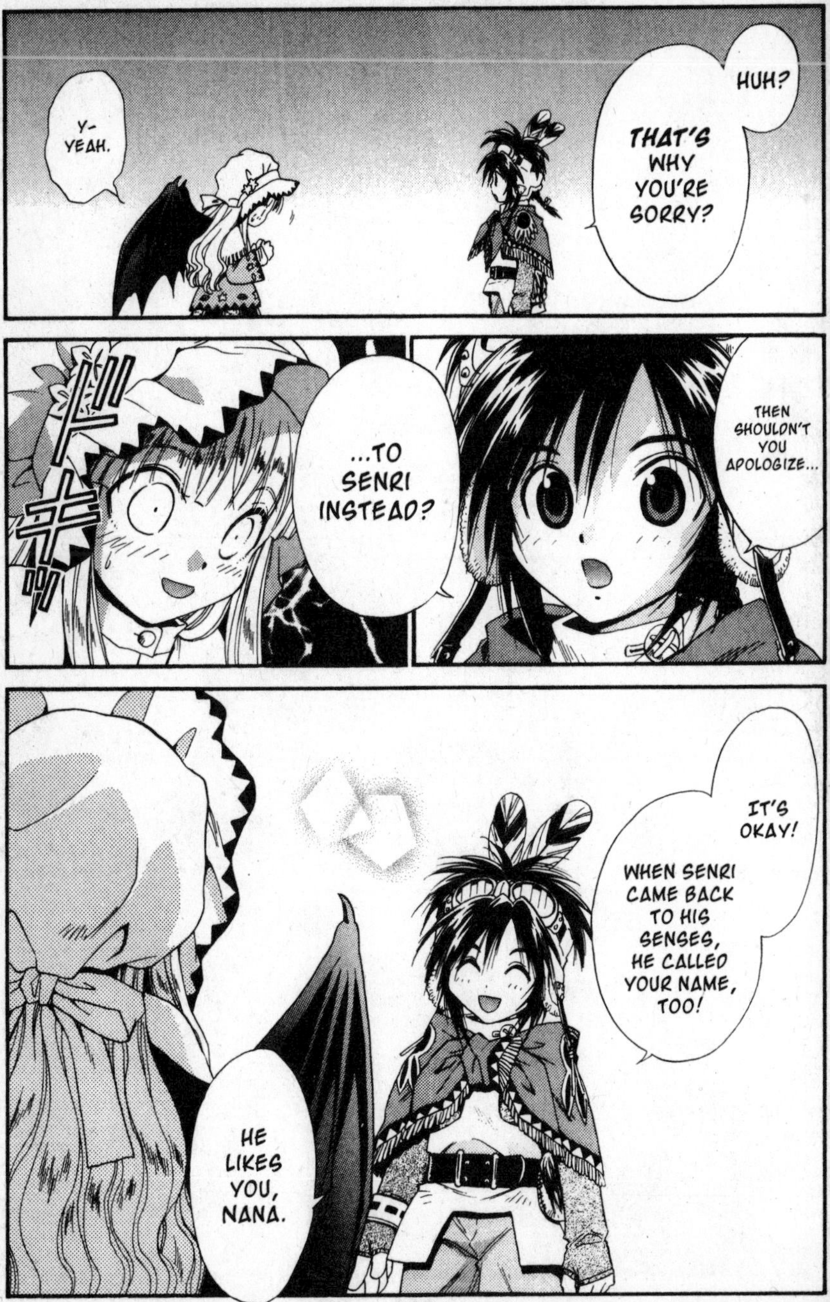
HUH?
THAT'S WHY YOU'RE SORRY?
Y-YEAH.
THEN SHOULDN'T YOU APOLOGIZE...
...TO SENRI INSTEAD?
IT'S OKAY!
WHEN SENRI CAME BACK TO HIS SENSES, HE CALLED YOUR NAME, TOO!
HE LIKES YOU, NANA.

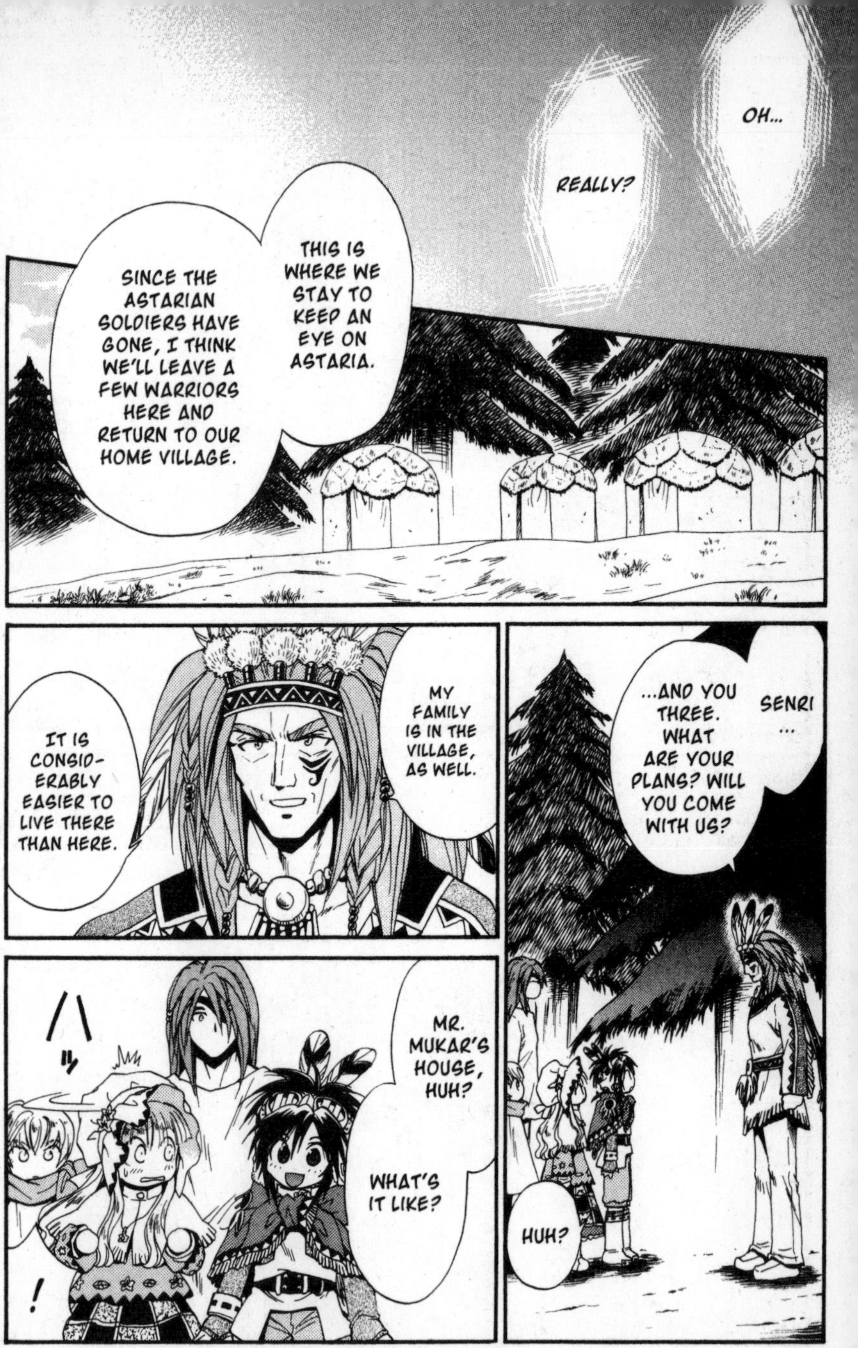
OH...
REALLY?
THIS IS WHERE WE STAY TO KEEP AN EYE ON ASTARIA.
SINCE THE ASTARIAN SOLDIERS HAVE GONE, I THINK WE'LL LEAVE A FEW WARRIORS HERE AND RETURN TO OUR HOME VILLAGE.
SENRI ...
...AND YOU THREE. WHAT ARE YOUR PLANS? WILL YOU COME WITH US?
HUH?
MY FAMILY IS IN THE VILLAGE, AS WELL.
IT IS CONSID-ERABLY EASIER TO LIVE THERE THAN HERE.
MR. MUKAR'S HOUSE, HUH?
WHAT'S IT LIKE?

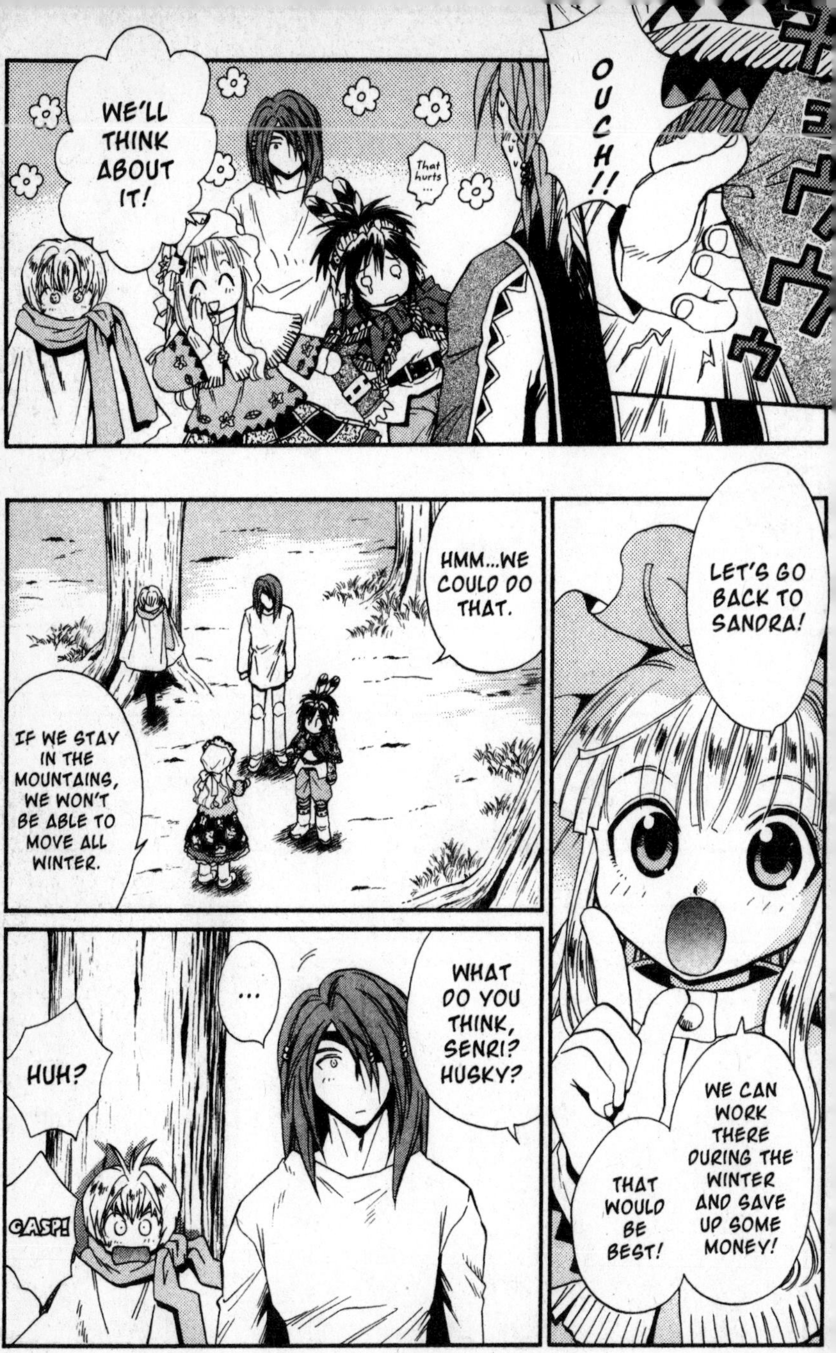
OUCH!!
That hurts...
WE'LL THINK ABOUT IT!
LET'S GO BACK TO SANDRA!
WE CAN WORK THERE DURING THE WINTER AND SAVE UP SOME MONEY!
THAT WOULD BE BEST!
HMM...WE COULD DO THAT.
IF WE STAY IN THE MOUNTAINS, WE WON'T BE ABLE TO MOVE ALL WINTER.
WHAT DO YOU THINK, SENRI? HUSKY?
...
HUH?
GASP!

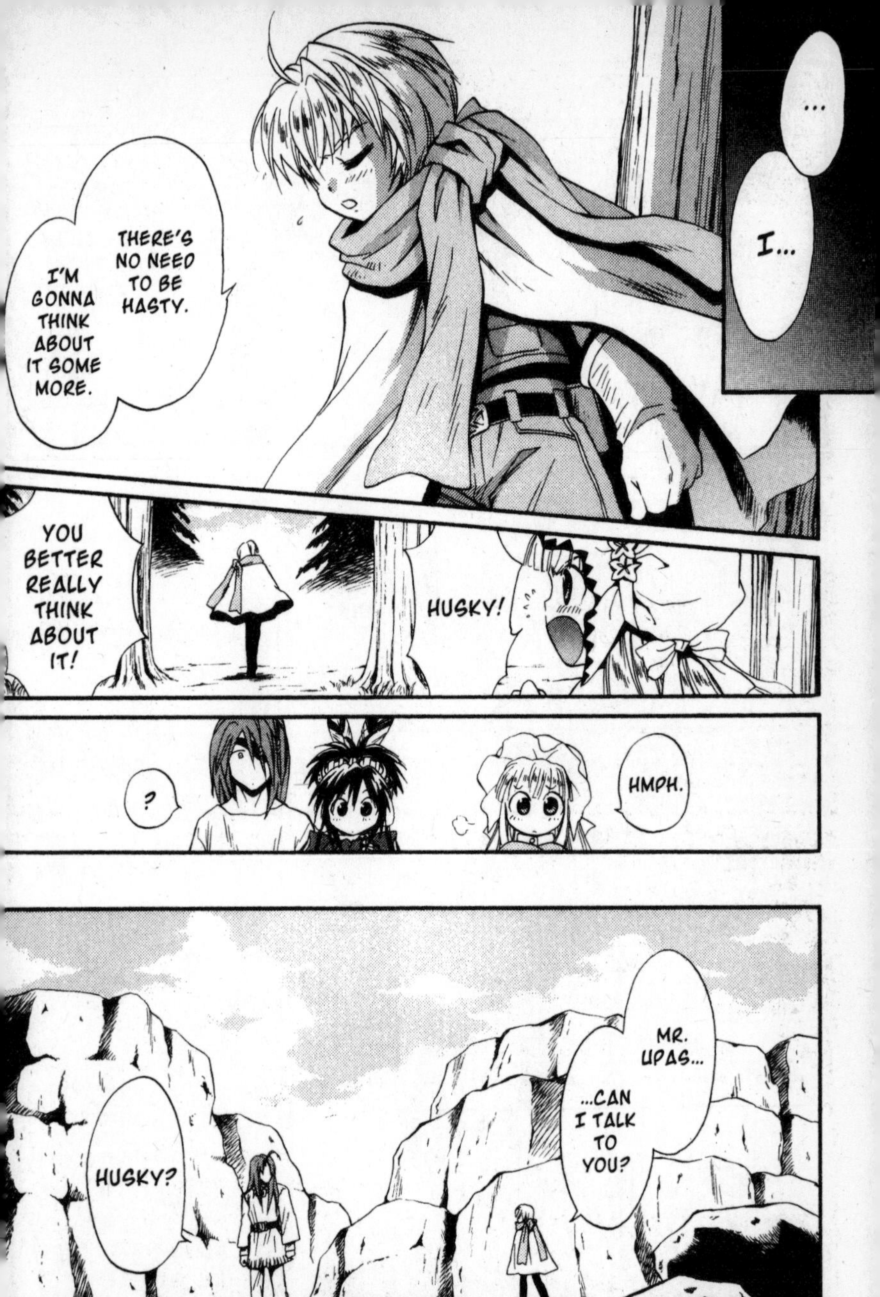
...
I...
THERE'S NO NEED TO BE HASTY.
I'M GONNA THINK ABOUT IT SOME MORE.
HUSKY!
YOU BETTER REALLY THINK ABOUT IT!
HMPH.
?
MR. UPAS...
...CAN I TALK TO YOU?
HUSKY?

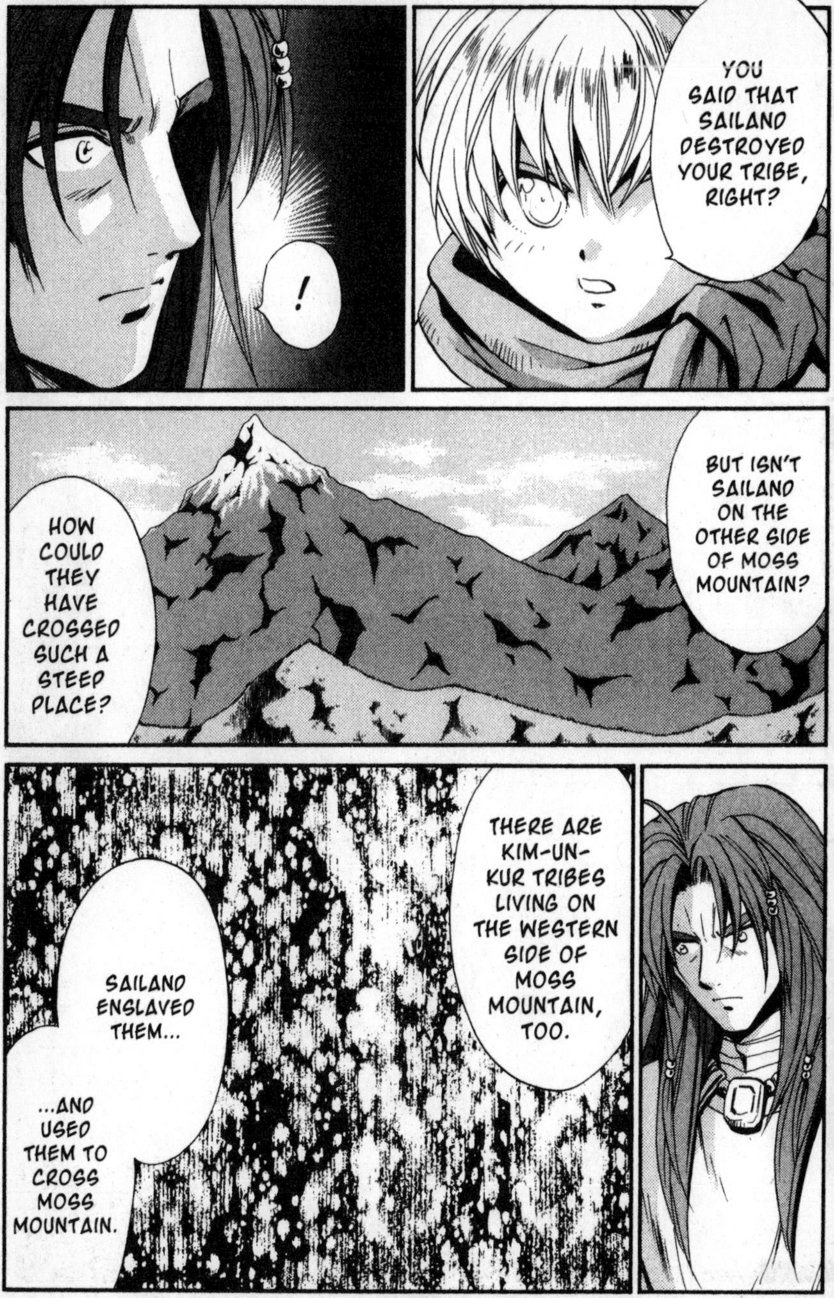
YOU SAID THAT SAILAND DESTROYED YOUR TRIBE, RIGHT?
!
BUT ISN'T SAILAND ON THE OTHER SIDE OF MOSS MOUNTAIN?
HOW COULD THEY HAVE CROSSED SUCH A STEEP PLACE?
THERE ARE KIM-UN-KUR TRIBES LIVING ON THE WESTERN SIDE OF MOSS MOUNTAIN, TOO.
SAILAND ENSLAVED THEM...
...AND USED THEM TO CROSS MOSS MOUNTAIN.

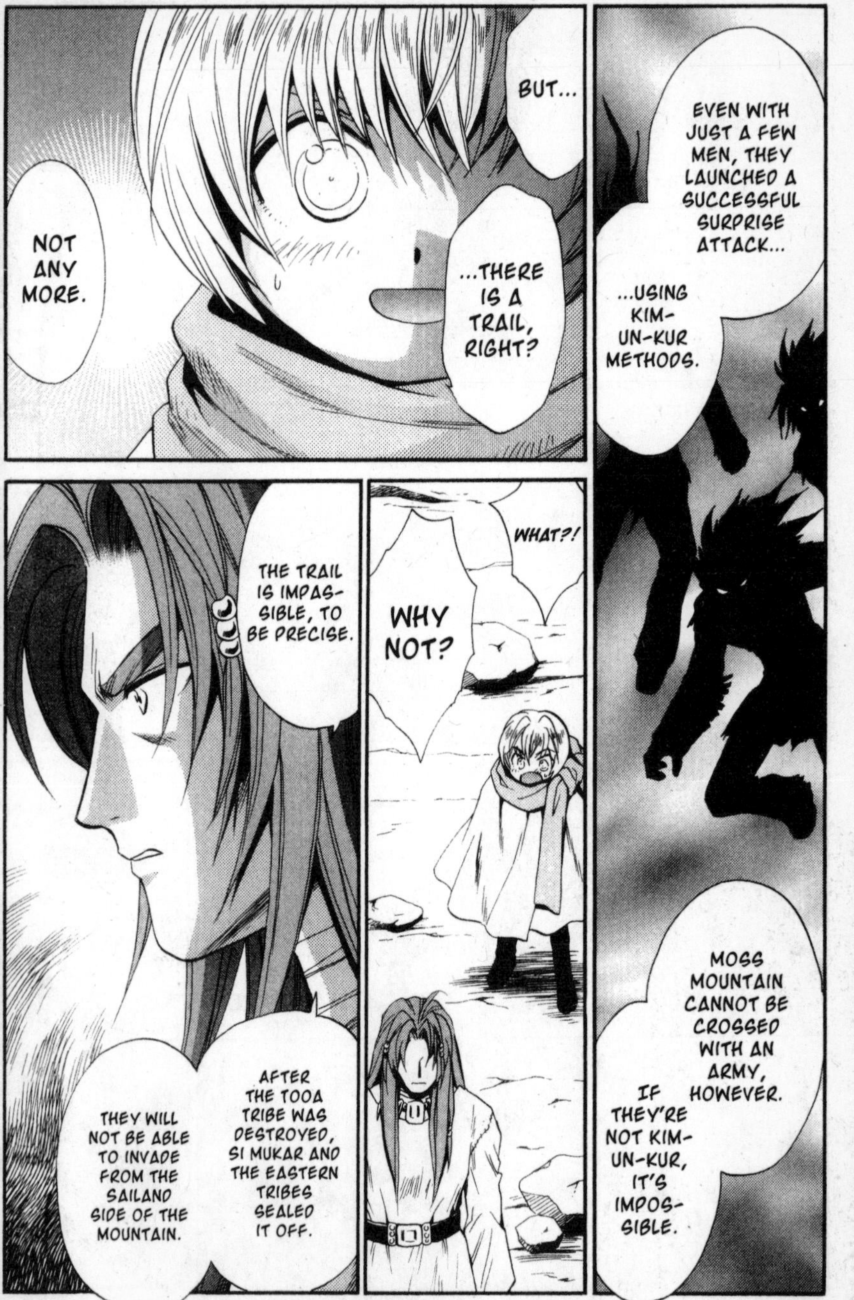
EVEN WITH JUST A FEW MEN, THEY LAUNCHED A SUCCESSFUL SURPRISE ATTACK...
...USING KIM-UN-KUR METHODS.
MOSS MOUNTAIN CANNOT BE CROSSED WITH AN ARMY, HOWEVER.
IF THEY'RE NOT KIM-UN-KUR, IT'S IMPOSSIBLE.
BUT...
...THERE IS A TRAIL, RIGHT?
NOT ANY MORE.
WHAT?!
WHY NOT?
THE TRAIL IS IMPASSIBLE, TO BE PRECISE.
AFTER THE TOOA TRIBE WAS DESTROYED, SI MUKAR AND THE EASTERN TRIBES SEALED IT OFF.
THEY WILL NOT BE ABLE TO INVADE FROM THE SAILAND SIDE OF THE MOUNTAIN.

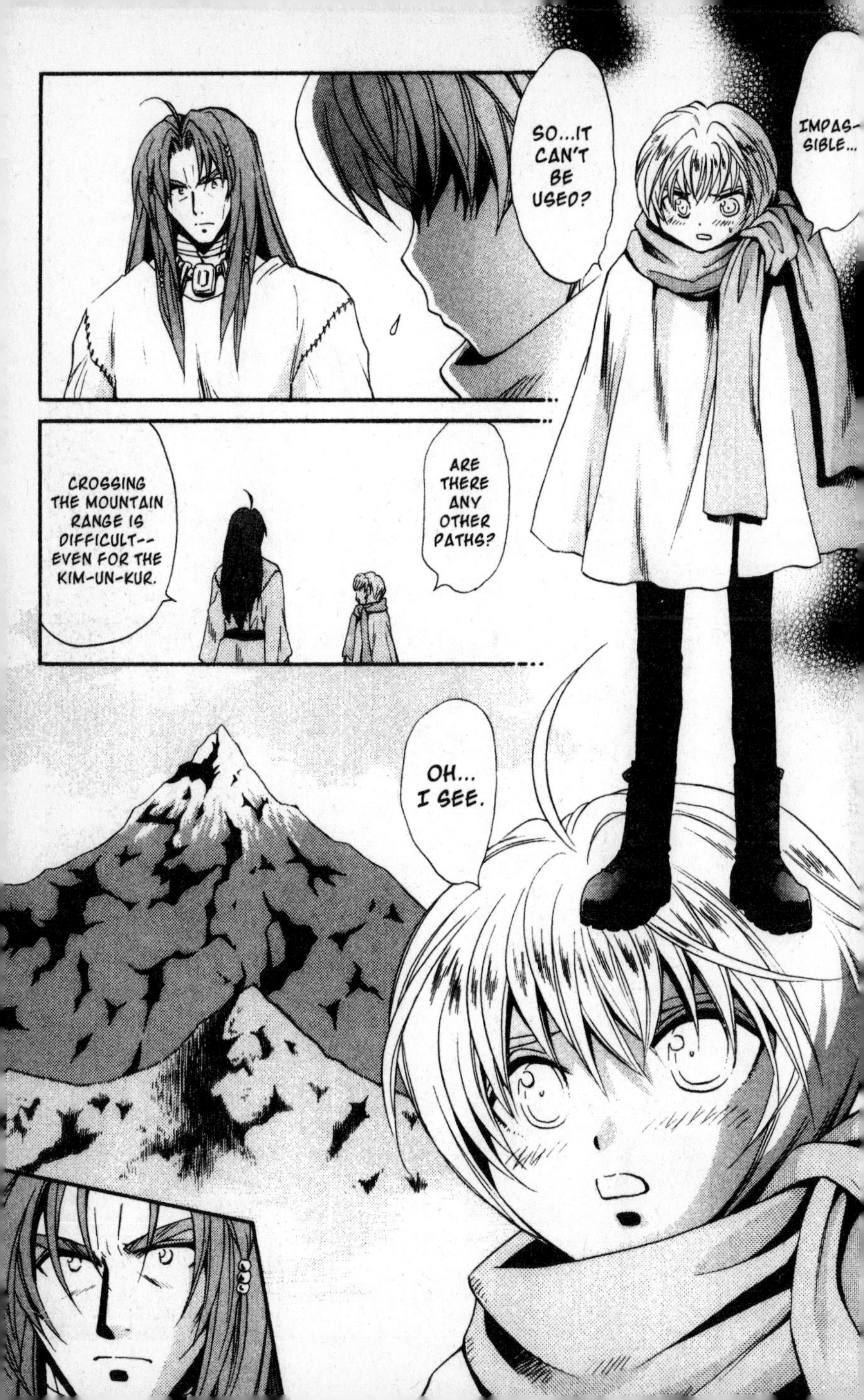
IMPAS-SIBLE...
SO...IT CAN'T BE USED?
ARE THERE ANY OTHER PATHS?
CROSSING THE MOUNTAIN RANGE IS DIFFICULT--EVEN FOR THE KIM-UN-KUR.
OH... I SEE.

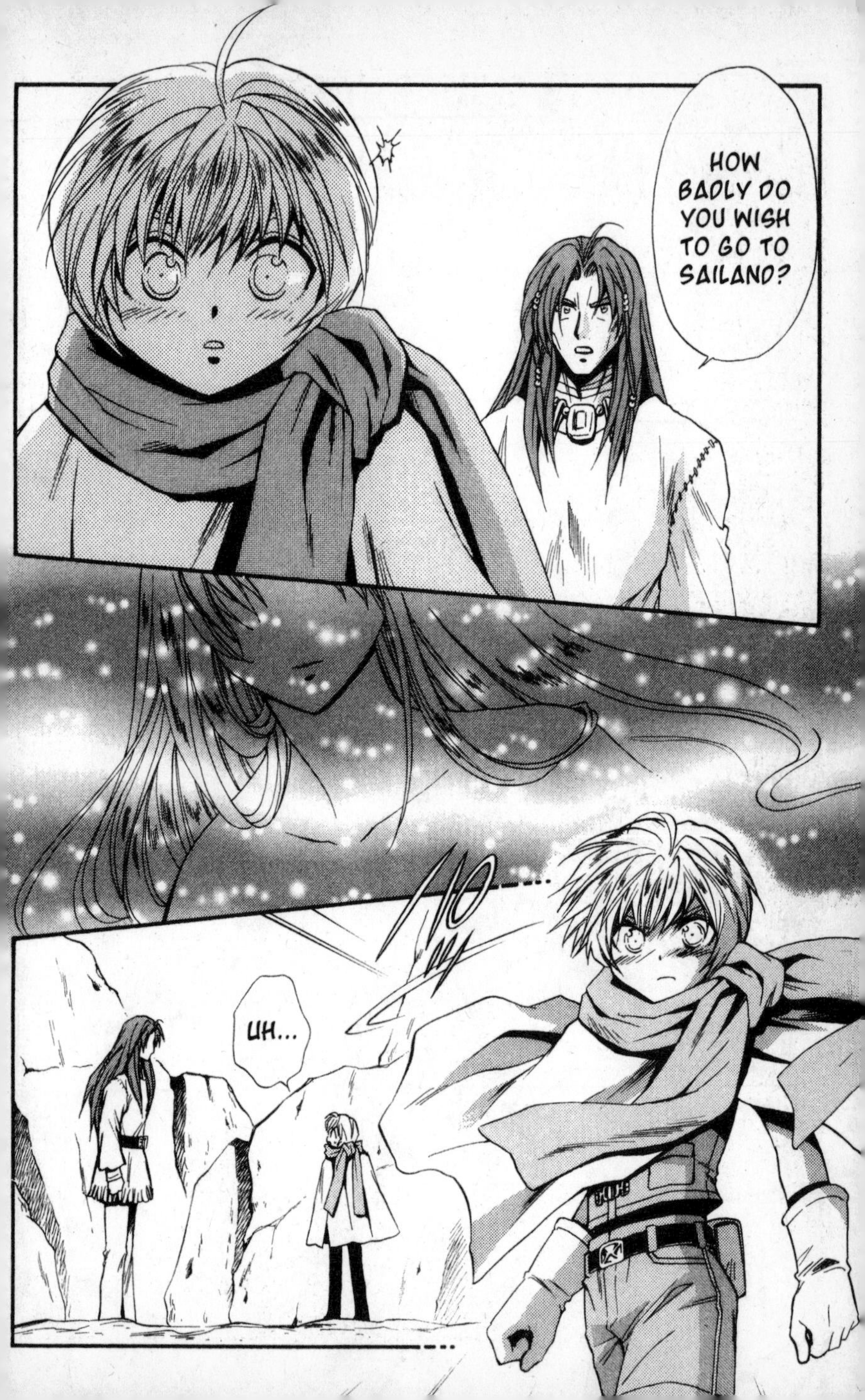
HOW BADLY DO YOU WISH TO GO TO SAILAND?
UH...

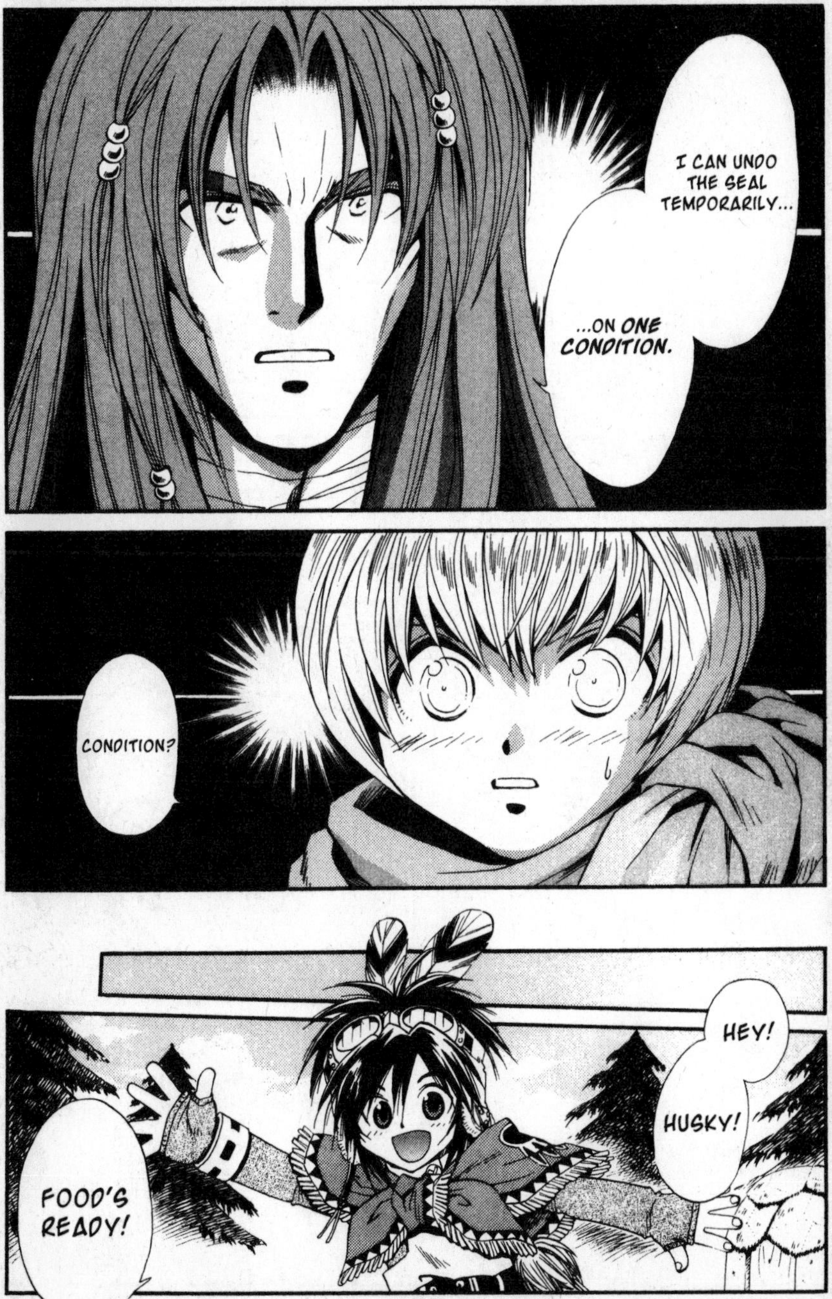
I CAN UNDO THE SEAL TEMPORARILY...
...ON ONE CONDITION.
CONDITION?
HEY!
HUSKY!
FOOD'S READY!

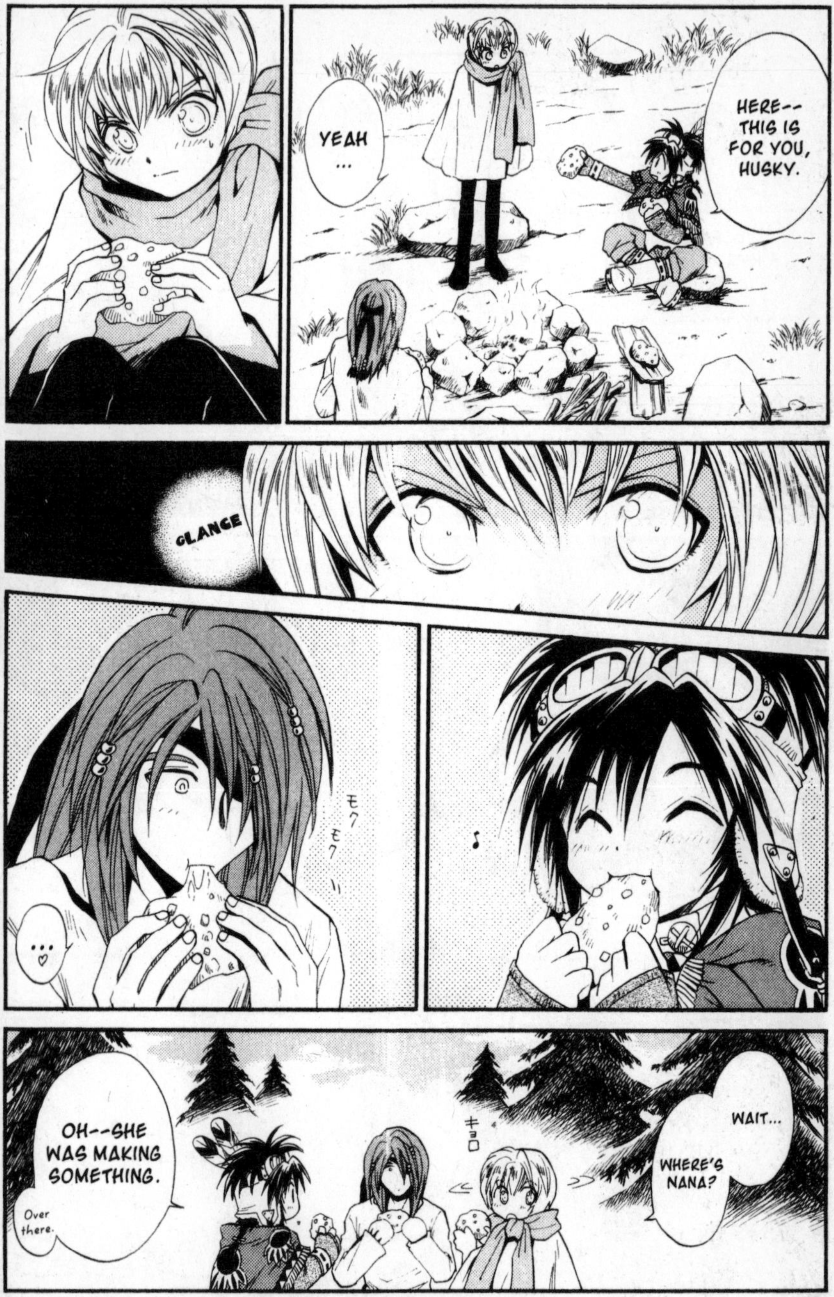
HERE--THIS IS FOR YOU, HUSKY.
YEAH ...
GLANCE
モク モク
...♥
WAIT...
WHERE'S NANA?
キョロ
OH--SHE WAS MAKING SOMETHING.
Over there.

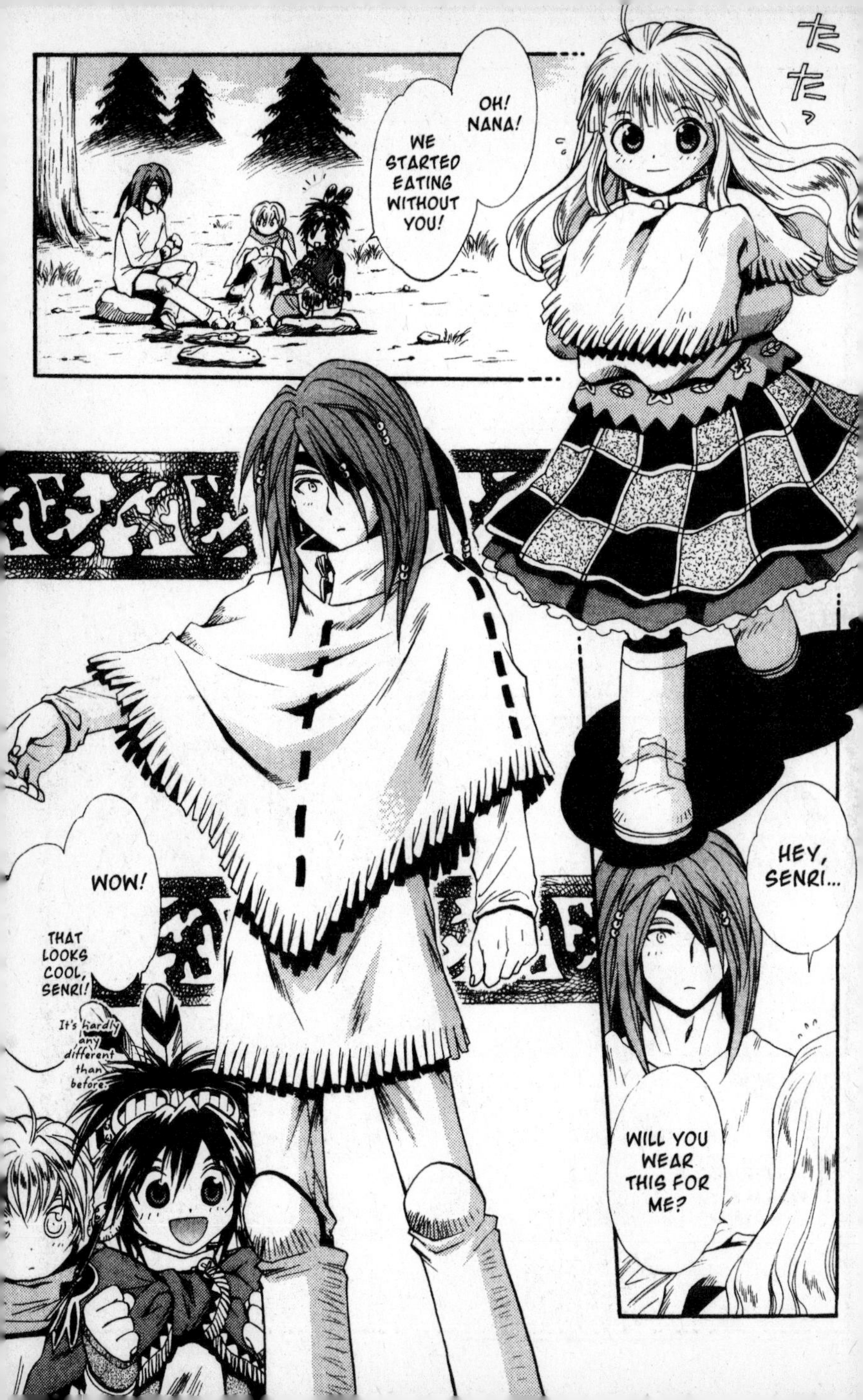

たたっ
OH! NANA!
WE STARTED EATING WITHOUT YOU!
HEY, SENRI...
WILL YOU WEAR THIS FOR ME?
WOW!
THAT LOOKS COOL, SENRI!
It's hardly any different than before.

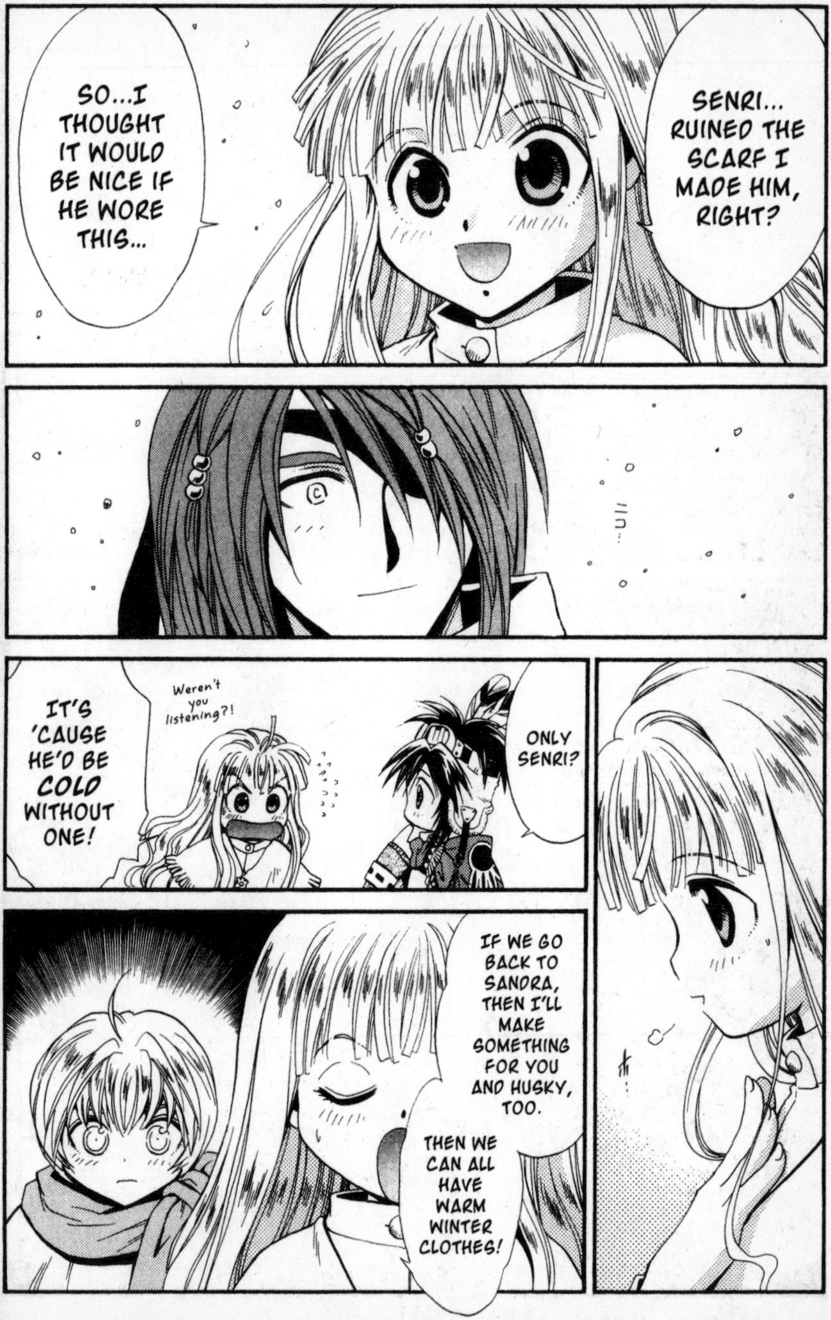
SENRI... RUINED THE SCARF I MADE HIM, RIGHT?
SO...I THOUGHT IT WOULD BE NICE IF HE WORE THIS...
ONLY SENRI?
Weren't you listening?!
IT'S 'CAUSE HE'D BE COLD WITHOUT ONE!
IF WE GO BACK TO SANDRA, THEN I'LL MAKE SOMETHING FOR YOU AND HUSKY, TOO.
THEN WE CAN ALL HAVE WARM WINTER CLOTHES!

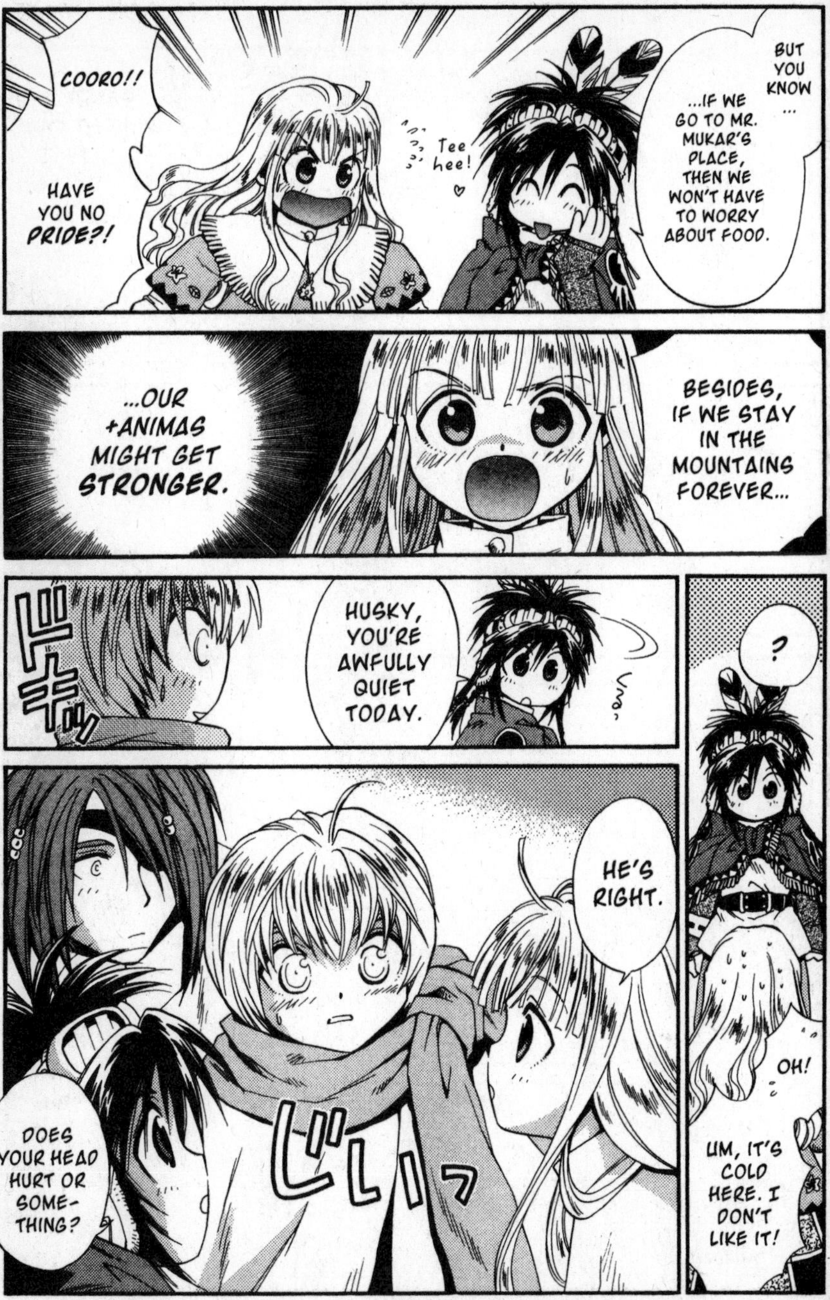
BUT YOU KNOW...
...IF WE GO TO MR. MUKAR'S PLACE, THEN WE WON'T HAVE TO WORRY ABOUT FOOD.
Tee hee!
COORO!!
HAVE YOU NO PRIDE?!
BESIDES, IF WE STAY IN THE MOUNTAINS FOREVER...
...OUR +ANIMAS MIGHT GET STRONGER.
?
OH!
UM, IT'S COLD HERE. I DON'T LIKE IT!
HUSKY, YOU'RE AWFULLY QUIET TODAY.
HE'S RIGHT.
DOES YOUR HEAD HURT OR SOMETHING?

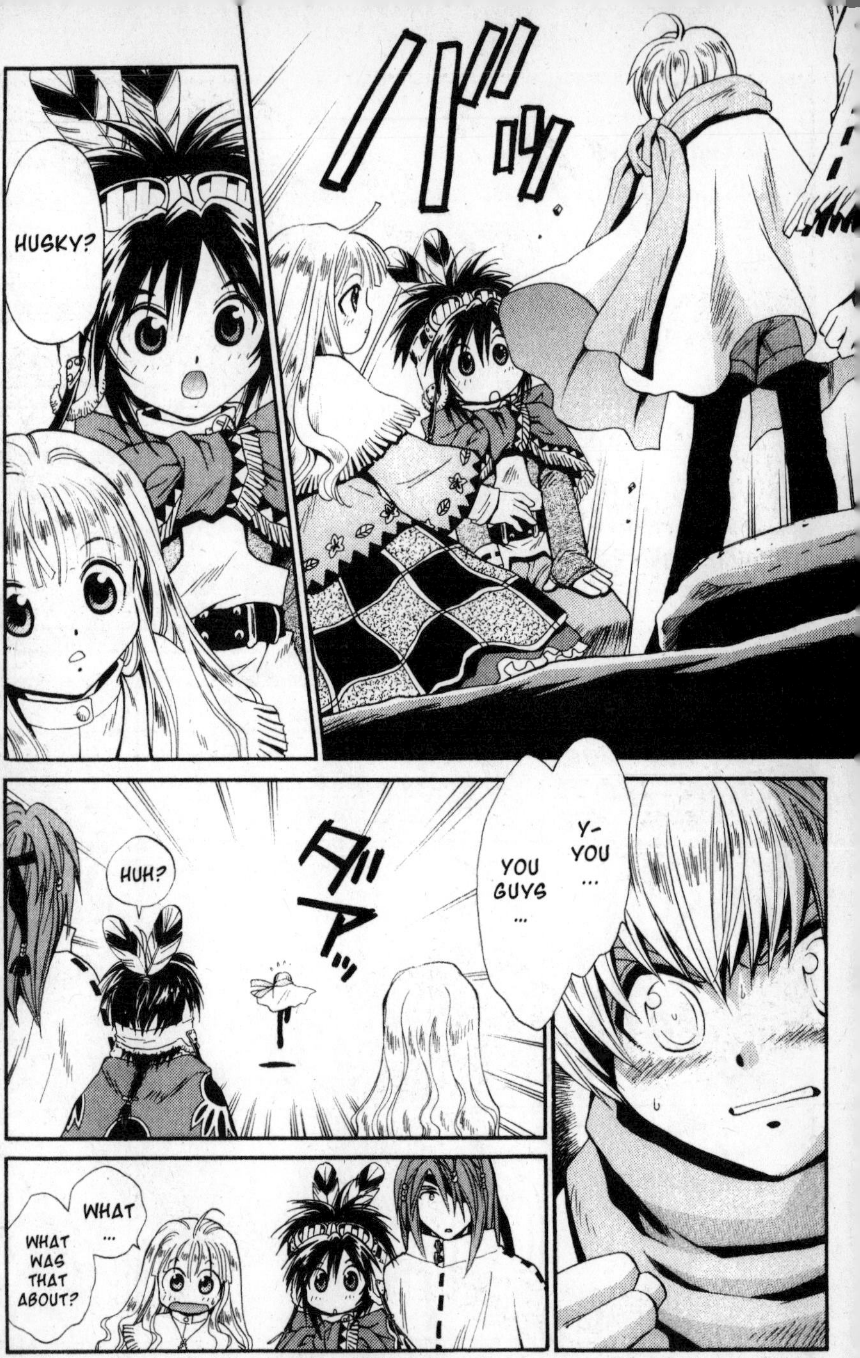
バッ
HUSKY?
Y-YOU ...
YOU GUYS ...
HUH?
ダァッ
WHAT ...
WHAT WAS THAT ABOUT?

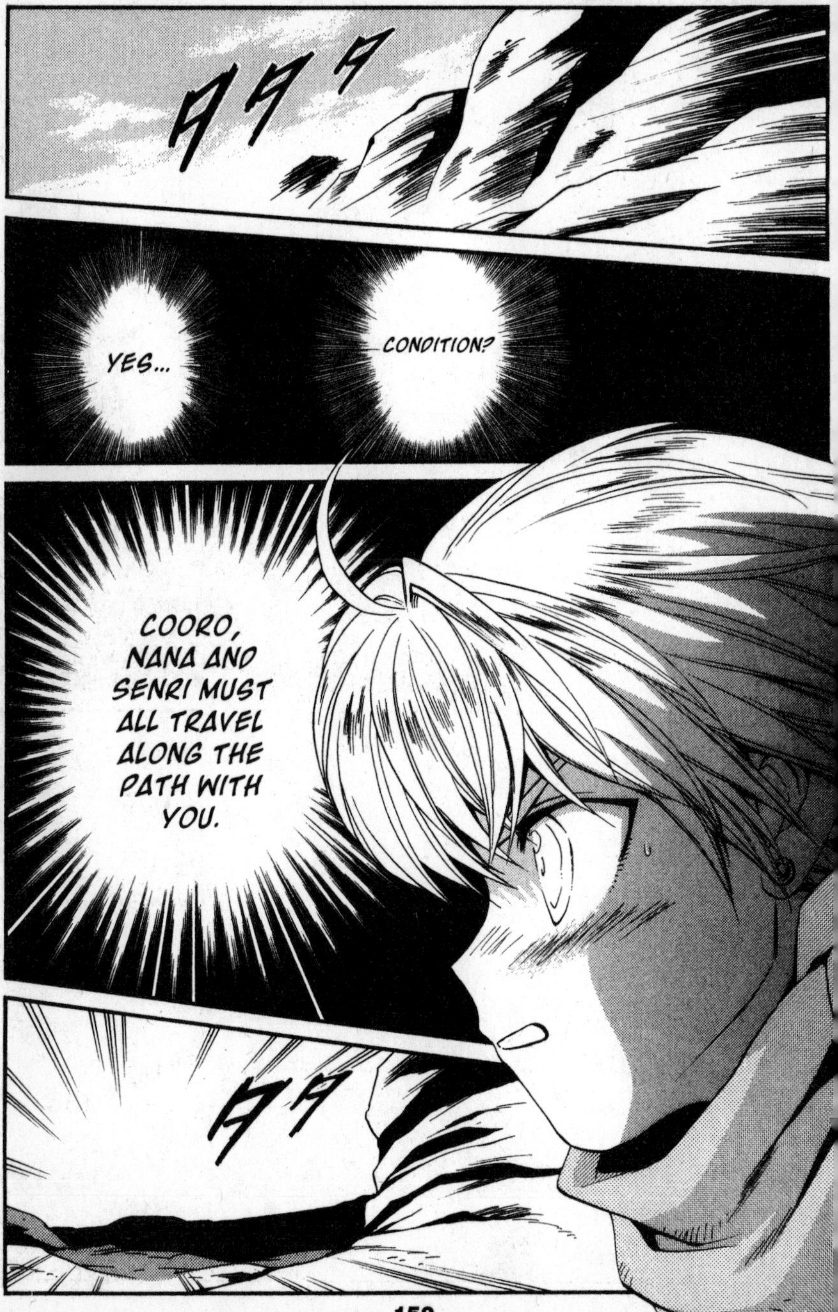
CONDITION?
YES...
COORO, NANA AND SENRI MUST ALL TRAVEL ALONG THE PATH WITH YOU.

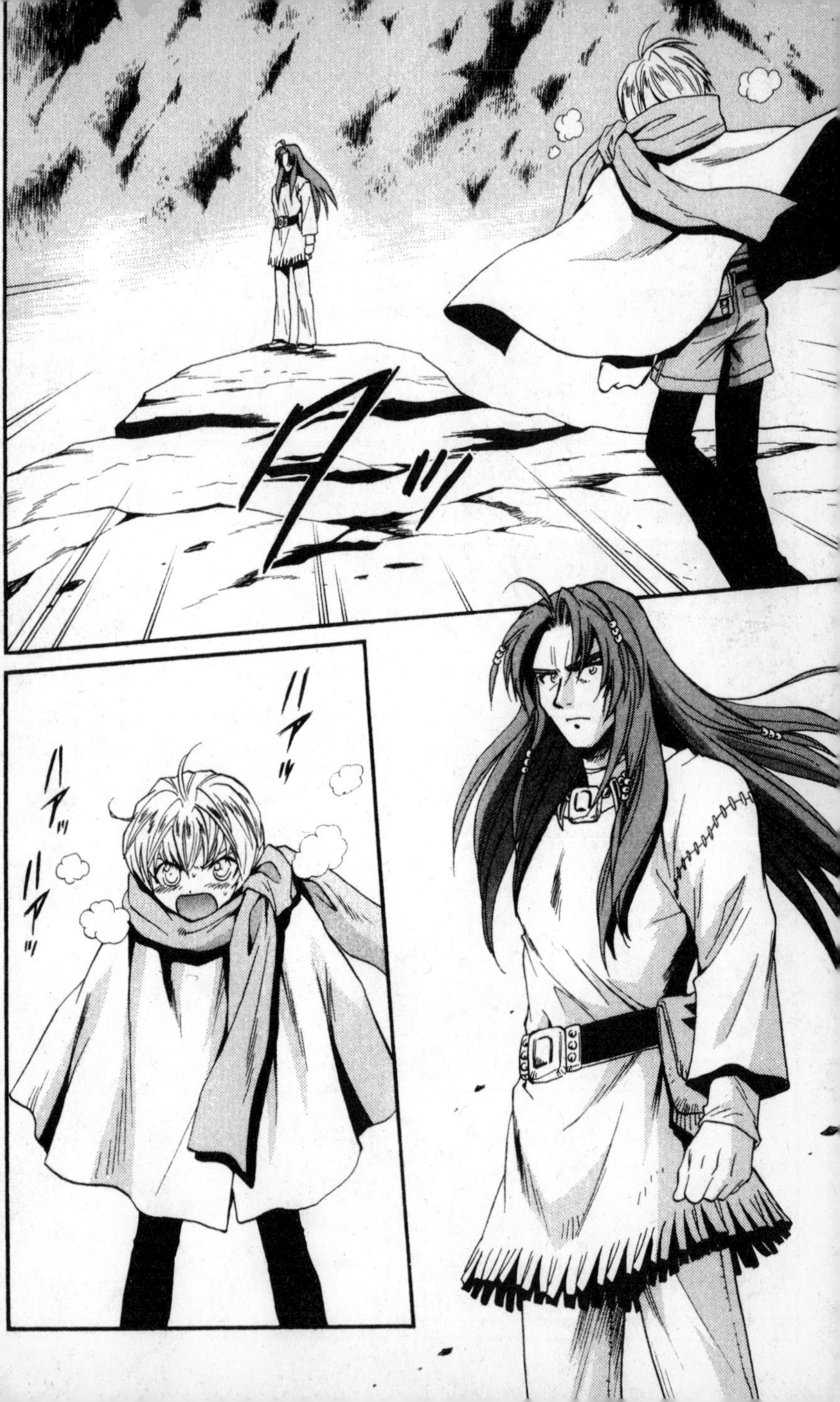
ダッ
ハァッ
ハァッ
ハァッ

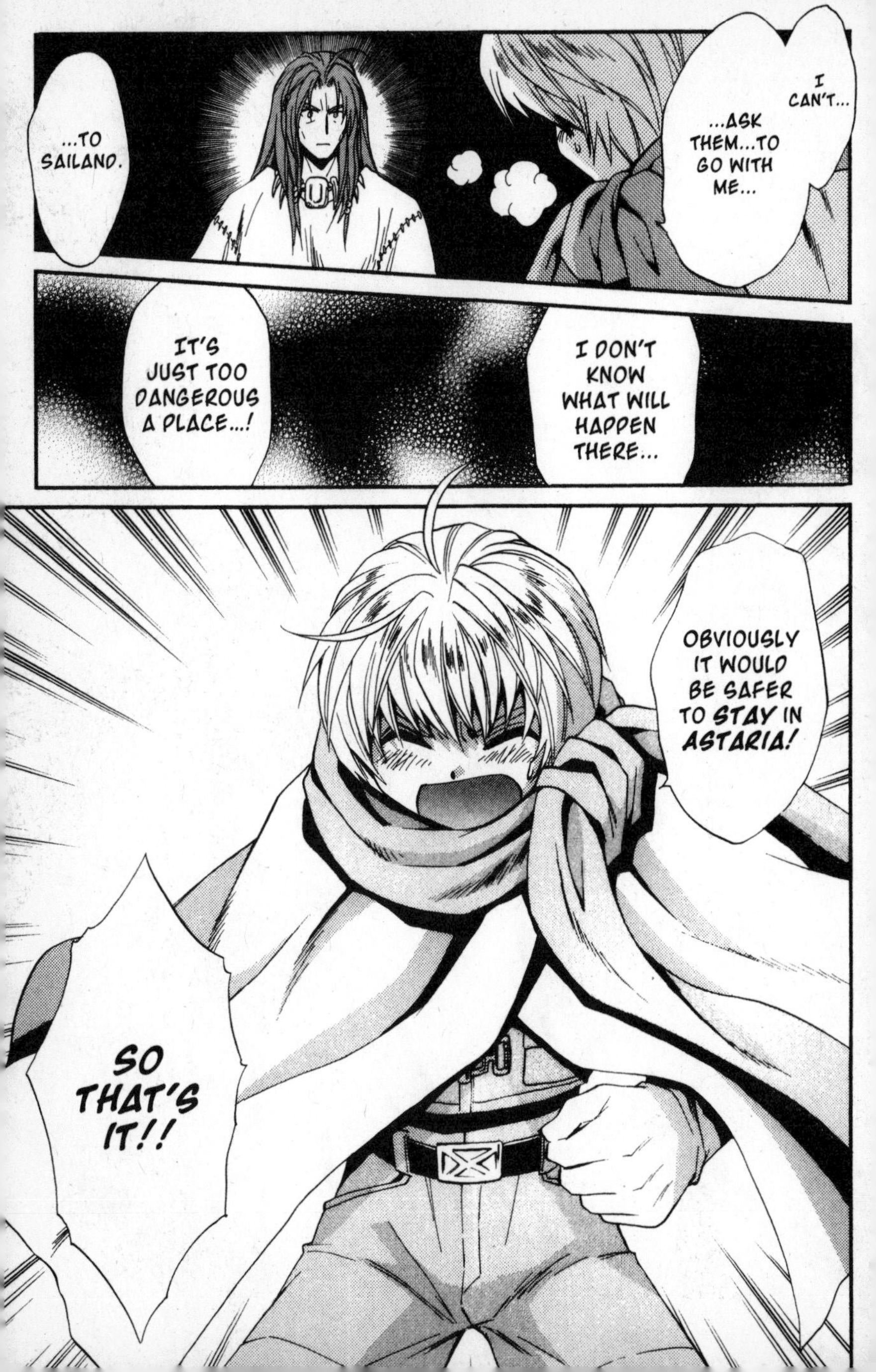
I CAN'T...
...ASK THEM...TO GO WITH ME...
...TO SAILAND.
I DON'T KNOW WHAT WILL HAPPEN THERE...
IT'S JUST TOO DANGEROUS A PLACE...!
OBVIOUSLY IT WOULD BE SAFER TO STAY IN ASTARIA!
SO THAT'S IT!!

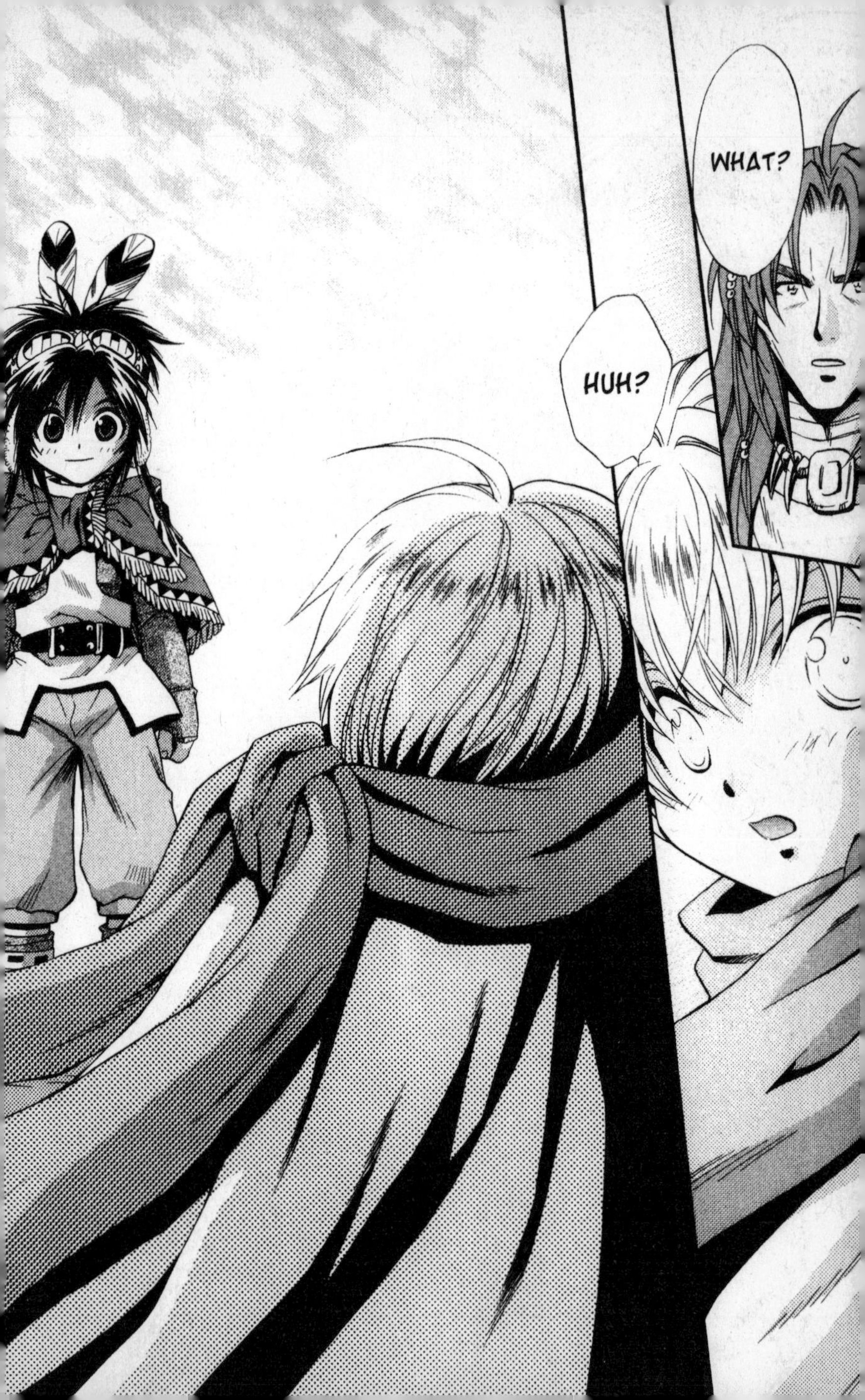
WHAT?
HUH?

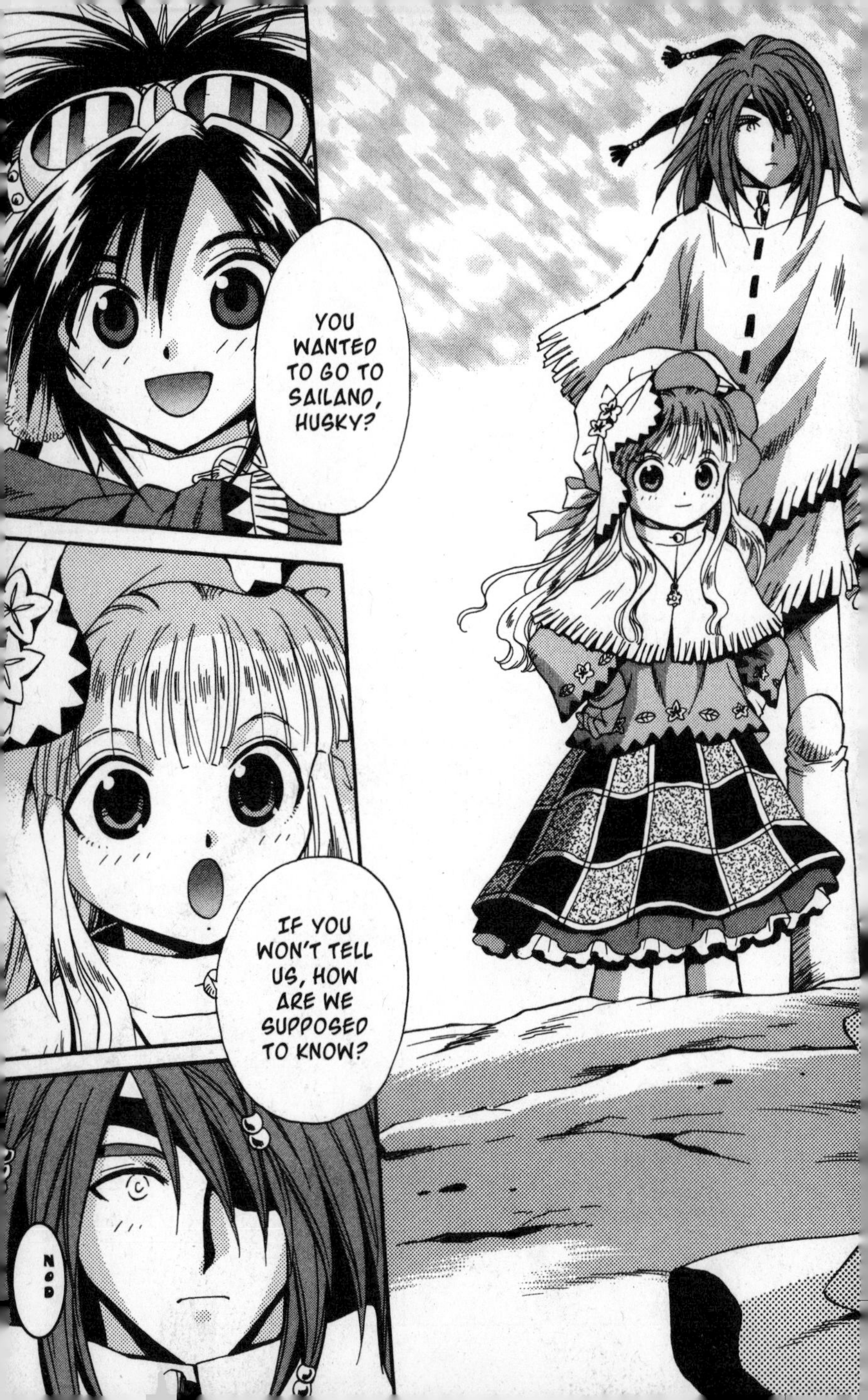
YOU WANTED TO GO TO SAILAND, HUSKY?
IF YOU WON'T TELL US, HOW ARE WE SUPPOSED TO KNOW?
NOD

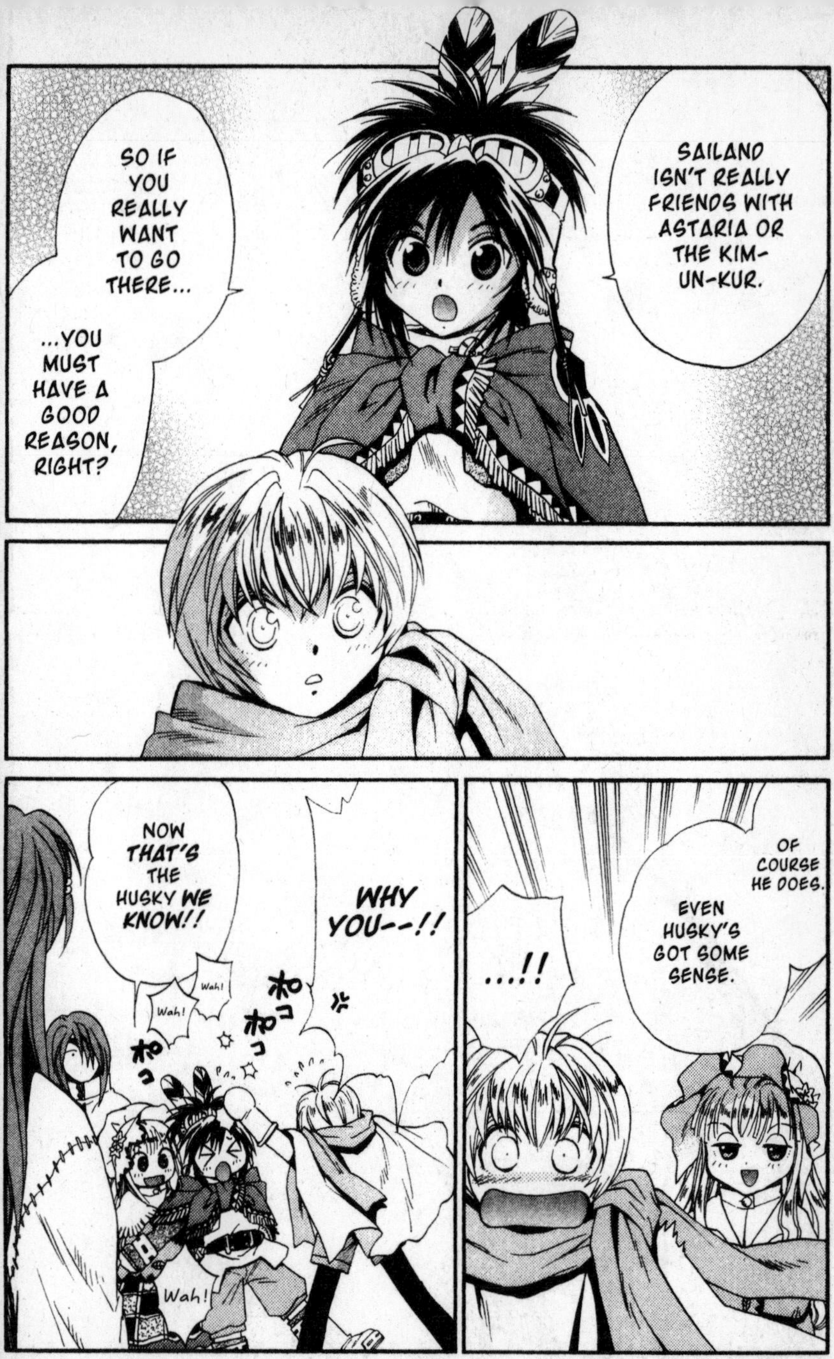
SAILAND ISN'T REALLY FRIENDS WITH ASTARIA OR THE KIM-UN-KUR.
SO IF YOU REALLY WANT TO GO THERE...
...YOU MUST HAVE A GOOD REASON, RIGHT?
OF COURSE HE DOES.
EVEN HUSKY'S GOT SOME SENSE.
...!!
WHY YOU--!!
NOW THAT'S THE HUSKY WE KNOW!!
ポコ
ポコ
Wah!
Wah!
ポコ
Wah!

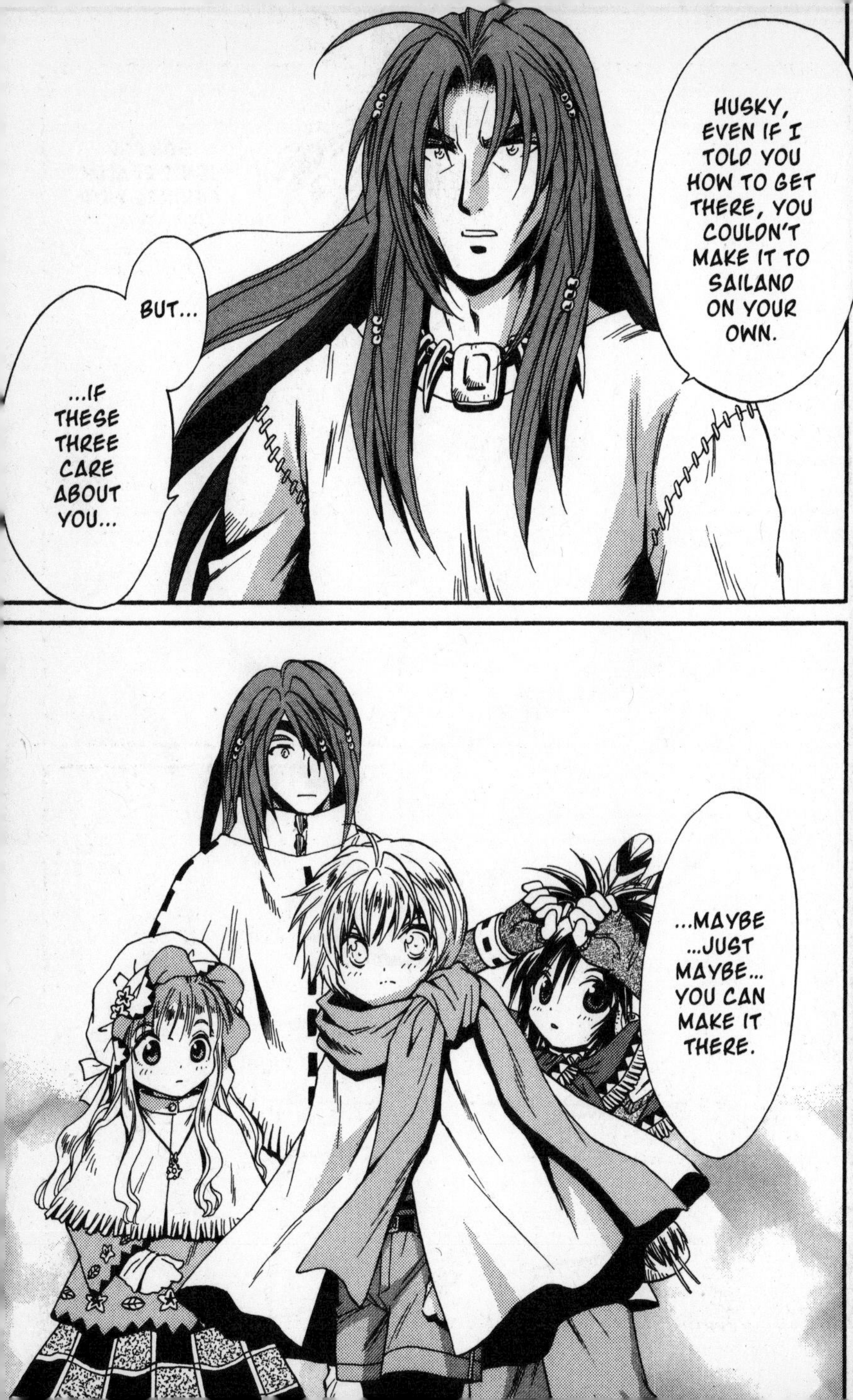
HUSKY, EVEN IF I TOLD YOU HOW TO GET THERE, YOU COULDN'T MAKE IT TO SAILAND ON YOUR OWN.
BUT...
...IF THESE THREE CARE ABOUT YOU...
...MAYBE ...JUST MAYBE... YOU CAN MAKE IT THERE.

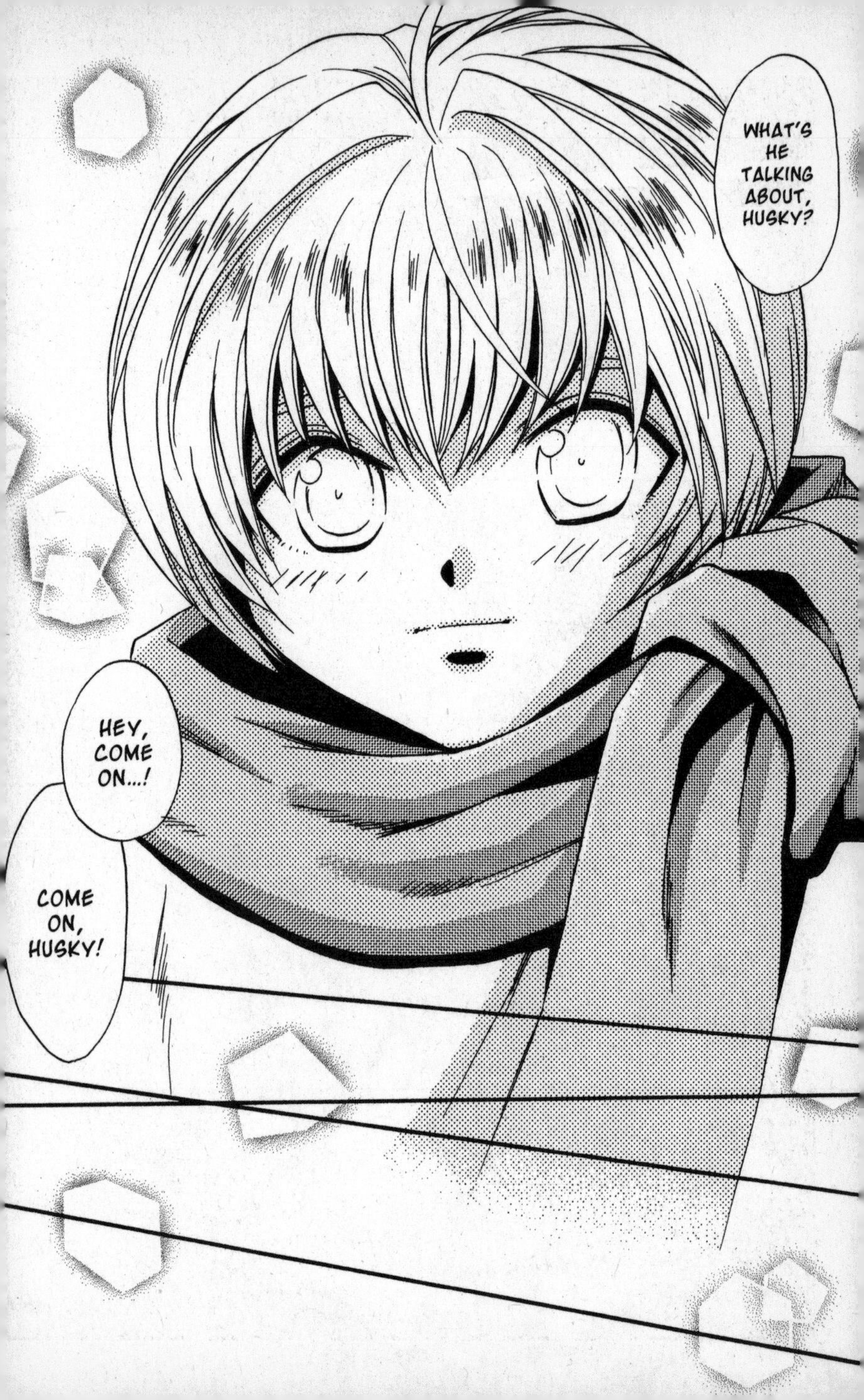
WHAT'S HE TALKING ABOUT, HUSKY?
HEY, COME ON...!
COME ON, HUSKY!

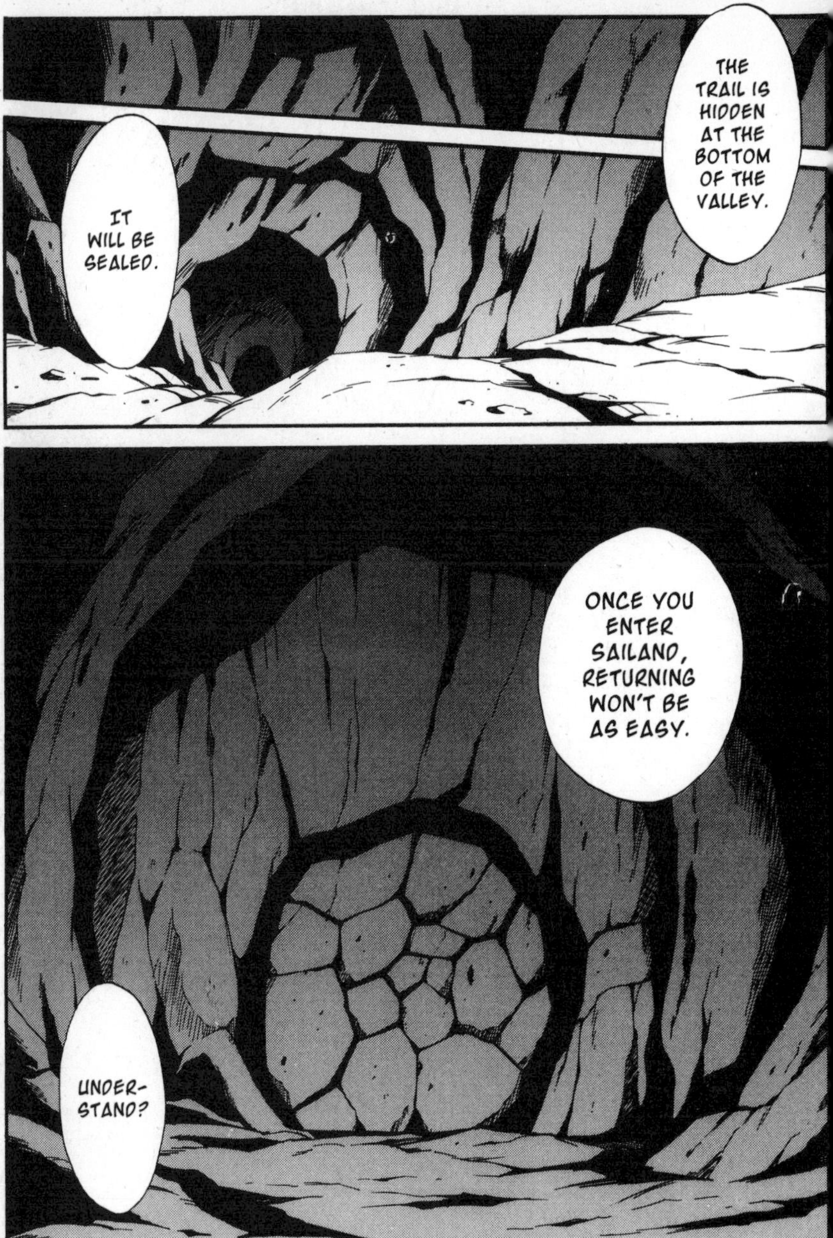
THE TRAIL IS HIDDEN AT THE BOTTOM OF THE VALLEY.
IT WILL BE SEALED.
ONCE YOU ENTER SAILAND, RETURNING WON'T BE AS EASY.
UNDER-STAND?

Disappearing

WHEN WE USE THE ERASER AFTER INKING...
OOPS!
HIS HAND DISAP-PEARED!
This part has been inked.
It's a divine message from our ancestors...
I must have gotten distracted.
...THESE THINGS HAPPEN OFTEN.
Oh, dear...!
ESPE-CIALLY WITH SENRI.
OOPS!
HIS MOUTH DISAP-PEARS A LOT.
Since it's almost like his mouth doesn't exist anyway.
IS IT OKAY TO LEAVE SENRI'S MOUTH OFF?
...
HE NEEDS IT.

Chapter 32:
A Story in the Snow

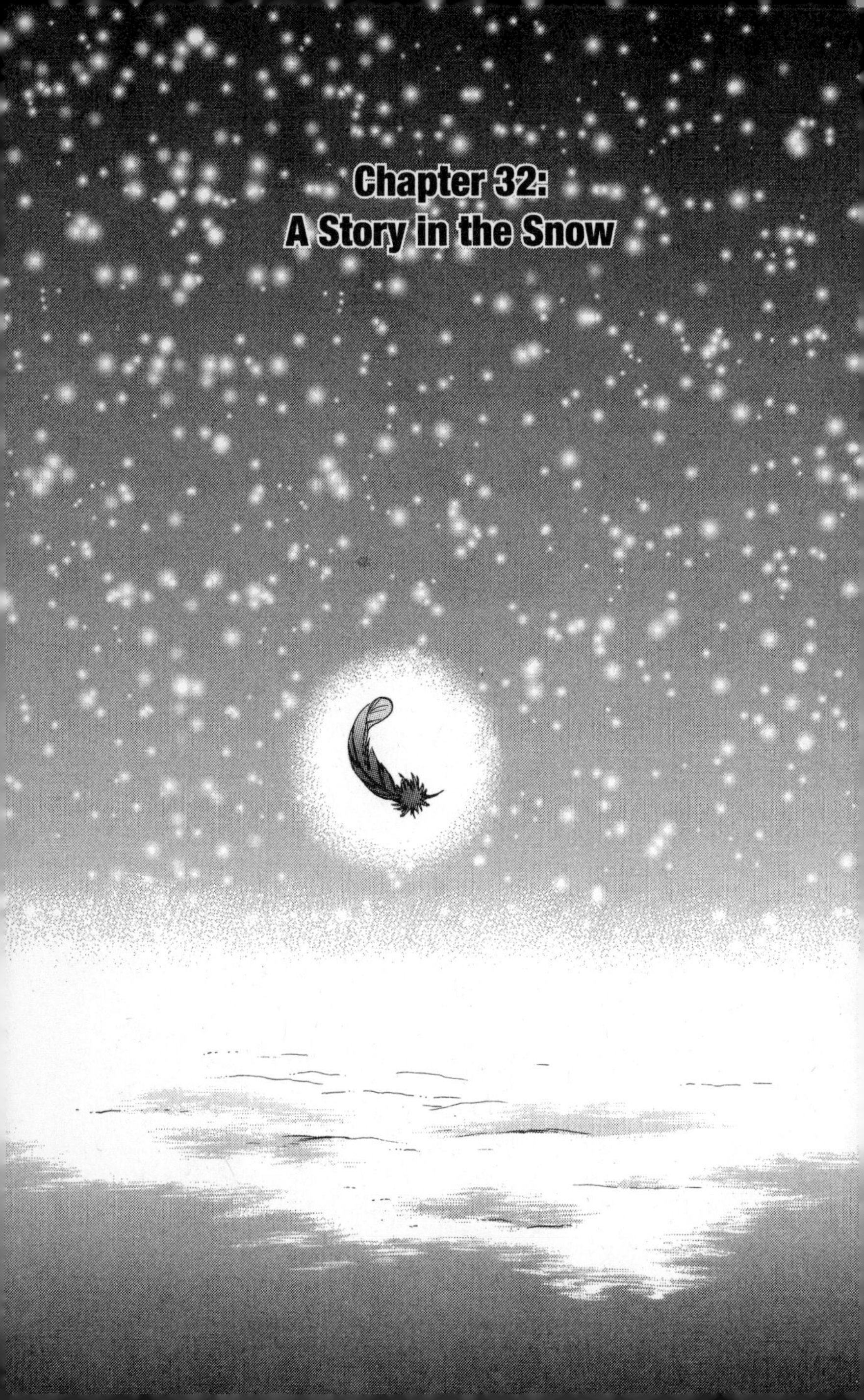

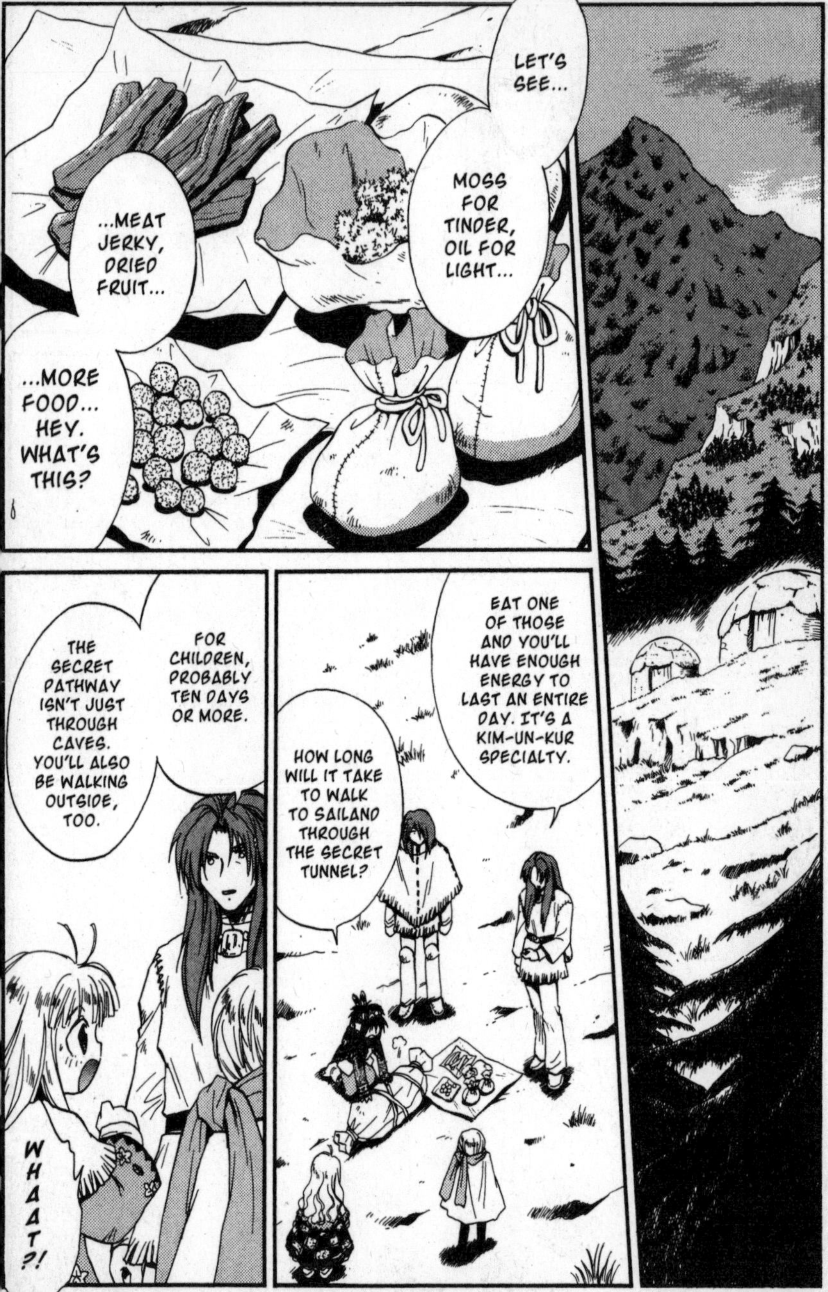
LET'S SEE...
MOSS FOR TINDER, OIL FOR LIGHT...
...MEAT JERKY, DRIED FRUIT...
...MORE FOOD... HEY. WHAT'S THIS?
EAT ONE OF THOSE AND YOU'LL HAVE ENOUGH ENERGY TO LAST AN ENTIRE DAY. IT'S A KIM-UN-KUR SPECIALTY.
HOW LONG WILL IT TAKE TO WALK TO SAILAND THROUGH THE SECRET TUNNEL?
FOR CHILDREN, PROBABLY TEN DAYS OR MORE.
THE SECRET PATHWAY ISN'T JUST THROUGH CAVES. YOU'LL ALSO BE WALKING OUTSIDE, TOO.
WHAAAT?!

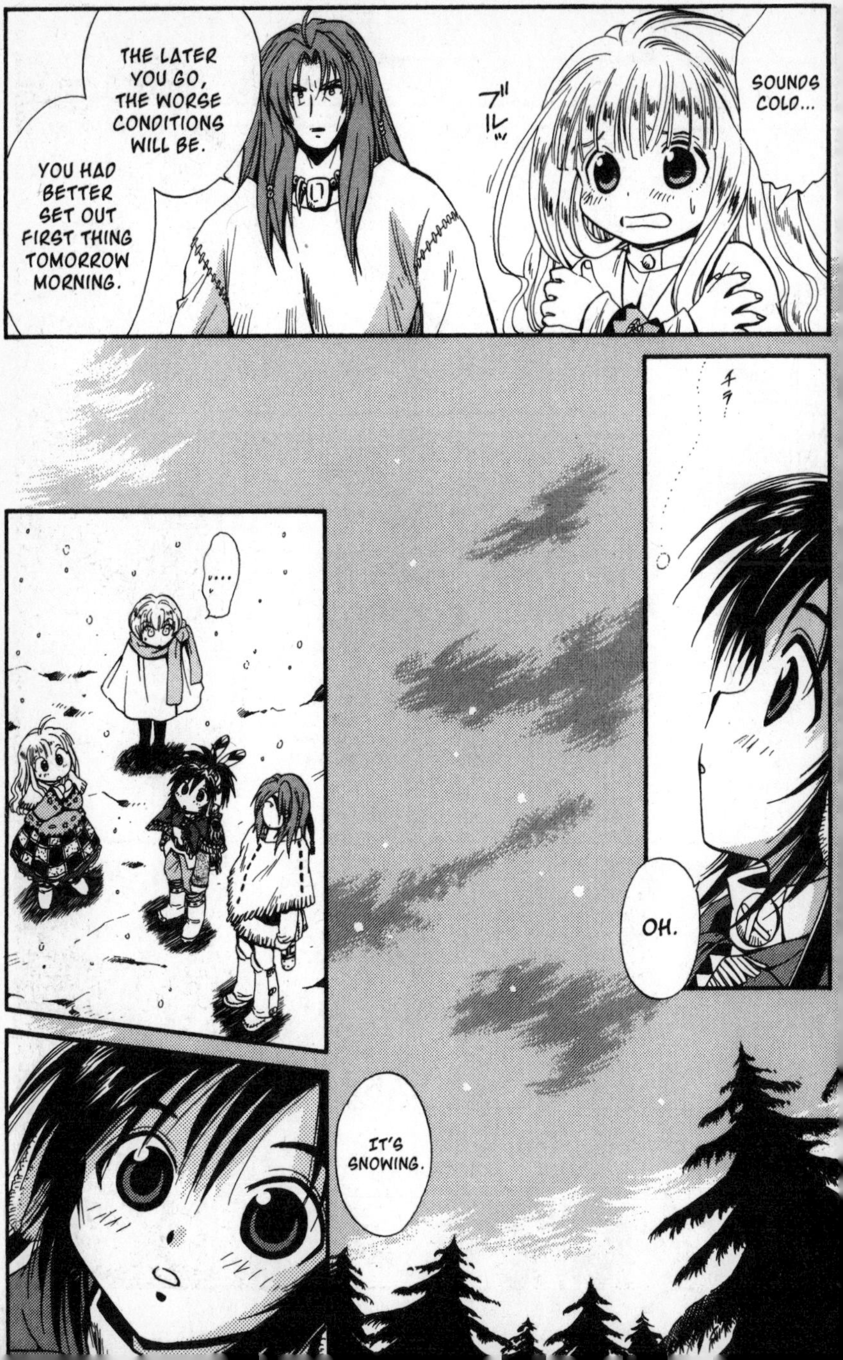
SOUNDS COLD...
ブルッ
THE LATER YOU GO, THE WORSE CONDITIONS WILL BE.
YOU HAD BETTER SET OUT FIRST THING TOMORROW MORNING.
チラ…
OH.
...
IT'S SNOWING.

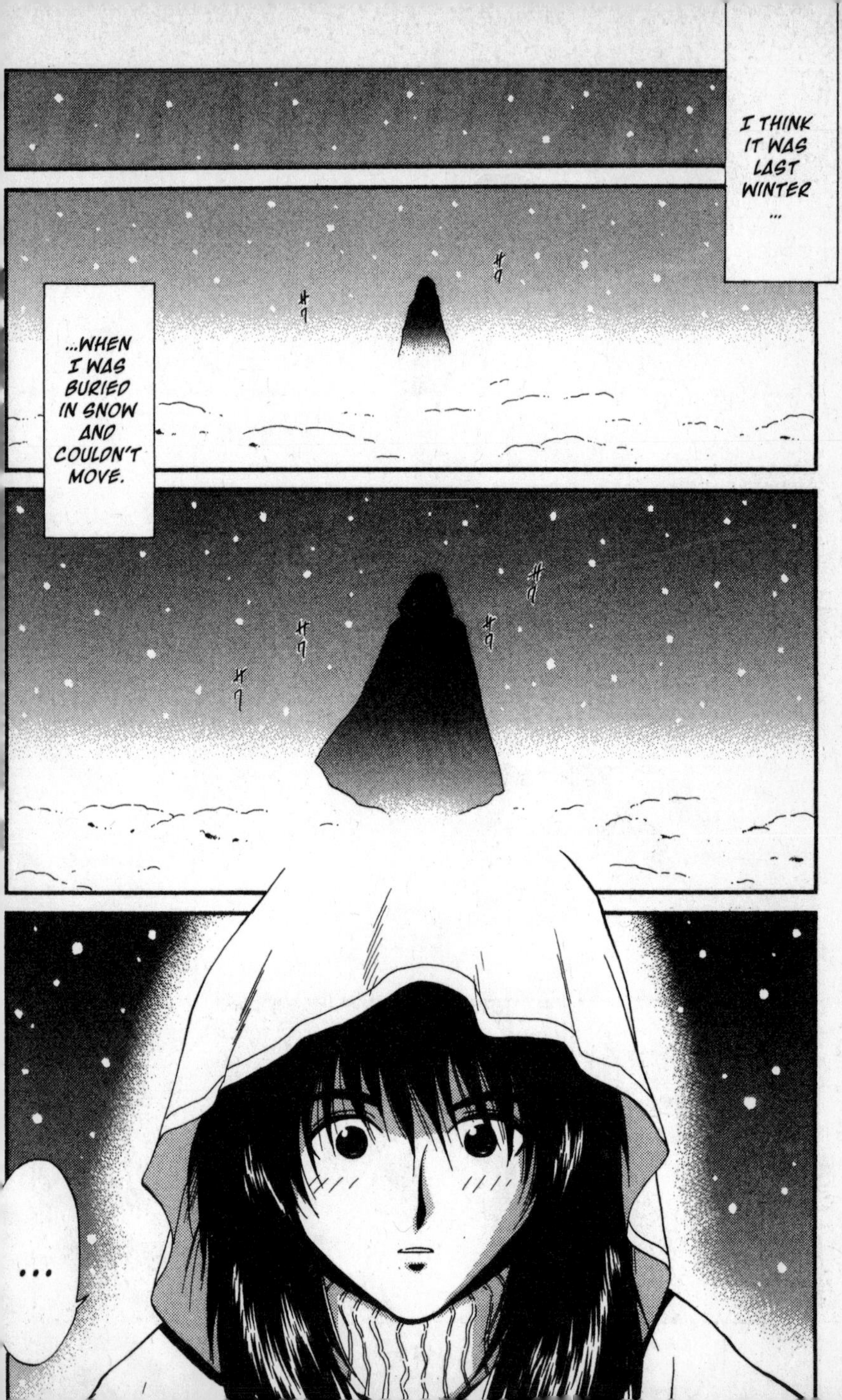
I THINK IT WAS LAST WINTER ...
...WHEN I WAS BURIED IN SNOW AND COULDN'T MOVE.
...

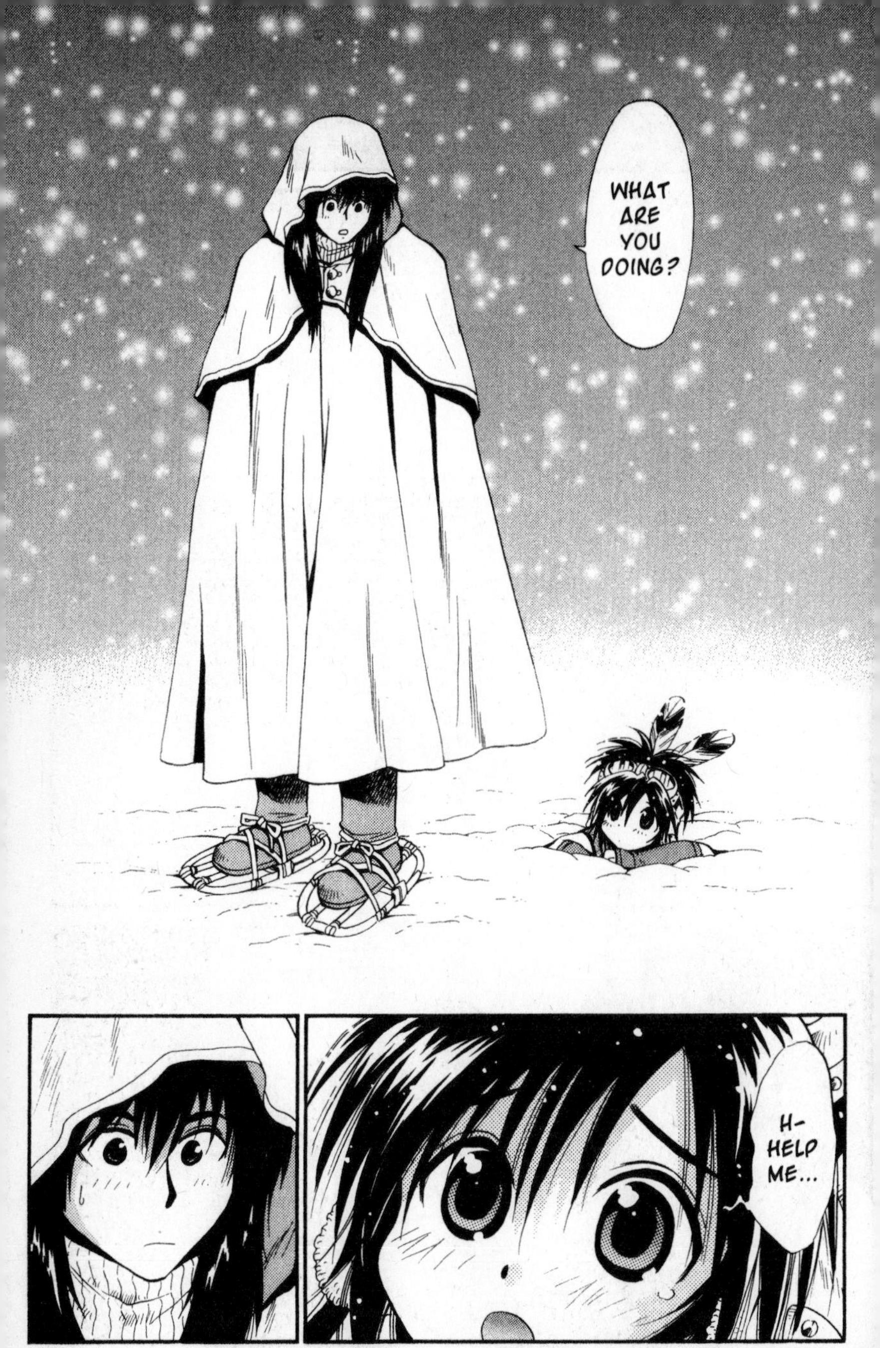
WHAT ARE YOU DOING?
H-HELP ME...

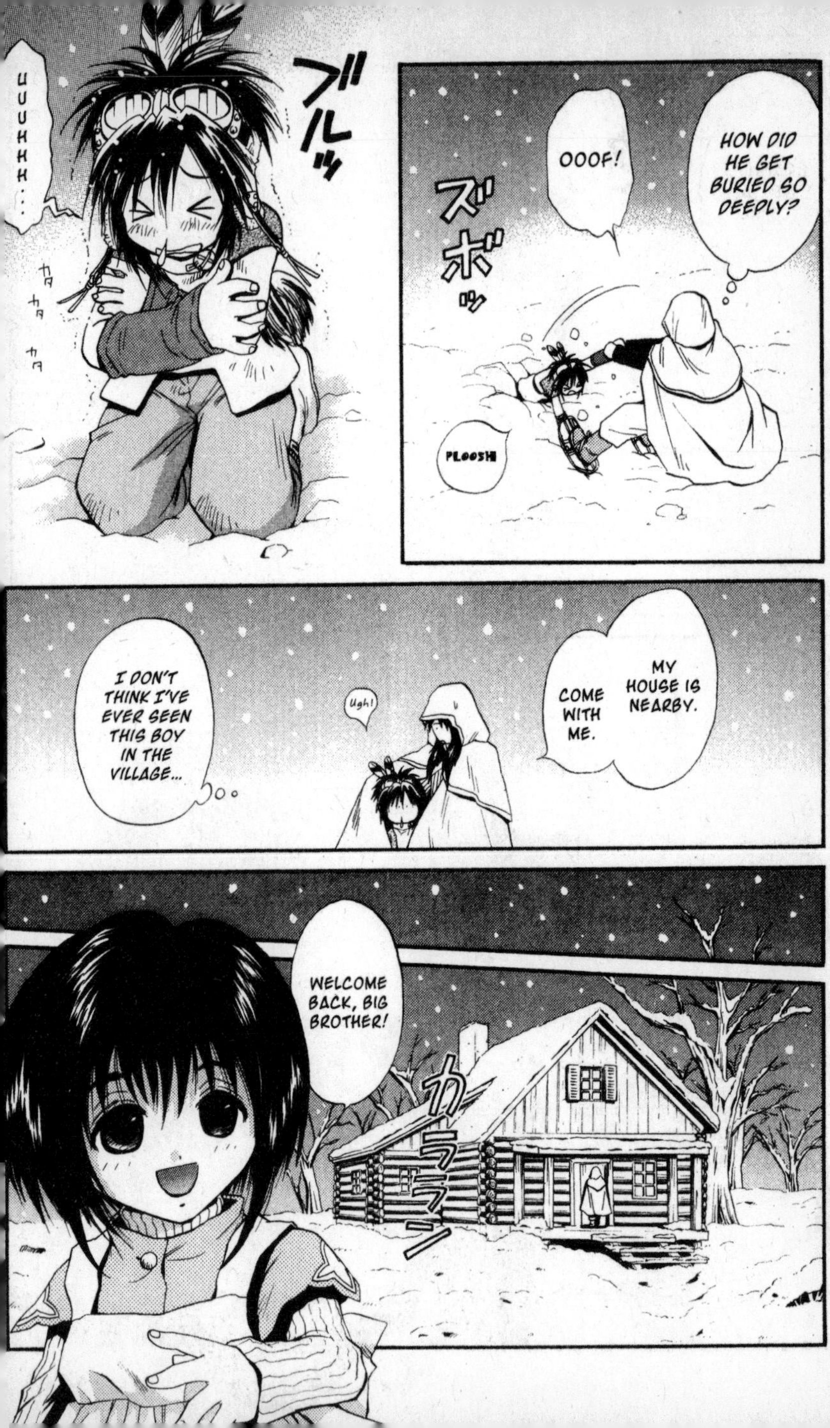
HOW DID HE GET BURIED SO DEEPLY?
OOOF!
ズボッ
PLOOSH
ブルッ
UUUHHHH...
カタカタカタ
MY HOUSE IS NEARBY.
COME WITH ME.
Ugh!
I DON'T THINK I'VE EVER SEEN THIS BOY IN THE VILLAGE...
WELCOME BACK, BIG BROTHER!
カララン

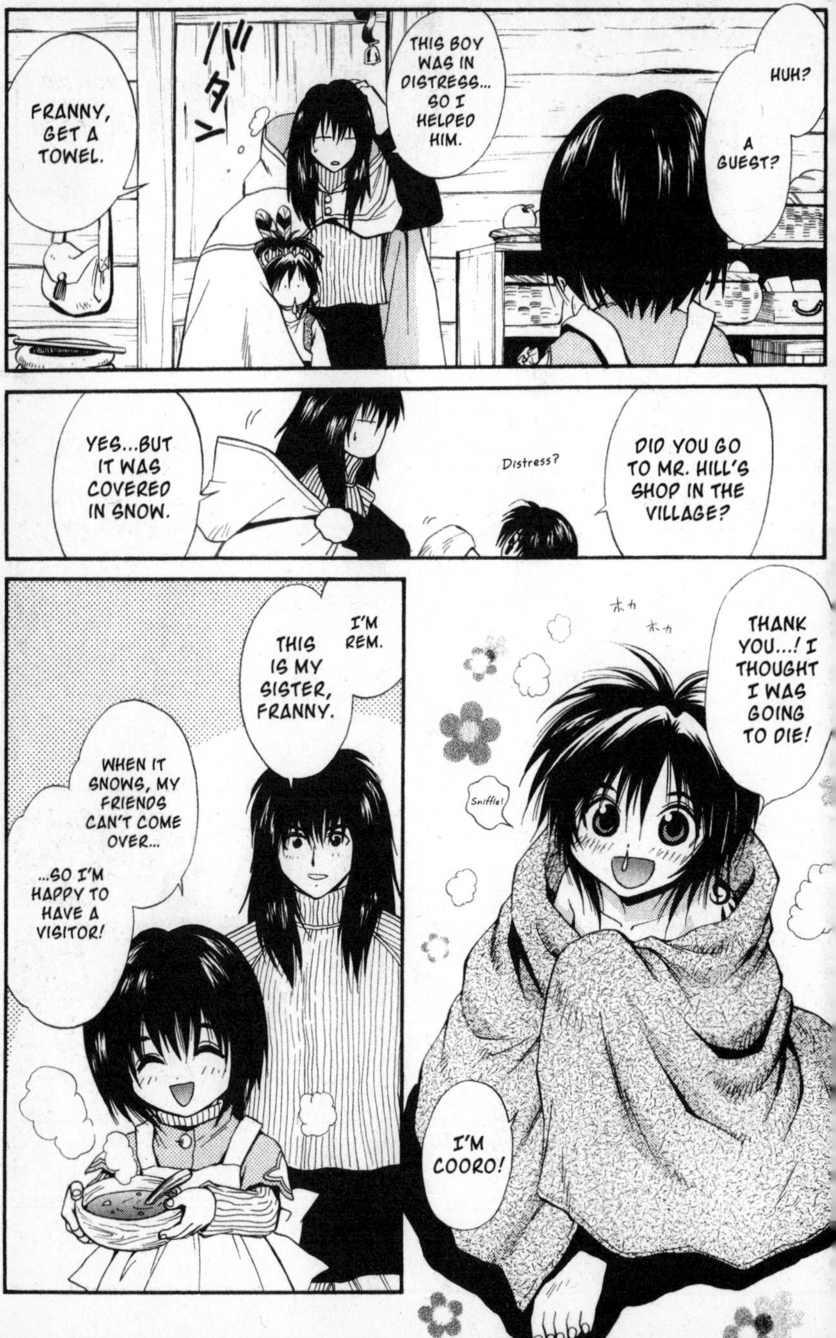
HUH?
A GUEST?
THIS BOY WAS IN DISTRESS... SO I HELPED HIM.
バタン
FRANNY, GET A TOWEL.
DID YOU GO TO MR. HILL'S SHOP IN THE VILLAGE?
Distress?
YES...BUT IT WAS COVERED IN SNOW.
THANK YOU...! I THOUGHT I WAS GOING TO DIE!
Sniffle!
I'M COORO!
I'M REM.
THIS IS MY SISTER, FRANNY.
WHEN IT SNOWS, MY FRIENDS CAN'T COME OVER...
...SO I'M HAPPY TO HAVE A VISITOR!

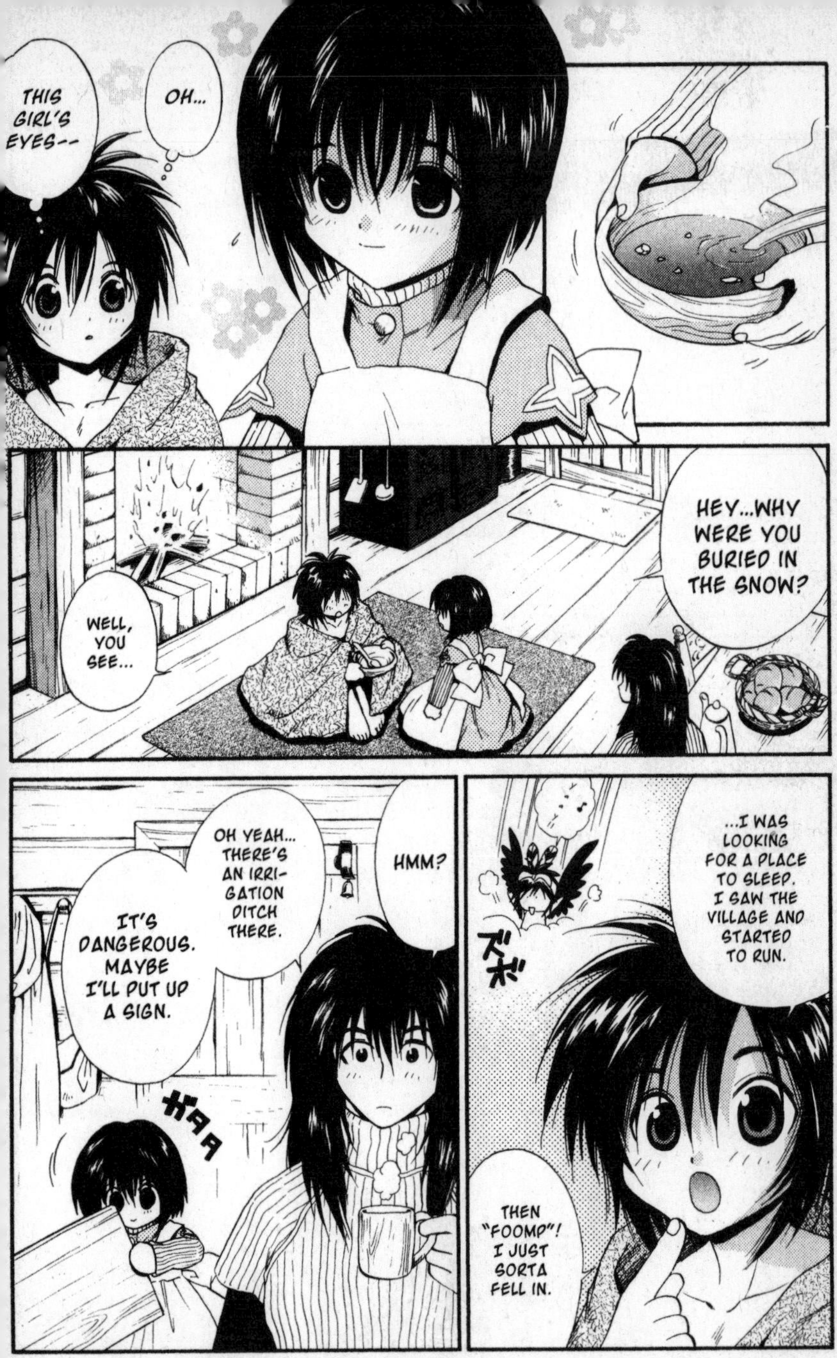
OH...
THIS GIRL'S EYES--
HEY...WHY WERE YOU BURIED IN THE SNOW?
WELL, YOU SEE...
...I WAS LOOKING FOR A PLACE TO SLEEP. I SAW THE VILLAGE AND STARTED TO RUN.
ズボ
THEN "FOOMP"! I JUST SORTA FELL IN.
HMM?
OH YEAH... THERE'S AN IRRIGATION DITCH THERE.
IT'S DANGEROUS. MAYBE I'LL PUT UP A SIGN.
ガタタ

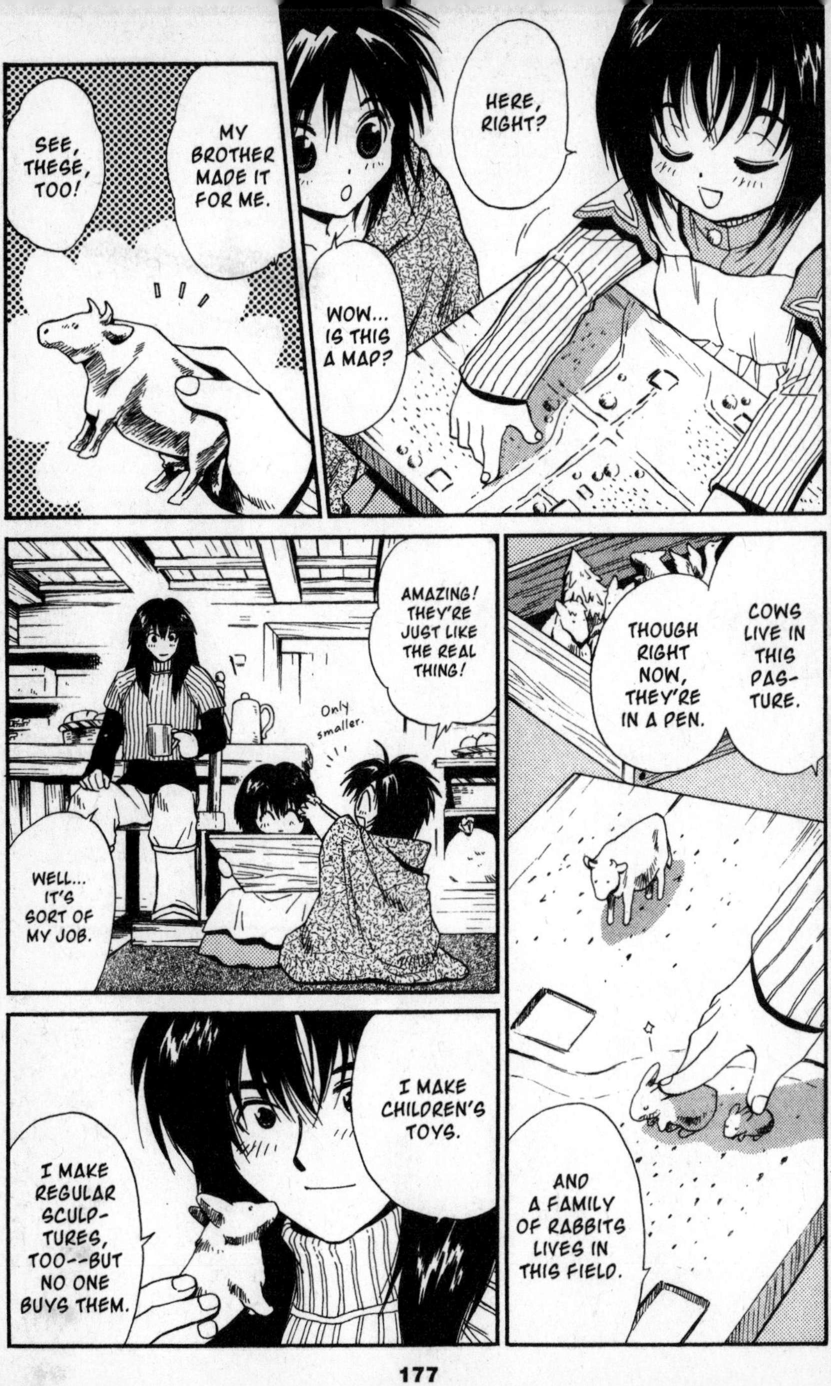
HERE, RIGHT?
WOW... IS THIS A MAP?
MY BROTHER MADE IT FOR ME.
SEE, THESE, TOO!
COWS LIVE IN THIS PAS-TURE.
THOUGH RIGHT NOW, THEY'RE IN A PEN.
AND A FAMILY OF RABBITS LIVES IN THIS FIELD.
AMAZING! THEY'RE JUST LIKE THE REAL THING!
Only smaller.
WELL... IT'S SORT OF MY JOB.
I MAKE CHILDREN'S TOYS.
I MAKE REGULAR SCULP-TURES, TOO--BUT NO ONE BUYS THEM.

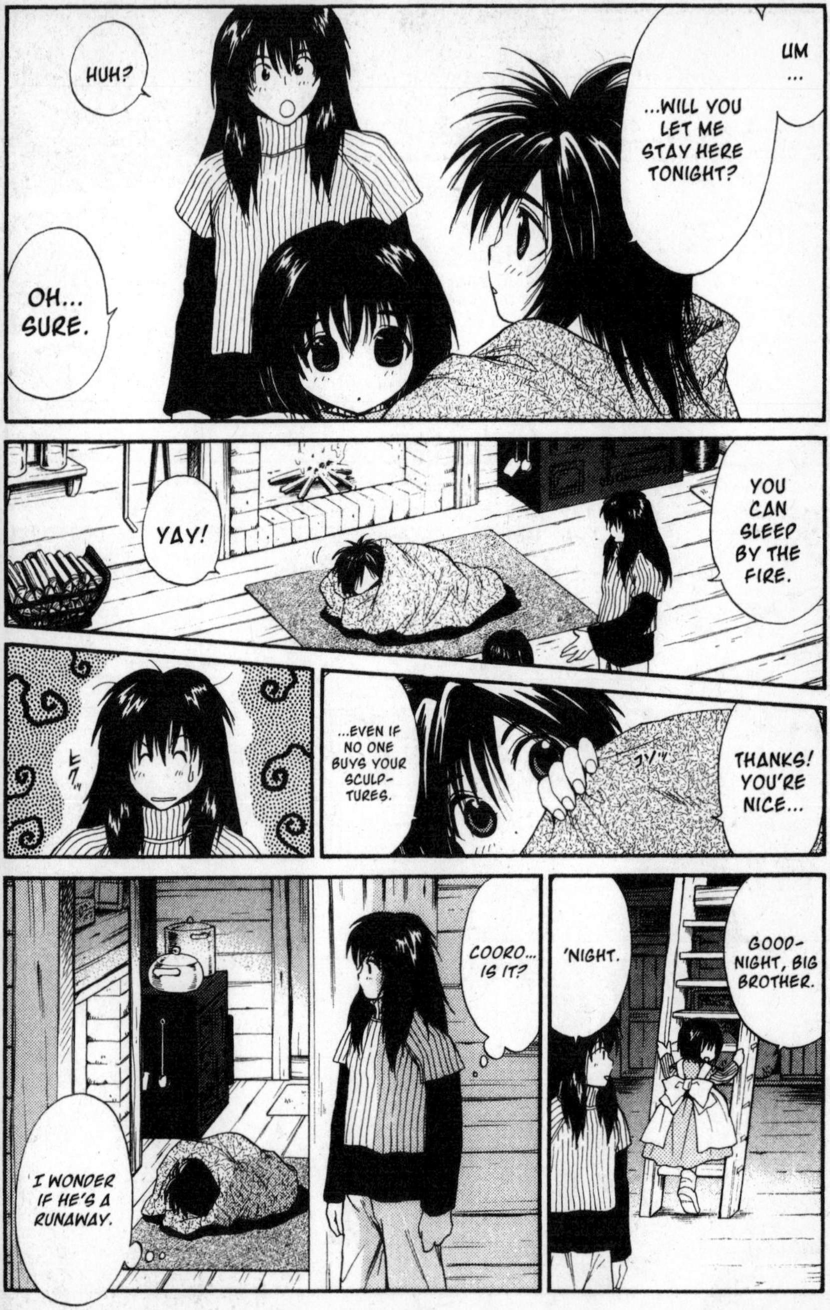
UM ...
...WILL YOU LET ME STAY HERE TONIGHT?
HUH?
OH... SURE.
YOU CAN SLEEP BY THE FIRE.
YAY!
THANKS! YOU'RE NICE...
...EVEN IF NO ONE BUYS YOUR SCULP-TURES.
GOOD-NIGHT, BIG BROTHER.
'NIGHT.
COORO... IS IT?
I WONDER IF HE'S A RUNAWAY.

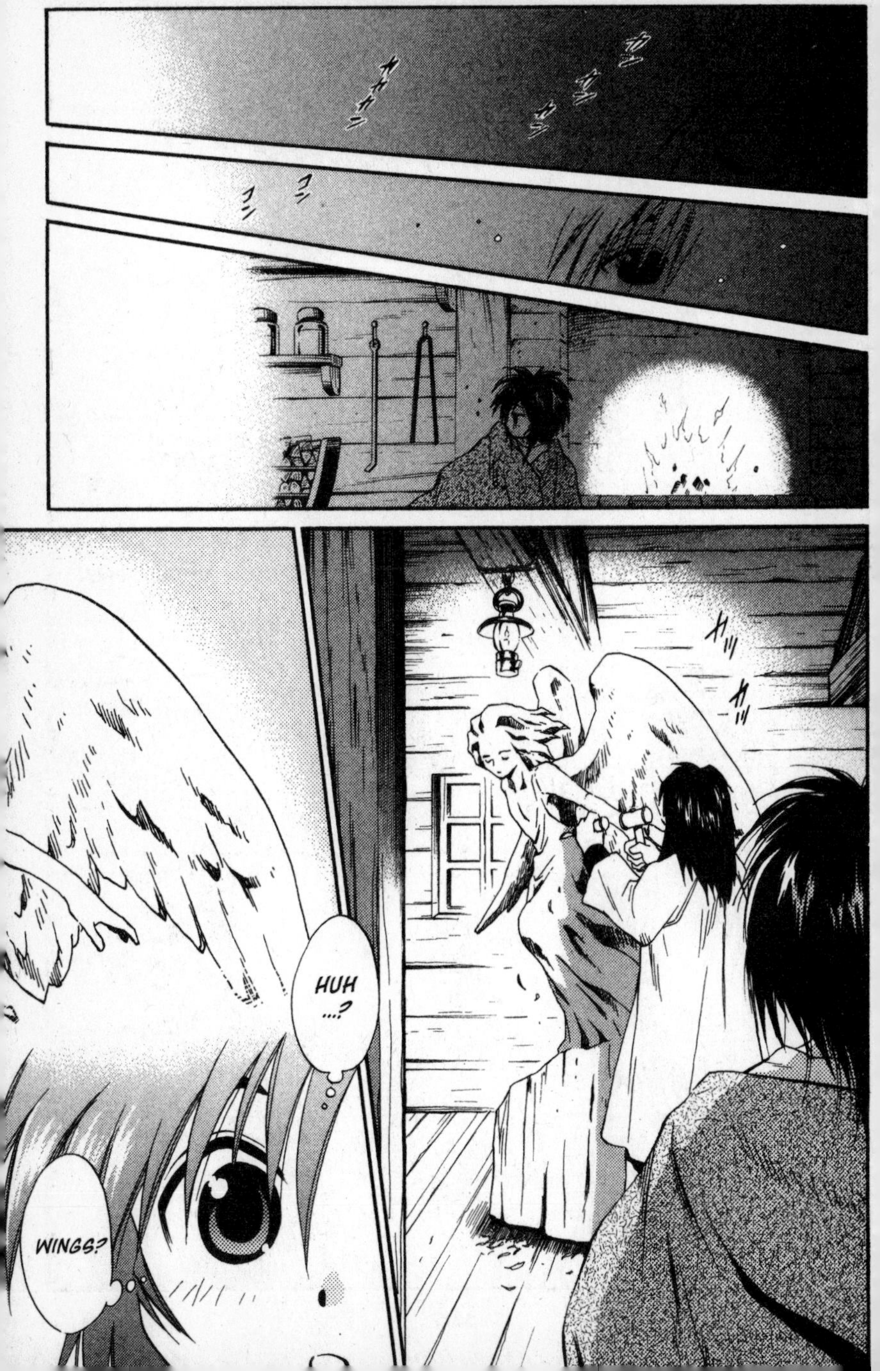
HUH ...?
WINGS?

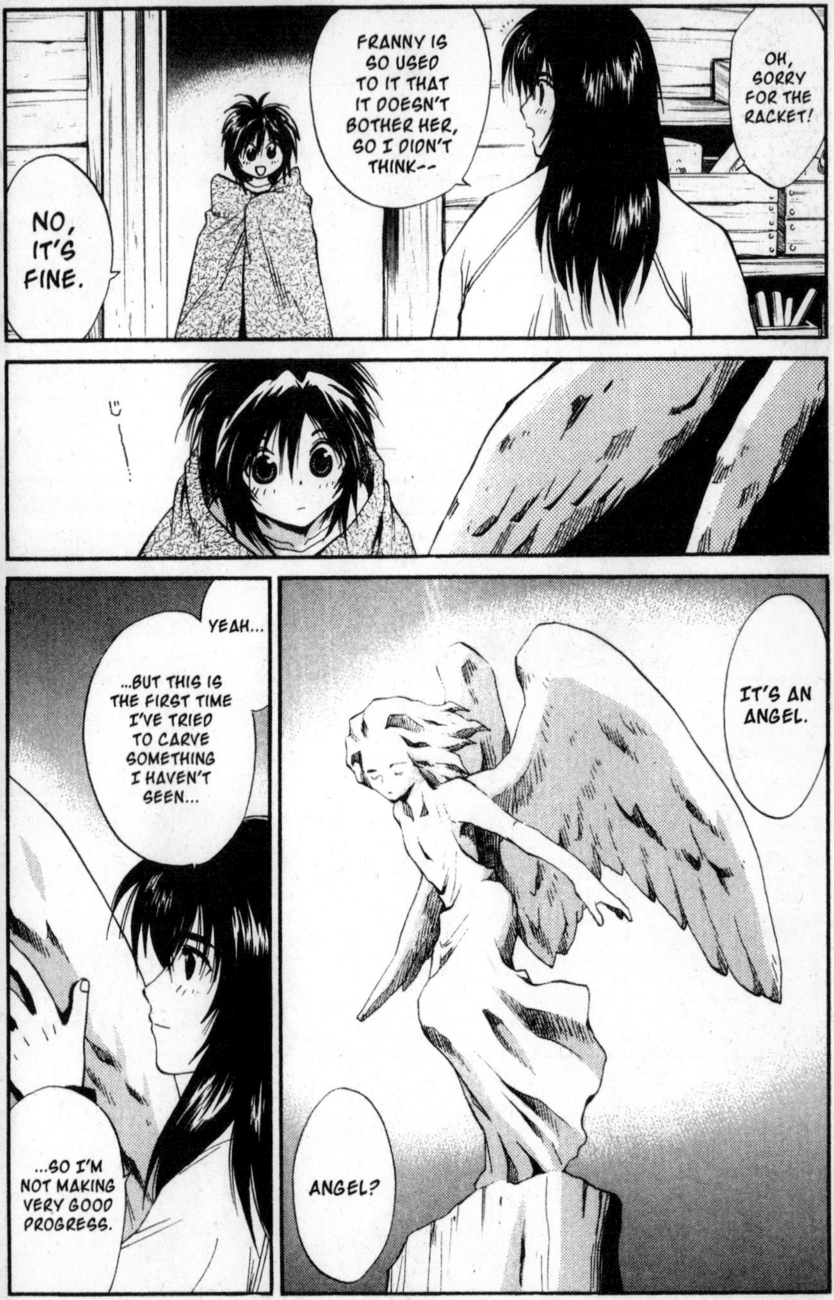
OH, SORRY FOR THE RACKET!
FRANNY IS SO USED TO IT THAT IT DOESN'T BOTHER HER, SO I DIDN'T THINK--
NO, IT'S FINE.
じー
IT'S AN ANGEL.
ANGEL?
YEAH...
...BUT THIS IS THE FIRST TIME I'VE TRIED TO CARVE SOMETHING I HAVEN'T SEEN...
...SO I'M NOT MAKING VERY GOOD PROGRESS.

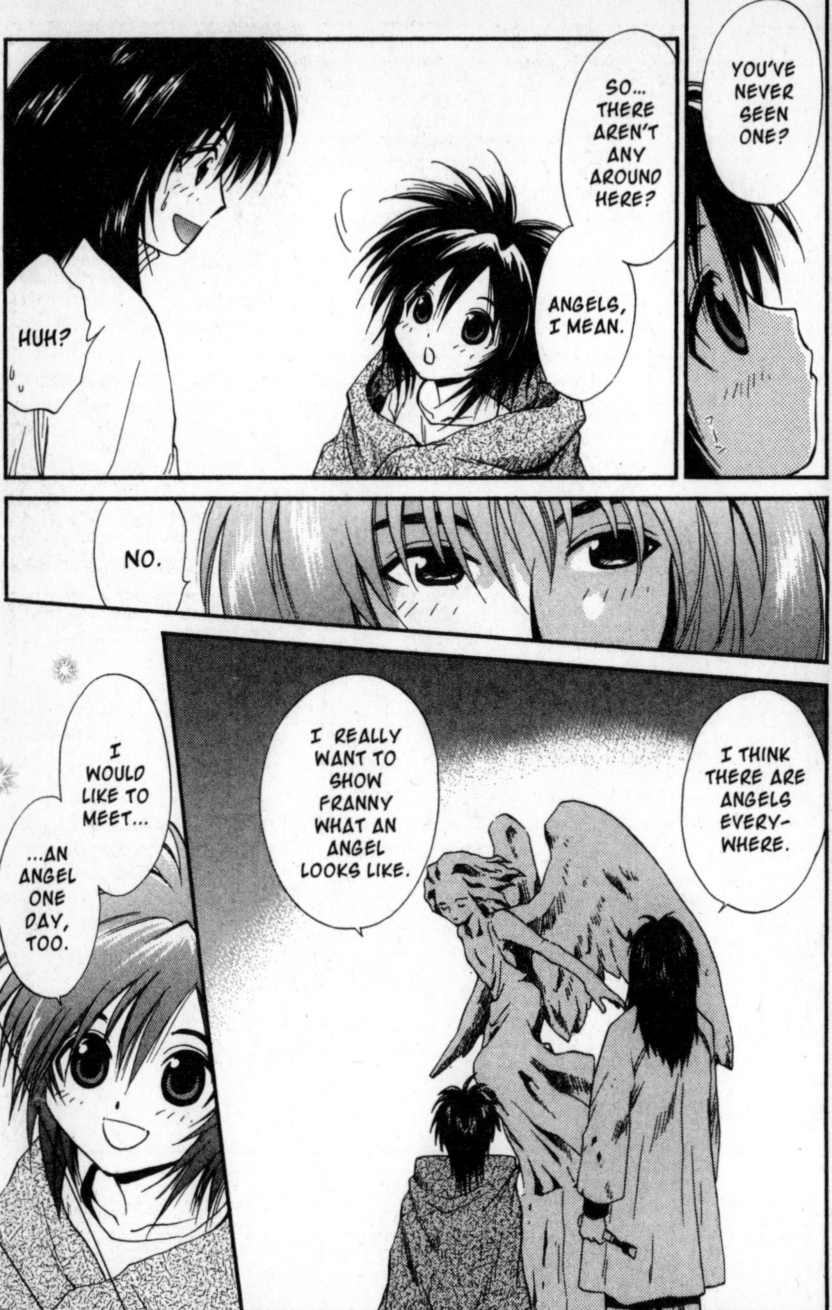
YOU'VE NEVER SEEN ONE?
SO... THERE AREN'T ANY AROUND HERE?
ANGELS, I MEAN.
HUH?
NO.
I THINK THERE ARE ANGELS EVERY-WHERE.
I REALLY WANT TO SHOW FRANNY WHAT AN ANGEL LOOKS LIKE.
I WOULD LIKE TO MEET...
...AN ANGEL ONE DAY, TOO.

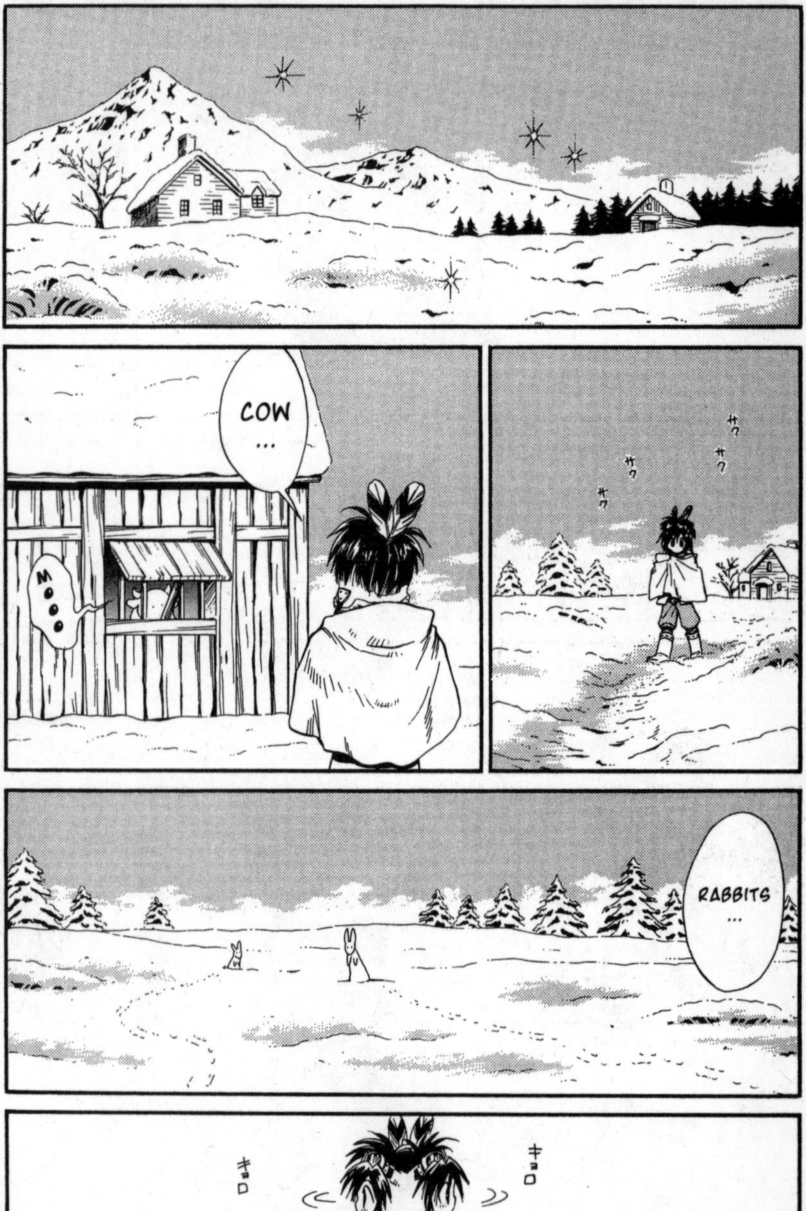
サク
サク
サク
サク
COW ...
MOOO
RABBITS ...
キョロ
キョロ

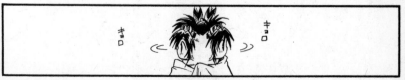

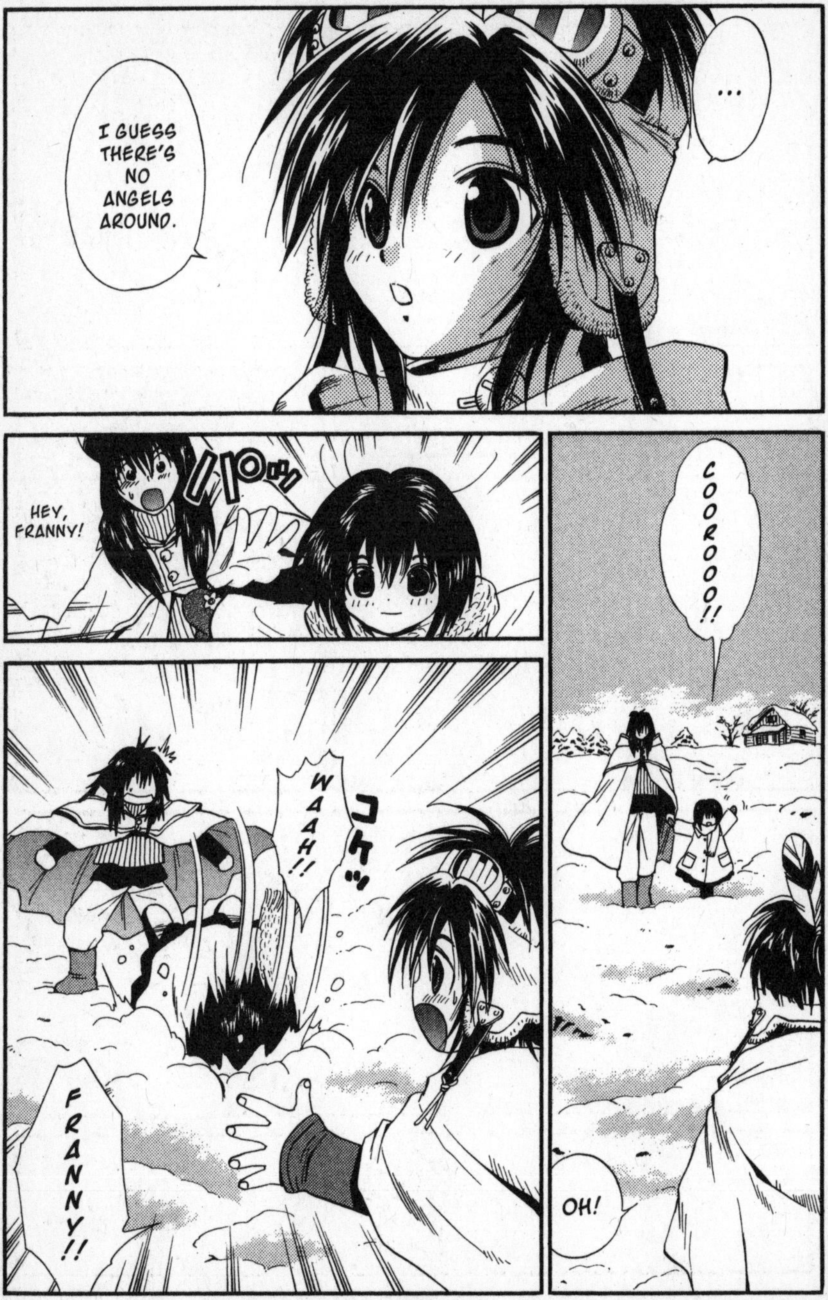
...
I GUESS THERE'S NO ANGELS AROUND.
COOROOOO!!
OH!
HEY, FRANNY!
WAAH!!
コケッ
FRANNY!!

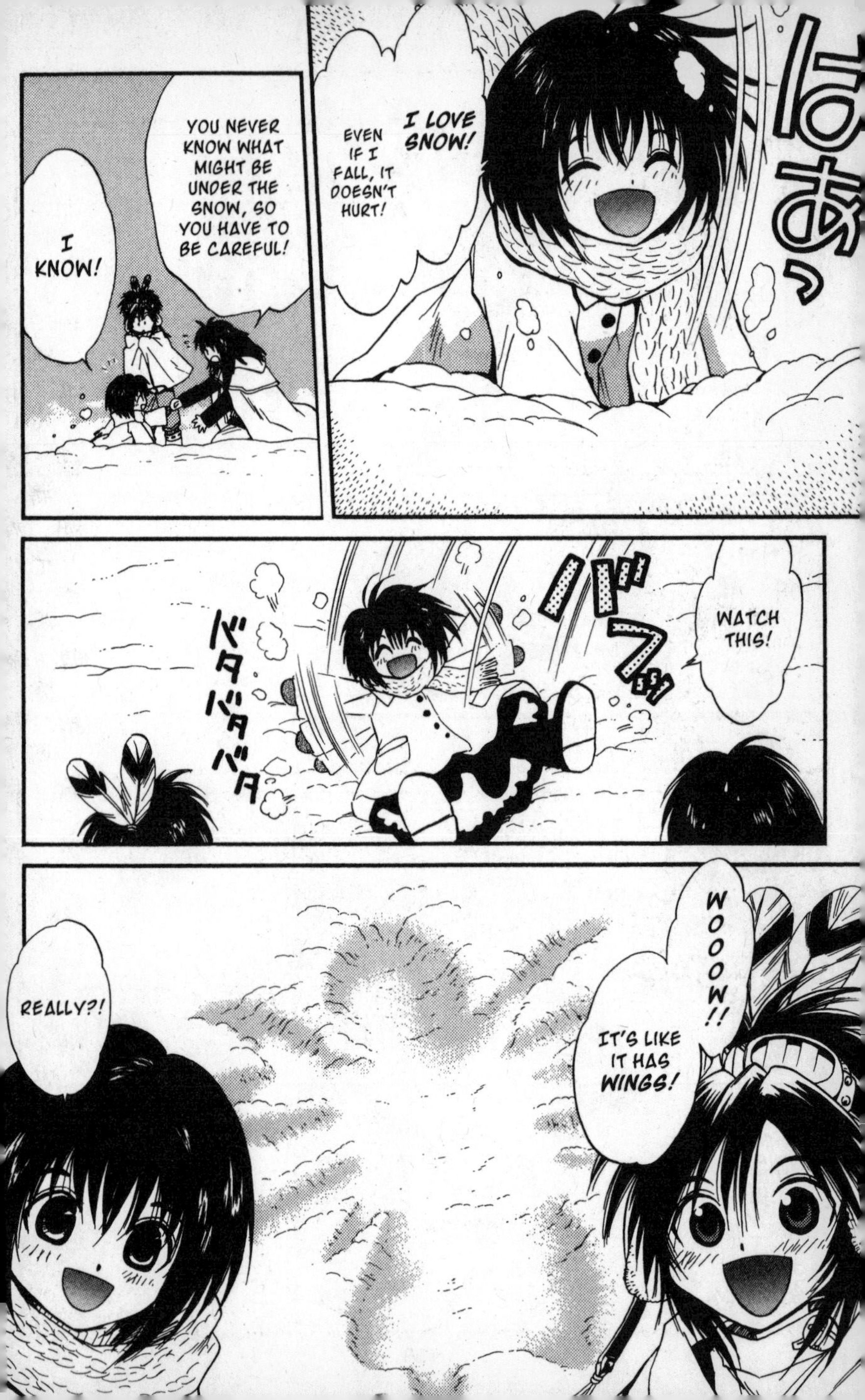
はあっ
I LOVE SNOW!
EVEN IF I FALL, IT DOESN'T HURT!
YOU NEVER KNOW WHAT MIGHT BE UNDER THE SNOW, SO YOU HAVE TO BE CAREFUL!
I KNOW!
WATCH THIS!
バフッ
バタバタバタ
WOOOOW!!
IT'S LIKE IT HAS WINGS!
REALLY?!

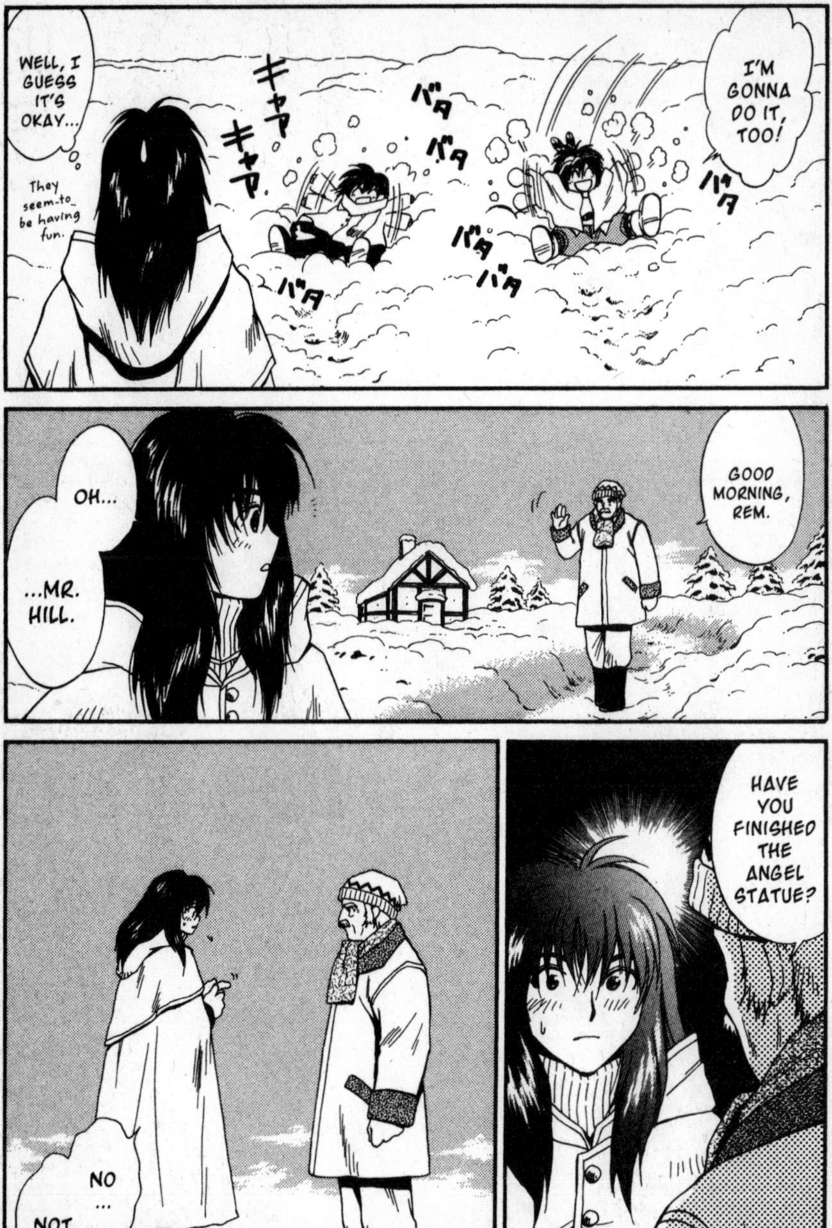
I'M GONNA DO IT, TOO!
バタ
バタ
バタ
キャア
キャア
バタ
バタ
バタ
WELL, I GUESS IT'S OKAY...
They seem to be having fun.
GOOD MORNING, REM.
OH...
...MR. HILL.
HAVE YOU FINISHED THE ANGEL STATUE?
NO ...
NOT YET.

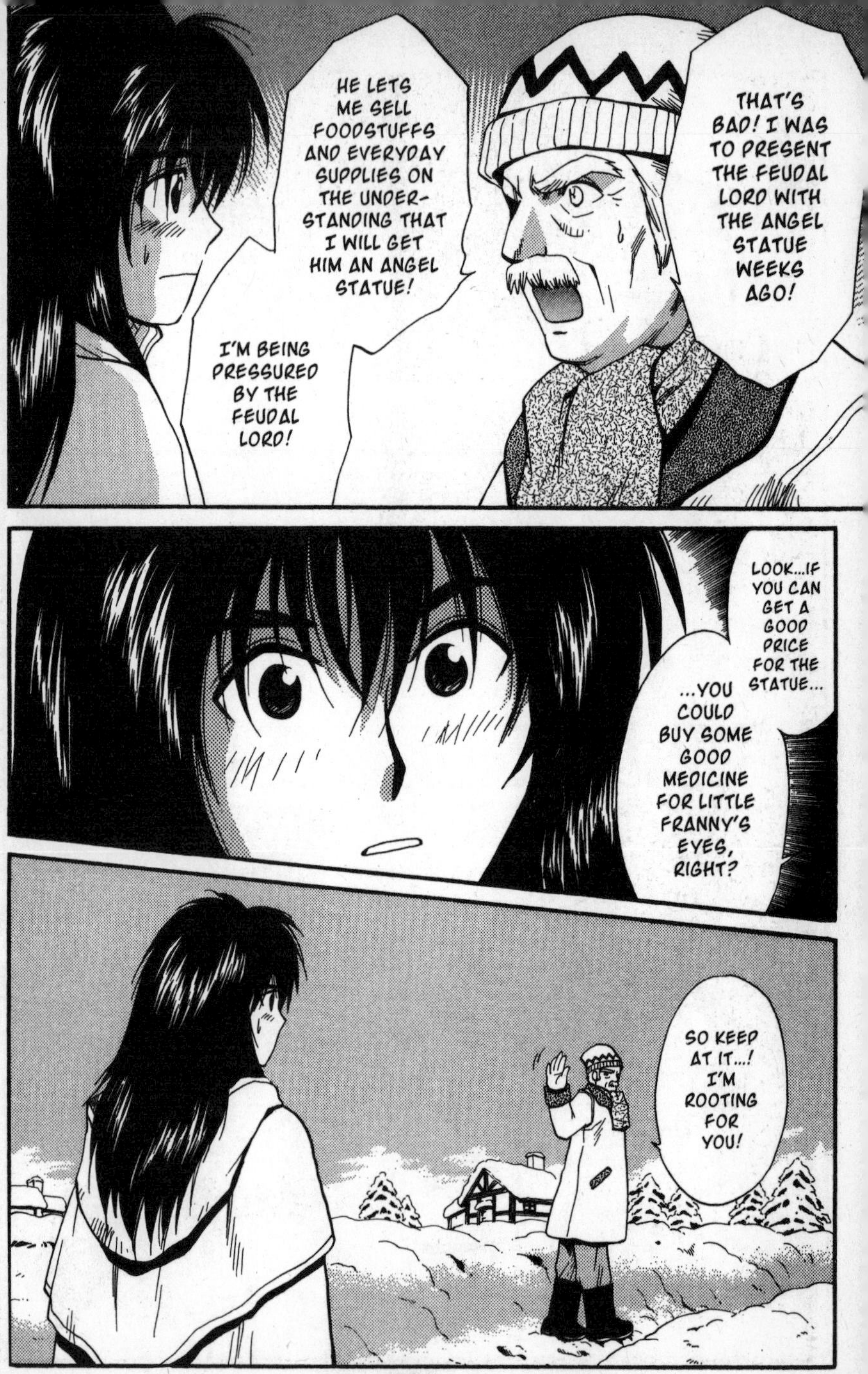
THAT'S BAD! I WAS TO PRESENT THE FEUDAL LORD WITH THE ANGEL STATUE WEEKS AGO!
HE LETS ME SELL FOODSTUFFS AND EVERYDAY SUPPLIES ON THE UNDER-STANDING THAT I WILL GET HIM AN ANGEL STATUE!
I'M BEING PRESSURED BY THE FEUDAL LORD!
LOOK...IF YOU CAN GET A GOOD PRICE FOR THE STATUE...
...YOU COULD BUY SOME GOOD MEDICINE FOR LITTLE FRANNY'S EYES, RIGHT?
SO KEEP AT IT...! I'M ROOTING FOR YOU!

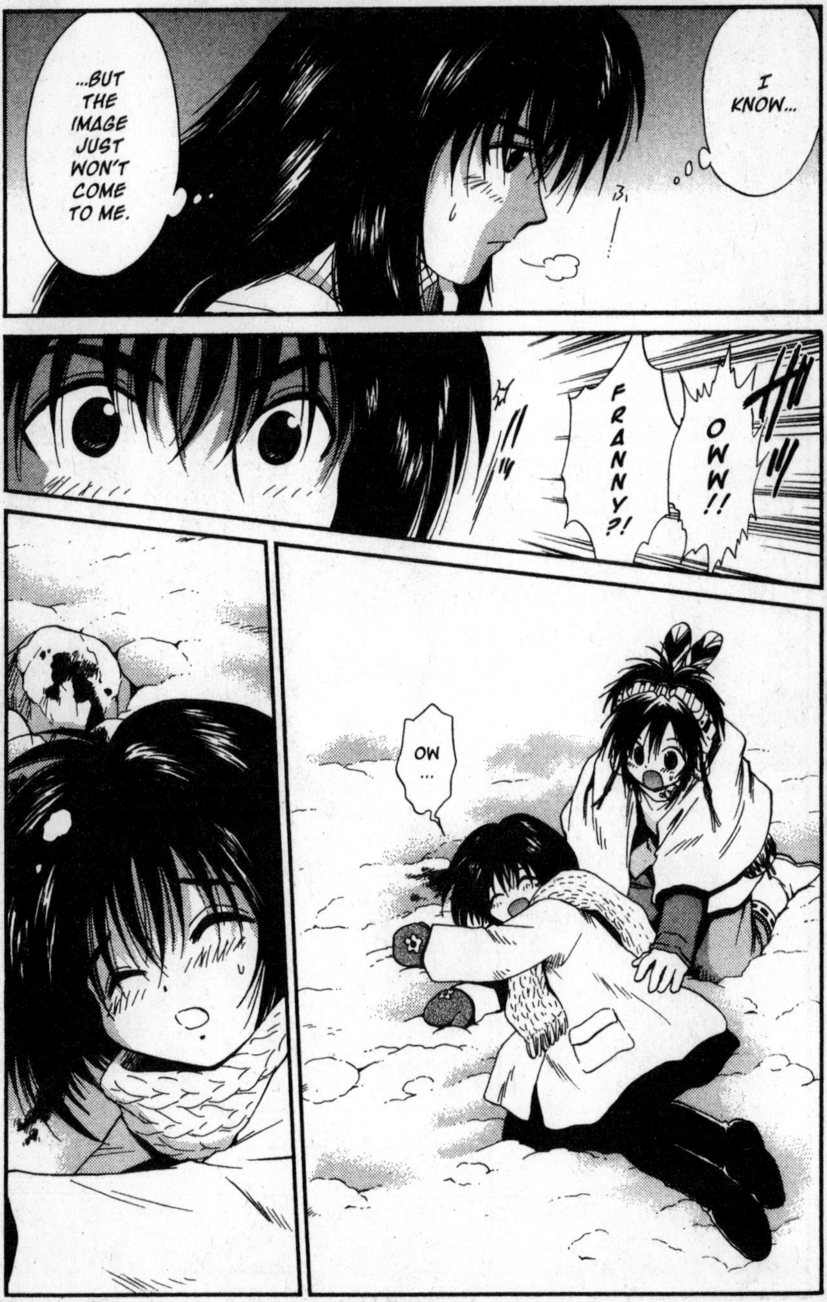
I KNOW...
...BUT THE IMAGE JUST WON'T COME TO ME.
OWW!!
FRANNY?!
OW ...

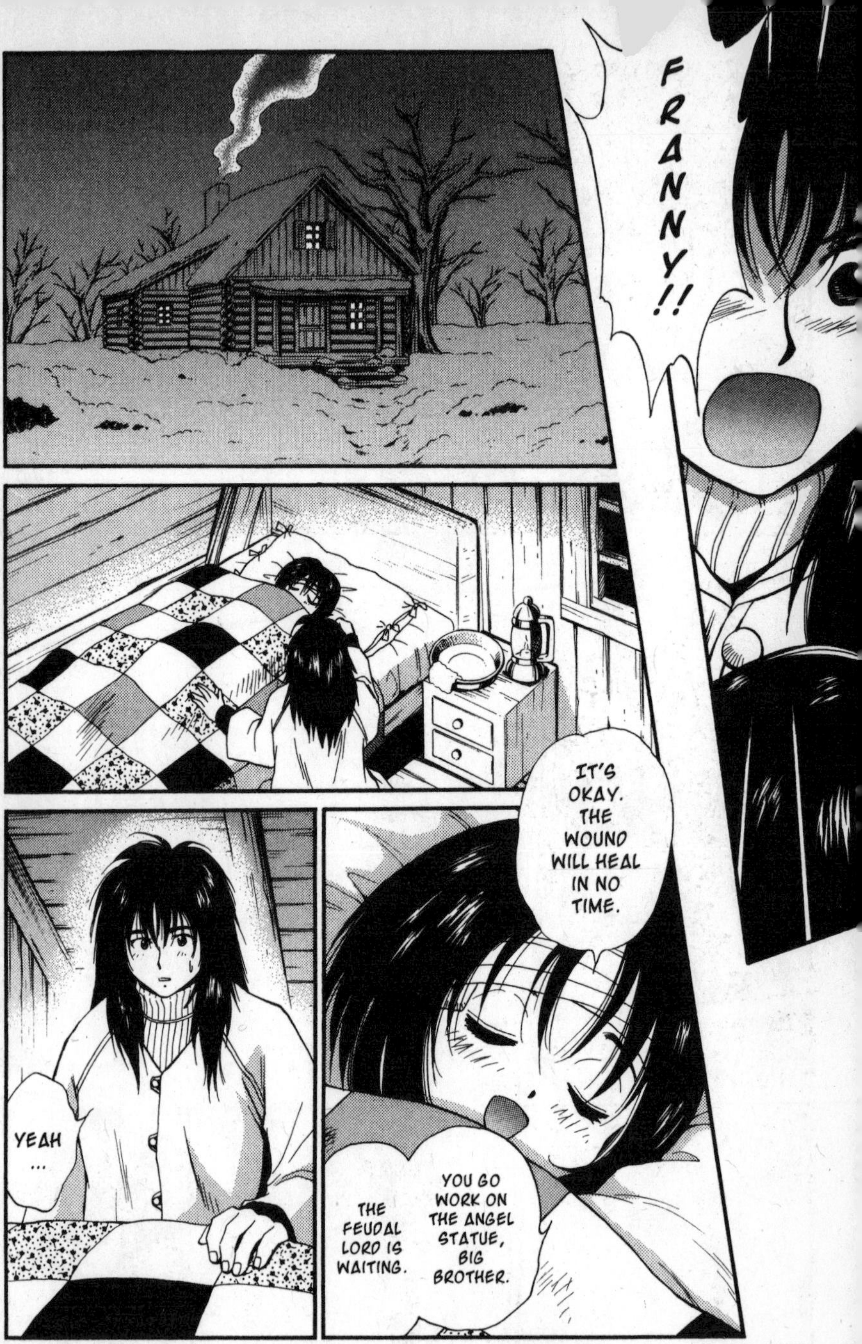
FRANNY!!
IT'S OKAY. THE WOUND WILL HEAL IN NO TIME.
YOU GO WORK ON THE ANGEL STATUE, BIG BROTHER.
THE FEUDAL LORD IS WAITING.
YEAH ...

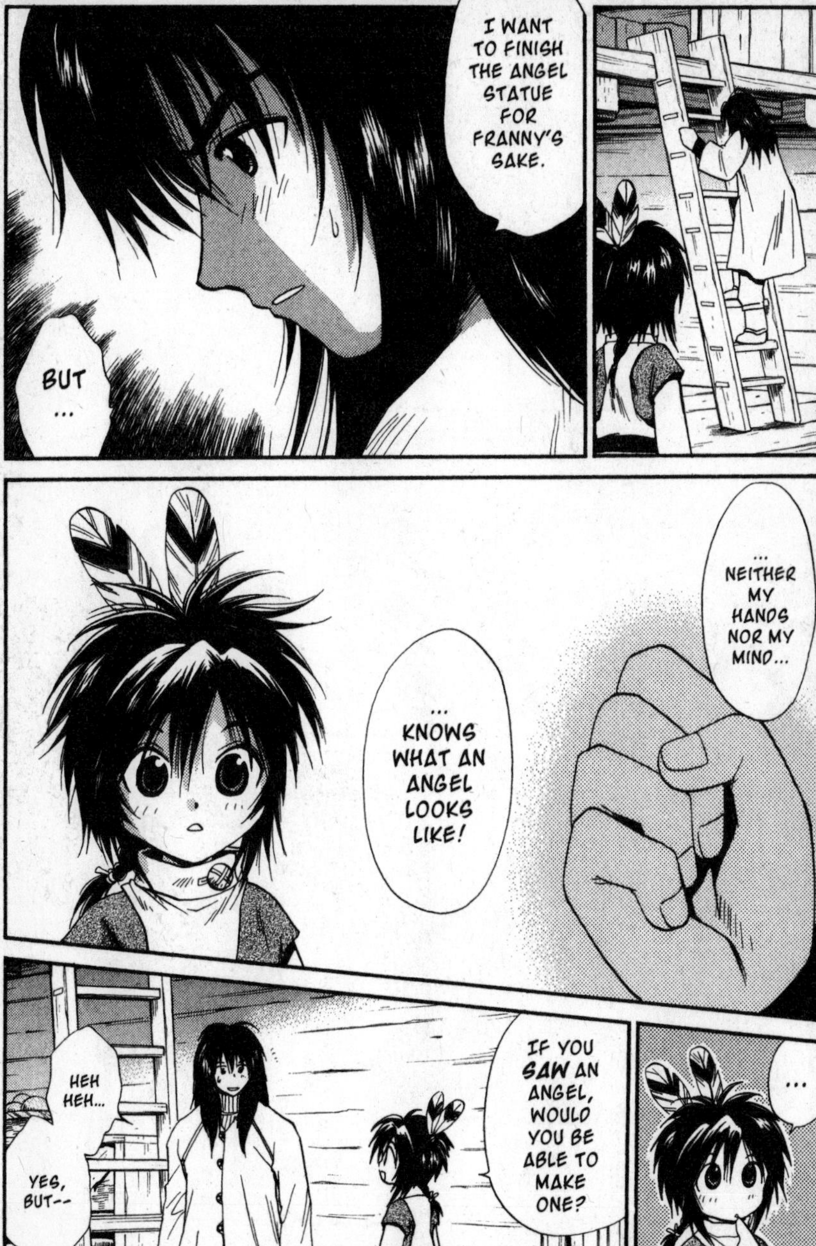
I WANT TO FINISH THE ANGEL STATUE FOR FRANNY'S SAKE.
BUT ...
... NEITHER MY HANDS NOR MY MIND...
... KNOWS WHAT AN ANGEL LOOKS LIKE!
...
IF YOU SAW AN ANGEL, WOULD YOU BE ABLE TO MAKE ONE?
HEH HEH...
YES, BUT--

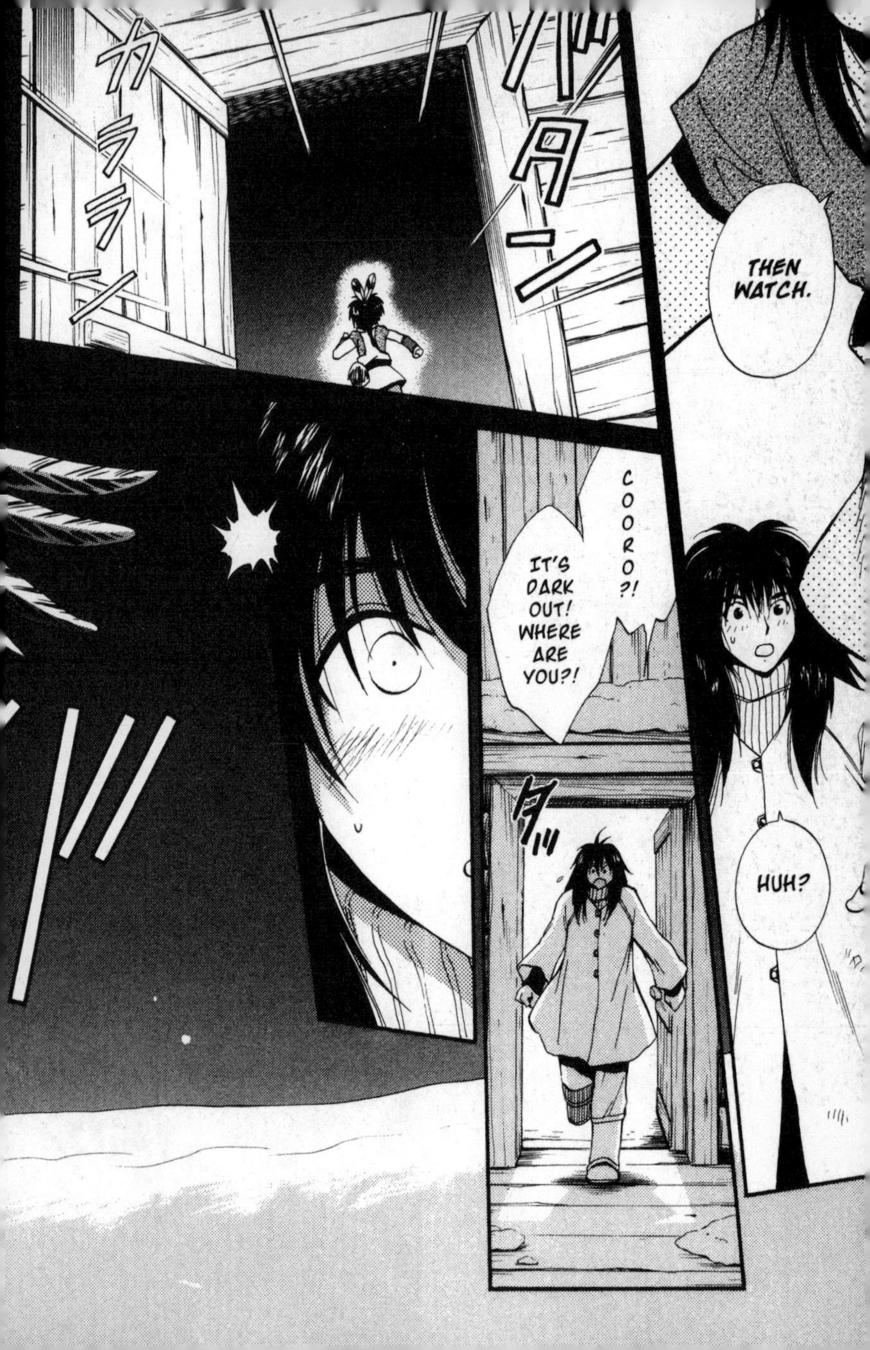
THEN WATCH.
HUH?
ドアーン
カラララーン
COORO?!
IT'S DARK OUT! WHERE ARE YOU?!
ダッ

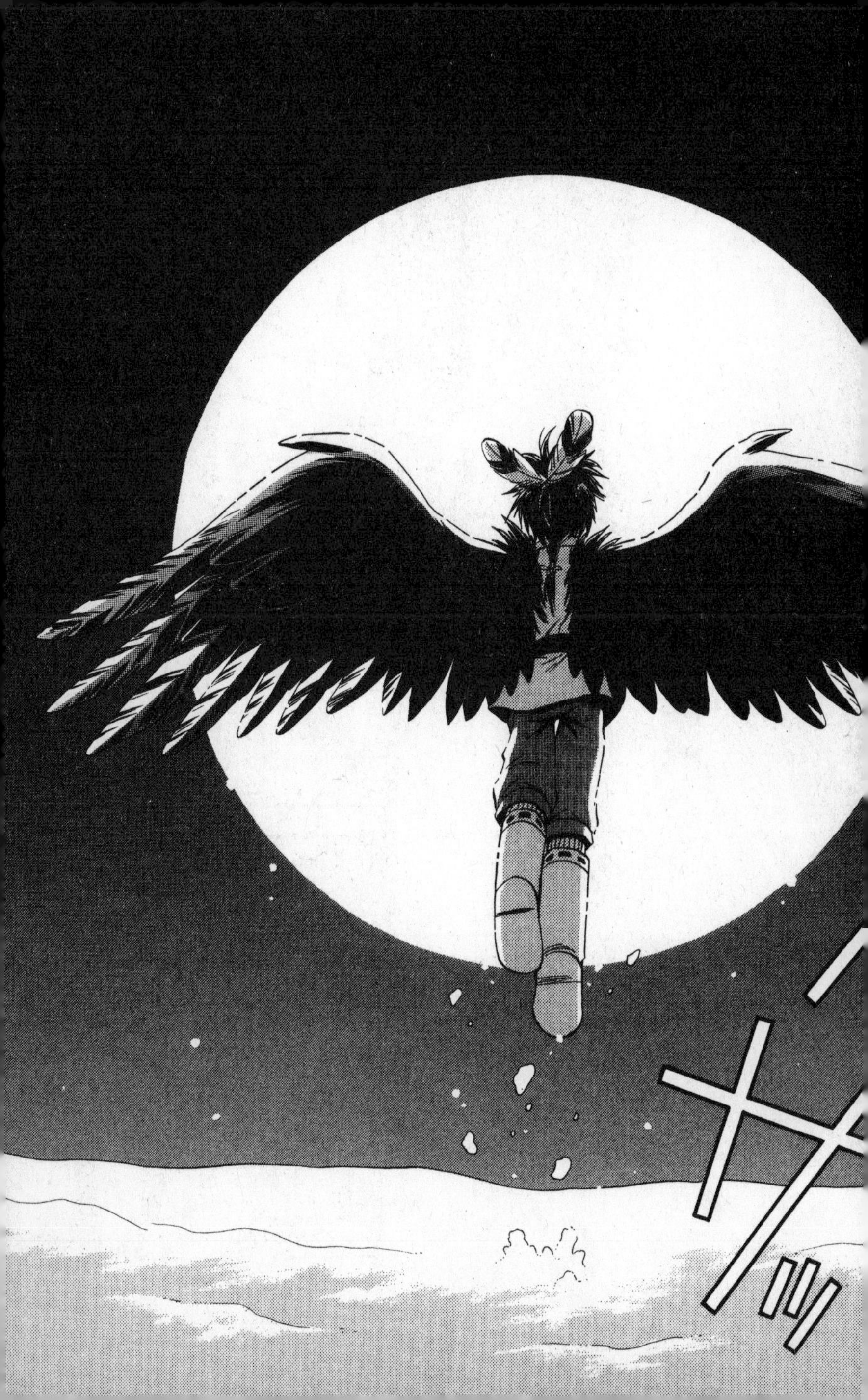

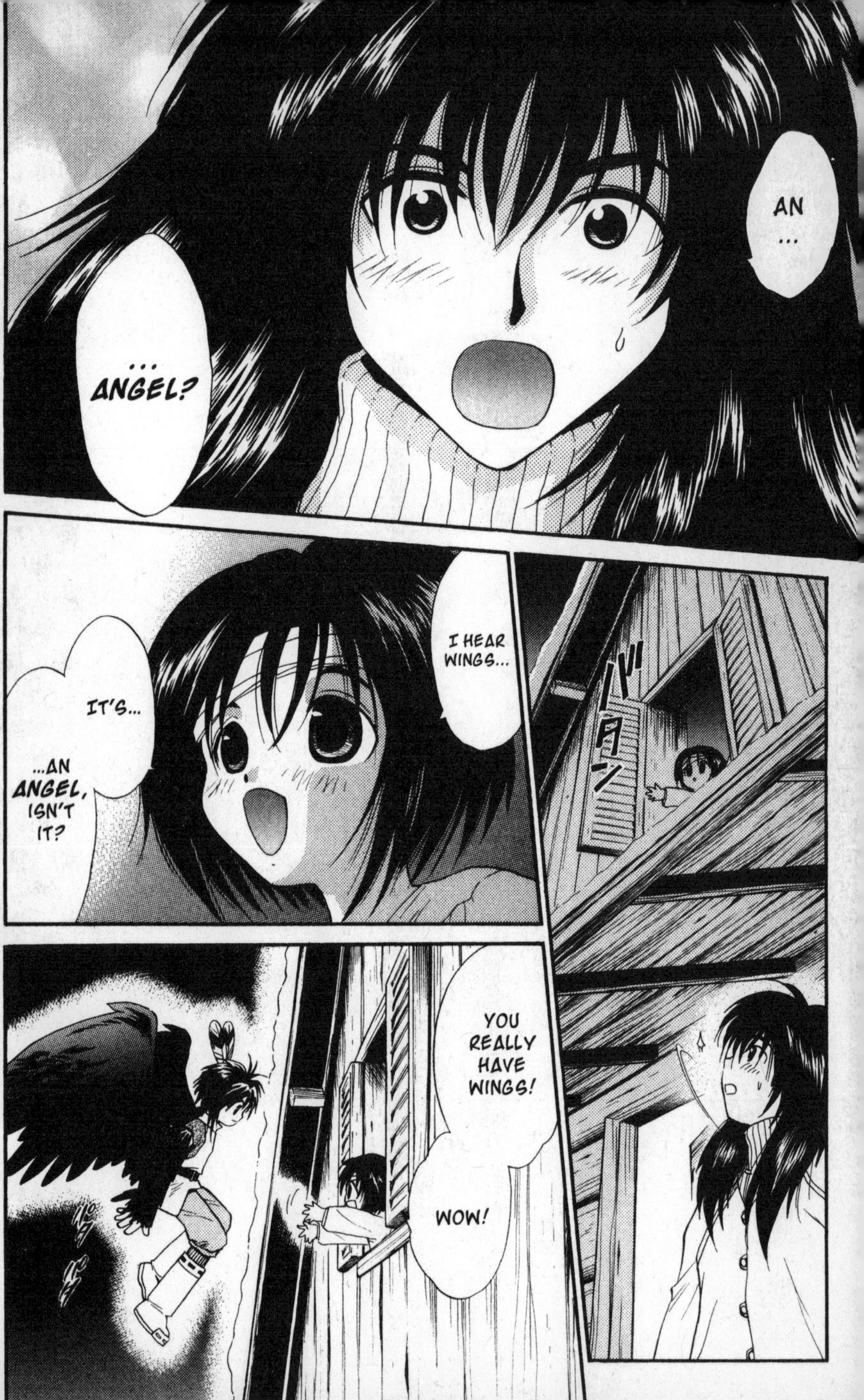
AN ...
... ANGEL?
バタン
I HEAR WINGS...
IT'S...
...AN ANGEL, ISN'T IT?
YOU REALLY HAVE WINGS!
WOW!

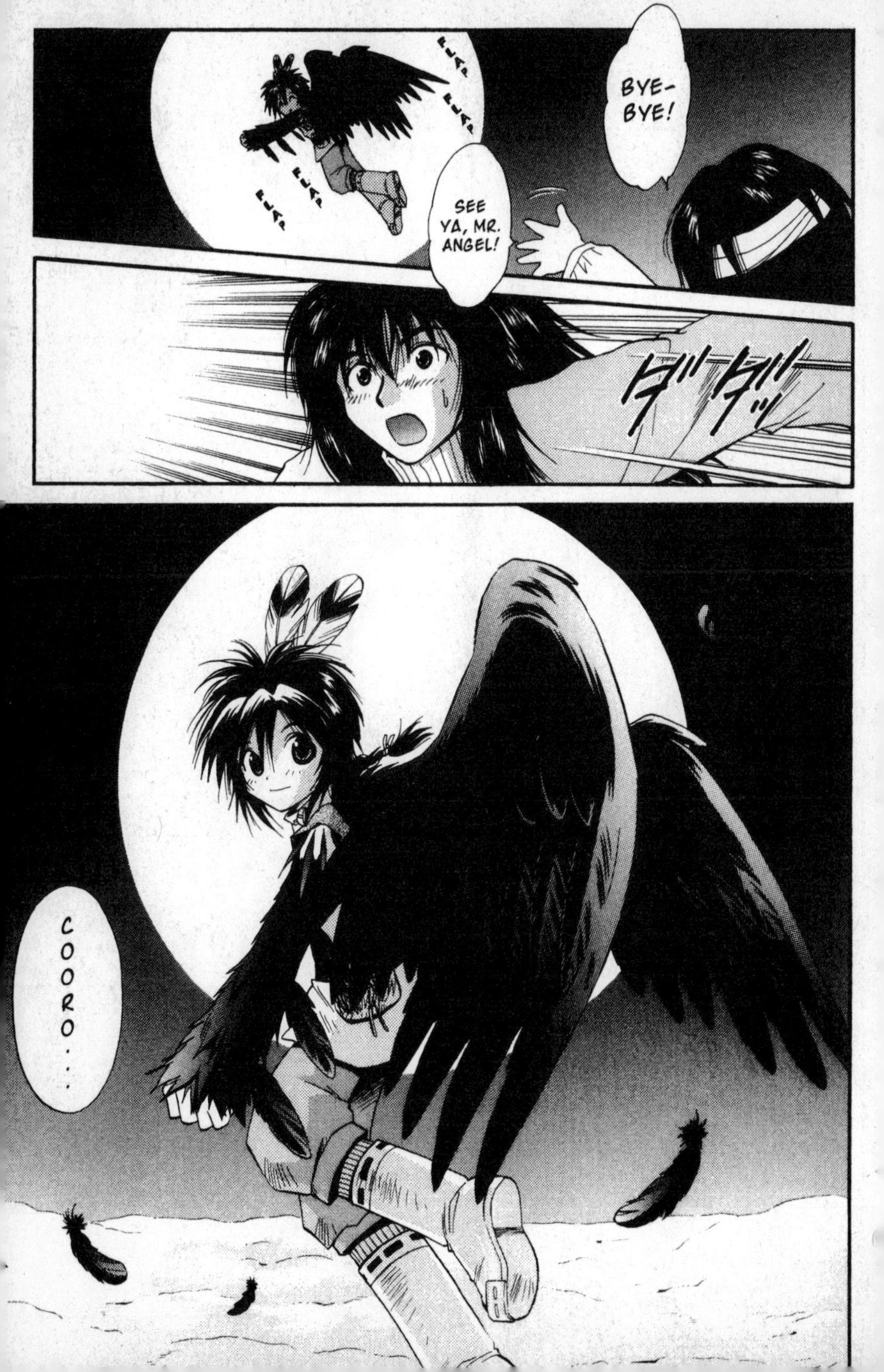
BYE-BYE!
SEE YA, MR. ANGEL!
FLAP
FLAP
FLAP
FLAP
COORO...

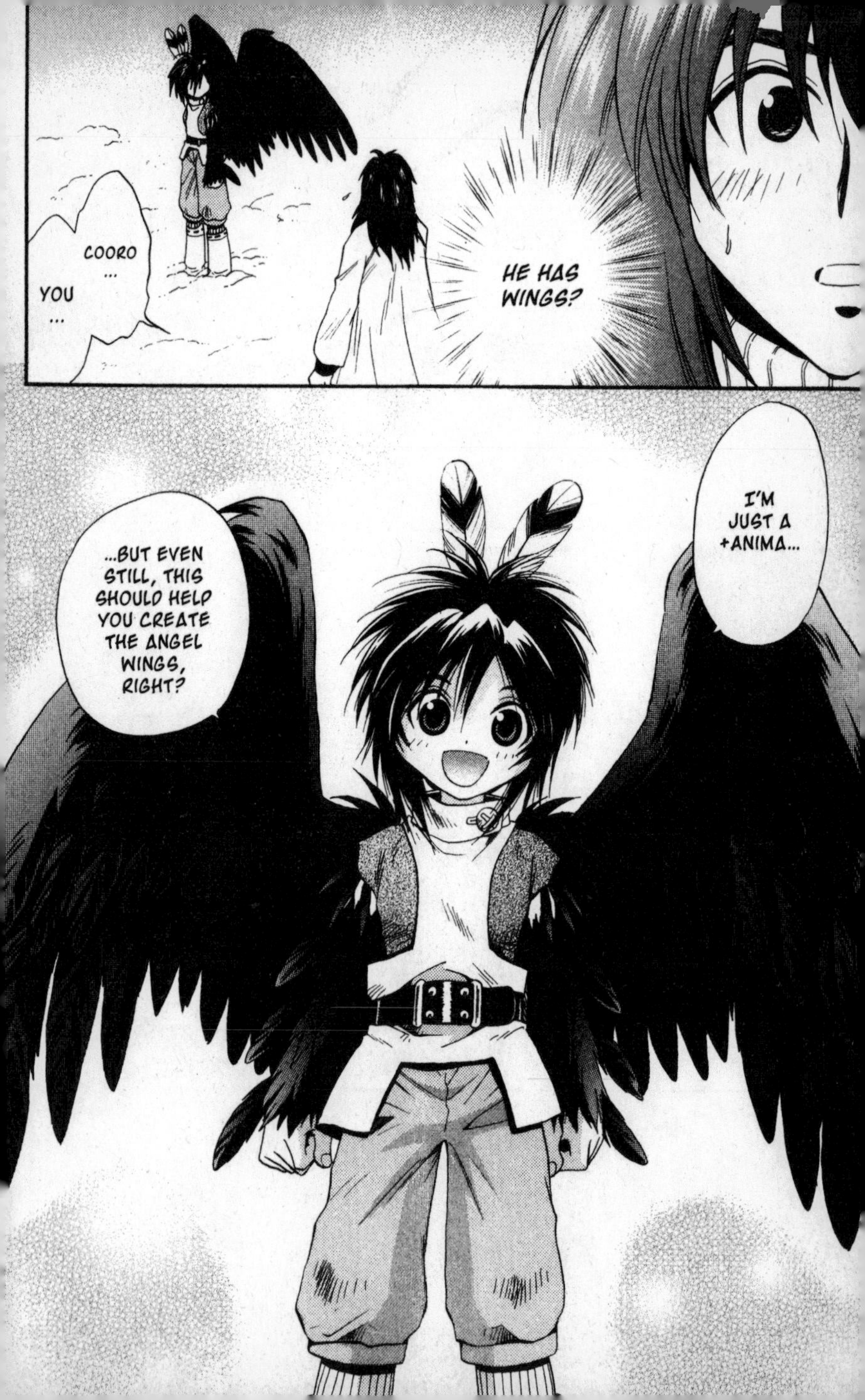
HE HAS WINGS?
COORO ... YOU ...
I'M JUST A +ANIMA...
...BUT EVEN STILL, THIS SHOULD HELP YOU CREATE THE ANGEL WINGS, RIGHT?

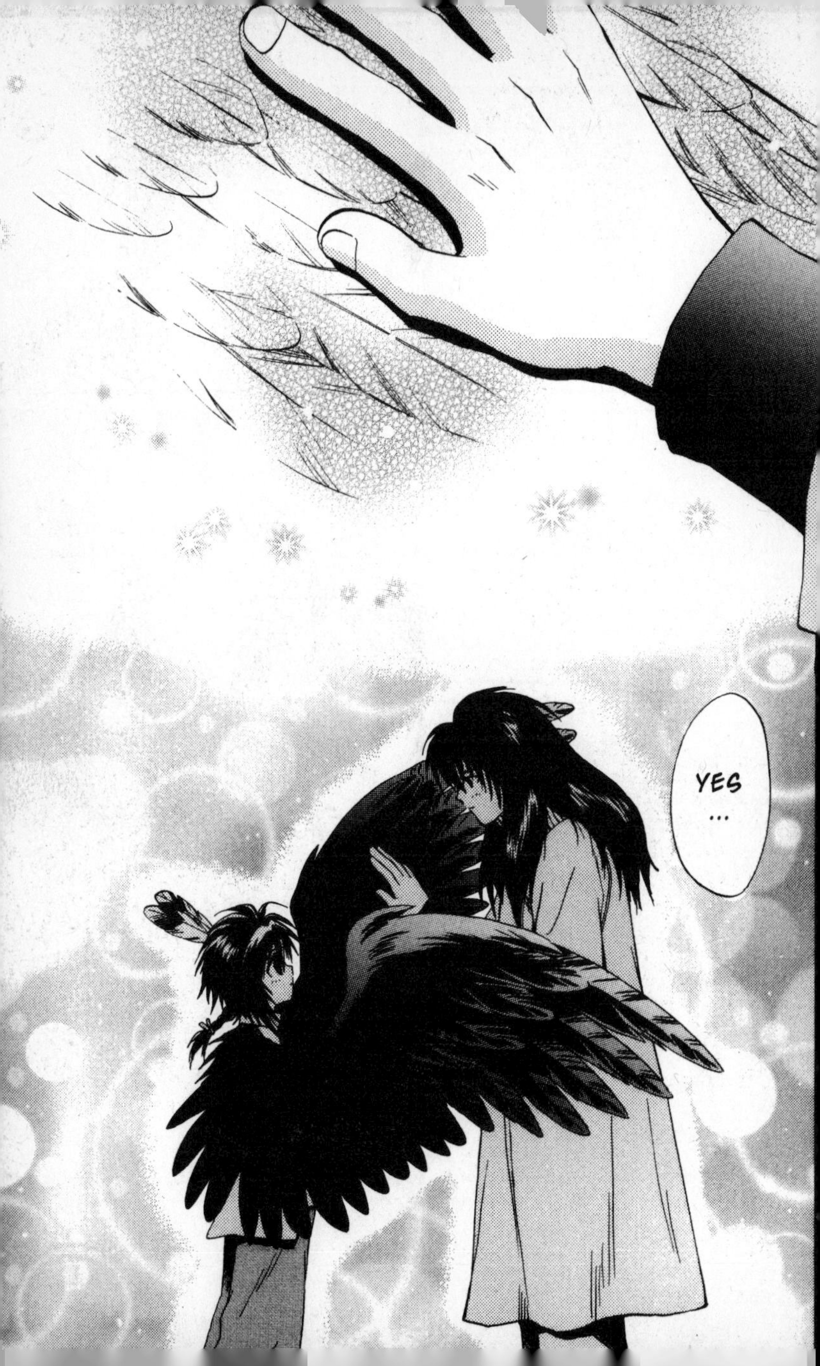
YES
...

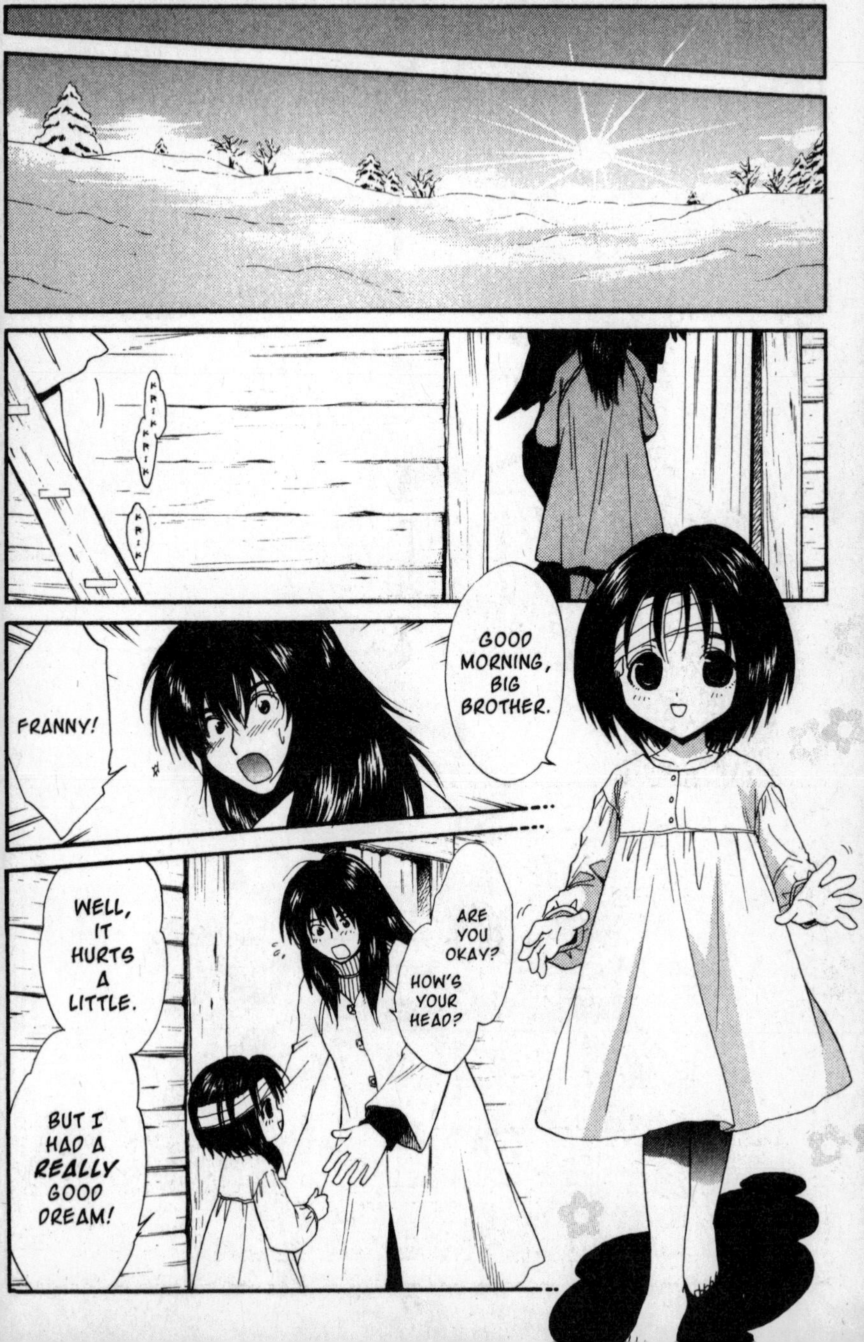
KRIK KRIK
KRIK
GOOD MORNING, BIG BROTHER.
FRANNY!
ARE YOU OKAY?
HOW'S YOUR HEAD?
WELL, IT HURTS A LITTLE.
BUT I HAD A **REALLY** GOOD DREAM!

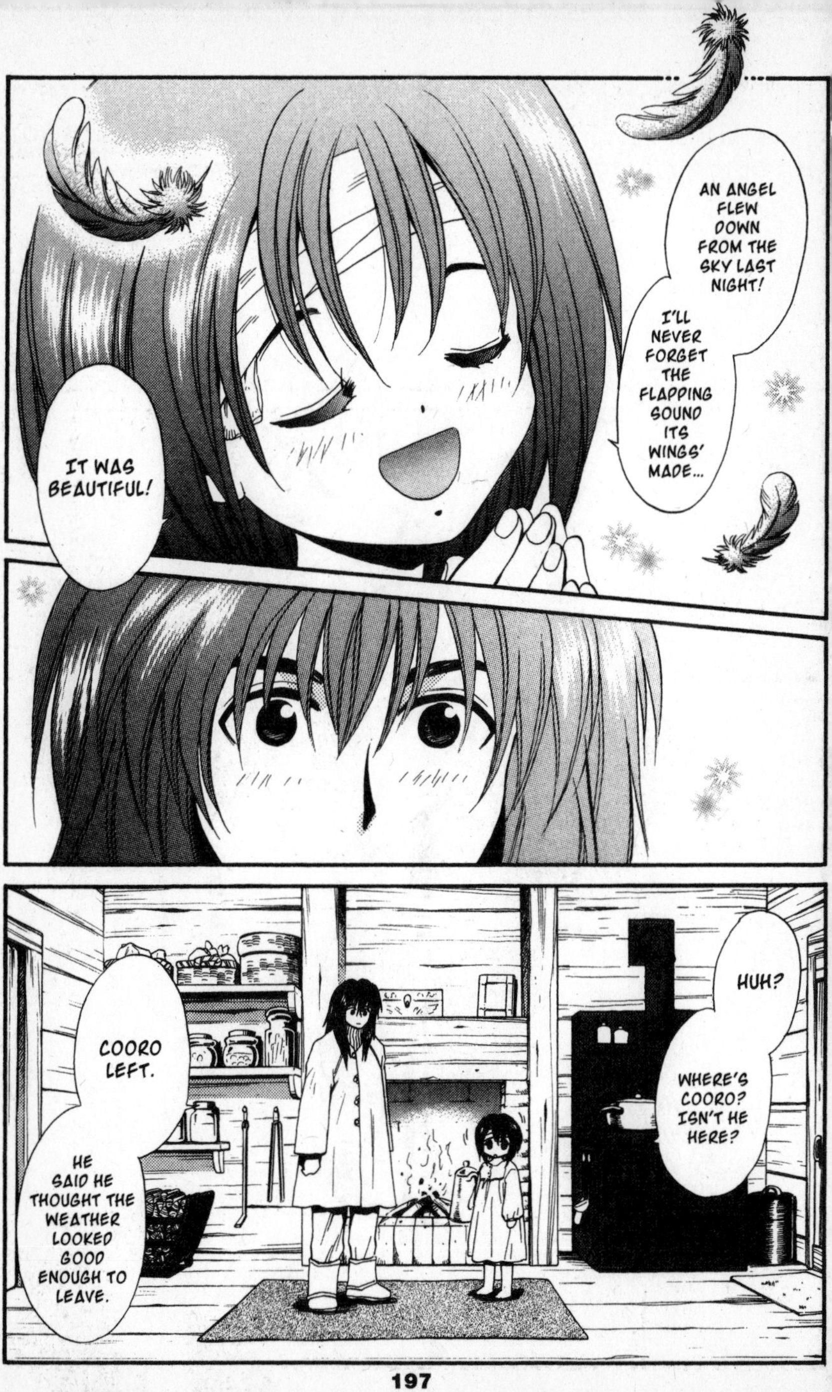
AN ANGEL FLEW DOWN FROM THE SKY LAST NIGHT!
I'LL NEVER FORGET THE FLAPPING SOUND ITS WINGS' MADE...
IT WAS BEAUTIFUL!
HUH?
WHERE'S COORO? ISN'T HE HERE?
COORO LEFT.
HE SAID HE THOUGHT THE WEATHER LOOKED GOOD ENOUGH TO LEAVE.

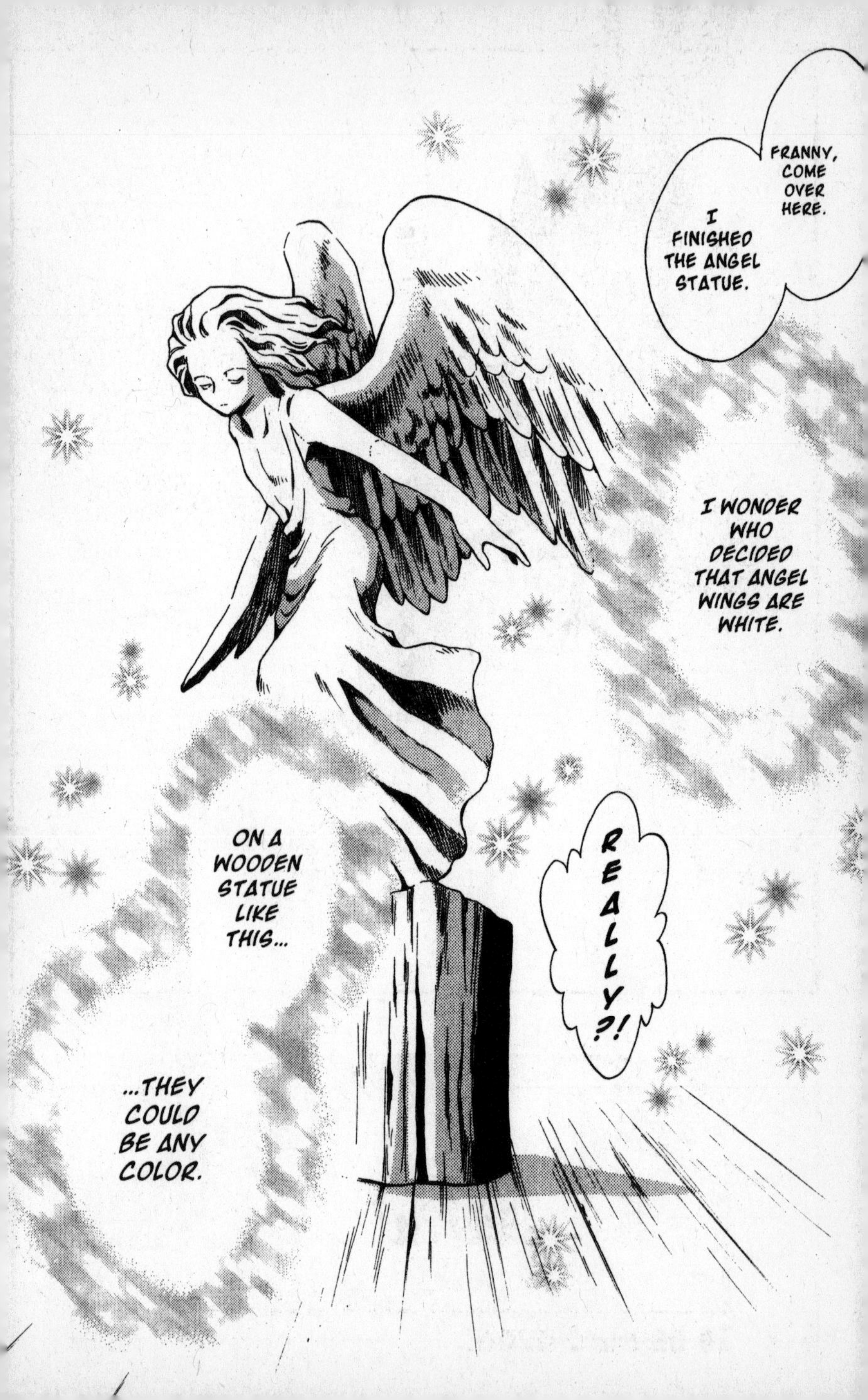
FRANNY, COME OVER HERE.
I FINISHED THE ANGEL STATUE.
I WONDER WHO DECIDED THAT ANGEL WINGS ARE WHITE.
REALLY?!
ON A WOODEN STATUE LIKE THIS...
...THEY COULD BE ANY COLOR.

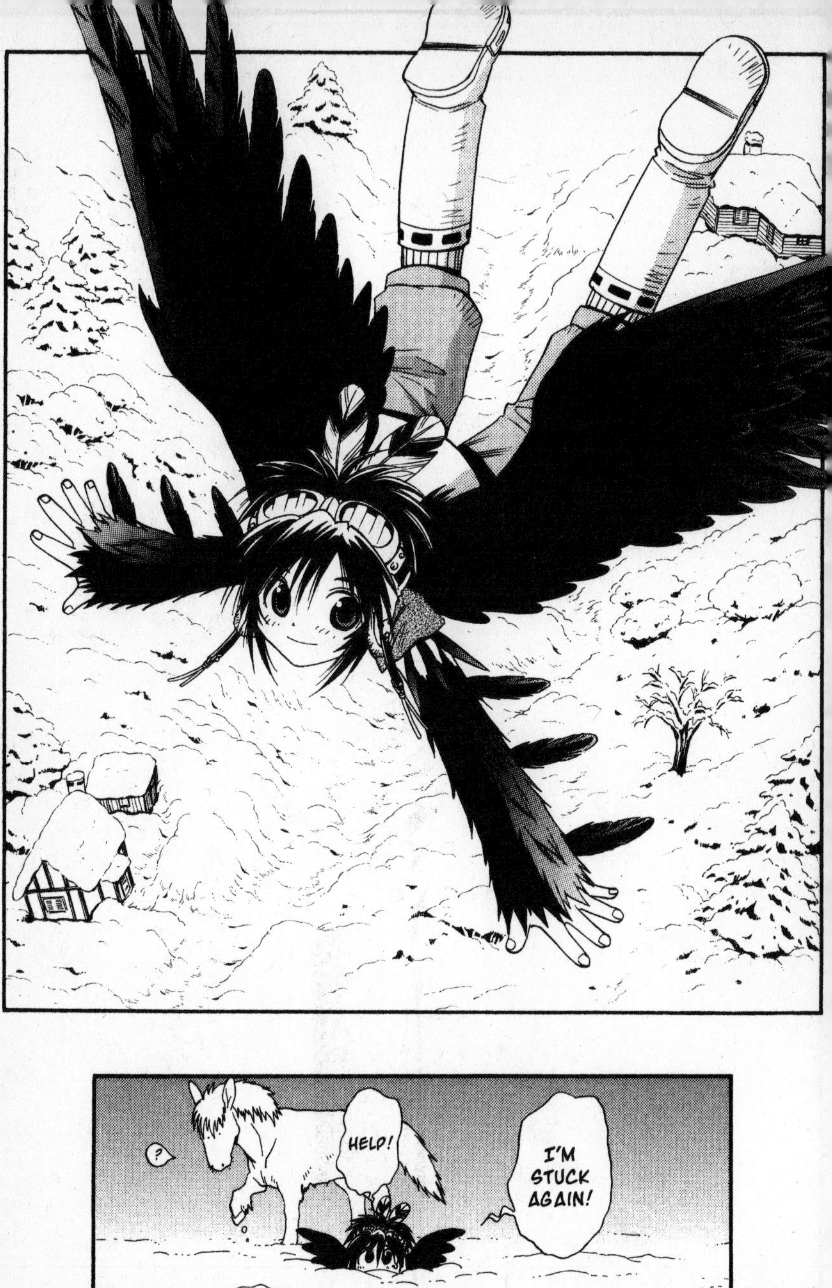
I'M STUCK AGAIN!
HELP!
?

To be continued...

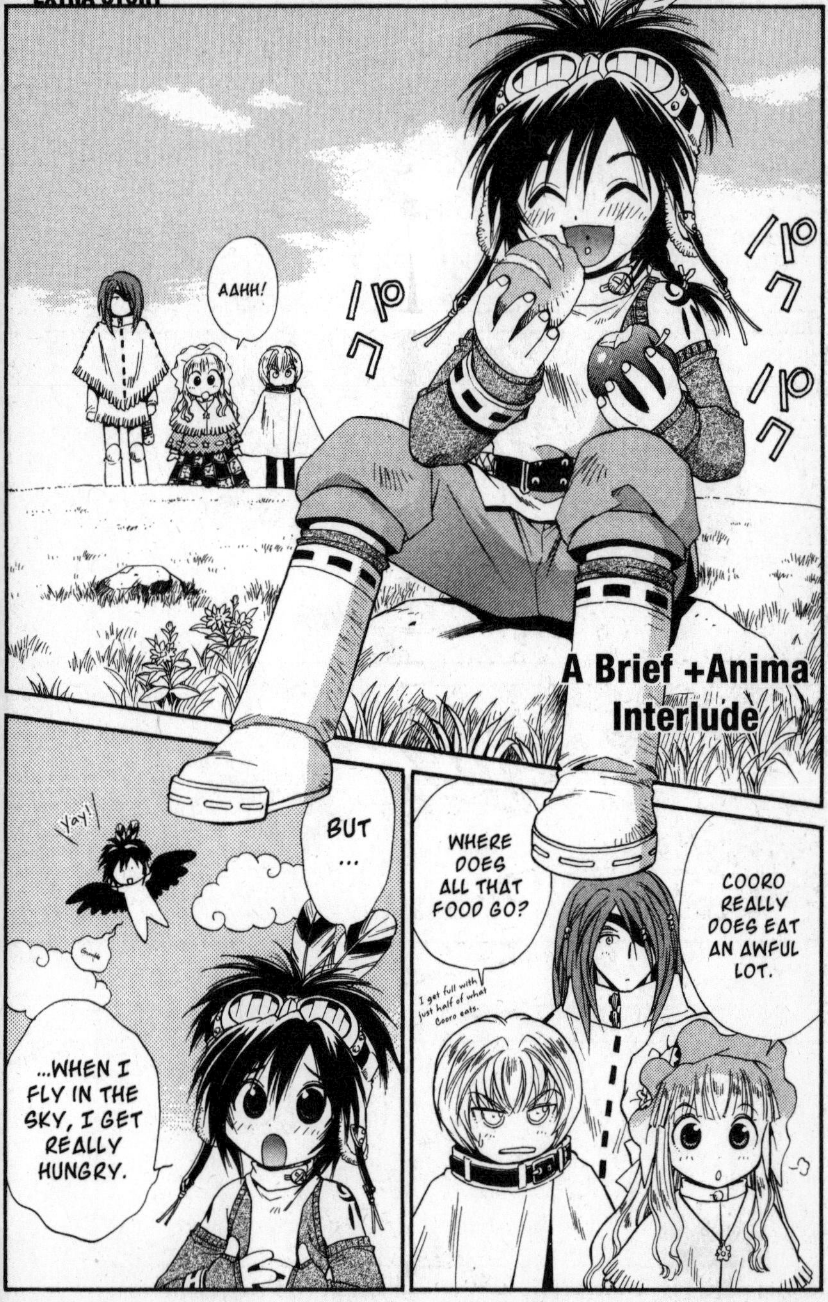
パク
パク
パク
AAHH!
A Brief +Anima Interlude
COORO REALLY DOES EAT AN AWFUL LOT.
WHERE DOES ALL THAT FOOD GO?
I get full with just half of what Cooro eats.
BUT ...
...WHEN I FLY IN THE SKY, I GET REALLY HUNGRY.
Yay!

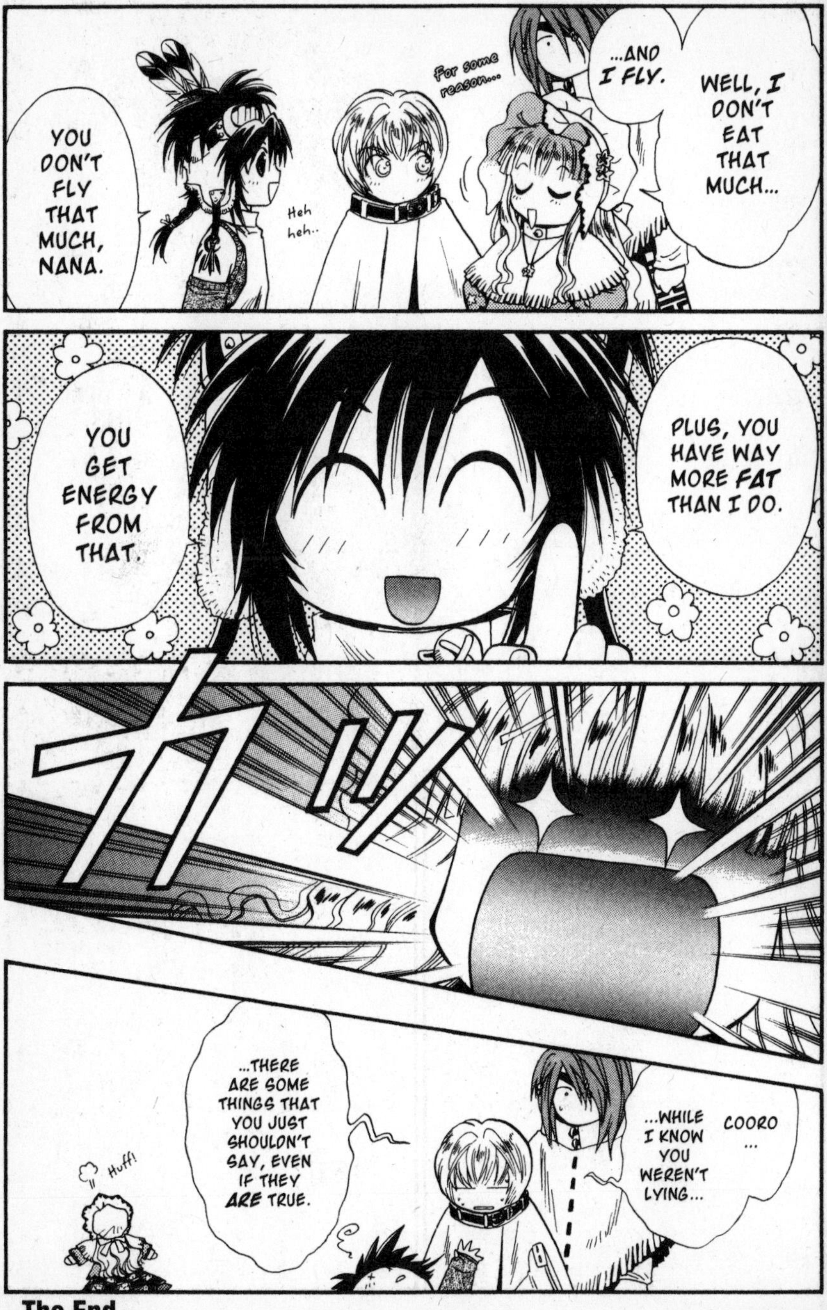
WELL, I DON'T EAT THAT MUCH...
...AND I FLY.
For some reason...
Heh heh..
YOU DON'T FLY THAT MUCH, NANA.
PLUS, YOU HAVE WAY MORE FAT THAN I DO.
YOU GET ENERGY FROM THAT.
カッ
COORO ...
...WHILE I KNOW YOU WEREN'T LYING...
...THERE ARE SOME THINGS THAT YOU JUST SHOULDN'T SAY, EVEN IF THEY ARE TRUE.
Huff!

The End

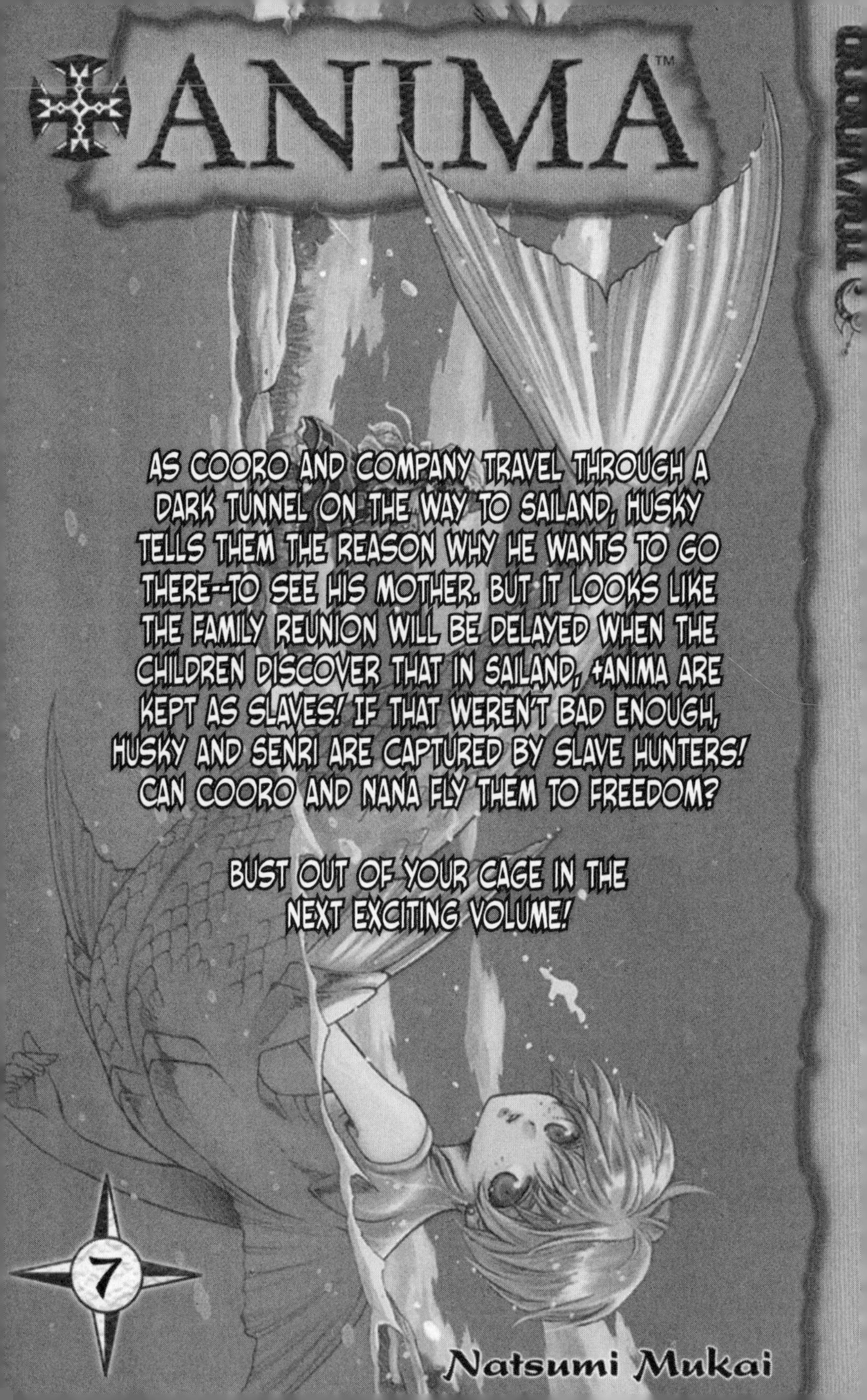
+ANIMA™
TOKYOPOP
AS COORO AND COMPANY TRAVEL THROUGH A DARK TUNNEL ON THE WAY TO SAILAND, HUSKY TELLS THEM THE REASON WHY HE WANTS TO GO THERE--TO SEE HIS MOTHER. BUT IT LOOKS LIKE THE FAMILY REUNION WILL BE DELAYED WHEN THE CHILDREN DISCOVER THAT IN SAILAND, +ANIMA ARE KEPT AS SLAVES! IF THAT WEREN'T BAD ENOUGH, HUSKY AND SENRI ARE CAPTURED BY SLAVE HUNTERS! CAN COORO AND NANA FLY THEM TO FREEDOM?
BUST OUT OF YOUR CAGE IN THE NEXT EXCITING VOLUME!
7
Natsumi Mukai

Ageha lands the job of a lifetime— making her sister's wedding dress!

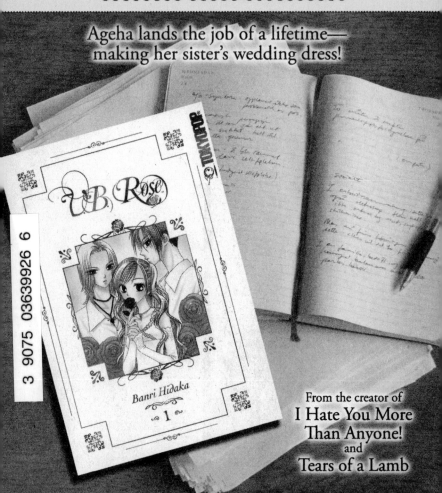

VB Rose

Banri Hidaka

1

3 9075 03639926 6

From the creator of
I Hate You More Than Anyone!
and
Tears of a Lamb

Pure shojo bliss full of weddings, frills...and romance!

Despite being shocked and heartbroken by her sister's upcoming marriage to the most boring man alive, Ageha quickly jumps in to help when the wedding dressmaker hurts his hand! Thus begin her adventures working at Velvet Blue Rose, the super-exclusive bridal-design shop run by two super-hot guys!

ROMANCE

T TEEN AGE 13+

© Banri Hidaka

FOR MORE INFORMATION VISIT: WWW.TOKYOPOP.COM

STOP!

This is the back of the book.
You wouldn't want to spoil a great ending!

This book is printed "manga-style," in the authentic Japanese right-to-left format. Since none of the artwork has been flipped or altered, readers get to experience the story just as the creator intended. You've been asking for it, so TOKYOPOP® delivered: authentic, hot-off-the-press, and far more fun!

DIRECTIONS

If this is your first time reading manga-style, here's a quick guide to help you understand how it works.

It's easy... just start in the top right panel and follow the numbers. Have fun, and look for more 100% authentic manga from TOKYOPOP®!